RECORDS MANAGEMENT HANDBOOK

Records Management Handbook

Second edition

Ira A. Penn
Gail B. Pennix
Jim Coulson

Gower

Published by
Gower Publishing Limited
Gower House
Croft Road
Aldershot
Hampshire GU11 3HR
England

Gower
Old Post Road
Brookfield
Vermont 05036
USA

Reprinted 1994, 1996

IA Penn, GB Pennix and J Coulson have asserted their right under the Copyright, Designs and Patents Act 1988 to be identified as the authors of this work.

British Library Cataloguing in Publication Data

Penn, Ira A.
  Records Management Handbook. – 2 Rev. ed
  I. Title
  651.5

  ISBN 0–566–07510–5

Library of Congress Cataloguing-in-Publication Data

Penn, Ira A.
  Records management handbook / Ira A. Penn, Gail Pennix, Jim
  Coulson. – 2nd ed.
      p.   cm.
  Originally published: 1989.
  Includes Index.
  ISBN 0-566-07510-5
  1. Public records – United States – Management. 2. Public records –
  Great Britain – Management.   I. Pennix, Gail.   II. Coulson, Jim.
  III. Title
  JK468.P78R44   1994
  354.410071'4 – dc20   93-48279
                                                                  CIP

Typeset in Times by Raven Typesetters, Chester.
Printed in Great Britain at the University Press, Cambridge

Contents

The authors

Ira A. Penn, CRM, CSP, FAI, is a senior management analyst with the US Federal Government and the Editor of the *Records Management Quarterly* published by the Association of Records Managers and Administrators. An internationally known author and speaker, he is the recipient of the Emmett Leahy Award for records management excellence and has been involved with management analysis and records management for over 30 years.

Gail B. Pennix, CRM, is an independent consultant in Boston, MA associated with the Records Improvement Institute. The holder of an MLS from Simmons College in Boston and with 20 years of professional records management experience, she has taught records management courses at university level, authored several articles, and lectured at various seminars.

Jim Coulson, CRM, FAI, is President and Senior Consultant with Records Improvement Institute, Westboro, MA. He has been active in records management for 24 years as a records analyst, microfilm supervisor, filing systems sales representative, senior executive, and consultant. A developer of automated records management software, university lecturer, and author, he regularly conducts records management seminars for organizations throughout North America.

List of figures and tables

Figures

Tables

Foreword

J. Michael Pemberton, PhD, Associate Professor,
Graduate School of Library and Information Science,
The University of Tennessee, Knoxville.

We can lick gravity, but sometimes the paperwork is overwhelming. Wernher von Braun.

In recent years, the public has begun to understand what information managers have known for some time: the volume, power and value of recorded information have risen dramatically. In seventeenth-century England a person would neither encounter nor use as much information in a lifetime as is found today in any Sunday edition of the *New York Times*. The world's first technical journal was published in 1660; today, more than 80,000 such journals are published worldwide, and the number of scientists in the world now represents a staggering 90 percent of all scientists who have ever lived. Thus, in a sense, social progress can be measured by information output and a correspondingly expanding knowledge base.

Our ability to *use* information effectively can be either enhanced or diminished by the huge volumes of it that are available. While more information can lead to better decisions, on the other hand, the volume of information – whether at the business or the societal level – must be matched with an ability to control and to provide access to it as needed. Because of its great volume, power, and impact, the information resource is one that must be managed effectively to be of value.

Before World War II, little thought was given to information management. However, the 'paperwork' necessary to run the war machine taught the corporate sector that effective organizations run on good information resources, and, during the 1950s and 1960s, there consequently emerged a continuing focus on 'records management' as a way to control the volume of records, reduce their costs and increase their quality.

Like other management disciplines, records management has become a specialization within the larger parent discipline of management. Marketing management, financial management, personnel management, facilities management – all these center on a particular aspect of the management of larger enterprises. The focus of records management is on the creation, evaluation, storage, access, retrieval, duplication, dissemination, use and disposition of recorded information. Today, recorded information is the lifeblood, as well as the corporate memory, of virtually all organizations. Our everyday business records have a host of powers which many seem to take for granted; among other things, they enable all types of organizations to:

Control	Notify	Insure	Guide
Enable	Authorize	Mandate	Explain
Instruct	Protect	Verify	Authenticate
Entitle	Track	Empower	Terminate

In sum, records permit organizations to function!

Records management has evolved around a specific body of knowledge which is generally contained in the many textbooks that have been published over the years. Yet unlike other book-length treatments of the subject, written mostly by academics, the *Records Management Handbook* is prepared by three widely known and successful practitioners who have set records management into the conceptual, integrative and management-based context in which it belongs. While the *Records Management Handbook* might well be used as a text at university level, its contributors take an effective, 'real-world' approach to the development of an organization's records management systems. Rather than issue a mind-numbing stream of details which can soon become out of date and which may apply only to a limited range of organizations, the *Handbook* lays out, in clear terms, a road map detailing the procedures and processes that must be followed – regardless of type of organization or environment – to develop a sound records management program. The authors assume that any effective program will have as its primary goal getting the right information to the right people, in the right form, in the right order, in the right amount, at the right time, and at the lowest reasonable cost. More than any other book in the field, the *Handbook* raises the questions which must be intelligently confronted during the development of such a program. Also, to its credit, instead of treating technology in separate chapters as though it were an exotic relative of records management, the *Handbook* properly integrates it where it belongs – throughout the text.

This second edition of the *Handbook* has been strengthened in several ways. A consistent adherence to the framework of the information life cycle in developing sections of the book provides an important intellectual anchor for the user. Additional management techniques (for example, cost/benefit analysis) are provided where useful, as are graphics, tables, formulae and sample forms, new to this edition.

Two groups of readers will profit most from the use of the *Records Management Handbook*: those new to the field who need guidance in developing a program from the beginning; and those who need a standard to evaluate how well they *might* have designed their program had they used the *Handbook* to begin with!

Preface to the second edition

As with the first edition, this second edition of the *Records Management Handbook* was written for the practitioner. Although suitable for use as a college text, the intention of the authors is to provide a practical reference for records managers, analysts, and other information management professionals.

With any revised publication, the obvious question from the reader is, 'What's new?' The answer in this case is, 'Almost everything!' For many years, literature on the subject of records management has dealt almost exclusively with the management of paper records. For the second edition of the *Records Management Handbook*, the authors have brought a multimedia perspective to the subject, promoting the concept of using the correct medium for the application, regardless of type. This approach recognizes the steady trend in records management toward the use of machine-readable media for the storage and retrieval of records, yet it acknowledges that over 90 percent of business information is still paper oriented.

Also included in this second edition are proven management strategies for initiating or improving a records management program. The methods advocated have been developed and refined by the authors in their advisory work with literally hundreds of organizations in the public and private sectors. In presenting these strategies, the shifting media paradigm has been taken into account. Many opportunities for the automation of records management functions are explored.

In addition to a predisposition for dealing with the paper medium, records management literature has generally focused on the management of inactive records. The aim of this book is to provide more balance in the treatment of all phases of the record life cycle, from creation or receipt through ultimate disposition.

The material included in this second edition has been carefully organized in three sequential parts to support the work of the records management professional. The authors hope that it will prove useful and helpful to the readers as they pursue the challenge of managing records and the information they contain.

Acknowledgments

In some respects, revising a book is more difficult than creating an original one. Not only must new material be developed, but decisions must be made as to how it will be incorporated with the previously existing text. Second (and third) guessing is common and it often seems that one cannot see the book for its chapters. It is good, in this situation, to have help.

The authors are indebted to Marti Fischer, CRM, Debra K. Gearhart, CRM, FAI, and J. Michael Pemberton, Ph.D. for their invaluable assistance in reviewing the manuscript. Additional thanks are due to Sue McNaughton, Senior Editor at Gower Publishing Co. Ltd, whose unstinting support made this second edition possible.

The authors also wish to acknowledge their fellow records management professionals within the Association of Records Managers and Administrators and the Institute of Certified Records Managers who have provided encouragement, assistance, and, perhaps most importantly, friendship over the years.

Part 1

Introduction

INTRODUCTION

Records management is concerned with the management of information. Both the public and private sectors need information to function properly; if that information is mismanaged or is not available, organizations might cease to exist. As government and business have expanded during the twentieth century, so has the need for information and records management.

In examining the records management function in Chapter 1, as much importance has been placed on management as on records, and this is studied further in succeeding chapters. We have considered that management is a practical function and that records management, the concern of the whole organization and not just an individual, is a staff function.

Chapter 2 examines the concept of the life cycle of information – its creation, its maintenance and use, and its disposition. These three phases form the basis of records management programs, and it is on this concept that the effective, efficient and economic use of information is founded.

Chapter 3 deals with record media. The variety of media available today presents new challenges for the records manager. Understanding the various media alternatives and the technologies associated with them is paramount if effective record systems are to be developed.

1

The records management function

We live in an information society. This is not something that will happen or is happening; it has already happened. Information is our basic resource, and information is our product.

Although we consume more food than ever before, only 3 percent of the workforce is engaged in agriculture. Although we consume 'hard goods' at an ever increasing rate, only 14 percent of the workforce is involved in manufacturing. By contrast, over 50 percent of the workforce is employed in offices and 80 percent of the office employees are considered to be 'information handlers.'

What is this information that has taken over the economy so completely in only a few short decades? There is probably no single answer to that question. Depending on the philosophic approach one might take, information could be considered to be raw facts, commonly referred to as data, or it could be knowledge, which would be the same facts evaluated, organized and synthesized into meaningful intelligence.

Regardless of the definition one wishes to ascribe to information, there is little doubt that it all has to be managed. Information must be managed so that it can be used. The usability and usefulness of information can mean the difference between the success or failure of an organization. Unmanaged, data are relatively useless, merely a conglomeration of unrelated details. Unmanaged, knowledge is not worth much more than the original data from which it was derived – not updatable and, possibly, not even retrievable.

If we accept that information must be managed to be usable, where do records fit into the picture? The answer is quite simple – records *are* recorded information. Indeed, a record may be defined as *any information captured in reproducible form that is required for conducting business.*

Obviously, within this broad definition there are limitations. A standard dictionary, for example, would meet the criteria just described, yet is most certainly not a record. The determination as to what constitutes a record is based on the context in which the information is created. The standard dictionary may well be required for conducting business, but it was not specifically created by or for the particular organization using it.

We may wish to enhance the definition of a business record, therefore, to suggest that it is any information that is:

- recorded on any physical form or medium
- generated or received by a business enterprise as evidence of its organization,

3

functions, policies, decisions, procedures, operations, and internal or external transactions
- valuable because of the information it contains.

Records require a specific type of management. It is not sufficient to manage records like other forms of information because they are a distinct category of information and must be treated accordingly. Distinguishing between library material and records may serve to illustrate this point.

Library material must be managed. The information in various books, periodicals, and published monographs would not be a usable resource if it were all just thrown in a big pile in the middle of the library floor. But library material is received in a historical manner. Library material is not specifically created by or for the library. The library obtains information after the fact, places it in logical order so that it is readily available to the users, and disposes of it when it is obsolete. The library's concern, therefore, is information maintenance and disposition.

Records, on the other hand, must be managed by the organization that originates them from the moment they are created. How records are created and what information they contain is as much a records management consideration as is the maintenance of that information while it is being used, and its ultimate disposal when it is no longer needed.

An author would not ask a librarian for advice about the content or format of a book prior to its publication. A creator of records, however, might well pose that question regarding information to a professional records manager.

Data versus records

The difference between the information used to record the validity of a business contract, and the summary information used to speed up the processing of its day-to-day transactions, is worth exploring. The best way to do this is to focus on three key terms in our definition of a business record – physical form, evidence, and value. It is these terms that differentiate the management of business information into two distinct and separate subsets – records management and data processing.

As the term record (or, sometimes, document) implies, this information is permanently etched on a medium or physical object such as paper, microfilm, magnetic tape, videotape, or magnetic or optical disk. The types of records captured and stored on these media include text, maps, photographs, and drawings. The discipline and standards for the capture, storage, and management of information in a meaningful format is the substance of **records management**.

Data (both textual and numerical), on the other hand, is information that is raw or unformatted in that it is constantly being updated, edited, manipulated, and moved about irrespective of its physical storage medium. Even in the early days of business, when all information was written or printed on paper, data was extracted from documents to speed processing, or to produce summary reports. Most contract documents were typeset on 'legal-size' paper, and most summary information was more swiftly handwritten like the now historical hand posted accounting ledgers. Because virtually all of this summary information was numbers, computers were first conceived to deal strictly with data. Hence the original name of working with computers was **data processing**.

The media for data today are almost exclusively magnetic-electronic, such as tapes and disks, or specialized compact laser optical disks. Within an organization, information in the form of data is extracted from source documents, which are created or received by the organization, to keep management updated on the status of day-to-day operations, or to allow employees faster access to the facts. Information in the form of physically structured data-records, on the other hand, provide the evidence or proof of these business transactions, should they be required by regulation, litigation, tax audit, and so on.

An example of how these two subsets of information management relate in business could be found in the execution and administration of a house mortgage. The original mortgage document is dated, the terms and repayment schedule are clearly stated, and the agreement is signed and sealed by both the mortgager and the mortgagee, legally binding both parties to the terms of the transaction. Other documents involved in the transaction might be a survey map of the property, blueprints of the home and buildings, land transfer agreements, and proof of a legal title search.

All of these records are permanently stored in a physical form on some medium – almost always paper for this type of transaction – as evidence of the existence of a business transaction and the terms which govern its execution. However, during the execution of a mortgage, the party holding the mortgage (mortgagee) may, for example, want to inform the party who owes the money (mortgager) of the current financial status of the mortgage (as it is always wise to stay in regular contact with your debtors). This data is usually generated by a computer which automatically compares payments to interest obligations, prepares a dated credit/debit statement, and reports the net outstanding balance. Another example of why data is extracted from the documents might be for a report in response to an executive of the mortgage company who wants to see a summary of performing and non-performing loans. These statements are not in themselves legally binding, but are for status and comparison purposes only. They reflect the current status of the legally binding contract evidenced by the documents (records) previously discussed. It should be obvious from this discussion that records have administrative value and legal value. They also have research value and historical value. All of these values and their access and storage implications will be described in detail in this book.

Records management and data processing, then, should be viewed as indispensable, complementary building blocks in the information structure. While it is important to understand the relationship between the two, the focus of this book will be on the management of information as documents, or records management. As we will see in later chapters, however, there are new technologies being used to automate the management and storage of records. The ability of these computerized systems instantly to make available full documents or custom iterations of data, may someday render obsolete the distinction between data and records.

WHAT IS RECORDS MANAGEMENT?

Having defined a record, it is not too difficult to go one step further and define records management. We simply say that records management is the *management of any information captured in reproducible form that is required for conducting business*. But while this is certainly a definition in the classical sense, it is similar to the original record definition in that it requires additional explanation. This explanation is necessary, not so that we will have a further understanding of the terms 'information' or 'record,' but so that we will have some understanding of the functions of 'management.'

Management

Much has been written about management. Advanced degrees in management are offered at the most prestigious universities throughout the world. Yet an individual can become a manager with no prior training or knowledge of the subject. This is not meant to be derogatory to managers but it shows that it is necessary to look at the subject of management from an objective viewpoint, not from the perspective of one who is awestruck.

First, management is not a science. Although management literature abounds with various theories and principles, they are not applicable in the same manner as scientific knowledge is applied. Secondly, management is not an art. Although that word has been used to describe the discipline, such description is totally erroneous and is usually only proposed by those persons who are desperately arguing against the idea of management being a science.

Management is a practice. It is performance based on knowledge, skill and responsibility. If managers are to be effective they must practice management using all three of these attributes. Through this practice the purpose and scope of the organizational mission should be defined; work should be organized logically so that employees achieve a high level of productivity; and a relationship between the organization and the society in which it operates should be maintained.

If the manager as practitioner seems somewhat ethereal, consider the manager as administrator. A manager must carefully administer the organizational resources available so as to obtain the maximum possible productivity from them. While this may not, on the surface, seem like an inordinately difficult task, the magnitude of the problem comes more clearly into focus when one considers that the primary resource in most organizations is people. As an administrator of people, a manager is responsible for creating and maintaining a working environment where groups of individuals can perform efficiently and effectively toward the attainment of the organization's goals.

The organization's goals referred to here are those of the organization as a whole, for example, the corporation, academic institution, law partnership or government agency. The goals of any entity within an organization, such as a division, department or branch, must be consistent with the overall organizational goals or they become, by definition, antithetical to them and the organization will be destroyed from within.

Although this seems obvious when stated in a theoretical manner, the concept, when implemented, often becomes distorted. It is not uncommon to find entities within an organization that seem to have lost sight of the reason for the organization's existence. One of the main reasons for this problem is the misunderstanding of the functions of line and staff.

Within all organizations there are two types of functional entities: line entities which have direct responsibility for accomplishing the objectives of the organization (production, marketing, sales); and staff entities which support the line in their efforts (personnel, accounting, purchasing). In general, the characteristic that distinguishes line from staff is that staff operate in an advisory capacity unless specifically delegated functional authority. Using the personnel function as an example, unless the managing director of a corporation specifically delegates functional authority to the director of personnel, the personnel department would only be able to advise in matters of hiring, firing, employee relations, etc., and all actions/decisions would have to be made by the managing director. To avoid the bottleneck that would inevitably occur from such an arrangement, functional authority for personnel activity is delegated from the managing director to the director of personnel. For that particular functional area, the staff entity has authority over the other line areas within the organization.

How the delegated functional authority is handled by the staff entities is the key to a successful operation. Far too often, staff managers and staff personnel forget that regardless of the functional authority delegated, their one and only purpose is support of the line entities. No organization exists to perform staff functions. An automobile manufacturer exists to produce cars, not to prepare budgets. A transportation authority exists to operate buses and trains, not to prepare press releases. A department store exists to sell merchandise, not to perform employee appraisals. Whenever the staff entities exercise their delegated authority in such a manner as to become nuisances, or become so large and powerful that the line entities appear to be working for them, instead of vice versa, then the organization has reached a critical stage of bureaucratization and is, for all practical purposes, internally hemorrhaging.

It should not be inferred from this discussion that a line manager should have no interest in, or responsibility for staff activities. That is the exact opposite of the situation. A line manager is inherently responsible for dealing with functions such as personnel, budget, and public relations as part of the practice of management. To ignore responsibility for these areas is to be guilty of mismanagement. It is the prioritization of activities and the overall balance that is important, and in this respect the records management activity may be viewed in perspective. Records management is a staff function.

The records management function

Records management is a logical and practical approach to the creation, maintenance, use and disposition of records and, therefore, of the information that those records contain. With a viable records management program in operation, an organization can control both the quality and quantity of the information that it creates; it can maintain that information in a manner that effectively serves its needs; and it can efficiently dispose of the information when it is no longer valuable.

A complete records management program encompasses a multitude of disciplines including forms, reports, correspondence, directives, mail, files, copying, retention scheduling, vital records protection, archival preservation, and ultimate disposal. Each discipline has its own particular principles, practices, methods, and techniques for accomplishing the necessary end results, and certain technological tools that may be employed to help in achieving the results more efficiently, effectively, and economically.

Because a records management program consists of so many diverse elements, a professional records manager must be a combination generalist/specialist. Essentially, the function requires specialized subject matter expertise in several interrelated disciplines. Although it might, on the surface, appear that the design of a form and the determination as to the long-term value of the information it contains are two entirely unrelated activities, we will see, when the life-cycle concept is discussed in Chapter 2, that one is very much dependent on the other. The records manager, therefore, must be able to relate all the various elements together and to explain the relationships to persons at all levels within the organization.

The explanation aspect of the records management function cannot be over-emphasized. For while the records manager will have delegated functional authority to plan, organize, and direct the records management program, the successful operation of that program will require the cooperation of the line (and other staff) entities that the program is designed to support. Cooperation from within these entities will be more readily forthcoming if the people understand why they are being asked to perform a certain activity and are not just told to do it.

The records management function is unique in an organization because although it is a staff operation, and therefore basically overhead, it could be considered as an 'invested overhead' in that unlike most staff areas it has the potential for saving more than it costs. Figures from the US government have shown that a return on investment of 20 to 1 on records management system improvements is not unusual. In developing countries, the return would be even higher.

But while the savings which can accrue from a records management program are substantial, they must be placed in proper context. *The savings are not the rationale or justification for the program and should never be considered as such. The records management program must exist because the function of managing recorded information is a necessity. The savings are merely a bonus that may be obtained from managing the information efficiently.*

One of the major areas of contention in organizations that have established records management programs is the integration of the information handling technologies into the program operation. Although not always considered to be a part of records management, these associated technologies (such as word processing, micrographics, optical character recognition, etc.) are a legitimate records management concern in so far as they are used for creating, maintaining, using, or disposing of recorded information. While records management is often thought of as being synonymous with the term 'paperwork management', nothing could be further from the truth. There is nothing in the records management definition that is media specific. 'Reproducible form' is not limited to paper. Information captured on a microform, a magnetic tape, or an optical disk is just as much a record as that captured on an 8½ × 11 inch (210 × 297mm) piece of paper. As such, it must be managed and the equipment that is used in conjunction with it must be managed concurrently.

Whether or not records managers should have the delegated functional authority to manage and control the associated information technologies is not the issue. The point is that records managers, as a part of their basic records management authority, must at least be involved in matters such as equipment selection, placement, and utilization procedures to ensure that all recorded information receives proper treatment.

RECORDS MANAGEMENT IN HISTORICAL PERSPECTIVE

Records management, as a profession, is a relatively new concept. Even the term records management was unheard of until the mid twentieth century. But records management as a function has existed for some 7,000 years.

Around 5000 BC, the people of the Sumerian civilization produced the first records. These written documents are not just considered to be records today because they are a record of a bygone era. They were created to be records by those originating them. The Sumerian records dealt with business matters such as taxes, loans, and inventories, and they were managed by the temple priests who controlled the Sumerian economy.

Obviously, the management of these clay tablet records was somewhat primitive. But the fact that they were created and kept at all was a major advance for civilized society.

During the New Empire period in Egypt (1530–1050 BC), creating and managing records was a significant government operation. Likewise, in Babylonia, records management was an important function during the reigns of both Hammurabi (1792–1750 BC) and Nebuchadnezzar II (630–562 BC).

The records of ancient civilizations were housed in the libraries of the rulers. Such repositories would today be considered archives, but that distinction was not made at the time. Early 'libraries' contained business records and later evolved to contain collections of literature and information on science, medicine, and religion.

As the centuries passed, the record media changed. Clay gave way to papyrus and parchment, and these, in turn, slowly gave way to paper. Except for this media transition, improvements in recordkeeping techniques were slow to develop. Why this was so is a matter for conjecture, but, at the risk of oversimplifying, it could be said that improvement had not yet become a necessity. Information was recorded by that portion of the population that was literate – priests, teacher/philosophers, scribes, rulers, nobles, and landed gentry – and the recorded information was referenced by that same literate segment of society. Proportionately, there were few people creating documents and few people using them.

There is evidence that a case file system was established in Rome around 1200 AD, and that statutes regarding records retention and disposition existed in the city states of Northern Italy during the same period. These records management principles, however, like many other managerial principles developed over the centuries, seem to have had little application and were relatively short-lived. They came and went until rediscovered at a later date.

It was not until the fifteenth century that any lasting records management innovation was developed. At that time the registry system (in which all incoming and outgoing documents are numbered and entered into logs or registers) was established. Although the registry system is cumbersome, it was an improvement on the previous non-existence of a system. And although archaic by today's standards, it is still in use over much of the world.

In 1789 the Archives Nationales was established in France. This institution provided for unified administration of archives, including the records of public agencies, and developed many of the archival theories subscribed to today. In 1838 the British Public Record Office Act was passed, establishing the principle of a centralized public record office under the direction of a records administrator. In 1877 a British Order in Council authorized destruction of valueless material, and in 1889 the first General Records Disposal Act was passed by the United States Congress. Except for the previously mentioned brief efforts in Rome in the thirteenth century, no routine and systematic disposal of unneeded records had ever been done before. In 1913 the US Bureau of Efficiency was created. For the first time the use of labor-saving office equipment was studied and promoted. In 1934, the National Archives of the United States was established and, within that Federal agency, the life-cycle concept of records management was developed.

With the development of the life-cycle concept, records management went from being a series of sporadic and unrelated efforts to an organized, structured, and logically-based approach to creating, maintaining, and disposing of recorded information. Because it is the foundation of all records management principles, practices, methods, and techniques used today, the life-cycle concept is discussed in detail in Chapter 2.

RECORDS MANAGEMENT TODAY

In the historical section of this chapter, it was suggested that advanced records management concepts were not developed earlier in time because they were not yet necessary. The need for records management came to the fore, however, in the US as a result of the mountains of 'paperwork' in the military and civilian effort during World War II. We now see that not only are sophisticated records management principles and practices necessary in today's information-oriented society, but that they are absolutely critical to its continued survival.

Governments at all levels establish requirements for maintaining records. Almost all business transactions depend on the proper creation and maintenance of recorded information. Decisions in court cases have resulted in proper records disposal becoming an important factor in day-to-day business operations. Quite simply, an organization today cannot ignore its records any more than it can ignore the working conditions of its employees or the environmental concerns of the community in which it is located.

As important as these factors are, however, there is another one which is even more necessary to consider. That is, the changing record media and the advent of electronic recordkeeping. Traditionally, records have been created and kept on paper. As long as information is on paper it can be seen. As long as the paper exists it can be found. A paper document that is misplaced or misfiled may cause inconvenience and the expenditure of excessive funds to locate, but it is retrievable given enough time and effort. With electronic recordkeeping this may not be the case.

When information in electronic form is updated, the previously existing information is lost. Electronic database operations may not provide for back copies or chronological files which can be referenced to obtain the original data. Information stored on electronic media can be adversely affected by dirt, heat, smoke, abrasion, and even the magnetic impulses of an ordinary telephone. Information being entered into electronic storage can be totally wiped out by a power surge or a power loss. Information filed electronically is not retrievable by anyone who does not know the type of system used to file it, and is retrievable by virtually anyone who does.

The issues just described are not automated data processing issues; they are not management information system issues; they are records management issues because they directly relate to how recorded information is created, maintained, used and disposed of. Their resolution, therefore, is dependent on how recorded information is managed.

Additionally, there is the matter of information substantiation. Paper documents have long served the business community with an accepted tradition of judging the verity of information. As this medium is replaced by magnetic, optical, holographic, and others as yet undefined, the business community will appear to be left without a foundation for information substantiation. The foundation, however, was never paper documents. The foundation was the proper management of records. Over one hundred years of common business practice of relying on paper documents for substantiation of information yielded a perception that the two, paper media and records management, are inextricably linked. This is not the case.

The requirement for the substantiation of information still exists, regardless of the medium of the record. New techniques, policies, procedures, and standards for any new media will take time to be developed and will require the focus of an organization-wide brain trust to become as comfortable with it as with the old paper ways. It is essential, however, for organizations to understand that the need for the substantiation of information is growing as it becomes harder and harder to identify and authenticate the sources of electronic information databases. To meet this growing need, records management is undergoing a metamorphosis. The very life of most organizations will depend on their investment in facilitating this metamorphosis, as information technology brings about an impending revolution in business administration.

Why we require substantiation in business is quite simple. The world of business can be a world of dispute. These disputes most often center on the amount of money owed, the responsibility of the other parties in respecting the rights of others in the execution of their business, and the ownership of certain properties, be they real estate, asset, trademark, copyright, or other. Ultimately these disputes, if not handled in the normal course of business transactions end up in the courts of the land. And just as in any civil or criminal dispute, there are uniform rules of evidence for the substantiation of business transactions and communications.

These uniform rules of evidence pertaining to business records strictly define the relative strengths of information that are used to substantiate claims in a court of law. They vary from the weakest third party oral hearsay evidence to the strongest witness-supported, notarized, signed, and sealed paper documents that have been created at the time of the transaction in question in a standard reporting format for that type of transaction.

Lest we think then that records management in the modern office is solely a job for the legal counsel of the organization, let's examine what the roles are in the substantiation of business records. The roles are not unlike the roles of the courts, the legislators, and the police forces in the execution of justice in society. There needs to be a force to design policy and procedure to ensure the substantiation of business transactions. There needs to be a force to audit adherence to these policies and procedures and to bring forward those who are not complying, and there needs to be a force to decide in these cases whether compliance is in fact there and, if not, to take some action to ensure future compliance. A task force made up of the legal counsel, internal audit, the relevant department heads, information systems, and the records manager brings to the table the varied perspectives and responsibilities within an organization, ensuring that all the roles in the substantiation of information can be addressed.

Without responsible individuals who are concerned about these records management issues, and with technology often causing the splintering of information from documents, an organization is constantly in danger of ending up with no substantiating documents to record a transaction. The common, yet inadequate, reaction to this dilemma by senior management has been to keep everything 'just in case.'

Even if organizations can afford to pay for the space to house these records, this response to such an important business issue is little more than hiding one's head in the sand. Although this strategy is perceived to lower the organizational risk of losing a key litigation, it will in fact over time raise and complicate the risk. Right now enough paper documents are probably still being produced and kept to support the organization's evidential needs. However, it has been proven over time that the tendency when using automated systems is to become more lax about protecting such information (e.g., backup). Business records on organizational personal computers are a perfect example. The issues pertaining to the management of records in the modern office must be addressed immediately.

The lack of a well-defined strategy for the substantiation of business information within an organization will prove to be a fatal barrier of entry to the new information technologies which will soon be critical to the competitive positions of companies worldwide. Applying the principles and precepts espoused in this book will ensure that organizations have a solid foundation on which to build as they enter the twenty-first century.

2

The information life cycle

Records do not just materialize on desks, in file cabinets, or in computer storage; people create them and put them there. While this may seem obvious to anyone reading this book today, it was not so obvious prior to the mid twentieth century. The approach to records management from about 5000 BC to about 1945 AD was basically one of attempting to 'keep track of it all.' The fact that 'it' (records) existed because someone had made a conscious effort to capture information in reproducible form had never really been considered.

THE LIFE-CYCLE THEORY

When the life-cycle concept was developed in the United States, people began to realize that there was something that could be done to control the creation of records. If that something was done properly, maintenance, use, and disposition of the recorded information would be much less of a problem. The life-cycle concept may be easily understood. The theory is that recorded information has a 'life' similar to that of a biological organism in that it is born (creation phase), it lives (maintenance and use phase), and it dies (disposition phase). Figure 2.1 illustrates the various phases. Each of the phases has various elements associated with it and functional activities are performed within each element.

Within the creation phase, which also includes receipt of records externally created, there are elements such as forms, reports, directives, and correspondence; during maintenance and use there are elements such as files, mail, communications, appraisal, active storage, security, and vital records. Within the disposition phase there are elements such as storage in records centers, archives, and ultimate disposal. All records go through these phases, some faster or slower than others, and some faster at some phases than at others.

Creation

There are various ways in which a record is created. An individual writes a letter or memorandum to a business associate; a form is sent to a job applicant who must complete it and return it to the organization that has the vacant position; an existing record is placed

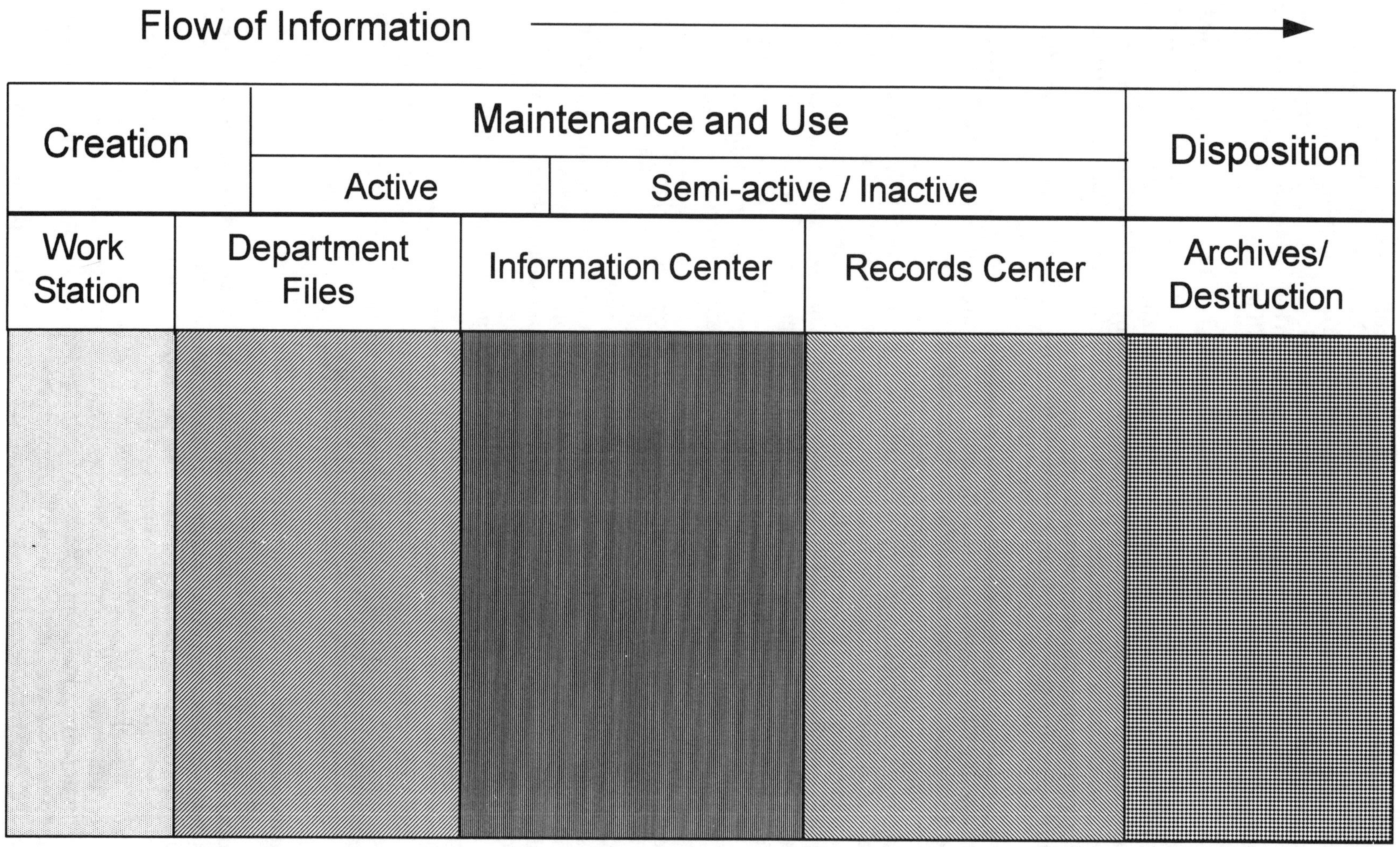

Flow of Information →

	Creation	Maintenance and Use			Disposition
		Active	Semi-active / Inactive		
	Work Station	Department Files	Information Center	Records Center	Archives/ Destruction

Figure 2.1 The phases of information flow

13

on a copying machine and, in a matter of seconds, one becomes two; and so on. There are, of course, different levels of effort involved in creating these records. It does not take a whole lot of time or intelligence to duplicate a record on a quick copy machine. To write a letter or complete a form, however, might involve considerable research. A report might have to be reviewed and edited by a number of people. So before a record is created some thought should be given to the necessity for its existence. If it is unnecessary, it should not be created.

Records creation most often occurs at the personal level with the records staying within a person's workstation under that person's control. Workstation filing systems are usually not controlled by the records manager as they tend to reflect the individual paperwork styles of the individual. The records management discipline at this level will become more important, some argue essential, in the future with the handling of electronic records, particularly from personal computers.

Seventy percent of the cost of information is in records creation, and yet superfluous records are created unnecessarily in almost all organizations on a daily basis. A letter is written when a phone call would have been perfectly adequate. A form is completed in triplicate and only two copies are used. Reports are required even when the response is negative. Little consideration is given to the most fundamental question: '*Is it necessary to capture the information in reproducible form?*'

Obviously there are instances where the capture is not only desirable, but absolutely imperative. One does not conclude treaties, contracts, and multinational mergers without adequate documentation. But assuming that a record should be created, there are still the additional questions regarding how it is to be created. What exactly is it that constitutes 'adequate' documentation? Is a 400-page report necessary, or will a two-page memorandum do the job? Do we want the information to be in a consistent format, necessitating use of a form, or can it just be obtained in a random manner? What type of directive will be needed to ensure that those who are involved in the creation process are aware of the various requirements?

These are the types of issues that must be dealt with when considering records creation. When they are not dealt with, creation quickly becomes proliferation, and the successive phases of life become increasingly more difficult. Because situations differ, the answers to the questions will necessarily differ as well. The goal of a records management program is not to develop a set way for handling all of the various problems and conditions, but to establish a sound methodology for evaluating the situations so that the most appropriate course of action can be taken in each instance.

Additionally, questions regarding the future life of the information must be asked prior to the creation process. Although the maintenance and use activities can obviously not take place until the information has been created, the maintenance and use systems must be developed at this early stage so that when the information does come into being it can be stored and retrieved in an orderly and efficient manner. Thus we begin to see the interrelationships of the various phases.

Maintenance and use

For proper maintenance, all questions regarding information storage and retrieval systems must be answered. As already stated, they should be answered before the records are created because the answers will determine the way in which information is captured.

This phase requires that records be managed both on the file folder and the record series levels. Files management usually comes into play when the record moves out of the workstation into a more central department location, easily accessible by several users. An efficient departmental filing system can be designed using an organizational standard but tailored to the reference needs of the department.

As records become less active, their treatment evolves from the use of specific file folders to their maintenance as record series. This does not mean that individual files are no longer accessed and retrieved, only that the series as a whole takes on more importance in supporting business needs. When we use the term **record series**, we mean *a group of related records, filed together, used together, and which can be evaluated together for retention purposes.* Checks and project files, ledgers and contracts are record series. Correspondence can form series; correspondence related to departmental administration may make up one record series, and correspondence related to outside organizations another.

Just because a record ceases to be fully active does not mean that it should cease to exist. Its existence may be required by statute or regulation, or it may be desirable for historical reference purposes. Nor does it mean that it, and the larger record series, should be accessioned by the archives immediately, for it may, after a given period of time, lose all value.

Disposition

The disposition that is made of an inactive record will depend on the value of the information that it contains. The value of information is measured sometimes in minutes and sometimes in centuries. The information in a memorandum from the company managing director regarding the annual staff party, for example, may be needed only until the party is over. The information in a letter from the same individual discussing the corporate strategy for avoiding a takeover may be deemed historically significant and kept permanently.

If information is considered to be of a permanent nature, it must be captured in reproducible form in a manner that ensures permanence. Thus, disposition should be considered during both the active and semi-active phases. For example, if information is known to be archival at the time it is originated, it can be captured on 100 percent rag bond paper, maintained and used appropriately, and archived at a predetermined time. However, if information is not considered to be archival at the time of origination, but is determined to be archival at a later date, it could be recaptured at that later time in a different form such as microfilm, and the film could be processed to archival standards to ensure permanence. Again, we see the interrelationships of the various life-cycle phases.

INTERRELATIONSHIPS

We have referred to the interrelationships of the phases. There are interrelationships between the various elements as well. For example, the active files element is interrelated with the records center element inasmuch as the amount of space needed for remote storage is dependent on the volume of records in the active files and the frequency with which they become inactive. Similarly, the vital records element is related to the security element because, but its very nature, a vital record must be protected and stored securely. Or again, scheduling relates to appraisal. In fact, the purpose of appraising records is to determine the value of the information they contain during the various life stages so that a schedule may be developed to provide guidance on proper record handling, transfer, media conversion, storage, etc. Likewise, scheduling relates to archiving and to final disposition, both of which are possible last steps in the information life cycle.

There is an additional relationship to be considered besides those of phases and elements and it is, perhaps, the most important relationship of all. The relationship between the people in the organization and the records is one which may be examined when seeking to develop or improve a records management program.

Figure 2.2 illustrates the person/record relationship. The concentric rings represent the various life-cycle phases starting in the center with creation. As the life cycle continues, the volume of records increases. Concurrent with this increase in volume is a shift in focus

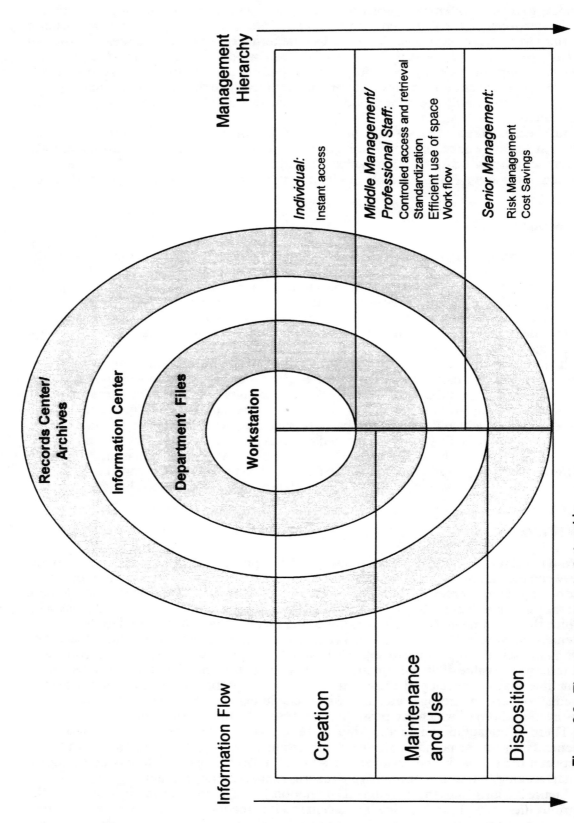

Figure 2.2 The person/record relationship

16

regarding the overall records program and the issues related to it.

Persons working with records in the creation phase are most interested in the immediate availability of information to do their jobs. They are usually not concerned about retention requirements, standard filing systems and storage costs. Indeed, they are often resistant to efforts to improve information handling systems because they are afraid of relinquishing control over what they perceive to be 'their' records.

As we move through the middle circles, the emphasis shifts to middle management concerns regarding such things as multi-use access and retrieval, standardized filing systems and equipment, work flow, and office space efficiencies. Middle managers are concerned that the records are available to get the job done, but they see the job as larger than a single individual.

At the outer circle, or disposition phase, senior managers are the people primarily concerned about records. They view records (information) from the perspective of risk management and cost savings. To a limited extent, senior managers may be concerned about archival factors as well, thinking about the corporate history and their roles in it.

THEORY TO PRACTICE

The life-cycle concept of records management is, like most theories, relatively valueless unless it is put to use. The idea is to implement the theory and turn it into practice. If we consider the life cycle as the basis for a total records management program, we can see that it affords great potential for the effective management of recorded information. However, as far as interrelationships and interdependencies are concerned, it can be seen that all of the phases and all of the elements must be managed in a unified and coordinated manner if significant program effectiveness is to result. This is where the management aspect comes into play. The various records management elements all require planning, organizing, directing, and coordinating, and, obviously, the overall records management program requires that those managerial functions be performed as well. Establishing, organizing, and managing an effective records management program is the subject of Part II.

TECHNOLOGY

In addition to the phases and elements, we must also consider the technologies of records management and their relationship to the information life cycle. Technologies are tools. Their purpose is to make information handling easier, more efficient, and less costly. They can do these things if they are properly used. But technologies are merely the means to an end – not the end themselves. As such, they must be fitted to the function, not vice versa. Devices such as computers, optical character readers, facsimile transceivers, and laser printers should be looked at no differently than filing equipment, and should, therefore, be obtained only to fill a specified need.

Care must be taken to ensure that the implementation of technological improvements does not get out of hand. Life-cycle management efficiencies can be completely eliminated when technology is misapplied. In certain situations technology can actually slow down rather than increase productivity and can increase rather than decrease the cost of operations. Electronic mail can be disastrous if documentary evidence is needed for litigation. A microfilm conversion can cost much more per record than storing hard copy documents in a record center.

With the advent of electronic recordkeeping, the technological issue becomes even more involved. One must be concerned not only about the medium on which the information is captured (magnetic tape, floppy disk, optical disk), but about the equipment on which the medium depends in order to be read. With paper this is not a problem. Assuming that the document has not been destroyed, the information it contains is easily readable. Even with a microform (other than ultrafiche) the recorded information can be read in an emergency with very unsophisticated magnifying lenses. But with electronically-encoded media, there is only one way to get the information out. The electronic equipment that reads the codes must be available – and operable.

Given the rapid changes in technology, the machine availability issue is a major records management consideration. Organizations which make a wholesale commitment to electronic media may find themselves archiving machines and spare parts as well as records, or investing in massive media conversion efforts in order to eliminate the equipment dependency.

3

The evolution of record media

It took thousands of years for an inexpensive, readily available, easily transportable, publicly acceptable medium for the capture of information to evolve. That medium, of course, is paper. During the last one hundred years, people have been educated in standardized reading and writing practices using paper. The various writing instruments invented to mark paper have required remarkably similar skills for operation, and even the markings are based on a universally understood, standardized set of symbols – the alphabet and the number system. It is easy to understand, then, that in this world of automation the paper record has been and will remain an important medium for the capture of information.

Paper, however, is no longer the only medium available for recording information. Microforms, achieved through traditional microphotography and through digital representation of information via laser, for example, have become more cost-effective in particular applications. The storage and retrieval of information on these new media has also brought promises of increased productivity in the office because of their facility to be routed automatically through digital networks to a worker's desktop. In fact, although most experts have recently extended their estimates of when it will practically occur, they agree that white-collar productivity will only increase substantially when office workers master more of this technology and rely on and generate significantly less paper.

There is a new sobriety amongst all information professionals in the 1990s about the complexity of achieving the vision of the 'paperless office'. It is generally agreed that it will be a considerable length of time yet before information storage on paper media is reduced to even 50 percent of the holdings of a usual organization. However, it cannot be denied that progress is being made in this direction and certainly a 'less papered' office will result.

Typically there are three barriers to any new technology. First there is a technological barrier as to whether or not a new concept is physically transferable into a commercially viable product. Next there is the market (or economic barrier) question of whether the product can be produced at a reasonable enough price to make it attractive to the mainstream of prospective applications. Third, and usually the toughest and hardest to break through, is the operational feasibility.

If the new concept is revolutionary (as could easily be argued for a paperless office), the culture of the existing organization may make the introduction of the new concept seemingly impossible. Some historical examples of change on a similar scale that witness this phenomena are: the Luddites reaction to new cloth manufacturing concepts; the reaction to 'horseless carriages' at the turn of the century; the reaction to mass production techniques in the 1920s; and the reaction to world class (sometimes called cellular) manufacturing in the 1980s. The scope of such change in the office today is comparable to the scope of these mentioned innovations. Many people fear this change for some of the same reasons. They fear that they are not equipped with the skills and experience to do their job properly using these new tools. They fear that the increased productivity promised with these tools will result in massive unemployment. It is little wonder that any significant momentum towards a paperless office is being hampered by these fears and lack of skills.

In the meantime, the prevailing office practice is an integrated approach to records management or, essentially, the use of the most cost-effective media for information capture. The choice of medium in each individual case depends to a great extent on a number of factors such as how a record is created, whether it originated inside the organization or was sent from another organization or individual, the access requirements of the information, and whether the records must be a signed original document or a copy. In addition, to complicate this issue further, the cost-effectiveness of a record medium may change at various stages of a record's life span, due to changes in the manner and frequency of its use.

Form should follow function

It is a basic records management principle that the use of information should determine the medium on which it is placed, not vice versa. While this principle may seem obvious, it is often disregarded with the result being poorly functioning records management systems.

All records are not created equal. Different types of records serve different purposes and have different values. Treating all records equally is not management, but chaos. Take, for example, a simple business letter. In the process of writing a business letter, several types of records are created. There is the draft (which may, in fact, be drafts, involving several iterations of the record), the final (which gets sent to the addressee), and at least one record copy of the final (which gets filed somewhere in the originating office).

When paper was the only option, the process of developing a letter was something like the following. A draft was typed by the author and then given to the reviewer. If the draft was not acceptable, the reviewer marked it up and sent it back to the author. The author retyped it and sent the second version to the reviewer along with the first marked-up version. The reviewer compared the second to the first and either accepted it or changed it again as necessary. With the submission of each subsequent modification for review, the preceding versions were attached as reference. Sometimes, the reviewer would go full circle, and end up with a fifth version that was closer to the first than to the third or fourth. Eventually, a final was developed and sent, a 'record copy' made and filed, and the series of drafts disposed of. When sufficient time had passed, the record copy was perhaps transferred to a records center, disposed of, archived, etc.

Within the above scenario, the draft of the letter was considered to be important while it was being actively worked on, but once the final had been created, the draft's importance diminished substantially. The record copy of the final, however, was as important as the original, because the original was sent off to the addressee and the copy was all that remained in the originating office.

It is necessary to understand the various record values and uses when considering media, because technology has vastly changed the creation process. It is now possible, through the use of a Local Area Network (LAN) for the author to key the draft into a computer and transmit it electronically to the reviewer who makes modifications to the electronic file (no hard copies have been created) and transmits the modified version back to the author who then uses the modified version to print a hard copy to be sent out.

The improvement here is obvious. Rather than go through five drafts only to arrive back at the starting point, we have, essentially, a first time final. (The signatory could always change his mind and initiate further revisions at hard copy stage, but psychologically, persons are less likely to do so on finals than on drafts.) There are no hard copy drafts to dispose of because they were automatically eliminated by the reviewer as the modifications were made. The question arises, however, 'What about the originating office record?'

Is a hard copy record made of the final and filed in the old-fashioned way? Or is the electronic file considered to be the official record? If a hard copy record of the final is made, is there provision for deleting the electronic file so as to ensure proper disposal of that duplicate record? If there is no hard copy record of the final, but the electronic file is considered to be the record, is that record legally adequate given that there is no authenticating signature on it? Will it be sufficient to keep the file in internal computer storage or will it have to be transferred to some external medium such as a floppy disk? How will the organization ensure that the file, whether internally or externally stored, is maintained and ultimately disposed of properly?

Suppose we are not dealing with a simple letter, but with some important policy document. In that instance, there might be a need to keep not only a record copy of the final, but of all of the drafts as well so that later researchers will be able to follow the course of the policy's development. Obviously, the system wherein draft one is automatically eliminated with the creation of draft two is not going to work. Record copies of all versions will have to be made before they are transmitted for modification. In fact, the situation gets even more complex. When one of the requirements is for future researchers to be able to understand the intent of the individuals developing the policy (as would be the case, for example with legislation, regulation, labor contract negotiations, position papers, etc.), then keeping the electronic files will be sufficient only if the LAN system allows for annotations, embedded hidden notes, redlining, and vision tracking, and then only if the information contained within those features is reproducible along with the text of the document. Without the necessary system features, potentially significant historical information is likely to be lost.

The medium may not give you the message

The primary usage difference between paper and all other media is that paper can be read using only the human eye. All other types of media require some additional apparatus. The importance of this distinction cannot be overstated.

What must be considered, when contemplating using any medium other than paper, is that not only must the information be appropriately cared for throughout its life cycle, but the equipment necessary to read the information must be adequately maintained as well. For information with a relatively short life span of a few years, equipment maintenance may not present much of a problem. For information with a life span of a decade or more, the problems will be enormous.

Of course, there is an alternative, and that is conversion. Even today, the state of technology is such that a record residing on almost any medium can be converted to reside on almost any other medium. The question is not one of feasibility, but of practicality. The cost of new equipment purchases and the effort associated with media conversions could well have managers longing for the good old days of the quill and scroll.

Maintaining the global approach

None of the foregoing is to suggest that the use of alternate media should be avoided. To the contrary, using advanced technologies and alternate media may be expeditious, economical, and effective. Rather, the cautionary message is included to reinforce the idea that things must be looked at from a global perspective and that **the entire life cycle of the information must be considered at the records creation stage**.

Choosing the medium upon which to capture information is one of the toughest decisions on which a records manager has to advise. The best preparation for making decisions about the medium to be used for capturing information at any point during a particular record's life is a thorough understanding of all the available media and a thorough understanding of the fundamentals of records management. In this chapter, then, we will look at an overview of available media. Further discussions on the use of these technological tools, relevant to the subject at hand, will be included when we deal with the fundamentals of records management throughout the rest of the book. In addition, the final chapter is totally dedicated to exploring the opportunities and pitfalls of implementing these new media and their systems into the modern office.

PAPER

Paper is by far the oldest record medium still in current use. Although there have been many improvements made over the years, the basic structure of paper today is the same as it was when the Chinese invented it circa 105 AD, that is, interwoven cellulose fibers.

The quality and durability of paper are determined by the materials and processes used for its manufacture. Cellulose comes from either cotton or wood and the process for converting the fibers into paper involves the use of acid or alkaline chemicals, heat, and various types of pressure. The processing does not render the organic fibers inert. All paper is chemically active and subject to deterioration. Generally, the highest quality and longest lasting paper is acid free with a high rag content, but even that product will break down due to light, heat, humidity, dust, fungus, air pollution, insects, vermin, and heavy usage.

This is not to say that the medium is volatile. Even a low-grade, acidic paper has a life expectancy of about 50 years when properly stored and handled and, with archival preservation, paper can last hundreds of years. But paper is most often not properly stored and handled (a photosensitive facsimile document placed on a sunny window sill will last about two hours), and so the prudent thing is to understand the conditions to which the material will be subjected before making a selection.

MICROFORMS

Microforms are miniaturized, photographic images on film. Three types of film are generally used to create microforms: silver halide, diazo, and vesicular. There are also dry silver, thermoplastic, and photoplastic films, but they are not widely known. The films come in a variety of formats. There are rolls (100–250 feet long (30–76m) strips of images wound on reels), fiche (individual card size pieces of film with images arranged in a grid pattern), jackets (plastic holders about the size of fiche containing small strips of film), and aperture cards (essentially large punch cards made of paper stock with a cutout area to house a single filmed – usually 35 mm – image). No one film or format is appropriate for storing every type of information.

The great advantage of microform over paper is the reduction of space needed for storing information. Microform images are reduced anywhere from 20 to 150 percent or more. Ninety-eight standard 8½ × 11 inches (210 × 297mm) documents can be placed on a piece of microfiche which measures only 4 × 6 inches (102 × 152mm) at a reduction ratio of only 24 percent. The great disadvantage of microfilm compared to paper is that to use the information on those documents the reduced images must be magnified so that they are readable. This necessitates having equipment such as 'readers' and 'reader printers' available.

Two acronyms, COM and CAR, need to be mentioned here as they will inevitably come up in any discussion regarding the use of microforms. Neither COM nor CAR is a record medium. Computer Output Microfilm (COM) is a system for producing microfiche by having a computer directly generate the images onto the film (i.e., there are no original paper documents). Computer Assisted Retrieval (CAR) is an information storage and retrieval system which utilizes a computer to find the images stored on various microforms.

Many people regard microforms as suitable only for long-term record storage where their advantages of size and stability easily justify the apparent labor and expense of their preparation. Unfortunately, this point of view does not take into consideration the many other benefits of microforms over hard copy.

As the costs of storage, labor, information distribution, and paper products rise, microforms become increasingly attractive, particularly where low-cost information distribution to a limited audience is essential. Libraries and educational institutions have long subscribed to micropublishing services as an alternative to the high costs of publishing small volumes of print materials. One of the most widespread business uses of microforms is computer output microfiche (COM). The ability to photograph information from computer screens directly on to microfiche has proven to be particularly cost effective for the wide distribution of lengthy computer reports.

If micrographic systems have so much going for them, why are they not being more universally embraced to replace hard copy systems? Microphotography is indeed an important technological advance. Let's look at how it fares in all three tests that govern the feasibility of a different medium for records storage and retrieval other than hard copy: technological feasibility, economic feasibility, and operational feasibility.

Technological feasibility

The technological feasibility test indicates that the necessary technical breakthroughs have been made which enable the production of at least laboratory working models of all equipment and supplies used in a process. In the case of microfilming this would require a reliable hard copy transport device, a camera, and switches for the microfilmer, as well as a film that produces an image that can be read in the required detail and a reading device to assist the human eye in reading the processed film. In some form or other, all of these components were available prior to 1900, and all have been significantly improved since that time.

Economic feasibility

A new process should justify any extra cost in dollars to the organization. Some of the major barriers to the market or economic feasibility of a new microfilm system are listed here.

Source document preparation for filming

Each piece of paper to be filmed must be individually prepared by removing staples, paper clips, and pins and by repairing ripped documents. The cost of this tedious clerical process is often as much as all other costs of image conversion combined. This cost can be significantly reduced. Hard copy handling practices aimed at limiting stapling and paper clipping of documents and supported by ongoing staff awareness training can make a significant difference in the cost of source document preparation during later conversion efforts to any media.

Filming and indexing

Although new technologies provide high-speed filming and automatic coding of image documents, much of this process is still a labor intensive, hence expensive, effort. Indexing, in particular, can be an overwhelming task if the indices required are beyond a simple name or number. An organization-wide classification system standard simplifies this process and makes later document retrieval more reliable.

Film processing, error/quality scanning

Poor quality image capture due to overlapping documents as they feed through camera transport devices, or poor lighting conditions producing blackouts or overexposure, require expensive refilming and reindexing. New technologies have eliminated much room for error, but quality control steps can still be expensive and are often ignored in considering the initial economic feasibility of an application.

Special viewing equipment

Once document images are captured on a microform, special viewing equipment is required by any user of this information. In organizations where active files are captured on film this could require every employee having a microform viewer. In cases where a hard copy of the image is required, the employee would then require access to an even more expensive reader printer. Besides the device cost, space in the user's workstation must also be made available. Even if this sometimes significant extra cost in floor space is incurred, often users are reluctant to use microforms at all. It seems that although improvements have been made to viewing equipment in the last ten years, recent surveys show that users continue to be dissatisfied with the readability of microforms for regular document access.

Operational feasibility

Besides overcoming the normal culture resistance to any change, a new process must also fit into the way an organization operates; in other words, it must have operational feasibility. Sometimes a micrographic system creates delays or requires a complete reorganization of the way records are processed. The following issues identify some of these operational barriers to the use of microforms.

Delay in information availability

The nature of today's competitive business world requires that information be distributed for use as soon as it is available. Any medium on which documents are recaptured must possess storage and handling advantages that clearly outweigh the disadvantages of not having document availability during an image capture process. This factor often limits the viability of using a microform because users are unwilling to have access restricted due to the capture process early in the life cycle when both the value of the information and the value of the conversion are greatest.

Incompatibility with annotation

A piece of correspondence often travels through many hands as it is processed. During this journey it is often annotated with notes about phone or face-to-face communication with the correspondent. These additional bits of information often clarify the points contained in the letter and become an integral part of the letter. A microform does not lend itself to this type of annotation. A hard copy must be regenerated, annotated, then refilmed and cross-referenced if additional information is added.

Admissibility as evidence

A primary use of documents is to provide evidence that transactions occurred as purported. Documents recording financial, contractual, and other legal information in particular often serve as evidence of these transactions in courts of law. Most countries have 'evidence acts' that specifically govern the type and format of information admissible as evidence in court. In the United States the federal government and 30 states have adopted the Uniform Photographic Copies of Business and Public Records as Evidence Act (UPA), developed in 1949 and the Uniform Rules of Evidence, developed in 1974. The states that have not adopted these two laws have either their own statutes or some form of the Best Evidence Rule. In some cases these laws do not permit the destruction of paper originals after source document microfilming. It is a good practice to research applicable state laws to determine their specific requirements.

Because of this admissibility ambiguity, it is common for corporate legal counsels to demand the hard copy when they go to court. Few, if any, are interested in fighting the uniform rules of evidence issue when they are trying to protect the interests and rights of their organization in other matters. If this results in a company retaining the original paper documents, in addition to their recaptured microimages, then the paper originals become the best evidence and must be managed carefully so that they can be retrieved for legal or regulatory defense. This extra cost of storing and managing the hard copy documents may be enough to sway the economic feasibility to outweigh any daily administrative reference advantages of using a microfilm copy.

It should be noted, however, that microforms are more readily admitted as evidence in courts than their magnetic or optical counterparts (at the time of writing). This is in part due to the nature of photography having more safeguards against tampering with the information captured on the media than has digitization and in part due to better defined standards for filming than for digitization. The most admissible microform records are produced when the micrographic program is integrated into 'the normal course of business' with official written policy and procedure governing its use.

When are micrographics appropriate?

So far we have concentrated mainly on the negative features of microforms. The sophistication of modern micrographic equipment and the growing expense of office space to store hard copy records has, however, made microphotography viable for many records systems. The following list, though not exhaustive, identifies attributes of a record system that might be a candidate for moving from a hard copy system to a micrographic system.

Attributes indicative of a microfilm application

- More than one user needs the same file at the same time.
- It requires multiple distribution or recurring transportation of records.
- Material is being lost from, or misfiled in, file folders.
- Vital records are not being adequately protected.
- Record reference is to an individual document not a unitized record.
- Individual documents are identical in size, thickness, and color and are indexed simply by a number (such as checks, invoices, purchase orders, credit card receipts).
- Records are created, then seldom updated.
- Saving space is an overwhelming consideration.
- Long-term storage (at least fifteen years) is required.

- Users must have hundreds or even thousands of files at their fingertips (such as in the case of a telephone service hotline).
- The slow speed of computer output on paper is a bottleneck in the data processing operation.
- File users are capable of changing from using paper to using microforms.

Although it is clear that there are many opportunities in an organization to use micrographics for positive economic and operational impact, it is unlikely that it will replace hard copy in business. Microfilming is a proven technology nonetheless and should be integrated into the records management program where the application warrants. The most prevalent applications continue to be COM reports and vital records backup.

Seldom, if ever, is a mass microfilming of hard copy records a wise strategy if done simply to relieve space congestion. Studies have proven that based on space savings alone, it requires twelve to fifteen years (depending on space costs) to recoup the total costs of a microfilm conversion. Further it should not be seen as a panacea for those beleaguered with messy or ineffective hard copy systems. The most effective conversions to microforms have proven to be those where a streamlined, properly organized hard copy system already existed.

DIGITAL STORAGE MEDIA

When one speaks of 'computerized' or more properly 'digitized' information, one is generally referring to information stored on either magnetic or, more recently, optical media. Both use digital technology to accomplish the end result. Digital media are entirely different than either the paper or microform media we have discussed. With digital media there is no 'image' as we are used to thinking of one. Computers reduce images to a series of 0's and 1's, hence the term digitize. A user of digital media is therefore completely dependent upon the equipment which interprets these digital codes to obtain any usable information or to view the image on a computer display.

Magnetic

Magnetic media are constructed of a metal or plastic base coated with a metallic oxide. The digital codes are placed on the medium by an electromagnetic 'head' that magnetizes or demagnetizes small areas of the metallic oxide coating.

There are three basic types of magnetic media: tape, diskette (sometimes referred to as a 'floppy disk'), and hard disk. As a general rule, data access is faster on a hard disk than on a diskette which is, likewise, faster than tape. A key consideration, for records management purposes, however, is that tapes and disks can be removed from the equipment they are used with, whereas hard disks are built in. (There are some exceptions to this rule.)

A capacity comparison between various magnetic media is difficult. Determining the amount of data that can go in a given space is not simply a matter of calculating reduction ratios for a standard size document as it is with microfilm. For one thing, the capacity of the medium varies with the type of coating and the type of head used. For another, the number of documents that can be stored digitally is dependent on the amount and type of information found on the documents.

The amount of digital storage space required by a typical machine-readable document such as a word processing file or spreadsheet is dependent on the amount of information it contains. Likewise, the more complex the information (i.e., if there are graphics as well as text) the more digital storage space will be needed. Digitized images of documents can take up to ten times the magnetic storage space of the regular machine-readable variety.

All magnetic media are volatile. The magnetized coatings are especially sensitive to electronic forces. (A diskette placed next to a telephone could be erased by the electromagnetic impulses from the ringer.) Humidity, smoke, dust, and other pollutants can adversely affect the metallic oxide and destroy valuable data. Multiple backup copies are required to ensure against data loss. Additionally, proper equipment maintenance is imperative if the medium is to remain usable. There is no such thing as 'archival' magnetic media. With very careful handling, information can last for several years. For information that is important, a transfer to another medium for long-term retention is a must.

Optical

Because of the volatility of magnetic medium there has been a consistent need for a more stable medium for the long-term capture of documents that can still be read and manipulated by computers. In the mid seventies a viable medium called optical disk, which combined the stability of microforms with the computer recognition of magnetic media, was announced. Since that time many variations of optical media have been developed to specifically address a wide variety of business records applications. The concept of storage on these various optical media is the same.

Optical media consist of disks which are made up of layers of polycarbonate and aluminium or rare earth metals. Data is digitized onto the metallic layer with a laser beam that creates bubbles or marks. The data is subsequently read by another laser beam that measures the change in reflection or refraction as the light is focused on these bubbles or marks.

As discussed, there are various types of optical media and much of the technology is still in the evolutionary stage. Most common are Compact Disc–Read Only Memory (CD–ROM) discs which are distributed with pre-recorded information and are primarily used for electronic publishing. There are also Write Once Read Many (WORM) disks on which information can be recorded and read (but not erased) by a user. Then there are erasable optical disks which will allow recording, erasing, and rerecording in much the same manner as one uses magnetic diskettes.

Capacity-wise, optical media are subject to the same variables as magnetic media in that the amount of digital storage space required depends on the amount of data a document contains and its complexity. In terms of volatility, optical media are far more stable than magnetic media and even more stable than paper. Optical disks can certainly be destroyed, but a stray electron floating through the air or a spilled cup of coffee won't do it. At this point, however, optical disks should not be considered as archival. Although there have been claims of a 50 year life for information on optical disk, such claims are unproven. A more realistic life span is ten years. The major risks with optical media at present are due to the lack of industry-wide standards.

Optical media and the paperless office

When asked whether it was possible to program a certain application, a programer once said that anything is possible given enough time and money. In this spirit and witnessed by the unprecedented breakthroughs in technology and the continual downward spiral of prices, it is hard to believe that anything as simple as records management could not be possible. With the continuing penetration of computers into both our business and personal lives there has been a continuing dream finally to get rid of the slow and linear paper recordkeeping systems and replace them with a combination of magnetic and optical systems. This dream of a paperless office is not new.

The term and 'would be' trend, 'paperless office', originated in the late 1970s. It seemed to make sense at that time given the following reasons:

- Minicomputers which aimed price and capability at the specialized data processing requirements of a department, rather than the whole organization, were successful, and it seemed to make sense to data processing staff that continued development of these machines could lick the records problems too.
- Personal and departmental filing systems were a disaster in almost every organization and paper was the visible culprit. Senior management supported the data processing developments because they thought if they could get rid of the paper, they would have the whole problem solved.
- People in the data management areas, generally did not have a firm understanding of the special differences between handling information as data and handling information as documents.
- Optical disk storage subsystems were developed in the mid 1970s and by the end of that decade were showing the incredible promise of solving previous data processing issues for information permanency and finally fulfilling everyone's dream of getting rid of all the paperwork.

Evaluating the opportunity of a paperless office, or more appropriately the increased use of magnetic and optical media for records storage and retrieval, requires an appreciation of why it has not happened as yet. Even though the technological barriers of digitized storage on optical disk have been solved and the technology continues to improve and decrease in cost, we have been experiencing a stall in universally embracing imaging technology not unlike the stall towards embracing personal computers experienced in the early 1980s. The feasibility issues are not unlike those discussed previously for micrographics use.

Technological feasibility

The technological feasibility test indicates that the necessary technical breakthroughs have been made which enable the production of at least laboratory working models of all equipment and supplies used in a process. In the case of imaging business records this would require a reliable hard copy scanning device, a rudimentary software for indexing and cross-referencing of the scanned documents, as well as a medium that produces a lasting image that can be read in the required detail and a reading device to assist the human eye in reading the image. Literally hundreds of companies now have working installations of such imaging systems.

The technological barriers that are now being solved are:

1   more interchangeability/interconnectability of equipment and media
2   more standardization of machine software and applications software
3   faster processing speed in desktop computers
4   faster throughput in office networks
5   faster refresh and display rates for large video display terminals
6   faster scanning devices, equipped with more accurate optical character recognition.

Economic feasibility

Most of the developments before the early nineties were in mainframe and minicomputer imaging systems. While these systems were very powerful they had many of the same problems that have made people move to personal computers (PCs) for their data processing needs. The biggest problem was expense. These systems often required proprietary hardware and software that was not available in the open competitive market. The trend now is to LAN-based imaging systems that make use of existing PCs, peripherals, and networks. In fact, imaging has become more about software with the only discrete imaging hardware becoming peripherals, such as scanners and storage sub-systems. Imaging application software has also become compatible with the mainstream operating systems. This has brought imaging from being an independent system not associated with the rest of the office computer systems to being just another data type to join text, sound and video in a multimedia information system. This evolution is parallel to the development of PCs in the eighties. The economies of scale that drove their downward pricing are expected to influence imaging.

The other major barrier to imaging is the high cost of converting from a traditional paper system to an optical disk system. Some vendors have suggested that it is not necessary to do a backfile conversion. They maintain that if you go forward from today imaging your records that within a few years, everything will be imaged. Some systems have been installed with this methodology, but usually there is a grim realization that for a couple of years the organization is actually slowed down in its work as users struggle to reference two parallel records systems. The impact of a backfile conversion must be carefully studied before proceeding. There is, however, a way to have a significant impact on the amount of information that must be scanned and indexed in a back file conversion. This is to implement a corporate records retention schedule and corporate standard-ization in records management practices. In addition, a company should educate its staff in records management principles and methods. The combination of these approaches can cut the cost of a later backfile conversion by as much as 70 percent.

Operational feasibility

One of the most intimidating factors to those considering a move to an imaging system is the lack of standards, procedures and experience to meet evidence admissibility concerns in a court of law. These issues are now being solved and while the courts still have not drafted standards for the admissibility of imaged records, some of the US government regulatory agencies, such as the Securities Exchange Commission (SEC) have established policies for their use.

As barriers to the technology, economy and admissibility of imaging systems dissolve, the final determinant will be how fast the average office worker is inspired to use them. Imaging systems will only become the mainstream records filing and retrieval systems when they are integrated into the day-to-day personal workstation level. It is at this level in an organization that information is created or received. If records are created or received in digital form, by word processors or electronic mail (including electronic data interchange – EDI), they can be stored quickly and efficiently without ever hitting paper. If they are created or received in paper format, they can be desktop scanned immediately and summarily indexed by the people that best know the information and hence where to file it. If every individual is doing this 'in the normal course of business', a general relaxing of admissibility concerns for non-erasable optical storage media should be expected. As well, the one significant remaining economic barrier – media conversions – would disappear as 'many hands make light work.'

Summary

Advising users within a corporation on which is the best medium for their recordkeeping application is one of the most difficult responsibilities of the records manager. There is no one correct answer. As we have already discussed, the prevailing office practice in the midst of this confusion is an integrated approach to records management or, essentially the use of the most cost effective medium for information capture. The trend in records management, however, is unmistakably toward the use of more media that are machine readable. As this trend continues the records manager must become far more technologically aware than is the norm for records managers today. Organizations also have to change as they stretch to assimilate new ways of doing their work. One of the most effective programs that an organization can undertake to prepare for the use of new technologies, and also significantly to limit the cost of their implementation, is a records management program. In the next part of the book we will discuss the proven strategies for the implementation of such a program.

Part 2

Records management improvement strategies

INTRODUCTION

Without a structured program or adequate organization, the effective management of records and information could not be carried out. Under the overall charge of a records manager, who must have senior management support, an organization will include all the functions mentioned in Chapter 1 and examined in detail in later chapters. The organization must be flexible and provide sufficient expertise to cover not only program operations but also policy development and evaluation.

Chapter 4 examines a traditional pyramid organization but considers that records management is more suited to a matrix management structure. It also discusses the importance of people in the organization and their selection and training.

Understanding how the records management program supports the business goals of the organization is central to ensuring its success. Chapter 5 looks at improvement strategies, including planning and strengthening managerial relationships.

In order to maintain the effectiveness and efficiency of an organization, it is necessary to monitor management operations closely. Chapters 6 and 7 discuss how this might best be done and examine in detail the techniques of management analysis, including preparation, project management, data collection, problem solving, drawing conclusions, evaluation and implementation.

Chapter 8 applies the data collection techniques to the physical inventory of the organization's records. This first and most important step in the proper control of records is the only way to ensure the success of the management analysis process and to provide a true assessment of the problems that need to be addressed.

4

Organizing an integrated program

The major prerequisite for establishing a records management program is a top level manager who is convinced that such a program is needed. Top management support is the key to success for every type of line or staff operation and records management is no exception.

A top manager who realizes the importance of records management will delegate the functional authority for such management to a competent, professional records manager and issue an authorizing directive establishing a comprehensive records management program at a level commensurate with other staff functions such as budgeting, personnel, or data processing. While the size of the program will depend on the size of the overall organization, the records manager must be an individual who will develop and expand it to match the organization's growth and who will foster that growth through the effective management of its recorded information. Such an individual should possess a variety of managerial skills and abilities, among which are communicating, goal setting, motivating, decision making, problem identifying and solving, and change facilitation.

The records management program directive, or policy statement, is the official charter for performing all records management functions and should, therefore, be written in terms as broad as possible. Included should be a reference to a total, comprehensive records management program which provides for the management of recorded information throughout its life cycle. By establishing the program on this basis, all records management elements are included and all functional activities are able to be performed. Depending on the way organizational directives are to be written, the records management charter might also incorporate a statement of program objectives and the outline of specific program responsibilities. If the organization is one which subscribes to the ISO 9000 series of standards for quality management, the records management program directive is the place where the quality documentation and records issues of those standards (ISO 9004, Section 17) should be addressed.

Once the directive is officially approved and issued, no further authorization should be necessary for any program activity as long as such activity falls within the range of the authority which has been delegated and stays within budgetary constraints. This is not to say, however, that the records management staff can operate in a totally independent manner and receive no guidance from higher authority. In fact, for some functions, the input of senior level managers is not only desirable, it is an absolute requirement. But most records management program activities such as conducting inventories, developing referencing systems or reviewing the operation of information storage and retrieval systems, can be routinely performed without receiving specific top management approval because such approval was inherent in the issue of the program charter.

Those issues which require decisions at a level of authority higher than that delegated to the records manager should be discussed by a senior level records management committee. The committee, which should be a formally established body chaired by the records manager and consisting of members including legal counsel, accounting or tax personnel, internal auditing manager, data processing manager, director of administration, and other key figures in the hierarchy as appropriate, should deal with overall policy issues and should provide input for decisions of critical import such as vital records determination and retention scheduling.

The committee serves two extremely important purposes. First, it provides high-level managerial expertise to assist the records manager in problem solving and decision making, and, second, it serves as a communications forum to ensure that senior managers are appraised of records management issues and have the opportunity to offer suggestions for future program initiatives. This second factor is extremely important from a 'political' standpoint. If senior management officials are a part of the records management development process, full cooperation is much more likely at the time initiatives are undertaken.

WHY ORGANIZE?

Organizations do not have to have a formal structure in order to function. Indeed, it has even been suggested that a certain organizational ambiguity is preferable because such an arrangement forces people truly to work together to get things done. Whether the structure is formal or informal, however, some organizing is necessary. All things being equal, people generally work more effectively if they know the who, what, where, why, and how regarding the organization in which they are employed.

Organizing is a managerial concept second only to recordkeeping in age. It is basically the logical grouping of activities necessary to obtain objectives, the assignment of each grouping to a manager who has the responsibility to supervise it, and the provision for coordination and communication between all of the organizational entities.

Traditional organization

Records management functional activities appear to lend themselves quite well to being organized in the traditional manner, that is, into a functionally divided hierarchical pyramid. A traditionally structured records management program might be organized as shown in Figure 4.1. (Note: No attempt is being made to try to include every possible functional activity or element in these illustrations.) This structure seems to be logical. The correspondence and policy elements, for example, are shown grouped together under one program manager (this would depend, of course, on the organization's size and the workload involved); management of the technologies of desktop publishing and copy management are placed in this unit (the majority of the work produced using these technologies is either correspondence or policy related); and there are analysts to do the necessary professional work and clerical personnel to provide support.

The files element also shows a program manager, with clerical and professional personnel, correspondence and security, and the technology of micrographics (appropriately placed since micrographics is merely an alternative medium for information storage and retrieval).

All in all, it might be thought that the structure in Figure 4.1 represented a model records management program. Indeed, it is the type of structure found in many organizations. But consider the nature of the records management effort. Why does an

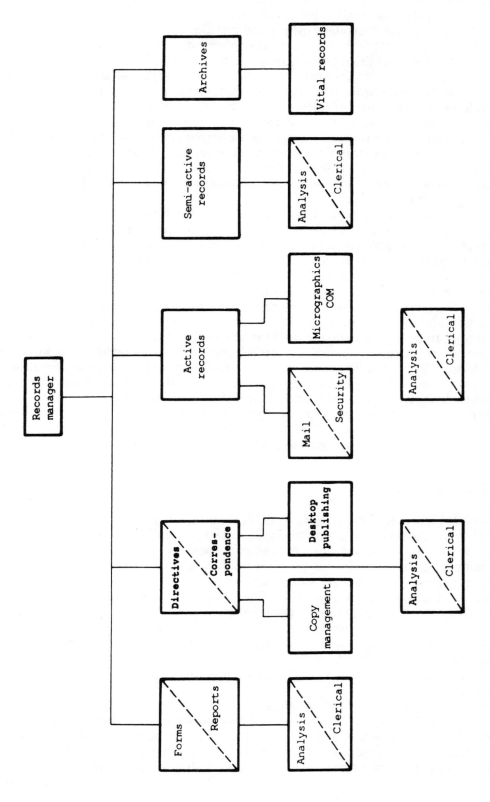

Figure 4.1   A traditionally structured records management program

organization establish a records management program? As discussed in Chapter 1, the records management program should be established to manage the information captured in reproducible form that is required for conducting business. As discussed in Chapter 2, the program should be based on the life-cycle concept which necessitates a multifunctional approach because of the interrelationships and interdependencies.

Even though Figure 4.1 shows no program fragmentation (the records management functions are placed under the records manager), there is complete compartmentalization wherein each element is in its own box with its own separate staff. Even though coordination and communication are possible, each element is still a separate entity and the individuals within those entities may have a somewhat restricted or parochial approach to things because of this separateness. For example, an individual may be capable, by nature and training, of being a multidisciplinary management analyst. But if that person is called a micrographic analyst, and is working in a micrographic operational environment, and reports to the head of the micrographics area, it is highly unlikely that that person is going to be able to sustain the global perspective necessary for doing broad-based management analysis work.

In that same vein, consider the difference between the functions of records management systems, procedures development and implementation (retention scheduling, forms analysis and design, media conversion), which require highly skilled multidisciplinary professional efforts, and those of records management operations (files transfer to inactive storage, forms replenishment, desktop publishing production, document preparation for microfilming) which can be routinely handled by well-trained clerks and technicians. The probabilities are, given the segmented structure, that at any given time there will be either too much or too little work for the professional employees in the various units. It is not reasonable within this type of arrangement to think that professional workers can be laterally shifted between units to achieve workload/staff balance. Although it would be possible to send a forms analyst to the policy area for two weeks or two months, it is poor management practice to do so. Even under the best of conditions such shifts are disruptive and often result in morale deterioration.

The pyramidal organization, like the pyramid itself, provides great stability, but virtually no flexibility. For an effective and viable records management program, managerial flexibility is of paramount importance.

An alternative approach

In contrast to Figure 4.1, there is the organization structure illustrated in Figure 4.2, usually referred to as a matrix or grid management structure. This type of arrangement is reflective of the tasks and activities necessary to achieve the objectives of a records management program, provides for their accomplishment, and gives virtually unlimited flexibility to a records manager to place resources where they are needed.

The matrix structure works as follows. One records manager is responsible for the overall program. Reporting directly to the records manager are two distinct categories of professional. Across the top of the grid are shown the policy and operations managers responsible for the direction and maintenance of the records management program elements, and down the left side of the grid are shown the management analysts whose function is the study, development, and implementation of records management systems and procedures.

In terms of policy development and program operations (operations being essentially the 'control' activities such as maintenance of inventories and the 'production' activities such as desktop publishing and microfilming), the matrix organization would not function much differently than the hierarchical pyramid organization previously described. But in terms of records management systems and procedures development and implementation, the matrix structure is very different indeed. By having an independent staff of

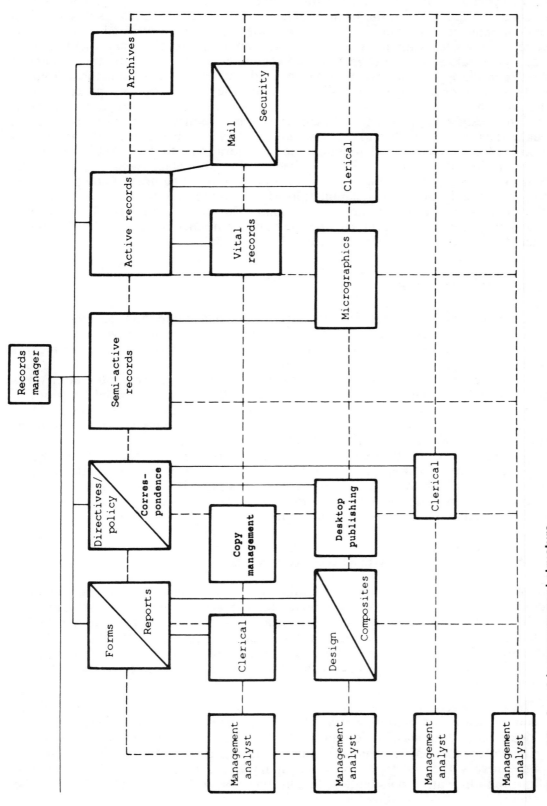

Figure 4.2 A matrix management structure

37

multidisciplinary management analysts, each system and procedure can be viewed from a global perspective. A request for a new form, for example, might be processed as follows: The request would go from the form originator to the forms area just as it would in a pyramidal organization. Then, however, the request would be forwarded to the records manager who would assign the review project to an independent management analyst. The analyst would study the form from the viewpoint of how it related to a system of records, considering the information which would be captured on that form from an overall organizational perspective, and coordinating the forms design and procedures for its use with the various forms users and with all of the necessary records management operations personnel to ensure that the captured information would be correctly handled throughout its life cycle. When the review and analysis was completed, the form would go back to the forms area for final adoption and incorporation into the forms inventory.

Theoretically, the process just described could take place within a pyramidal organization. As a practical matter, it almost never does. The great advantage of the matrix structure is the virtual elimination of the organizational barriers which are artificially imposed by the hierarchical pyramid. The matrix structure allows records management program policies and operations to be maintained in a stable structure while the analytical functions are able to be carried out in a fluid structure.

PROGRAM MANAGEMENT

The purpose of creating an organizational structure is to facilitate the accomplishment of goals and objectives. The primary goal of a records management program – life-cycle management of recorded information – is obtained by efficiently managing the records management elements in an integrated manner.

Overall program management is needed to ensure that the necessary integration takes place. Included in program management are the well-known managerial functions of planning, organizing, directing, staffing, controlling, communicating, decision making, etc., all of which have been written about in great detail in the myriad of management textbooks that are available in various libraries and book stores.

Organizing has been dealt with here because, although matrix management is not a new concept, it is certainly atypical and because the structure uniquely fits the records management functions. We will also discuss staffing because it has been traditionally one of the biggest records management problem areas, and program evaluation because it has not been written about in any significant form.

CHARACTERISTICS OF A RECORDS MANAGER

Successful records managers will be those who can work independently, often in isolation, to achieve results. They must be self-motivated and must constantly seek out and work with all users of information within the organization. Although fairly well established in the United States and Canada, records management is in some respects still in its infancy in most other countries, and those who are establishing it within their organizations must be innovative. Records managers and the staff they select should have the following characteristics:

● The ability to consider new ideas, new possibilities, new ways of doing things. Never content with 'just muddling through,' the innovative records manager is always looking for better ways to do things, at less expense, and with greater efficiency.

● The determination to achieve results. Refusing to be crippled by tradition or bureaucracy, they will try every avenue until they are successful. They will be able to imagine alternative possibilities, finding one that will work. They will never be stalled or aimlessly waiting for encouragement.

- The freedom from concerns about status. They may have to get their hands dirty moving boxes in a records center. They may be improperly placed in the organization structure. These factors should not matter to the innovative records manager, who cares more about creating and establishing an important program than about status.

Innovative records managers will be introducing change into their organization and, when they start hiring, need to surround themselves with a team of innovators. They must always be working not only toward efficiency, but toward improvement. The management analyst who can only streamline a form, instead of recognizing that it can be eliminated if certain simpler procedures are introduced, will continually cling to tradition and to what is familiar. This kind of conservatism will ensure the kind of records management department that does nothing to solve problems, and merely adds to the bureaucratic snags. A strong team of creative individuals can, on the other hand, transform an organization's information structure.

Learning and training for the role of a records manager

While other functions in an organization will have been clearly defined and described, records management often does not have that luxury. Records managers must create or discover their functions and the procedures to follow, then educate the rest of the organization about them, and convince people that they are necessary. A procedures manual will rarely have a section on records management; the records manager will have to write it, and then have it included in the manual. To work alone like this in creating records management policies and procedures requires a certain blind confidence, stamina, and some independence. It is also necessary to have the patience to explain, over and over again, the purpose and importance of records management.

The job of a records manager can be said to cover three roles. Initially, he/she is a problem solver, then a troubleshooter, then a creative designer of new approaches to, and uses of, information and records.

In the first stages of records management, problems have to be discovered and analyzed. The solutions proposed will have to be carefully planned and implemented. Where new procedures are implemented, it will take time for them to become so much a part of the routine that the original problems do not recur. The stage of discovery and analysis leads naturally to implementation.

Once the proposals are implemented, and there is a satisfactory records management program in place, the second stage can begin. This can be either stagnation or innovation. After months of exhausting effort, explanations, and training, records managers will justifiably want to sit back and watch their program operate efficiently, and take pride in all of their accomplishments. However, if they do so, people will begin to forget about them and their program, and fail to see the purpose of their presence. This is the stage at which people, many of them professional records managers, have asked, 'What more is there for the records manager to do? Once the new procedures are accepted and followed, isn't the records manager superfluous? Couldn't the program be supervised by someone at a clerical level?' Some records managers deal with this by having well publicized, yearly campaigns to clear out offices of old records. This raises the records management profile, and temporarily increases record center usage statistics. It is hardly enough to justify a full-time employee with a manager's salary and responsibility.

Records managers must assume two new roles, that of the troubleshooter and that of the creative designer. In the former, they are constantly looking for new problems with records and information and solving them using their management analysis skills. This means that they have to visit offices, talk with people, look at records and equipment, and always offer assistance. Sitting in an office and sending out reminding letters will only make the records manager an anonymous irritant. In order to be aware of new developments or changes in procedures or structures, all of which affect records and information, the records manager must go out and know what people in the organization are doing.

The role of the creative designer develops out of the knowledge gained from the original study, and subsequently consolidated and built upon. Once all of the information that is created, held, and needed by the organization is known to records managers, they can then begin to see where combinations or separations would be a better use of the information. They also can begin to see completely new uses of the information. Instead of simply solving a problem or fulfilling a need, they can propose new ways to exploit a resource. Whether it be as basic as setting up a paper recycling plant for those mountains of shredded documents, or as complex as turning disparate groups of information into a single database, there is much that a creative records manager can and should be doing long after the program is established.

THE STAFFING CHALLENGE

Management has often been defined as getting things done through people. Records managers should, therefore, make every attempt to get a sufficient number of high caliber people for their staff so that the things can get done in an expedient yet effective manner. Typically, records managers have had a difficult time accomplishing this feat. For one thing, being a relatively young profession, there have not been that many records management professionals around to choose from, and, for another, the number of positions on a records management staffing table has usually been somewhat under that which would be ideal.

Records managers, however, do not have to be limited to using their own staff. Although that is the most preferable situation, alternative sources of labor must sometimes be found. The two most common methods of augmenting a records management staff are the employment of outside consultants, and the establishment of an organization-wide records management liaison network.

Consultants

The advantages of using consultants are basically the same as the advantages of having independent management analysts on the staff – specialized experience and expertise, an unbiased viewpoint, ability to concentrate on one job at a time, and a global perspective. (A discussion of the management analysis function will be found in Chapter 5.) Additionally, however, because consultants are not on the staff and are completely unaffiliated with the organization, there is an aura of credibility surrounding them which is often quite significant in terms of the way their work is accepted by senior management. Although this 'credibility factor' is based more on emotion than on logic, it is a reality and must be considered when staffing a records management program.

A consultant can do all the types of work that a management analyst would do, but usually does not. Consultants' efforts are mostly confined to studying problems rather than implementing solutions, implementation being a time-consuming and therefore expensive process. This latter factor is an extremely important one. A study which results in a report that sits on a shelf gathering dust is not much more valuable than a study which was not done at all. When the staffing-by-consultant alternative is being considered, therefore, thought must be given to the total amount of funding that will be necessary to see the project through to completion, not just to the amount that is necessary to get the project started.

It is useful to have someone from the records management staff involved with the consultant on a continuous basis. If an entire consulting team is being brought in, one member of the records management staff could be assigned to be a team member. If the effort is a smaller one, then, at a minimum, regular meetings with the consultant should be held. Without continuous, open communication regarding the consultant's activities, the records manager may be placed in the position of losing some control over that aspect of the program in which the consultant is involved.

Liaison network

The second alternative source of staffing is the records management liaison network, established by having the manager of each organizational entity designate an individual to act as a liaison with the records management staff. Indeed, it is valuable to establish a liaison network even if the records management program is sufficiently staffed. Having a 'friend on the inside' is always a good idea, and the liaison network can provide friends organization-wide.

The key to liaison effectiveness is in developing reasonable expectations. Liaisons are not substitute staff professionals as are consultants. They are not expected to perform studies, or write reports. What they can do is to provide information about their own organizational entities to the records management staff and foster the idea of using sound records management techniques among their co-workers.

Persons who are selected to serve as liaisons should receive training in basic records management principles and more advanced training should be provided if interest and receptivity are shown. Since it is difficult to conceive of a records management program suffering from having too much help, the liaisons should be encouraged to become as involved in the various projects as they want to be. The psychological implications for individuals at the working level are just as significant as they are for the persons on the records management committee. If people think about a project or system as their own, the job of convincing them of its worth is usually not necessary.

Even when liaison personnel are not involved in any particular records management project within their own organizational entity, they should attend periodic meetings so that they might keep abreast of what is happening throughout other parts of the organization. These periodic meetings are opportune times to present short workshop sessions to reinforce the training already received, and to elicit people's ideas and suggestions.

In addition to the obvious support and assistance that liaison personnel can provide, they may also prove to be a source of talent should records management staff vacancies occur. Internal organizational transfers are sometimes easier to effect than external hires, especially during periods of austerity. If a records manager can cultivate an in-house resource pool to draw from, the staffing job will be significantly lessened.

Selecting and training the team

Training in records management has traditionally been very limited. At the professional level within the US and Canada there are a few degree programs for the discipline, but not within the schools of 'management.' In continuing training programs there are some one- or two-day seminars offered by the professional associations. Thus, most of those working as records managers have been trained for some other profession, and it is this situation that records managers must face when they hire their staff.

Equally important to consider is the kind of experience in information work applicants will have had. The more exposure to management techniques and analysis, the better qualified they will be to assist in the management, as opposed to the mere maintenance, of records and information. Even the records clerk or analyst must have some initiative and creativity if the team is to effect worthwhile changes. The techniques of training and staff development are covered thoroughly in numerous publications and will not be repeated here.

The areas in which training should be pursued for each records and information management level are as follows:

1   The director of information
      Business administration
      Data processing/personal computers/networks (PC LANs)
      Records management
      Archives
      Library services
      Information law
2   The records manager
      Management and management analysis
      Information studies (either via library or archives training)
      Imaging/micrographics
      Marketing
      The essentials of data processing/PC LANs
3   The records management analyst
      Management analysis
      Forms and reports management
      Indexing and classification
      Stock control or warehouse management
      The essentials of data processing/PC LANs
4   File supervisor
      Basic records management program procedures
      Personnel supervision
      Supplies management
5   The records clerk
      Basic clerical skills
      Indexing and classification
      Filing procedures, including rules for alphabetical filing
      Correspondence analysis.

Because of the lack of a standard curriculum in which all of these subjects can be learned, staff will have to be sent to courses sponsored by a variety of schools and organizations. This can, however, be an advantage, for it allows the records manager to select carefully the training to be received, and to structure it according to each individual's, and also the organization's, needs.

PROGRAM EVALUATION

The ultimate test of records management program effectiveness is whether the recorded information is available to those who need it when and where it is needed. Add to those criteria the manner in which it is made available (efficiency), and at what cost (economy), and a complete program evaluation can be made.

A program evaluation is essentially a type of internal audit. Whether the evaluation is conducted by an organization's internal auditor or (staff) inspector, however, is not significant. What is important is that the evaluation be done.

A records management program evaluation should be conducted at least bi-annually. If the internal auditors are unavailable to perform audits of a single program on such a regular basis, the records management staff analysts should conduct a 'self-inspection' instead. Because of the nature of the management analysis position, such individuals are easily able to perform self-inspections. In this respect, it should be pointed out that the prime purpose of a program evaluation is not inspection to uncover waste, fraud, and abuse, but review to determine the extent of effectiveness, economy, and efficiency.

Evaluation should encompass all elements of a records management program and should consist of a two-part review. Part one can be a checklist type of examination wherein a comparison is made between textbook theory and operating realities. The greater the similarity between the two, the better the program. Part two of the review should include a study of an existing system which is considered to be operating smoothly. By examining the storage of files, retention schedules, etc. relating to a system which is perceived to have no (or few) problems, one can assess the effectiveness of the records management program fairly accurately. If, upon review, serious problems are found with any aspect of the information flow, whether in the phases of creation, maintenance and use, or disposition, there is a good possibility that some defect exists in the related records management program area. If, on the other hand, the system is found to be operating smoothly, it can be reasonably construed that the records management functions are being effectively performed.

5

Setting the scene for improvement

As the office evolves into a more complex electronic environment, so too records management is evolving into a new level of intricacy as a discipline. The prerequisites required for this new level are either management skills or tools that are part of an analytical approach to records management. And as the information systems of the office evolve, records managers are developing and redefining these recognizable skills and tools even further to ensure their continuing value in the process.

MANAGEMENT EXPECTATIONS

Senior managers have certain expectations of managers on any team responsible for making organizational improvements. They are looking for proficiency in:

Planning processes for the business including:

- understanding the rationale for planning
- knowing the value of anticipating and shaping change
- defining the key result parameters
- relating plans for the records management program to organizational interests and aspirations
- relating plans for the records management program to operational (departmental) interests and aspirations.

Managerial relationships and responsibilities including:

- understanding and knowing how to influence organizational practices
- contributing to and supporting senior management decision making
- dealing with alternative leadership styles
- helping to build a culture that encourages commitment.

Management analysis including:

- motivating staff to help collect data through inventories and interviews
- using/teaching techniques for problem analysis and decision making
- knowing how to introduce and manage change.

These management abilities are part of the expectations of all managers in the organization who are responsible for allocating and managing the organization's resources. The responsibility of the records manager is to add value to the management of traditional records, as well as to the evolutionary change process to electronic record-keeping. This work not only affects the quality of the information resource, but it impacts on the work of every employee in the organization. To fulfill these broad responsibilities records managers have refined a definitive set of tools and skills pertinent to managing the records and information resource and to dealing with the various constituencies of the organization.

PLANNING PROCESSES

The daily orientation to detail, required by activities such as retrieving inactive records from an off-site records center or developing effective filing systems, sometimes makes a records manager overly focused on specific problems – and less concerned with the overall organizational impact of innovation. Senior management, however, is oriented to this type of overall thinking and planning, called **strategic planning**. In other words, they expect the daily programs to carry on uninterrupted, but still demand to see some overall plan to any new innovation or program. This is particularly true when a significant expenditure is required. The challenge of records management, then, is formulating and internally marketing a long-term records improvement plan to maximize access and retrieval and minimize risk while simultaneously organizing and implementing the tactical programs to keep the organization operating on a daily basis.

Strategic planning is planning that is visionary and long-range in nature. It deals with an organization's stated mission and its long-term goals. Strategic plans are derived from an analysis of how senior management views the business environment in which it anticipates it will be working and how it can act to achieve the corporate goals in such an environment. This plan provides guidance for the actions taken at the operational levels of an organization.

Senior managers know that a productivity increase in the office can stretch scarce budget dollars and can make a direct impact on the bottom line. They also accept that productivity gains are usually accompanied by capital investment. When funds are scarce, senior executives consolidate spending on the priority programs and projects that will best help the organization meet its goals and objectives as defined in the **corporate strategic plan**. The prevailing emphasis in these plans is on increasing the quality of service to the organization's customers and the quality of its product. This emphasis is almost always in the context of streamlining the business and of lowering the overall cost of doing business.

It is the records manager's responsibility to be familiar with the strategic plan and to determine how the records management program can facilitate the achievement of the stated organizational goals. Information systems (IS) managers have long realized the benefits of producing an information plan for the organization in response to the strategic plan. Most organizations refer to this plan as the **corporate information strategy**. It is updated annually but covers three to five years into the future. The purpose of this strategy is to track a migration path for hardware, software, and staff resource requirements in response to senior management's vision for the business of the organization.

The records manager must be aware of the impact that strategic decisions will have on operations in order to be able to adjust records management operations in accordance with them. For instance, a corporate strategy which focuses on growth through acquisitions and mergers might call for a far different response than does a strategy that focuses on improving operational efficiency through cutbacks and layoffs. Let's then look at the elements that should be considered when developing a records management strategy for an organization.

The strategic records improvement plan

A strategic records improvement plan is the blueprint for records management in the organization. It needs to be synchronized with the goals, objectives and activities of the rest of the organization. Each new request for expenditure is then put forward in a context of the overall corporate strategy with clearly defined objectives. Instead of gratuitous statements about the importance of properly managing records, there are distinct measurements for the success of the plan and its component projects. Most successful records improvement strategies clarify corporate philosophy and policy in three areas of records administration.

The relationship of records managers and other organization information managers

The plan should clarify the relationship of records management with information systems. This is usually accomplished by integrating the strategy for managing the documents, files and records of the organization with the strategy for data processing and management information systems. Documents and data are most effectively managed as two complementary building blocks in the information structure of an organization, not as separate entities. A coordinated corporate information strategy that defines the character and role of each of these blocks is critical in preparing to take strategic business advantage of new technologies such as imaging. This integration of information disciplines ensures that an organization can take full advantage of the latest information technologies while continuing to meet its responsibilities for the substantiation of its information holdings.

The scope of the records management program

The plan must address the management of all records and related information, regardless of the media on which they are recorded. This management must be applied continuously and consistently as the records and related information flow through the organization. A flow is created as information is processed by multiple departments, being handed on to the next department to continue its part of the transaction (the interrelationship of inventory control, purchasing, receiving, and accounts payable, is a classic example of this flow of virtually the same information on very similar records – the purchase requisition, the multiple copies of purchase order, and the invoice). Since information does not know any departmental boundaries, it cannot be managed in organizational parcels. The emphasis should be on streamlining the complete information flow rather than on the classic cycle of throwing isolated vendor solutions at departmental filing symptoms.

The responsibilities for records management

The plan must empower all staff to seek continuous improvement in the way they handle recorded information. The emphasis must be daily on the elimination of any waste of space, supplies, equipment, and time, in all areas of creating, processing and storing records. This culture, and the resulting attitude and actions, contribute directly to raising the quality of work and to lowering the cost of doing business. An essential part of this culture is the positioning of all records as the property of the organization and not of any individual.

MANAGERIAL RELATIONSHIPS

It is not enough simply to present requests for expenditures to management in a long-term context. Senior managers want to know how these expenditures will affect the daily routine of the organization. They are pressing their departments to be profit centers and want their department managers to be entrepreneurs. This means making them not only responsible for getting results but also for how they get results. Getting support from these managers will not only require consensus on the value of the opportunity presented in the strategic records improvement plan, but also on the details of preparing and implementing such a plan.

Department managers are interested in who on their staff will be involved or affected, the timing of any changes, and how it will reduce their budget. Even if they feel that the initiative serves the organization in general, they will often resist any funding or staffing participation if they feel it doesn't directly benefit their department. This is a quandary when trying to present the opportunity of records management. Information and its management is not constrained by any organizational boundaries. In fact, many of the benefits of better records management are gained by streamlining the interdepartmental flow of records.

Sometimes the solution to this quandary is to bring a group of department managers together and to present a plan that shows incremental benefit to them all. The administrative managers for facilities, personnel, finance, and legal should not be overlooked at this type of meeting. Each of these administrative groups has an agenda for saving space, headcount, or money, and/or for defending the organization in an audit or litigation. Their support will exert pressure on the operations managers and senior management. Gaining their support will require showing how the records management program can further their agenda. There should be a clear context for how the records improvement initiative will relate to these other administrative management entities in the organization, for example:

- *Facilities management operations*. Any cabinets, equipment, or space requirements should fall within any established corporate facilities standards, and/or future plans.
- *Purchasing management operations*. New records equipment or supplies need clear specifications of their necessary attributes, so that the purchasing group can acquire the most effective equipment at the best purchasing terms.
- *Finance management operations*. Cash flow, funding, budget, and cost-benefit are all important issues to the records manager and senior management.

In the end, there is no secret to influencing department managers about an increased opportunity to manage efficiently the records that are created, stored or passed through their department. They want to study the detailed costs and benefits to them in a professional plan. And they will want to hear about this improvement from a management individual or group that they feel is competent to implement the plan before they commit any departmental resources. Records managers can fulfil these expectations and at the same time improve their own analysis and recommendations through the application of professional analysis techniques. These techniques are often referred to as management analysis.

MANAGEMENT ANALYSIS

Management analysis is a term used to describe the activities of individuals in organizations who study organizational structure and operations. On the basis of the studies performed, the management analysts advise managers on ways of increasing efficiency by doing work better, faster, or cheaper.

Management analysis is not a new concept. Over the years those performing the analytical functions have been given a variety of titles. In the early part of the twentieth century such persons were known as 'efficiency experts'; in mid century the title was 'organization and methods examiner'; and, today, an alternative name for management analyst is 'internal consultant.' Although we will refer to management analysis in this book, the title is not the important factor. Regardless of which label has been applied in the past, there has been little question as to the necessity for the work that is performed.

Part of a manager's responsibility is the concern for an organization's methods and procedures. But managers have to divide their attention between several areas relating to their particular programs, many of which tend to seem more urgent than the methods and procedures by which those programs operate. Put another way, getting the job done takes priority over how it gets done, and not until it stops getting done does the way in which it gets done become an issue.

So just as personnel specialists might be available to assist busy managers with employee recruitment, management analysts are available to help managers improve methods and procedures. Management analysts can provide valuable help to managers because they:

- have an unbiased and independent viewpoint
- study the organization from a global perspective
- concentrate on one job at a time
- have specialized experience and expertise.

This latter factor, specialized experience and expertise, is especially important in records management analysis work. The entire information life cycle must be considered when designing a records system. It is possible that to create even a simple system an analyst would have to understand forms analysis and design, printing, desktop publishing, mail, filing, micrographics, inactive storage, vital records, and archival preservation. Management analysis assignments vary widely in scope: they may include examinations of office procedures, reviews of the organization of entire departments, and specific studies in areas such as office automation. Management analysts look not only at the work which is being done, but also at the purpose of it, and at the overall organizational requirements. With a records system especially, the analysis cannot be done in a vacuum. The manager who perceives the problem may not have the problem at all. What may initially appear to be a filing system deficiency may ultimately prove to be a mail operations deficiency – or vice versa.

Management analysis is a 'requested' service. Management analysts are not internal auditors or investigators who unexpectedly arrive on the scene. While the service is most often requested by the manager who wants to repair something, analysts can often do their best work when used as original system designers. It is far more cost-effective to design a system correctly at the outset than it is to redesign one after it is malfunctioning.

Management analysis is a staff function. Because of this, analysts recommend actions to managers, they do not direct them. It is unrealistic to think that all recommendations will always be accepted and implemented. Acceptance is based on four factors: the credibility of the analyst; the value of the recommendations; the manner in which the recommendations are presented; and organizational politics which, unfortunately, sometimes overshadow and negate the first three factors.

The timing of the management analyst's involvement very often determines the term used to describe the effort. For example, a review of an existing system is usually referred to as a **survey** or **study**. Development of a new system, on the other hand, is usually referred to as a **project**. Frequently, the recommendations of a study lead to initiation of a project. Semantically, however, surveys and studies are merely types of projects. This terminology issue is mentioned merely to head off any confusion that might result from encountering both terms in this book. The key idea to keep in mind is that the principles and techniques are the same regardless of what the effort is called.

Some dos and don'ts of management analysis

A management analyst should be familiar with organizational theory and practice and should have knowledge of the various subjects with which managers are concerned. While management analysis assistance is requested because of the management analyst's expertise, an individual analyst should avoid posing as a subject-matter specialist. This seeming contradiction is explained when one realizes that when dealing with a managerial problem there is usually not 'one best way' to solve it, and specialists may have an inherent bias towards their own area of specialization.

Management analysts need to know how to organize tasks, deal with people, collect, record, and verify information, draw and test conclusions, and prepare recommendations. They must operate in an independent and unbiased manner and be able systematically to collect and analyze data. Their recommendations must always be constructive and based on reason and logic.

The individual who is likely to be successful in management analysis enjoys working with people and systems, is not easily frustrated and displays energy, initiative, and self-confidence. Above all, however, a management analyst must possess an uncommon amount of common sense.

Using management analysis in records management

While there are a number of reasons organizations turn to modern technological advances, the decision to adopt and implement them requires careful attention. Tools such as work simplification are brought to bear on decisions when it is obvious that something is wrong (or at least that things can be significantly improved), but no one seems quite yet sure of what to do. While management is not science, this approach, based upon the method used by scientists in other fields of inquiry, attempts to bring the rigor associated with the physical sciences to the management of activities and decision making within an organization.

Management analysis is characterized by these features:

- the gathering of facts
- the breaking of complex steps into their basic elements
- the use of tentative solutions to problems as a guide to thinking
- the elimination of emotional bias
- the application of objective measurements
- the search for logical relationships between facts and results.

Combining management ability with this scientific approach equips the records manager with the powerful skill and tool set required to manage the diverse records media found in modern organizations. The ongoing complexity for records managers is knowing when and how to apply a variety of skills and tools.

Getting started

Working through the process of management analysis is an effective way for the records manager to solve records handling problems and to introduce change into an organization. In the next two chapters we will work through this process, step by step, to show how a records manager can integrate the general approach of management analysis into the specific work of records improvement.

6

Management analysis part one: preparation, project management, and data collection

Once a strategy for records management has been accepted by senior management, information systems, and the administrative and operational department managers, it is time to start the process of records improvement in the organization. To accomplish these improvements, the records manager uses the tools of management analysis as refined for use in records improvement work. These tools are employed throughout the process of data collection, analysis, evaluation, and implementation.

THE TOOLS OF MANAGEMENT ANALYSIS

The records manager's tool kit provides a unique set of skills to bring this scientific approach or 'management analysis' to the management of records in an organization.

Project management including:

- the ability to plan, estimate, schedule and direct a project.

Project team management including:

- the people skills to select and train team members
- the ability to involve, manage, and motivate workers from many different areas and levels of the organization
- the ability to facilitate the team meetings.

Process flow charting including:

- the ability to use/train others on automated flow charting software tools
- the use of flow charts to 'freeze the action' so that everyone can understand and agree on what is being done and how it can be improved.

Cost-benefit analysis including:

- the understanding of the concepts of opportunity cost when competing for diminishing resources
- the use of cost-benefit analysis as a formal tool in advocating a significant records management initiative.

We will discuss the use of these tools in the five step records improvement process:

1 Preparation for improvement
2 Project management
3 Data collection
4 Analyzing and drawing conclusions
5 Project evaluation and implementation.

The first three steps will be covered in this chapter. Steps four and five will be covered in Chapter 7.

PREPARATION FOR IMPROVEMENT

Meeting with senior management

One of the best ways to get any project under way is to do an initial briefing with senior management. Because even a well-conducted study is somewhat disruptive and intrusive, many people will object to it. Without the full support of senior management, the study will not be a success. This holds true for all records management programs generally. They usually require major reconsideration and changes, and these are often resisted. The records manager should find an ally in at least one senior manager, who will, when it becomes necessary, use authority to ensure cooperation.

Usually the briefing will only be twenty or thirty minutes in duration so it has to be carefully prepared and orchestrated. The records manager must do some advance preparation for a senior management meeting by reviewing previous studies or reports and documentation related to the activity to be evaluated.

These meetings give the records manager an opportunity to meet the organization's senior staff members in order to explain the reason for the study. It also gives them the opportunity of learning about:

- management's vision of information management
- management's concerns with access and retrieval
- management's concerns with legal or regulatory compliance risks

and of being supplied with information such as:

- organization charts
- functional statements
- position descriptions
- relevant statistics
- information about perceived shortcomings such as backlogs, customer complaints, high staff turnover, etc.

The ways in which the senior managers can help the study effort should also be discussed. Senior managers can, for example:

- appoint a liaison person (sometimes called a department coordinator) to help the analyst obtain materials, meet key departmental contacts or explain existing methods and procedures
- recognize that the scope of the study may need to be modified as the assignment develops and understanding of the problems increases

- consider the possibility of accepting a less formal final report so that it can be prepared more quickly.

The senior management memo

One of the most important things senior management can do is to request formally the staff members whose work is to be examined to do all they can to assist the analyst in obtaining the information needed. They need to ensure that the staff members of the organization to be studied understand the purpose of the study and realize that it is not designed to review the performance of individuals, but to review methods and procedures.

Before the effort begins, the senior manager should send out a general memorandum to all employees, announcing plans for a records management study. This memo should explain when and why the survey will take place, that it will require some time and cooperation from all employees, that confidential and even secret files on paper and computer will have to be seen and explained, and it should ask for full compliance and cooperation of all employees in the study (see the example shown in Figure 6.1). If a records management directive or mandate has already been produced, this memo may not be necessary, but it can't hurt and it could help.

MEMORANDUM

To: All employees
From: The Managing Director
Subject: Records Management Study

Our company has a serious filing and recordkeeping problem, and we have begun to take steps to find a solution. Starting next month, John Smith and a team of assistants will conduct an inventory of all files, computers and microfilm, within the company. They will ask all of you questions about your information and filing needs and problems. They will also require your attendance while they look through the files. Please give them all of your assistance. We apologize for the inconvenience but we are certain that the resulting improvements will make it all worthwhile.

Figure 6.1   The senior management memorandum

At the same time as this memo is sent, the records manager should obtain the necessary clearances to view any confidential or secret information. It may be necessary for others on the team to have this clearance as well, if there are large amounts of confidential files. Copies of the clearance or authorization should be kept at all times while doing the survey, and given to anyone who asks to see it. The same should be done with a copy of the senior manager's initial, authorizing letter. Many people will say that they have not seen it or have lost it. Rather than let this be an excuse for delay, simply give them a new copy from your supply.

Preliminary review

If, for some reason, the activities to be examined are well known to the analyst, it may be possible to draw up a work plan without a preliminary review. But if the activities are not known (which is usually the case) some preliminary review should be made to get a better understanding of the problems and to decide how best to carry out the study to obtain the most beneficial results.

The amount of information to be obtained in a preliminary review depends on the circumstances and on the individual analyst. Normally, only a general understanding of the work and the organization is necessary. But it may be that an unusual situation requires that more information about the organization structure or some specific procedures be obtained. Some areas for possible review include:

- the basic requirements of the work process; the amount of change to established procedures; relevant statistics for recent years; and trends related to workload
- estimated costs of activities for the operation as a whole and by sub-function when such figures are available
- the extent of delays and the nature of criticisms or complaints
- suggestions for systems improvement previously submitted by staff personnel
- the planning, controlling, and supervising methods of managers
- the characteristics of the individual work tasks
- the characteristics of the documents used in the process
- staff morale (comments or complaints about the process, the environment, the management style, etc.).

When the preliminary review is completed, a study cost-benefit assessment should be made as an adjunct activity to drawing up a detailed project plan. Management analysts are more appropriately utilized to correct serious systems defects than merely to making minor improvements to relatively smooth-running operations. Although there is hardly any system that cannot be improved in some measure, the aim should be to make the best use of the usually limited resources. If an early cost-benefit assessment indicates that the study is likely to result in improvements which will be negligible in comparison to the time which will be involved, the entire effort should be re-evaluated and possibly discontinued in favor of a more lucrative endeavor. If, however, a project is identified as a viable undertaking by the records manager or by a team on which the records manager is a member, then it is time to use one of the most important tools in the management analysis – project management.

PROJECT MANAGEMENT

Project management is a term frequently associated with the design and implementation of automated systems. It would be unfortunate to consider project management as limited to automated systems since its principles are clearly applicable to any type of project, automated or otherwise, and, in fact, were known long before automation was invented. Project management techniques are useful whether the project is conducting a micrographics feasibility study, designing a records storage facility, or developing a computerized information retrieval system.

It should be obvious that various types of projects require various levels of managerial effort. The level of project management should be proportional to the length, difficulty, and importance of the project. This is not to suggest that any projects that are undertaken are unimportant, but, in the real world, some things are just 'more equal' than others.

Any project requires resources – people, time, money, and sometimes equipment or other materials. Resources are characteristically dynamic in nature. Personnel changes, budget cuts, equipment availability, and the like, can alter the direction of a project at any given moment or even cause its demise. In this regard, the project manager, who in essence manages the project by directing and monitoring its progress in terms of a specific plan, must constantly be aware of the overall organizational situation.

The success of a project depends on the following factors:

- clearly defined scope and objectives
- clearly defined roles and responsibilities
- management commitment and support

- user/customer commitment and involvement
- clearly defined tasks and dependencies
- realistic scheduling of tasks
- cooperation among the participants
- realistic estimates of cost and effort
- periodic review and adjustment as necessary.

The following basic project management guidelines can help to avoid problems once the project is under way:

- There should be just one overall plan and schedule for the project.
- The plan must be comprehensive and detailed.
- Progress reports should specifically relate to the tasks on the plan and should be prepared on a regular basis.
- Time estimates should be regarded as commitments.
- Critical activities should be identified and closely monitored.
- Project review meetings should be held regularly, as the project demands.
- Project team members should be represented at review meetings and the representatives should have the authority to make decisions.

The project plan

It is said about Christopher Columbus that he started out on his voyage not knowing where he was going, did not realize where he was when he got there, did not know where he had been when he got back, and did it all on borrowed money. The end result, of course, was that Christopher Columbus discovered America. Few management analysts will be able to use Columbus's method and achieve the same degree of success. A plan is necessary before a study can be conducted.

A plan is, in some respects, a map for the voyage. While the analogy is not perfect, inasmuch as one will not know at the outset what the result will be, still the plan does help to guide the effort from point to point towards the ultimate goal of system improvement. A plan is any detailed method, formulated beforehand, for doing or making something. It is during the planning stage that the specifics of the study (scope, objectives, tasks, costs, etc.) are identified.

Scope

The scope is the extent or range of the study. It identifies the area within which action can take place and the limits between which variation is possible. This identification is not only what the study will cover or not cover. It includes who will be affected by the study and most important, any overriding constraints (budget, time, staff, etc.) that might affect the study, its timing, or its outcome.

Objectives

There is much debate over which comes first: goals or objectives. Since both are similarly defined as ends toward which efforts are directed, the term 'objectives' is used here to include both. Stating the objectives should be one of the first steps in the planning process. What happens more often than not, though, is that the objectives are either poorly stated or not stated at all. In larger studies, the scope and objectives should be distinct; in smaller studies there may be some overlap. Objectives describe the schedule, budget, and quality of the operation, and may relate to many different areas. A good objective is one that is clearly stated, reasonable (obtainable), and quantifiable. Objectives should be listed in order of priority. Failing to have written objectives or stating them in such a way that they conflict with one another will delay or misdirect the study.

Tasks

Once the scope and objectives are determined, task lists should be developed for each phase of the study. For each task, five specifications may be defined: purpose, functional description, resources/documents used, results, and completion criteria. The name of the individual to be assigned to the task should be included, as should the beginning and end dates and the time estimated for completion.

The project team

Through the eighties it became popular to improve work, not by studying the work, but rather by studying and buying technology. Many hard lessons later we have established that there must be a clear link between business and technology, always coming back to the business need, or the technology won't work. We have learned that no matter how effective new technology looks in a test environment, it is only as effective as the people doing the work in the daily activities of the organization. Project teams have always proven to be an effective way to collect data and to introduce and manage change. In general terms, the project team's mission is to bring into alignment the organization's goals, the people in the organization, and the most suitable equipment and methods. Also this model has recently proven to be an effective vehicle for introducing and managing technological change.

The management analysis process encourages the type of management and user commitment required in a project. However, all projects must have a project manager or leader. This could be the records manager, supervisor, or analyst, depending on the size and scope of the effort. The project manager should be an individual who can organize, lead, communicate, motivate and negotiate.

In addition, a project team of no more than ten people should be set up. Depending upon the nature of the project, the team could involve members of a particular department which may have the bulk of the expertise required or it could consist of representatives of the various areas affected by the project. Or it could be a small steering group that calls on others for expertise as needed. Whatever the model, the people involved should be able to collectively set up and operate as a team, deal extensively and sensitively with people, set up and test solutions, evaluate results, and prepare reports.

Selecting team members

One feature of emerging technology is that its introduction frequently cuts across organizational lines and patterns of communication. One example is electronic mail. Through either a mainframe computer system, or a personal computer network system, one worker can key in information to be shared with another worker. These systems are greatly reducing the amount of typewritten interoffice correspondence. They also ease frustrations that result from not knowing whether a message has been delivered, or from trying to reach another worker who is busy. It does raise a number of questions, however. Who is in control of the system? Is it the responsibility of the data processing department in which the computer resides or is it the responsibility of office services? Who provides training for workers in its usage? Who should have access to it? How is confidentiality ensured? What are the requirements for hard copy documentation? Which is the best system to purchase? How much will the system cost? In whose budget will it appear for approval? What modifications to the existing building structure will be required? How will the system be maintained?

Clearly, the answers to these questions cannot be provided by any one person nor should any one person assume responsibility for providing them. Answers will have to come from a variety of sources, such as data processing, purchasing, equipment vendors, records personnel, office services, maintenance, budget control, staffing, to name a few.

Depending on the nature of the project, a representative from each constituency may be a member on a technical support team that reports to the main project team. The main project team should primarily consist of members of the one group which is too frequently overlooked, but that is essential to the success of the system – the end users of the product or the system.

Those chosen from the end users group should:

- want to participate.
- not feel their jobs are at risk.
- come from a working environment where change is viewed positively.

To ensure that the necessary information and expertise is available to the project team, there should be ample opportunities for input from the organization's many functional areas.

Variations of team setup

Broad involvement of as many affected workers and advisors as possible can be encouraged with some variations of the traditional team setup. The responsibility for the project may be assigned to a particular department which may have the bulk of the expertise required or may be the principal user of the end product. In other cases, a full-time project team comprising a few members is assigned the project and other personnel are called upon as their input is needed. In still other cases, the project team includes full-time members from all the appropriate organizational functions. Whichever model is selected, the persons involved must collectively be able to set up and operate a team, deal extensively and sensitively with people, set up and test solutions, evaluate results, and prepare reports.

Estimating resource requirements

Another key element in the planning process is estimating the cost and effort required to complete the study. This is no easy undertaking, however, because there are several barriers which impede estimating and which can lead to inconsistent results. Erratic work methods, insufficient data, oversimplified analysis, lack of time to estimate or train in the estimating process, premature commitment, unrealistic administrative limitations, cost and scheduling edicts, ineffective communication, and lack of scope control all serve to inhibit accurate estimation. Estimating cost and effort should not be confused with scheduling, which comes afterwards or with the preliminary review which proceeds the project altogether.

The estimating process begins with an inventory of project team skills and experience. All members of the project team can be rated on a scale from 0 (low proficiency) to 10 (high proficiency) on their applications knowledge, technical skills, and productivity. Rating variance factors can be established, preferably by individual, or alternatively, by job title.

The detail of how to rate each of the three areas is as follows.

Knowledge factor. This is two-fold. The required level of knowledge (that which is needed to perform the job) may change from task to task depending upon the complexity of the topic. Required knowledge may be expressed in terms such as 'much' (detailed knowledge of the topic is required; the topic is complex), 'some' (proficient knowledge of the topic is helpful; the topic is not complex), and 'none' (background understanding of the topic is not necessary; the topic is easy). The staff level of knowledge refers to the experience (or lack of) brought to the task. This may be represented as 'experts' (extensive experience with the topic), 'proficient' (previous experience with and good knowledge of the topic), 'familiar' (acquaintance with and understanding of the topic; possibly without prior experience), 'related' (unfamiliarity with the topic, but good knowledge of related topics), and 'none' (no experience with this or related topics).

Technical skill factor. The technical skill factor of the person assigned to the task will vary based on the required skills for that particular task. An individual with multiple skills may have multiple skill levels, and a task may require one or more of the skills at any one level. Technical skills may be described as 'senior level' (expert with many successful assignments), 'middle level' (proficient with successful responsible assignments), 'junior level' (gaining proficiency with some assignments completed), and 'trainee' (novice with only classroom-type exercises or assignment experience).

Productivity factor. Variance in the productivity factor can have a considerable effect on both the cost and schedule of the study, and must, therefore, be carefully considered in the estimating process. The productivity factor represents the portion of an individual's day that is actually productive. It takes into account the usually ignored time consumers such as computer downtime, unavailability of resources, coffee breaks, travel, and un-scheduled meetings. Studies conducted on the amount of time spent productively during an average eight-hour day have shown that 5.6 hours may be considered the norm. Since this is only 70 percent of the time that is usually considered to be available (that is, eight hours), any plan based on the 100 percent figure is doomed to failure at the outset.

The number of work days and the cost of labor are easier to calculate than the individual variance factors. Most organizations have a breakdown of the charge rate for each job classification which includes annual salary, benefits, and overheads.

Once an inventory of the skills and experience of the staff has been made, the available work days and labor charges calculated, and the variance factors identified and computed, the cost and effort (measured as time spent) of each task may be estimated. The effort is best estimated for the individual rather than for the job itself since different individuals will have varying knowledge and skill levels. The task list developed initially can be referred to for time estimates to be incorporated into the estimation of effort. Computing the cost estimate for each task takes into account the labor charge rate for each job multiplied by the estimated effort. Additional costs include hardware and software, the involvement of outside consultants, special education and training required, facilities, supplies, and travel.

The estimating process, especially the personnel proficiency ratings, may, at first glance, appear to be an inordinate amount of work. The fact is, however, that before one can tackle a problem, one must know what resources are available to assist with the tackling. When undertaking a study, the staff personnel which make up the study team are the major resource. If the average proficiency level of the staff members is relatively low, the entire study is going to take longer because a learning curve is a time-consuming factor.

Scheduling

Scheduling is no more than planning to accomplish a task or objective at a certain time or date – a deadline. But within that simple definition lie the details for meeting that deadline. A well-thought-out schedule can result in evenly paced activities leading to satisfactory study completion. A poorly developed schedule, by comparison, can result in cut corners and/or missed milestones leading to dissatisfaction with the study and the people performing it.

Scheduling is the process of assigning resources to tasks. The schedule for a particular study should identify each task – its sequence, dependencies, assignee, duration, begin and end dates, and acceptable slack time. Schedules are driven by time, resources, or budget, so these and other constraints, such as task dependencies, planned (and unplanned) time off from work, personnel turnover, relocation, and hardware or software changes or upgrades must be considered.

One of the most popular scheduling tools is the scheduling chart. A scheduling chart graphically represents the entire study process. Two types of charts commonly used are Gantt and PERT. Because information regarding these (and other) charting techniques is readily available in management literature, only a brief explanation will be provided here.

A **Gantt chart** (the name comes from its originator, Henry L. Gantt) is basically a horizontal bar chart showing the chronological flow of tasks in order of task initiation. It can also be used to show the allocation of work days to an individual or group working on a particular task.

A **PERT (Program Evaluation and Review Technique) chart** is much more complex in that it is designed to indicate both task dependencies and the critical path (the segments with the longest duration) through the project. Rather than just indicating various task starts and finishes independently, each task is shown in its relationship to other tasks.

A scheduling chart is a good idea for most studies. The complexity of the chart, however, should be commensurate with the complexity of the job being charted. Generally, PERT charts are useful for scheduling large multifaceted projects such as designing and implementing a major computer installation or constructing a records center. For routine studies of office systems and procedures, a Gantt chart is usually sufficient. Persons with microcomputers will find that there are several commercially available software packages which will automate the scheduling process and ease the project monitoring task.

DATA COLLECTION

The theory of data collection

The most basic question in management analysis is, 'Does the job need to be done?' By job, we do not mean the individual functions of typing, filing, or processing microfilm, but the final result of all systems functions combined. If the system (and perhaps even the organization) being studied does not have to exist, it stands to reason that the individual functions being performed are superfluous.

If there is one area that could be said to cause inexperienced management analysts the greatest problem, it is accepting the philosophy that nothing should be taken for granted. But the fact is that performing useless work more efficiently does not increase the corporate profit. Far greater benefits can be derived from eliminating an unnecessary operation than from improving it.

It is not outrageous to begin an assignment which calls for reviewing a filing scheme by questioning the value of the files. It is not inappropriate to start a study for a potential microfilm conversion by asking why the paper documents are kept in the first place. It is not heretical to begin a feasibility analysis for an automated reporting system by asking what would happen if the manual system were abolished.

If an activity were not performed at all, what would be the result? If an activity must be performed, could it possibly be reduced in scale? A successful management analysis effort requires that everything be challenged, and the analyst must always keep in mind that just because something is, does not mean that it should be.

Systems and procedures must be studied from the perspective of those operating or performing them and also from the perspective of the persons or organizations being served. It is not always easy to balance the various needs and wants, but only with a full appreciation of all requirements and all points of view will it be possible to adequately determine if improvements can be made that will truly benefit those involved.

Assuming that the operation is to remain (which will be the situation the vast majority of the time), the total system should be reviewed generally at an early stage to see whether there are simpler ways of performing the various tasks. Not all problems are major ones, and often it is possible to make improvements simply by studying the basic operational requirements. For example, a system might have been well designed initially and subsequently become inefficient because of a workload increase.

Obtaining the overall picture is not always a simple task. It is often difficult to get a general understanding of the work methods and procedures because a great many people simply cannot explain what they are doing in any coherent fashion. Moreover, there may be great differences between the duties as officially described in the position descriptions and those actually being performed. Nevertheless, it is essential that the analyst clearly understand the entire mechanism before beginning to work on the component parts. Once the general understanding is obtained, the detailed gathering of data can begin.

When the organization is large and there are many analysts there should be a project manager. This person will be the primary liaison between the survey team and the staff of the department being surveyed. Because records management involves every part of the organization it is helpful to establish a task force for planning and overseeing the records survey. The task force acts in an advisory capacity during the survey planning. It also acts as a resource to the project manager throughout the survey. Depending on the survey's objectives, this task force might consist of the records manager, legal counsel, head of administration, and data processing manager.

Sources of information

The ways in which a management analyst can collect information are many and varied. The following are the most often used sources.

Existing documentation. Documentation such as organization charts, work distribution reports, production statistics, procedures manuals, and previous studies of the system or organization are usually available and provided by management or senior staff members.

Direct observation. The management analyst should examine the operational work methods and procedures and should discuss the job with those concerned. Occasionally, the analyst may perform some or all of the tasks to get a feel for exactly what is involved in the process.

Records. Information should be obtained about processes, actions, or decisions from both active and inactive records. Sometimes it will be found that employees are keeping 'personal' copies of correspondence, indexes, files, and other records in addition to the official ones. This type of personal material often contains a wealth of information. Its very existence may suggest that people have reason to believe that the official records are inadequate.

Outside research. Materials prepared by others outside the organization that relate to the subject. For example, when preparing a records retention schedule, applicable laws must generally be researched in a law library.

Questionnaires. These are useful to obtain data over a wide area (such as an interdepartmental study) or where one needs to know detailed information from geographically remote locations (such as branch or field offices). Questionnaires are better for collecting statistical information than narrative. It is difficult to word questions so that everybody will interpret them the same way, and people generally have neither the time nor the inclination to write meaningful responses to philosophical open-ended inquiries.

When questionnaires are used, specific response deadlines should be established and clearly indicated to the respondents. The deadline should be set in advance of the time when the data will actually be needed because people will inevitably be late with their submissions. Response times should be reasonable, yet not overly long. A short deadline will provoke complaints, and a long deadline will result in the questionnaires being put aside and forgotten.

Forms and logs. Often there is no relevant or accurate data on the system. When this is the case, such data will have to be collected as part of the study in order to have a baseline from which to make comparisons or projections. Because the data collected varies from study to study, forms and logs are usually not available as stock items and are, therefore, developed on an as-needed basis by the management analyst. An experienced analyst maintains a master set of such data collection devices used on previous studies or, at least, knows which reference materials contain model examples.

Interviews. Information about goals and objectives, relationships, authorities, attitudes, and general organizational atmosphere can often only be obtained by direct questioning. Interviewing, therefore, is one of the most important aspects of the management analyst's job. Successful interviewing requires a high degree of skill, because the purpose of an interview is not only to obtain raw data, but to get the ideas of the person being interviewed regarding potential system improvements.

Techniques of data collection

There are two management analysis techniques that when used together allow the expedient collection and validation of this information about the organization, target departments, the flow of information, the users, and the issues: work with the project team and interviews with key staff.

WORK WITH THE PROJECT TEAM

While it sometimes acts against a records improvement program or project that its implementation will affect a great many employees in the organization, it works for it in the gathering of data. Many of these stakeholders will participate in data gathering, if they feel assured that they can participate in the improvement.

The methods orientation of records managers makes them a good choice for project team facilitator. In highly technical projects, this may not be practical. However, it works well whenever there is a great deal of end user involvement because users are not usually technically oriented and feel more comfortable with a methods-oriented leader. The team meetings should have a set agenda with clearly defined objectives for each meeting. There should be some time built in to each meeting for some free-form brainstorming. The meetings should be less than ninety minutes. This time cap tends to encourage progress and discourage circular discussion. Short, well-organized, meetings also keep the team members enthusiastic about their project involvement while at the same time respecting their first priority of their regular daily jobs.

There are three stages of consensus that a group undergoes in order for them to take ownership of new ideas. The first stage is a frustrating reluctance to discuss anything negative, in case it be interpreted and communicated back as undermining someone. Once trust is established within the group (through non-judgmental facilitation by the team leader), the group slowly enters the second stage. This is a 'something that I've always wanted to say' opening of the flood gates. The facilitator needs to concentrate the group on translating all 'issues' into **business issues** over which the group has some control and may therefore change. Once the business issues have been identified and a group consensus on them has been reached, it is time to move on to stage three – how to solve these issues. This third stage is particularly difficult for lower level workers because they have rarely had control or authority over how things should be done.

During this three stage brainstorming of the issues, the work of the project team comprises a number of other tasks. Miniprojects are assigned to one or a group of team members to learn the most important requirements of the system. Any problems with the current system or processes must be studied in detail. The major barrier to proceeding from stage two to stage three is a group consensus on exactly what the present system does in detail and what the present requirements actually are. There is one analytical technique that is invaluable to the management analyst, and that is simplified flow charting discussed in detail in Chapter 7. The extensive data collection efforts can be collated and refined into 'as is' flow charts for all of the major functions that support the daily work of the area being studied. These charts are then analyzed and verified by the project team during 'analysis of the facts' project review meetings. This technique allows the group to stay focused and not become overly bogged down in detail or exceptions. Their multidepartmental representation allows them to focus on managing the records throughout the entire life cycle.

INTERVIEWS WITH KEY STAFF

Information about goals and objectives, relationships, authorities, attitudes, and general organizational atmosphere can often only be obtained by direct questioning. Interviewing, therefore, is one of the most important aspects of the management analyst's job. Successful interviewing requires a high degree of skill, because the purpose of an interview is not only to obtain raw data, but to get the ideas of the person being interviewed regarding potential systems improvements.

A large part of management analysis work consists of gathering facts. As important as facts are, however, they must be collected selectively because excessive fact-finding results in an accumulation of information which is difficult to analyze. The sole criterion for collecting facts is their relevance to the problem. In that context, the analyst should question specifically about the nature and amount of work, its purpose, the people who do it, the methods used, and the structure of the organization within which the work is being performed such as:

- *What work is being done?* Ask about the process – are people typing, filing, copying, writing, answering phones, attending meetings, etc.?
- *Why is the work done?* Is any part unnecessary? What would happen if it were eliminated? What are the results? Work on one process may seem to be justifiable yet when considered as part of a total system may be found to be duplicative, overly time-consuming, or just unnecessary.
- *How much work is being done?* Are the activities measurable? If so, have they been measured? If not, how do managers know when workers produce enough? Is there a backlog and, if so, when did it begin?
- *Who does the work?* Is the work efficiently and equitably distributed? Are the people sufficiently qualified and experienced? Could any of the work be done by persons of a lower grade, or, should higher graded personnel be employed for greater effectiveness? Is there adequate supervision? Is there too much supervision? (These questions will tie in with those relating to organization structure.)
- *Where is the work done?* Is the work centralized or decentralized? Would a different location be advantageous? Are working conditions adequate? Is necessary equipment conveniently located?
- *When is the work done?* Does the work proceed in a timely manner? Are there inordinate delays in the process? Are deadlines reasonable? Is the sequence of

events correct? Could steps in the later stages of the process be simplified or eliminated by modifying or extending an earlier step? Are inspections or quality control checks performed at the right time? Are there peak periods of work?

- *How is the organization structured?* Is the overall organization properly balanced? Are the lines of authority clearly defined? Is the supervisory span of control reasonable? Is the work divided evenly and logically? Are authorities and responsibilities delegated to the lowest level possible? Is there coordination between managers and staffs of the various units which must interact to get the job done? Are the downward and upward communication lines open?

Questions focusing on records management

While the questions in the above list will provide good information about the work, the people, the department and the culture of the organization, you may want to be more specific for records and related information during your interviews. Knowing exactly what information you want to get is the most important issue in interviewing. Draw up a list of questions that are asked of each interviewee. This way you can prepare parallel interview notes from which you can compare the answers to specific questions as you analyze the data. If there is some specific information that you want to get from an individual then it is alright to stray a bit from the list. However, the interview will go much smoother with less meandering in the conversation if you have a list of questions. The list also serves as a checklist so that you don't forget to ask any important questions. The following list has some of the more usual records management interview questions:

- How is the information stored? Note types, makes, models, and sizes of filing equipment, computers, terminals, reader printers, etc. Note also the arrangement of the information; for example, paper filed alphabetically on open shelves, or, individuals' personnel files held alphabetically on microfilm that is not blip-coded with rolls of film stored in chronological order.
- What changes are made in storage? Is paper microfilmed? How often and who does it? Is the paper destroyed? Where are the paper and film stored? Or are personal computer files always printed out? Are the disks kept? Where? Is the software kept with them? Are duplicates, backup disks, run? How often? Where are they kept?
- How long is the information needed in the way it was originally collected? If it is altered, how long is the altered form needed? How long are the reports or summaries of it needed?
- Who else uses the information, whether all or part of it, inside or outside of the organization?
- Does the user know what laws or company policies pertain to the information collected and used, or which government agencies have contacts with the company?
- How old is the complete collection of that kind of information?
- How much of it is there? With paper, give the number of feet or inches/cm or meters; with electronic information give the number of disks or amount of space on the mainframe.
- Is any of the information, old or new, duplicates or originals, stored elsewhere? Where? Who controls it? How often is it sent there?
- How is the accuracy of the originally collected information ensured?
- What security precautions are taken against theft, fire, flood, power failures, tape or disk erosion?
- What records or information training has the user had? Include awareness seminars, courses through professional organizations, in-house talks, as well as pertinent academic education.
- What problems or areas of improvement can the user identify? Note as much as possible of what the user says about any aspect of his/her information.

Opening communication

By asking the correct questions the analyst can often encourage others to provide meaningful information. Often the presence of an objective outsider who appears sympathetic to problems and eager to remedy them will stimulate people to think about their jobs in new and different ways and may also get them to offer valuable ideas and suggestions.

There is one other question that needs to be asked regarding an intangible, yet extremely important, area. The issue of staff morale is often an underlying factor behind office system deficiencies. No 'people system' (and almost all office systems are people systems) will function effectively if the people are discontent. The human mind, being as creative as it is, can find extraordinarily subtle ways to throw a wrench into the organizational works. Often employees may not even consciously realize that the wrench is being thrown, but the fact is that, given the same working conditions, people who feel good about their jobs and their employers will outperform those who do not.

A morale problem is usually the easiest to spot and the hardest to remedy. No amount of new paint, carpet, furniture, or equipment will adequately substitute for an evenhanded supervisor or a fair salary. Moreover, managers frequently do not want to deal with what are usually very uncomfortable or delicate issues. Providing specific recommendations for improving the morale conditions in an operation is usually not within the scope of the management analysis effort. However, it is necessary that an analyst who uncovers such a problem report it to management either as a part of the formal report, or, if more appropriate, in a special meeting called to discuss the situation.

The interviewing technique

There is no question that the interview of an individual about the information used and overseen requires tact, patience, perseverance, and diplomacy. The interview and inventory will be the introduction to records management for most people in the organization. The impressions that they form on this initial contact are, thus, very important.

Prying into people's private working lives is a sensitive operation. Pointed questions, opening drawers, reading papers and screens, pressing for explanations, all tend to put people on the defensive. The analyst should maintain an attitude of polite but firm efficiency, no matter how angry, insulting, or rude an interviewee may be. However, sometimes it will be wiser to stop, especially if an interviewee is visibly frightened by the whole process.

There will be numerous people who, because of fear, suspicion, or a generally obnoxious attitude, will refuse to cooperate with the analyst. There will also be encounters with difficult personalities, and it is important to retain a sense of humor. For many people a records survey is too much like the inspections of their rooms when they were children. Like children, they try one's patience, but are smarter than you may think.

Interview etiquette

Arrangements for an interview should always be made with the knowledge of the manager or supervisor in charge of the particular operation. Information regarding the general nature of an individual's job should be obtained beforehand so that the analyst can plan the course of discussion. The interview should be conducted informally and in a relaxed atmosphere. Questions should be carefully phrased so as to avoid implying criticism of the interviewee or their work. The person should clearly understand that it is the system being studied, not the people. While analysts must guide the conversation with their questions, they should listen more than they talk.

As much as possible, interviews should be scheduled so as not to interfere with work requirements. Some interruption, however, is expected. If the situation is at all likely to inhibit discussion, the management analyst must arrange to have an area where interviews may be held in private.

The length of the interview will depend, to a large extent, on the interviewee. The analyst should be aware of signs (body language, facial expressions, etc.) that the person has had enough. Several short sessions are better than one long one. Even under the best of conditions, people being interviewed often feel pressured and are apt to give inadequate or erroneous information if the discussion goes on too long.

Because a records and information survey can be very disruptive, it must be carefully scheduled with all departments. Introductory and explanatory appointments need to be made:

- Introductory appointments – it will be necessary to make a brief appointment with each department, simply to explain the purpose and procedures of the proposed survey. Give each department a copy of the authorizing letter and one of the survey forms to be used. After explaining how the department will be surveyed, ask for the names of key people within that area to be questioned. These will be the contacts who will escort and assist the surveyor. Once the procedure is fully explained and discussed, ask what problems the department head has with the records and information used in the department.
- Explanatory appointments – meet with each of the contacts to explain again, and in more detail, how the survey will proceed. If possible, and with the interviewee's permission, use a tape recorder. This minimizes the distractions involved with note-taking and allows more free-flowing conversation.
- Ask that all staff in the area be fully notified that the survey will take place and when. At this time, make the dates for surveying that department or area. Base the number of days spent in each area on the number of employees, giving approximately one day for every eight or ten employees.

Some final interview pointers

Note-taking during an interview is up to the judgment of the analyst. If the goal is to get a lot of detailed information, taking complete notes as the discussion progresses may be necessary. If the aim is to get general impressions, short notes may suffice. If the interviewee does allow the use of a tape recorder, it should be used with caution. The device can inhibit people from engaging in free and open discussion, and, additionally, can create more work for the analyst if the tapes have to be transcribed, edited, or summarized.

Be sure to follow your interview schedule precisely. Allow one free day a week for compiling notes, rescheduling appointments for people who missed the scheduled one, etc. Much of this scheduling can overlap with the actual survey, for example, make initial appointments and start surveying Department A; when nearing the middle of that survey, make initial appointments and schedule for Department B.

Additional points to be considered are:

- Refuse to participate in 'power games.' Pride, superiority, winning an argument have nothing to do with the survey.
- Ignore the 'offence is the best form of defense' kind of behavior.
- Do not fill silent pauses. It is an old defensive ploy to let sentences fade into excessively long periods of silence. The nervous analyst will fill these with senseless chatter and so, learn nothing.

- Always ask three basic questions:
  What do you like least about your current records system?
  What do you like best about your current records system?
  If given the opportunity, what would you change?
- Rephrase questions as many times as is necessary until they are understood and answered, however –
  Do not press a point too hard. Choose a different line of questioning for a few minutes, then gently return to the more difficult one. Often the key question 'why' can only be answered after the interviewee has been given substantial time to think about it.
  Verify everything by examining the records.
  Be sensitive to the reasons for fear of the survey. People's filing cabinets and computer files can often reveal many personal failings.
  Rephrase important points to ensure that you understood what was meant.
- Ask for comments and suggestions. Elicit ideas on methods, systems, procedures, or organization. A question such as, 'If you were in charge, what would you do differently?' can provide interesting results.
- Check the facts. Before the interview ends, review the ground covered to ensure that the information provided has been understood.
- Stay calm.
- Don't take anything personally.

There are no hard and fast rules to follow when collecting information. Analysts must be flexible and modify their techniques to fit the environment in which they are working. The following guidelines, which are applicable regardless of the methodology used, will help to ensure that accurate data are obtained:

- *Be organized*. Information should be collected systematically and verified as soon as possible after its collection. Notes should be neat, legible, and clearly identifiable. Files for the data obtained should be logically organized so that the information is easily referenced.
- *Obtain first-hand information*. Except at the beginning of a study when it is necessary to meet collectively with several of the principals who are concerned with the system or operation, the group method of fact-gathering should be avoided. It is better to have individual conversations with people so that information is more openly and accurately given, and sensitive issues are more honestly discussed. Supervisors should not be present during interviews with their employees. Although supervisors may wish to help by giving their own versions of how the work is being done, this information is often only valuable for comparison and should not be used in lieu of that which can be obtained from the worker.
- *Do not confuse facts and opinions*. Facts are facts and opinions are not. This does not mean, however, that all opinions are invalid. Opinions may be the result of much thought and experience and may provide information that is not available from files or statistics. The analyst should carefully weigh the value of any statements of opinion, regardless of the source, and accept only those which seem to have exceptional validity based on other factual information obtained or situations observed.
- *Obtain complete information*. The data collected must be truly representative of the overall situation. If the workload has significant cyclical fluctuations, collecting only data relating to one phase of the cycle will not be adequate. It may be necessary to work at certain times, on various days, or at certain points during a month or year. There may be great variations in the work methods used during the different periods.
- *Use definitive terminology*. The terms people use to describe work are often indefinite. Vague phrases such as 'coordinates,' 'deals with', and 'handles' are not

meaningful in an analytical context. The analyst should challenge such descriptions and find out what is really happening.

- *Do not overlook the obvious.* Operations of a routine nature, which may seem unimportant and mundane to the person who is doing them, may be quite important to the smooth functioning of the overall system. The analyst should carefully observe the working areas and question the purpose of all files, records, reference materials, or office machines which have not been specifically referred to and explained by the persons performing the work.

What if your data collection requires an inventory

We have thus far discussed in detail two management analysis techniques – working with project teams and interviewing – that effectively allow for the collection and validation of incredible amounts of information about an organization. In the following chapter we will discuss the next steps in the analytical process – analyzing, drawing conclusions, evaluating and implementing. Within the records management function, however, there is often an additional step that needs to be performed – the records inventory.

The records inventory is a critical step in the development or improvement of a records management program. It may be done at the start of a records management program to identify the current records of the organization, at the beginning of a records retention scheduling project to identify records series, or at the beginning of a vital records or archives program. The inventory allows the records manager to identify what records the organization is presently producing and to understand how these records are actually being handled and used.

The records inventory is not included in Chapters 6 and 7 because few management analysis efforts would include an inventory once a program is under way. However, because it is such a critical element of data collection, Chapter 8 details the issues, methods, opportunities and pitfalls of a records inventory.

Readers who are currently undertaking a project that involves conducting a records inventory may want to jump ahead and read Chapter 8 before going on to Chapter 7. The inventory techniques described there are meant to be coordinated with the project team and interview techniques discussed in this chapter. If an inventory is not indicated for a project or has already been completed, it is time to move on to the next steps in a management analysis – analyzing, drawing conclusions, evaluating and implementing.

7

Management analysis part two: analyzing, drawing conclusions, evaluation, and implementation

ANALYZING AND DRAWING CONCLUSIONS

There comes a time in every study when the data collecting ceases and the intensive data analysis begins. Analysis is the most important aspect of the work. During the analysis, thinking and reasoning are not confined to any particular stage of the assignment. As the work proceeds, the analyst is always comparing one bit of information with another, all the while keeping in mind the overall goals and objectives of the system or organization being studied. At the end of the data collection phase, however, the analytical effort becomes the predominant activity and is therefore considered as a separate function.

When analyzing office systems and procedures, there is no set of formulae which can be used to find the answers to the problems. While there are certain managerial theories which have been developed over the years on subjects such as supervisory span of control, and centralization versus decentralization, generally one will find that those theories are more easily studied than applied.

Effective analysis of information systems (whether manual or automated) requires that a common-sense approach be taken. The principles and techniques that one must know to design information systems (filing rules, forms design, database concepts, microfilm reduction ratios, etc.) can only be applied effectively in an overall environment of rationality. The underlying factor to consider is that the system must work, not just look good on the drawing board. Essentially, analysis is the mental process of reviewing all data which has been collected by questioning, asking additional questions, and then drawing conclusions. Figure 7.1 illustrates this process.

Although it is impractical to try and explain how one should think during this requestioning period, the following briefly describes the basic thought process which may be engaged in to achieve the most practical solution.

- Define the purpose of the work. Ensure that you have a complete understanding of exactly what is trying to be accomplished.

To get the facts – ASK:	ASK – WHY?	To make improvements – ASK
NEED What offices and what people receive the information? **What recipients use the information?** **What procedures describe the** origin, distribution and use of the information?	 WHY this need?	**NEED** How is the information used? Is it absolutely essential? How much does it cost? Is it worth the cost? Is there another source for all or a portion of this data?
PEOPLE Who requires this data? Who enters information on the basic document? Who extracts or manipulates data from the source document? Who analyzes the data? Who makes the decisions?	 WHY by these people?	**PEOPLE** Can the work be done by someone else? Can some or all of it be done by machine? Can any of it be done cooperatively? Do employees know their procedures? Is work performed at the right grade/level? Are duties related or varied? Are supervision and training adequate?
PLACE Where is the source document prepared? How many copies are made? Where are completed documents sent? How are they transmitted? Where is the information used? Where is the information summarized and published?	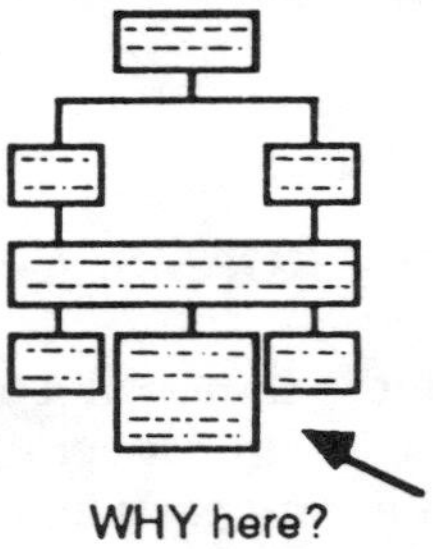 WHY here?	**PLACE** Is this the best place to prepare the source document? Is it closest to the source of information? Is it best equipped to do the job? Is equipment utilized for a variety of jobs, or just used for source data jobs? Could another office do it as well or better? Would another location speed transmission and use?
TIME What is the time schedule for obtaining the data? What are the deadlines for the final products? How much time is allotted to each process?	 WHY at this time?	**TIME** Is the time factor critical? Can peak loands be leveled by doing the job at a different time? Is the time factor realistic? Should frequency be altered? Can timing of related events be changed?
METHOD How is the source document prepared? What machines or tools are used? How is the information processed? Are there quality or production standards? Are production and quality controlled?	 WHY this method?	**METHOD** Is there a better or faster way for entering data on the source document? Can data on the source document be prepared in a machine language? Are processing steps taken in a logical order? Can any processing steps be eliminated? Can parallel processing be substituted for serial processing?

Figure 7.1   The analytical process

- Without any limitations, think of all the ways the work might be performed. Be imaginative, creative, and consider even idealistic schemes.
- Identify the problems inhibiting the accomplishment of the work and the situations that need to be changed.
- Consider how the ideas that you had in the second thought phase could help to overcome the problems identified in the third. Think of different methods for carrying out the entire procedure. Think of ideas that will improve both efficiency and effectiveness.
- Identify the restrictions and mitigating circumstances which would preclude implementation of the ideas proposed (for example, corporate policies, monetary limitations, legal requirements, etc.).

Common sense in analysis

While the effort, as stated, is a mental one, it does not mean that the analyst is confined to dealing with only mental images and abstractions. Spreadsheets (computerized or otherwise) may be used; statistical formulas may be applied; mathematical models may be constructed; and a whole host of other techniques are available as the situation requires. If the situation does not require the use of complex methodologies, however, it is better to leave them unused. The sophistication of the analytical process should be irrelevant to the manager who is seeking a solution to a problem. The only significant concern is that the solution be sound and workable.

Analysis, like records appraisal, requires a little skill and a great deal of common sense. Two common mistakes to be avoided are:

- Data obsession – whereby the evaluator is convinced that every tiny datum gathered on all forms must be incorporated into the evaluation. It must not. An evaluation is a sifting, not a reproduction, of the whole.
- Data glorification – whereby the evaluator sees every datum and every tally as deeply significant to the function of the records or information system. They are not. Inevitably, much of the data collected turns out to be useless.

The analysis of the study results must be made with the use for that information in mind. Records management is meant to improve records and information systems for the people who use them. A study that results only in a statistical report on completed forms is a complete waste of time. An evaluation should include consideration of the following:

- What records are useless and could be destroyed/deleted immediately?
- What records are inactive and could be removed to storage?
- What filing equipment could be emptied and removed or reused?
- What personal computers are improperly or inefficiently used?
- What records or information could be consolidated?
- What duplication can be eliminated or reduced?
- What records are insufficiently protected against loss?
- What records have archival value?
- What filing systems for paper, indexing systems for microfilm, and directory lists for electronic files need improvement?

Only when these questions have been considered can plans for improvement and new programs begin. Start by organizing the data gathered to provide the information necessary to meet the objectives of the study. If the study results are in machine readable form this organization will be quite simple.

Organizing the data for analysis

To meet most study objectives the study results should be organized by department first then alphabetically by record series within the particular department. If the study data is already in machine-readable form, there will be many options for data organization for evaluation. Examples are:

- record series – alphabetical by record series title for all departments; alphabetical by record series title for individual departments.
- active filing equipment – by type of equipment for entire organization; by type of equipment for individual departments.
- forms – by form number; alphabetical by form name; by form number and form name by department.
- reports – by report number; alphabetical by report name; by report number and report name by department.
- inactive records – by department by record series by volume; by department by record series by volume and destruction date.

The analysis of flow charts

A flow chart is a graphic representation of a process; in effect, a picture of a system. With an ordinary flow chart, symbols are used to represent documents, actions, and machines. A template designed for ordinary flow charting might have 18 to 21 symbols or more. Because everything that is happening in the system is represented, and because the symbols are not specifically identified throughout the diagram, the picture can get very confusing. Simplified flow charting, by comparison, uses between five and eight symbols representing only documents and machines. The action is described by brief narrative statements placed below the symbols, and each symbol is specifically identified every time it is used. Figure 7.2(a)–(d) clearly explains the process.

The flow charting process serves the analysis process in six ways:

1 It keeps the team focused within the scope of the project.
2 It isolates many immediate productivity improvements as these flow charts are analyzed by the project team.
3 It 'stops the action' so that the team can agree on the facts and not be bogged down in circular conversations about exceptions to the normal routine.
4 It makes it obvious to all that the improvement of records and related information services to the user community can have a significant impact on the productivity of the organization.
5 It graphically shows the relationships in the creation and use of both the documents and the data in the daily work of the area being studied.
6 It enables computer-prepared charts to have the major procedures itemized and numbered against the written procedures.

COST-BENEFIT ANALYSIS

Once all of the data has been collected and all of the alternatives identified, the next part of the management analysis is the rigorous evaluation of the investment opportunity. As we have discussed, the success of a records manager depends to a large degree on the ability to influence the organization's communication lines for the good of the system. In so doing, the professional must have the flexibility to be responsive to managers, peers, and subordinates while retaining some degree of independent perspective and action. However, even the best influencers and communicators have to live with some constraints

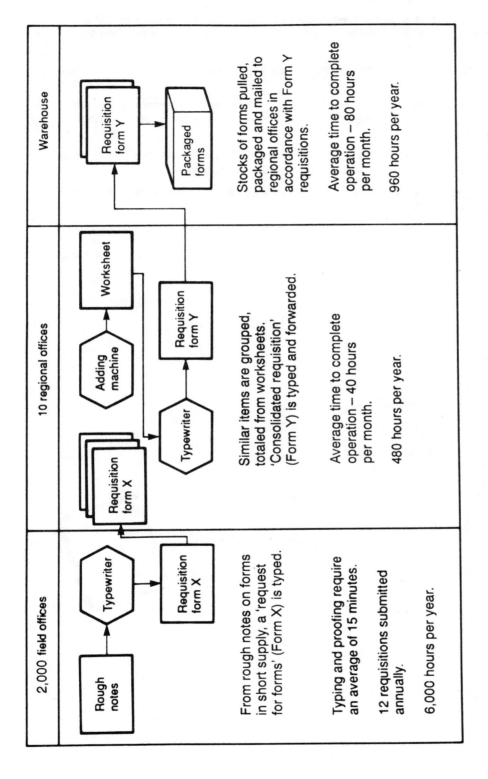

Figure 7.2(a) Simplified flow charting showing a basic manual system for processing form requisitions

71

Only a few basic rules are involved in simplified flow charts.

- Title. The chart should be headed with a title that clearly states the name of the unit being surveyed and the process under investigation. The column headings of the chart should show the office or work unit involved.

- Symbol identification. Don't force the reader to guess the meanings of any symbol. Clearly indicate what they represent.

- Accuracy. A flow chart should show exactly how a job is done or how it it proposed to be done. It is the analyst's duty to picture the work exactly as he/she sees it – or proposes it – based on careful observation and analysis.

- Brevity. Ensure that explanations are brief, clear and to the point. Use the explanations to make understandable the procedural steps covered by the symbols.

- Eliminate backtracking. Have continuous flow. If a document flows back to an office later in the procedure, make a new column on the chart for that step.

  Eliminate minutiae. Don't go into elaborate details unless they are vital to your explanations.

Example: If a form is prepared in five parts, but only one part is processed by the office being surveyed, show distribution of all parts, but give details only for the pertinent copy

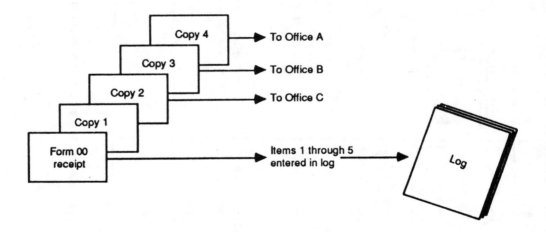

Figure 7.2(b)   How simplified flow charts are prepared

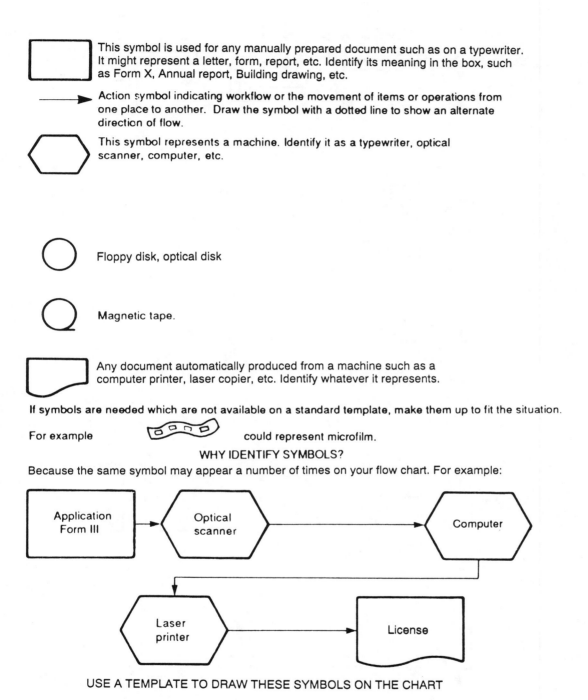

This symbol is used for any manually prepared document such as on a typewriter. It might represent a letter, form, report, etc. Identify its meaning in the box, such as Form X, Annual report, Building drawing, etc.

Action symbol indicating workflow or the movement of items or operations from one place to another. Draw the symbol with a dotted line to show an alternate direction of flow.

This symbol represents a machine. Identify it as a typewriter, optical scanner, computer, etc.

Floppy disk, optical disk

Magnetic tape.

Any document automatically produced from a machine such as a computer printer, laser copier, etc. Identify whatever it represents.

If symbols are needed which are not available on a standard template, make them up to fit the situation.

For example   could represent microfilm.

WHY IDENTIFY SYMBOLS?

Because the same symbol may appear a number of times on your flow chart. For example:

USE A TEMPLATE TO DRAW THESE SYMBOLS ON THE CHART

Figure 7.2(c)   The use of symbols in simplified flow charting

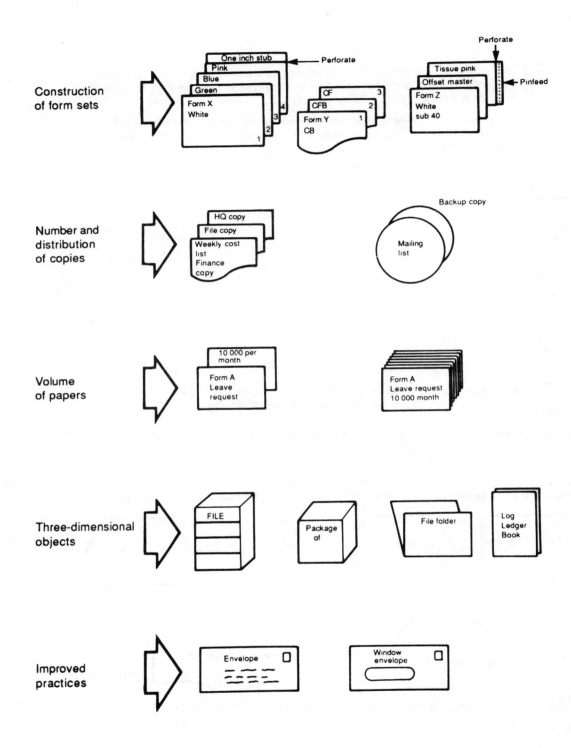

Figure 7.2(d)   Simplified flow charting: what symbols may illustrate

and are forced to base their recommendations on some assumptions. These need to be spelled out in the study.

Constraints and assumptions

The following assumptions or factors have direct impact on costs and benefits.

Financial constraints. The availability of funds for any initial or ongoing expenditure is not necessarily a green light for a project, but it is an important first step. Sometimes budgets can be modified or negotiated so that funds allocated for other things (that now seem to be less of a priority) can be reallocated to this new project. The discount factor applied to the calculations for evaluating economic viability should be obtained from the accounting department; the basis for salary levels from personnel and overhead costs from facilities.

Time factors. The period needed to implement the system and the stage at which it is anticipated that benefits will begin to accrue, should both be indicated. Graphs and timetables are very effective ways to present this information. The availability of staff to meet conversion deadlines should be addressed and confirmed with department managers.

Growth rates. Workload forecasting is a very subjective area. It is best to use historical trends to project growth and spell out any reasons for departure from past experience.

Psychological aspects. Elimination of any alternatives due to political considerations, such as the crossing of organizational boundaries or the resistance to automation, should be itemized.

Legal, regulatory restrictions. The nature of recordkeeping with respect to various laws can influence decisions. Restrictions or associated risks should be addressed.

Alternatives

Any one solution to a problem is not necessarily the best solution. In fact, it is important to define the level of performance that is required from a solution. Performance is usually not an all or nothing situation; more often it is a matter of degree. Sometimes a partial solution to a problem will meet 80 percent of the objectives and still leave substantial resources for other opportunities. In most situations, one alternative is to do nothing. The impact of choosing this alternative should be clearly set out. The best feasibility studies explore all viable alternatives. When presenting alternatives, the records manager must concentrate on meeting the objectives at the lowest possible cost. Often the investigation of a new technology creates a kind of emotional fervor that blinds everyone to this objective. All of a sudden, the problem is fitted to the solution instead of vice versa.

The elements of cost

Cost is the sacrifice, measured by the price paid to acquire goods or services. System costs can be subdivided into development costs and operational costs. **Development costs** include the salaries of the project analysts, the cost of file preparation and conversion of documents and/or folders, the cost of preparing new facilities, and the start-up costs associated with testing and documenting the new system. **Operating costs** include equipment and supply costs, rental or depreciation charges, operating personnel salaries, space, facilities, and overhead costs.

When determining the cost of a system or operation, then, there are four types of resources that must be considered. These are:

- direct personnel costs
- direct equipment, materials, and supplies costs
- other direct costs
- overhead costs.

Personnel costs

These consist of direct labor and fringe benefit costs. The direct labor cost is that portion of employee salaries that is chargeable to the system. The fringe benefits cost (which is expressed as a percentage of the salary cost) consists of allowances and services provided to employees in addition to their salaries.

To compile the direct labor cost for a system, two items of information are needed: first, the amount of time it takes to perform the system activities, and, second, the rate of pay of the personnel performing them. The amount of time can be expressed in either work hours or work years. When determining the direct labor cost, the actual salary rates should be used for existing positions if they are obtainable. If they are not obtainable, the median salary rate for the particular grade level should be used. Table 7.1 shows one method of computing the direct labor costs when the amount of time spent on an activity and the grades of the personnel performing the activity are known. Although the example used is for operational activity costs, the same procedure may be used for computing development and user costs.

Table 7.1
Direct labor operational cost

Activity	Grade	Annual salary ($)	Hourly rate ($)*	Time required per year	Total direct cost ($)
Source document preparation	230	36,750	17.61	50 hours	881
Source document coding	125	18,900		1 year	18,900

*The hourly rate is determined by dividing the annual salary by the number of working hours in a year (2087 used here).

The fringe benefit cost consists of retirement/disability, health and life insurance, and other employee benefits, such as work disability, unemployment programs, bonuses, and awards. The fringe benefit cost is expressed as a percentage of the salary cost expended on the activity. Fringe benefit costs vary considerably from organization to organization and should be determined on an individual basis. This percentage factor should be obtainable from an organization's budget office which determines the actual fringe benefit costs annually. Table 7.2 shows the procedure for compiling the fringe benefit cost.

Table 7.2
Calculating fringe benefit cost

Direct labor cost (developmental, operational, and user)	×	Fringe benefit cost factor	=	Fringe benefit cost
$500,000	×	10.5 percent	=	$50,000

Equipment, materials, and supplies costs

These refer to costs that are directly expended on a reporting system or activity. Examples of the types of equipment that may be included are computers, printers, microfilm readers, copiers, and calculators. Examples of the types of materials and supplies are magnetic tape, paper, microfilm, copier toner, printer ribbons, etc. In cases where equipment is used for more than one system, the cost should be pro rata so that only the share used specifically for the system being costed is included in the calculation. The equipment cost should include acquisition as well as transportation and installation costs. This cost should be amortized over a period of years depending on the useful life of the equipment and consistent with the organization's accounting procedures. The annual equipment maintenance charges should also be included. Table 7.3 shows the procedure for determining equipment cost.

Table 7.3
Sample calculation of annual
equipment cost

Item	microcomputer
Acquisition cost	$7,500
Annual cost on 5-year amortization ($37,500 ÷ 5 = $7,500)	$37,500
Percentage of time used for reports operations	95 percent
Annual equipment cost (except maintenance) $35,625 × 0.95 = $37,500	$35,625

Other direct costs

These consist of purchased services, and operations and activities for which fees are charged, such as data processing and printing charges. An example of this is the charge-back user fee imposed on an office for the time spent using a terminal to access a mainframe computer database.

Overhead costs

These are costs incurred by an organization to support the accomplishment of its overall purpose. These costs are called overhead, or indirect costs, because they apply to activities which benefit the entire organization rather than any one particular function or section. Included in overhead costs are the following:

- supervisory personnel salaries and fringe benefits
- clerical and technical personnel salaries and fringe benefits
- supplies and common distribution items such as telephones and electricity
- space and utilities.

Each organization concerned with developing a system for determining reporting costs should compute its own overhead rates. Before that rate can be computed, however, it is important to establish what overhead base to use in terms of the organizational levels to be included. This determination is based on the levels included in the system being costed. For example, if a system had been developed for a particular section, division, or office, the overhead base would be established at the commensurate organizational level.

However, if the system encompasses the entire organization, the overhead would consist of all the organization's supervisory, technical and clerical, common supplies, space, and utilities costs.

There are several ways of determining the overhead rate factor. One method is to obtain the ratio between an organization's direct purpose costs and its overhead cost. The steps for calculating this rate factor are as follows:

1   Obtain the total overhead cost for the organization affected by the reporting system. Be sure to exclude that portion of supervisory, clerical, and technical personnel costs attributable to the reporting system itself. For example:

	$
Supervisory (salary and fringe benefits)	1,140,000
Clerical/technical (salary and fringe benefits)	255,000
Supplies	202,500
Common distribution (telephone and other common terms)	132,000
Space and utilities	124,500
Total overhead cost	1,854,000

2   Obtain the total amount of the annual budget for that organization and subtract the total overhead cost from the budget figure. The remaining portion is the amount expended directly on the accomplishment of the organization's purpose. For example:

	$
Total budget	4,800,000
Total overhead	1,854,000
Direct mission cost	2,946,000

3   Compute the overhead rate factor for the reporting system by dividing the total overhead cost by the direct mission cost, as follows:

	$
Total overhead cost	1,854,000
Direct mission cost	2,946,000
Overhead rate factor	0.63
	(63 percent)

These costing procedures are applicable to any system, manual or automated. Care must be taken to use a consistent costing method when figuring the cost of old and new systems activities to ensure a subsequent analytical comparison of the two will be accurate.

Benefits

Benefits are defined in terms of a gain or improvement, good investment or saving and are usually divided into tangible (hard dollar) and intangible (soft dollar). **Tangible benefits** are the quantitative savings. These include the clerical salaries saved through headcount reduction or work reassignment, the salvage value of replaced equipment, the savings in floor space freed up, and any other operating benefits such as lower supply costs. **Intangible benefits** either increase value or reduce costs, but they are much harder to measure and define. Since they often represent more value than tangible benefits, it's worth the time and resources it takes to quantify them. The improved availability of information for decision making, potential for increases in sales or profits, and improved employee morale are good examples of intangible benefits. Measuring the success of such far-reaching goals requires putting them into a more specific operational context.

For example, these three examples may have been more precisely stated as, reduced time spent searching for information so as to lessen senior managers' hours worked in a day from ten to nine hours; increasing the sales of one specific product by 15 percent annually through better customer service; 20 percent more images processed per clerk due to increased morale. These benefits must next be translated into hard dollars. The best method to do this is the budget approach, where a department manager agrees to a headcount or other budget reduction based on the implementation of the records improvement program or project.

Since understanding the benefits of records management is integral to the discussion, let's take a closer look at what the general benefits are perceived to be.

Hard dollar savings

Records retention

The past thirty years of experience in hundreds of interviews by the records management community is reflected in a popular '1/3, 1/3, 1/3 rule of thumb':

> It holds that of the records found in an active system before a record management program is in place, approximately one third of them can be disposed of, because they no longer have any value; another one third can be sent to inactive storage because they have little current administrative value but still retain some long-term safeguarding value; only one third of the original files remain that are actually administratively active and should be organized into an efficient active filing system.

The savings in floor space alone is significant to any organization and particularly if consolidation of facilities is contemplated. This hard dollar savings is even more significant if the cost of equipment and supplies is also factored in. It would not be unusual for an organization to realize a 50 percent reduction in its filing supplies costs and a 40 percent increase in the space utilization of its filing equipment by replacing lateral roll-outs with lateral shelf filing equipment.

What is the probability that such savings can be realized in your organization? It should be noted that most companies that have records professionals and are reflected in the '1/3, 1/3, 1/3 rule of thumb' are Fortune 1000 companies. Also, most had been in business for a fairly long period of time before their records management programs were initiated.

Similar percentages can be found in many companies that are only five to ten years old. They have uncovered a high number of duplicate records, kept 'just in case,' which have resulted in over 25 percent of their records being ready for disposal in adherence to a new records retention schedule. In these cases, however, only 10 percent of the records in the active office were ready to be moved off-site to an inactive records center because of the youth of the organizations. This still amounts to a significant one third of the records being taken out of the active office environment where they take up valuable space and equipment, and generally interfere with the availability of the critical active information.

Soft dollar savings

Information availability

The most significant contribution of records improvement to any organization is the increased availability of crucial information to service customers and to carry on the day-to-day operations of the business.

This type of soft dollar savings is obtainable by all companies with a records management program. A streamlined active records system will increase the quality and timeliness of customer service, streamline the communications of the various operations, and reduce the costs of overall administration. Some organizations have successfully 'waded' into a program by designating two or three departments as 'pilot projects.' Then in this small controlled environment, these soft dollar benefits can be monitored and quantified in hard dollar terms, relevant to their companies.

Legislative/regulatory compliance

The exposure of most organizations to environmental, labor, tax, and trade record-keeping constraints, with the associated risks of ensuing litigation must be managed carefully. While a records improvement initiative does not guarantee the elimination of risk, it can significantly reduce the exposure. In fact, many Fortune 1000 companies have initiated their records improvement programs specifically to manage this risk. If the organization is relatively young, it works in its favor, as a sound program to manage this risk for all records can be initiated now without the painstaking (and expensive) process of inventorying thousands of boxes of old records.

Strategic business opportunities

It is generally agreed that over half of business documents which are now almost exclusively stored on paper, will be stored and retrieved on optical media by the year 2000. It is also generally agreed that the critical criteria for a successful imaging initiative is a solid hard copy foundation.

The tactical, cost and task reduction impact of an imaging application is generally high. Benchmark improvement norms reported from selected installations in major corporations include: transaction volumes per employee increases in the 25–50 percent range; staff reductions in the 30–40 percent range; floor space reductions in the 50–80 percent range; and reductions in transaction time by 50–90 percent.

Most large organizations will soon choose to adopt imaging technology to maintain their cost leadership and customer service position, or be forced by competitive advances in this direction to follow suit. Any proposal for a strategic records improvement plan and program should be predicated on positioning the organization on the solid recordkeeping foundation that will allow it to take full advantage of these strategic information tools.

Costing existing practices and systems

There is a strong case for ignoring cost as a justification for records management, and it rests on two points. The first is that the true value of records management is in the services it provides to the growing number of professional information users. As with many other staff functions, such as the data processing department, personnel, or the budget office, there is no question that they are legitimate and necessary regardless of whether they provide any 'return on investment.' The second point is that, if records managers sell their programs on cost savings alone, then, once those programs are established, they are often seen as unnecessary by management, which in many instances does not recognize the importance and value of managing information.

While it is true that improved information services must be the goal and reason for records management, it is also true that managing directors look at costs. For this reason, some simple costing exercises will provide the extremely valuable information of what current systems are costing the organization. The following sections give guidance as to how various costs can be assessed.

Space costs per linear foot

1 Add the total number of linear feet from the inventory forms (see Figure 8.1, p. 95) to get the total linear feet.
2 Add the number of square feet by equipment to get the total of square feet.
3 Multiply the number of square feet by the annual cost per square foot to get the annual filing space cost.
4 Divide the total number of linear feet by the total number of square feet to get the average number of linear feet per square foot.
5 Divide the annual filing space cost by the total number of linear feet to get the annual space cost per linear feet.

Materials cost per linear foot

1 Take the total cost of all filing equipment (available from the purchasing department, or from current sales brochures), with allowances for age of equipment, and the annual cost for filing supplies.
2 Divide the total equipment costs by the total number of linear feet to get the equipment cost per linear foot.
3 Divide the average number of linear feet increase per year (this can be obtained either from a storage facility or as an estimate from users during the interviews) by the annual supplies cost to get the annual supplies cost per linear foot.

Average storage costs per linear foot

1 Take the total number of years' records that have been stored in the offices (from the earliest date of the inventory sheets).
2 Divide the equipment cost per linear foot by the number of years records have been stored.
3 Add this to the annual space cost per linear foot to get the annual storage cost per linear foot.

Labor cost per linear foot

1 From the inventory forms, add up the total number of file references.
2 From the inventory forms, add up the total amount of time spent referencing.
3 Divide the time (2) by the number of references (1) to get the average time per reference.
4 Take the total number of linear feet in the office areas. (Do include storage cupboards, but do not include remote storage.)
5 Divide the number of references (1) by the number of linear feet (4) to get the average number of references per linear foot. (This may be a fraction.)
6 Multiply the references per linear foot (5) by the average time per reference (3) to get the average time per linear foot.
7 Take the average hourly secretarial pay (from personnel or published sources).
8 Multiply the average time per linear foot (6) by the hourly secretarial pay (7) to get the labour cost per linear foot.

Note: Be sure to use the same amount of time in all your calculations: hours, days, weeks, or months.

These costings can be done for the organization as a whole and/or for each department or division. They will be useful as additional reasons for making improvements, but should not be given undue emphasis.

Investment criteria

Another way of analyzing costs of a system or operation is from an investment standpoint. Since in most organizations departments are competing with each other for money, it's important to know how to evaluate all the different investment alternatives. The three most commonly used methods for making investment decisions are payback, return on investment or ROI, and discounted cash flow or present value. While most companies have an accounting department to perform the financial formulation, it is recommended that a management analyst have a good working knowledge of the method(s) used by the organization. On large projects someone from the accounting department is usually a member of the team doing the feasibility study.

Payback

The theory behind payback is simply knowing how fast the organization will recoup the money invested. Rules of thumb make payback under 12 months an excellent investment, 12–24 months a good investment (scaled accordingly), 24–30 months very skeptical, and over 30 months usually unacceptable unless there is some overriding strategic business opportunity at the end of the project.

The general formula for calculating a payback period is:

$$\frac{\text{cash outlay}}{\text{Net annual cash inflow}} = \text{payback period (in years)}$$

The payback model is widely used (though not as the primary model) because of the simplicity of calculation and the ease of understanding. The payback period is a measure which is especially suited to the early stages of an investment decision when the figures will necessarily be rough. It does not, however, take into consideration the life of the project. As a result of this shortcoming, coupled with no allowance for evaluating uneven cash flows, the payback period model is not very useful when choosing between alternatives.

Return on investment

In addition to the calculation of the payback period demonstrated above, accounting personnel consider the rate of return of the investment over the life of the project or, simply, return on investment (ROI). If a project has a life of several years, the organization will want to know how well it compares to other projects at the rate in which it returns the investment.

The general formula for calculating the accounting rate of return is:

$$\frac{\text{average annual cash inflow} - \dfrac{\text{required investment}}{\text{number of years of cash inflow}}}{\dfrac{\text{required investment}}{\text{number of years}}} = \text{ROI}$$

More simply stated this formula is:

$$\frac{\text{average net income}}{\text{average investment}} = \text{ROI}$$

This method is widely used as the primary method with some companies because it is fairly well linked to the impact on future income statements and balance sheets. Yet it explicitly ignores the time value of money and the cash flow patterns.

Net present value

When dealing with large sums of money, the above methods of comparing costs and benefits fall short of reflecting sound investment decision making in a number of ways. The principal shortcoming is that they do not take into consideration the rates of return an organization might earn if it invested the money elsewhere, such as in bonds or debentures. Nor do they take into consideration targets that an organization might set for the rate of return it expects to receive on money invested in particular projects or in the enterprise as a whole. And finally, they do not take into account uneven cash flow over a number of years.

Because of these shortcomings, accountants use present value calculations to determine the comparative worth of a variety of choices. In effect, the question the accountant asks is: If money invested today can earn this rate of return in the marketplace, will the money that must be invested today in this project earn an equal or better rate of return over the life of the project? In applying the present value concept to capital investment decisions, four considerations are involved.

Investment (cash outlay). Investment represents the incremental cash outlay required to install a machine, build a plant, or whatever the capital investment involves. For example, the cash outlay for a new computer system would involve the purchase price of the equipment, the freight in, and the cost of installation and start up.

Savings (cash inflow). Savings represent the incremental cash flow to be realized by making the investment. For a new computer system, the savings would be the net labor and any other value added. The savings are computed for each year of the estimated useful life of the investment.

Life. The life used in computing the return on investment is the useful or economic life of the machine, product, or project. This would be the shortest of the physical life, technological life, or market life. For example, if a computer is purchased, its physical life may be estimated at 15 years, but it will probably be obsolete in 7 years, so the useful life is the technological life – 7 years.

Rate of return. An organization determines an acceptable rate of return on a specific project, a class of projects, or an overall rate. In determining rates of return, computerized present value tables are used to perform the calculations.

PROJECT EVALUATION AND IMPLEMENTATION

The project team needs to play a major role in the analysis, developing conclusions and recommendations. This not only lends credibility to the results; it also places ownership in the hands of those who have the most to gain (or lose), thus sharing the responsibility of the success or failure of the project. Some of the recommendations are immediately implemented; others are further evaluated and refined for implementation. (Most team members also agree that the training and experience of the whole project process will be invaluable to them in seeking out continuous improvement in their daily routines long after the project is completed.)

Realistic objectives must be established for any major conclusions drawn, including a full range of alternatives to the problem. In some cases, more than one alternative may be tested by the project team and a comparative analysis incorporated into the project's design. This analysis and testing is often done in collaboration with the management steering committee. In the end, the success of the implementation will depend on the consensus of the project team that the chosen solution is the best course of action.

Once a recommendation has been chosen, a plan should be developed which sets out the implementation schedule to be followed. The plan should set out in detail each step in its proper sequence. Allocations of time and costs should be carefully estimated. Responsibilities for tasks should be assigned to the appropriate persons. Tasks should be checked to ascertain whether or not they can be accomplished to the satisfaction of the project team and the person to whom the task is assigned. Project management software can be invaluable for keeping track of assigned tasks and presenting a professional management image.

Recommended course of action

The recommended course of action should be based on its economic, technological, and operational feasibility. The economic feasibility should be obvious from the cost-benefit analysis. The technological feasibility should be innate to the experience and training of the affected staff. The operational feasibility can sometimes be elusive, because it usually depends on the human factors that must be taken into account when implementing the recommendations.

For example, operations questions, such as the following, need to be addressed. Will projected headcount reductions forecast with the new system be in the form of lay-offs, reassignments, or attrition? Are there any other major organizational changes planned in the same time frame that will interfere with implementation? Is the proposed staffing complement adequately trained and, if not, are they capable of being trained for this function? Who will do the training? Where will it be done? How should the program be introduced to the company in order to elicit employee support?

The report

When the analysis work is completed and the recommendations have been solidified, the management analyst must write a report to management detailing the findings and providing recommendations for improvement. Depending on the nature and complexity of the study, the report could take on the form of a two-page memorandum or a 100-page volume. One should not make the mistake of equating size with usefulness, however. As a general rule, smaller is better. Astute managers do not care how much a report weighs. What is important is the information that a report contains.

A complete and effective study report covers topics such as:

- *Executive summary* – give a brief overview of the study, highlighting the key points of its findings and analysis sections and summarizing the most important recommendations.
- *Background/rationale* – Why the study was done, for whom, by whom. Include begin and end dates. Add other significant data such as constraints or assumptions as appropriate.
- *Methodology* – Identify the universe (organization, geographic location, etc.). Identify the principals (study team, department heads, etc.). Explain the techniques used (questionnaires, interviews, sampling, on-site processing, etc.).
- *Findings* – Summarize the facts obtained which relate directly to the problems being solved. Except for explaining special circumstances or unusual occurrences, do not go into great detail. Rather, identify trends and patterns and generally outline the process.
- *Analysis* – Summarize the analytical thought process which led to the conclusions. Explain everything in an organized and logical manner so that the conclusions will be identified by the reader before reaching the next section.

SYNOPSIS

An inventory of the information held in Company A revealed that, in spite of a large number of personal computers, some 80 percent of the information is still held on paper. There are 4011 linear feet of paper, of which 25 percent, or 1003 linear feet, are inactive and could go to storage immediately.

The paper is stored in a variety of equipment types, from shelf files to heaps on bookcases and the floor, taking up 3071 square feet of office space. Approximately 750 square feet will be released by sending inactive files to storage and removing the emptied equipment. Of this information there are 743 different records series (documents which are always handled together) of which 37 percent is duplicative. Much of the duplication is on another medium.

There are no established retention periods for the storage, archiving, or destruction of the information. Neither are there sufficient protection procedures for vital records or for the information on personal computers and word processors. The organization of the information, in filing systems and on word processors particularly, presents a serious problem which will become much worse as the company grows. There is extensive duplication, incorrect distribution and uncertain filing requirements of reports on all projects.

The following report details suggestions for the establishment of a complete records management program to organize and protect all company information.

Figure 7.3   Synopsis of a records and information survey report

- *Conclusions/recommendations* – Outline specific steps to be taken. Present alternatives if appropriate. Include potential resultant cost savings when applicable.

As the introductory publication from records management, the report should be formal in tone, clear in style, and standard in format. It should begin with a brief, one page, synopsis of the contents (see Figure 7.3). Graphs, tables, and appendices should be kept to the minimum necessary to explain clearly the findings, but not so much as to reduce the impact of the recommendations, or as to bore the reader. It should include a table of contents, a table of illustrations, and be presented with a standard letter.

Formats, type styles, bindings, cover sheets, and other packaging specifications should be consistent with organizational standards. Unlike weight, the appearance of the product is important. A sloppy looking report may never even get read.

The initial report will be more important than any other produced by records management, for it will inaugurate all future programs. Sufficient time and care must be taken to ensure its excellence and thus, the approval of its recommendations.

The information in each section should be well organized and clearly presented. The above is general guidance. It may not apply in all instances and should be modified as necessary. For example, in a very short report the methodology section might be eliminated entirely. In a lengthy report, appendices might be added to provide supporting detail. Many analysts like to combine the findings and analysis sections as that often makes for a more easily followed presentation. For relatively long reports, an additional executive summary section may be added which compresses the essence of the entire presentation into several pages for review by senior management.

Variations on report structure

The report can be either inductive or geographical in organization. The first stresses subjects across the organization, the second stresses each department's or division's records systems. The following report organizations illustrate the point:

Inductive report structure
- introduction
- problems in filing systems

- problems in retrieval
- problems in storage
- problems in protection of vital records
- conclusions
- recommendation for improvements
- appendices

Geographical report structure
- introduction
- accounts department
- marketing department
- sales department
- production department
- summary of departmental systems
- recommendations for improvements.

Timing

The importance of the timing of when to ask for funding and when the project will start and end should never be underestimated. Obviously, if a company is coming off a good year and the prospects look bright for next year, there will probably be money available for investment in modernization and expansion. But other internal and external factors influence strategic business opportunities. Operational issues, such as running out of office space and forcing a renovation or a move to a new building, will sometimes exert extra pressure for the approval of a project that was undecided previously. Operational busy times should also be avoided for implementation. For example, year end is probably not a good time to install a new filing system in the accounting department.

Outside issues, such as a strategic move by a competitor to a technology like imaging to improve customer service, are also important decision motivators. Crises like litigation and audits certainly focus attention on recordkeeping practice. Other ordinary human factors such as the temperament, stress level and preoccupation of the decision maker should also be taken into consideration when considering the timing of presenting a request for expenditure.

Facilitating implementation

Selling the project must be done wisely, since there is always the danger that unrealistic expectations will arise. Vendors of equipment and overblown reports in trade publications may raise employee expectations, as can a management that is eager to reduce costs and improve profits. However, maintaining the enthusiasm of the people affected by the change is one of the key tasks of the project team. The tone of the project team's response to any inquiries will make or break the broad-based support for a change from the grassroots. Any suggestion or criticism of the new system should be welcomed as a legitimate opportunity to improve the final product. It must truly be 'our' new system, not the project team's or the vendor's.

Implementing new technological procedures, particularly if new equipment is involved, requires the inclusion of tasks that will make a smooth transition from old to new ways. In almost every organization, there are likely to have been instances where change has been attempted before. Sometimes, these will have resulted in failure, and the bad aftertaste may have to be overcome. While it is not suggested that the management analyst or project team refer to past failures, these should be dealt with as questions concerning them as they arise. Naturally, people who feel threatened by change will express concern.

This calls for eliminating as much ambiguity and uncertainty as possible and communicating as widely as is practicable to all organization members. Others will feel that their areas of responsibility or control are being infringed upon. They too must be kept informed and shown how they have a part in the overall plan. This may involve showing them what retraining they can engage in and what jobs will become available. If people still do not see themselves as being able to cope with the new scheme of things, methods need to be clearly set out by which they may direct their talents into new avenues fruitful to themselves and the organization.

MAINTAINING SUPPORT FROM SENIOR MANAGEMENT

Guiding senior managers through this process is also key to the success of the project. They are, after all, the 'resource allocators.' A project team under the auspices of a well-placed senior executive provides the most favorable communication line with senior management. Without this pipeline to the top, there need to be other established standards for the evaluation of the project. These should be tailored to the styles and aspirations of the senior executive group.

Managers must be fully vested in the change. They should be encouraged to raise critical questions, and the criteria for evaluating progress must be as hardheaded as possible. The key evaluation criteria should be:

- cost-benefit analysis including the total cost of conversion and implementation
- flexibility of the system not only for current needs but also of anticipated needs
- genuine need for the level of sophistication or equipment features being proposed
- vulnerability of the system to breakdown, sabotage, theft, and the loss of information due to accidents or incompetence
- availability of information from the system when needed
- reliability of vendor in providing training and service
- actual match of organization's needs and vendor's equipment
- compatibility of proposed equipment to equipment remaining in use after conversion.

Project control

Maintaining control of the project is essential. There are a number of ways control of the project can be lost. For example, the bandwagon effect may occur – other areas of the organization not associated with the project may decide to get on the technological bandwagon and on their own initiative purchase equipment. This may result in their acquiring unnecessary and, in some cases, incompatible equipment.

Control of the project may also be lost through impatience. This may come about in two ways. On the one hand, the initial results of the project may look so good that management decides to rush the project before it is completed; on the other hand, original time lines or goals may be unrealistic, and management becomes frustrated with the lack of progress being made and prematurely cancels the project. The records manager and the project team must stick to their guns as best they can. In both cases, agreement on a sound plan is the answer.

Final tasks for the project team

After implementation of the project recommendations, a final report from the management analyst and project team should deal with what requirements there are for follow-up, such as actual costs versus projected costs and long-term effects on staff turnover and training. Frequently, one project uncovers a number of other areas for attention, and this should be covered in the final report. Finally, what the project team learned from the experience should be reported so that the collective experience of the organization is enriched.

TRAINING

If the result of the project or study was the implementation of a new records mnanagement program, there is the matter of training to consider. Of course, persons using new equipment or performing new duties always have to be trained, but training, in this context has as its goal a positive attitude toward records management and ownership in the program. Everyone participates. Training, however, should be looked upon as never being finished. As the program expands to meet the needs of the organization into the next century, ongoing training in data processing systems, optical memory systems, and work simplification techniques are imperative to ensure that there will be a records management staff and user community capable of utilizing the new technologies when they are ready to be introduced.

Training programs are not a one-way street. The records management staff is continuously challenged to improve their procedures and stay in step with the changing needs in the user community. The ongoing success of the program is due in a large part to the ability of the servers and the users to listen and learn from each other.

For these reasons, training programs need to be developed at three levels to ensure the maximum compliance with records management policy and to encourage a global records management attitude and culture. These three levels are senior and upper middle management, records and related information users, and records management staff.

Senior and upper middle management

Orientation or marketing are probably more appropriate words than training at this level. Formal presentations should be scheduled about once every six months with particular attention to how the records management program is functioning and how it will continue to assist in attaining the goals and objectives of the organization. These presentations should be scheduled around strategic points in the records management program, such as the introduction of a study, the final report, a successful new technology implementation, an audit of cost savings for the past six months, etc.

Senior management is not particularly interested in education about records management unless there is something new that can help the organization strategically. The presentations, therefore, should not be entirely educational but lead up to a decision appropriate to management for something within the records management program. This may be something as simple as an introductory memo or something a little more complex like a major three-year funding initiative for document imaging.

Records and related information users

Training for the user areas should be covered from the manager or section head level to the clerical support groups. It should include head office and any regional or district offices. This training should also begin at the outset of the program.

While the records management staff gains an appreciation of the business of the user community, it is equally important that the users develop a positive attitude towards the contribution that the records management staff can provide. The format used here is two fold – first develop the right records management attitude and then begin the rigorous training in methods and procedures.

The first training priority is to have users understand the components of a records management program, understand the objectives of the program, and encourage them to take some ownership to the processes and procedures being introduced. While it is important for the records management staff to feel they have something to contribute, it is paramount to the success of the program to have the user community endorse them as a value-added comr onent.

This training ard orientation can be accomplished through in-house seminars of about 20 to 25 people at one time, audio visual presentations, and user manuals. The in-house seminars should last only 20 to 30 minutes. Any specific training, such as for a new automated records management system can be handled in a similar way. It should be supplemented with at least one week of concentrated hands-on training at the workstations in the user areas. Records management staff should be standing by to field questions and instruct one-on-one as required.

Audio-visual or slide presentations can be particularly effective at putting a very professional and succinct message in front of a lot of people in a short period of time. These presentations should be well rehearsed if they are done in person and very professional if done as an audio-visual because today's home videos and stereos have made most people very sophisticated in their viewing appreciation.

As the program expands, in-house courses on records management and the procedures to follow should be offered on a regular basis. A designated records management coordinator in each operating area should be appointed by senior management. They should receive more indepth training than their regular user counterparts. Their job is to coordinate with the records management staff on any new records management methods, procedures, or technology. They are also responsible for orientation of new employees to scheduling and disposal procedures and file operations in general. In addition, the records management staff should offer, about every four months, training seminars on scheduling and disposal procedures, subject file systems development, and any central file operations for all new employees of the organization.

Records management staff

Training for the records management staff should be ongoing and continuous. This subject was covered in Chapter 4.

8

Records inventory

Originally, a records inventory was done in order to identify all record series and the extent of their use, for the purpose of devising retention/disposal schedules. Records series are groups of records arranged in accordance with a filing system or maintained as a unit because they relate to a particular subject or function, result from the same activity, have a particular form, or because of some other relationship arising out of their creation, receipt, or use. The inventory was also focused on the systems used for maintaining and filing active records, and on gaining the information necessary for the establishment of forms and reports management programs.

This kind of inventory was centered around the filing cabinet and the mail room. It focused on the title of a record series, the type of documents it contained, and what method of filing was used in what kind of equipment. The records analyst wanted to know who originated documents, to whom they were sent, how important they were, how long they were needed in the office and later in storage, and when they could be destroyed. The records analyst would look through files and interview staff until he/she understood the purpose and actual use and value of the record series and its documents. Incidentally, this person would have a fuller understanding of the records flow and use in the organization than would any other person in that organization.

Now, it is this very understanding, this view of the whole, that is the true goal of management analysts. Before they can consider devising retention/disposal schedules, or making improvements in filing equipment or systems, they must consider the whole information structure of the organization. Who creates or brings in what kind of information? How do they use it? Why? Do they get all that they need? Do they share it? Can they benefit from information used by another department? Do the communications systems support or inhibit the transfer and use of information? Most importantly, what are the goals of the whole organization and what are its information requirements in order to achieve them?

The procedures of the records inventory are altered little by this change of emphasis and broadening of scope. More, it is the awareness of the analyst that must change, so that every question asked, while it may be about a small detail, will aim at an understanding of the full information source.

The initial information inventory is a gathering of all available information about existing records in an organization. This type of inventory is done not just to design a system, but to design a records management program for the whole organization. The inventory is the primary source of the information necessary to plan programs on retention scheduling, vital records protection, reports management, forms management, indexing systems, and records storage. It is an opportunity to discover all current recordkeeping problems and to anticipate future ones.

Later, when a records management program is established and operating, studies of a smaller, more specific, scope may be necessary. Examples of purposes for such studies might be to:

- provide a basis for establishing a vital records program
- gather information to determine what records should be microfilmed
- help plan the information requirements for a new building
- serve as a basis for evaluating the effectiveness of active filing systems
- identify all historically significant records in order to establish an archives
- inventory all equipment and supplies used for active records
- provide statistics for evaluating commercial versus in-house records center storage
- assess the appropriateness of a new technology, for example, optical disk, for the management of certain information
- determine the need for a policy regarding official records maintained in machine-readable form on executive workstations
- gather information pertinent to a feasibility study for organization-wide office automation.

The inventory must be planned carefully, so that all needed information will be obtained. It must be executed with thoroughness while causing as little disruption as possible. It can be expected to be time consuming; and also disconcerting if personnel are not properly informed in advance. In spite of the difficulty of doing an inventory, it is absolutely crucial to the creation of any records management program and, as the sole opportunity for gathering so much detailed information about the organization, it cannot be omitted.

WHY DO A RECORDS INVENTORY?

The greatest value of the inventory is that it gives, as one's first view of an organization's information, a reasonably objective and complete overview of the records, their real uses, and of the organization itself. Other reasons are:

- To know what information exists – While everyone will have a good approximation of what information they produce, no one will know all that exists in the entire organization. Before any changes can be suggested, the records manager must have a thorough knowledge of what actually exists.
- To know what the records are and the procedures for working with them – It is necessary to identify and have at least a basic understanding of the function of each type of record, including its path flow, who produces it and why, who needs it, what is done to it, the purpose it serves.
- To learn the users' information needs – No one will provide better (or worse) suggestions than some of the users. They know the information thoroughly and can give a history of how it was used, and of failed or successful programs in the past.
- To know all of the available storage media – Changing media is expensive. An organization may have just made a big investment in a particular medium of information storage, or may refuse to do so, or may have disparate and incompatible media. No suggestions or proposals can be made before there is a catalog of existing media (paper, microfilm, disks, etc.) and their uses.
- To obtain preliminary retention periods – Traditionally the main reason for performing the inventory, the preliminary retention periods allow one to begin preparations for a records retention program as soon as the inventory is completed.

Thus, the inventory will be the tool used to find out everything necessary for the design, justification, and establishment of a records management program.

DATA COLLECTION

Traditional view has it that the inventory should begin with the stored records, as a trial run, and there is nothing terribly wrong with this procedure. However, the stored records, in basements or remote buildings, are often mysterious, too old, too peculiar or idiosyncratic to understand. Trying to inventory them first often leads to a frustrating failure at the beginning of the project. It is better to do the stored records last, after becoming familiar with all of the active records, and then be able to make quicker and more accurate guesses as to what they might be. The best place to begin the inventory is in a small department that does not have urgent work, and in which at least one secretary or clerk has been working for a few years. In this environment, there will be enough time and knowledge to answer the questions about the records. The environment should also be relaxed enough so that those new to doing the inventory will be able to make a few mistakes without dire consequences. Departments with unique documentation, such as the accounts department, should not be one of those first to be inventoried.

After the letter of authority has gone out, and any specific management briefs concerning the inventory have been received, it will be necessary to decide exactly what type of information is to be obtained from the inventory, and for what reasons. If the object is to regain space from files, then the space taken by files and equipment will be important to quantify. If the main reason is to reduce costs, then the costs of files storage must be ascertained. Generally, the necessary information to find will be:

- Volume – The amount, in linear or cubic feet, of records and files, the number of terminals and computers, the number of filing cabinets. The storage space used on the mainframe computer, and the number of floppy disks used.
- Media – The different media on which information is stored, and how, if at all, they are linked: paper, microfilm, disks, audio-cassettes, etc.
- Creation – How and why is information created? Who creates it?
- Paths of distribution – To whom is the information sent, how often, why? Are people receiving reports or copies they no longer need, or no longer understand?
- Age – How old is the information on computer, in files, on microfilm? How old is the information in storage?
- Usefulness: active/inactive – How long is the information or record series needed in the office, how long in storage? When can it be destroyed?
- Document/Report/Form types – What kind exist? Who designs them? Who orders them?
- Organization – What kind of filing systems, codes, indexes are used?
- Legal requirements – What are the legal retention periods for any of the reports, forms, documents? What other legal requirements are there, such as specifications of what must be asked, how it must be stored, etc.
- Vital records – What records or information are absolutely vital to the survival and reconstruction of the organization.
- Problems – What problems do the users have with their files and information?

Methods for performing a records inventory

There are three basic ways to perform an inventory: by questionnaire, by committee, and physically. The first two are of less value because they provide the least amount of accurate data. Their advantage is the speed with which they can be done and the small number of people that need to be dedicated to managing the inventory.

Questionnaire

In this method, a questionnaire, asking about all of the topics in the list above is sent to each employee, or in some cases to each section head, asking them to describe the information and files that they create and use. There are many flaws in this method. Users see their work in the most narrow of contexts and cannot understand questions requiring a more general view. They may not understand certain terms, such as 'retention period', and so provide incorrect or insufficient answers. Questionnaires also take time, and everybody professes to hate them, so usually only 50 percent are returned. A last, and more serious, failing of this method is that the records manager will often have a very difficult time understanding descriptions of information that was never seen or discussed. However, if used as a preliminary exercise to the physical inventory, a questionnaire can give an initial map to the office and its problems, helping the records manager to plan the focus of the inventory more precisely. In very large organizations, of five thousand employees or more, this may be the only way.

Committee

In this method, representatives from each department meet with the records manager to describe and discuss what exists in the department and to apply preliminary retention periods. This almost never works as it takes a long time for the records manager to explain the reasons for the meeting, to deal with the personalities involved, and to get them to think alike about the information that they use.

Physical inventory

The physical inventory is generally the method preferred by records managers. It involves the use of trained records personnel, or a specially trained records task force, and, as a consequence, collects more reliable and complete information. The records manager and assistants go from department to department, room to room, looking into every file drawer and video display unit screen, asking questions, and filling out the forms. This method is, by far, the most time consuming and labor intensive, but it does yield the best results, giving a full, clear overview of the organization, its information, and its politics. It cannot be stressed strongly enough that this method of doing the inventory is the only one to be considered seriously. One of the key things to remember before starting is to reassure that confidentiality will be protected, security clearance has been obtained, that no secret records will be examined without a contact person present; and especially that the ultimate goal is to improve records and information systems for everyone.

Items to obtain before the inventory

Prior to the inventory, a few items should be collected and studied:

- Costs of office space per square foot/meter, including taxes, rates, and insurance. The costs should be obtained for each building where any records will be inventoried. If the costs are not available, or are believed to be confidential, then it is best to contact local real estate agents who handle similar commercial property in the area. The average figure, taken from two or three agents, should be close enough to be acceptable in any costing.
- Storage – the location and annual costs of any facilities used for records storage, for example, the basement in the building belonging to another company.
- Maps of all buildings, showing not only room and cupboard arrangements, but furniture, filing cabinets and terminals, if possible.
- Copies of contracts with all service bureau handling records and information for the company, such as commercial storage companies, microfilming bureaux, duplicating/printing/photocopying bureaux or rentals, computer services, etc.

- Equipment list showing all personal computers, photocopiers, microfilm cameras and reader printers, computer terminals, etc.
- Filing costs should be broken down into the annual costs, per department or ministry if possible, for equipment and filing supplies. If the purchasing department will not release these figures, they can be estimated from the average costs, as listed in catalogs, for the estimated annual purchase of equipment and supplies.
- Salaries for secretarial and clerical staff. If annual, average salaries for these job classes are unavailable, those published in the local press for similar jobs will do.
- Employee internal telephone list – crucial for making and changing appointments, or for asking directions to oddly placed offices.
- Staff organization structure charts – any diagram or list, showing reporting hierarchies, or connecting names with job titles, will be extremely helpful in understanding the flow of information.
- Procedure manuals – any procedure manual, for any function, will include valuable information on reports and correspondence procedures and titles.
- Forms – blank copies of all forms used will help with the establishment of the forms control files. While copies will be collected during the inventory, any that can be gathered, in response to a requesting memo, and cataloged in advance, will give a head start to the project.
- Copies of previous studies – obviously, if a study was once done on files, records, computers, secretarial or clerical services, archives, efficiency, etc., it will contain useful information, and give a solid foundation to the records manager's understanding of the organization, and will help to avoid duplication of effort.
- Copies of filing indexes and lists – even if outdated, these will help to understand not only the files to be inventoried in offices but those in storage.

THE INVENTORY FORM

Having decided on areas of emphasis and on the method of inventorying, a form can now be designed. It is unimportant whether it is a box form or a list of questions. This form need not be perfect. It is a worksheet, will be used for this exercise only, and will not be used by anyone but the records manager and the assistants. Ensure that the form is not full of records management jargon, so that people are not being asked questions that confuse them. Group the questions by subject on the form, to facilitate processing the information. Leave plenty of room for comments. A too detailed form will be wasted. At times, the inventory proceeds so quickly, that only the quickest notes, in shorthand, can be taken.

The records and information inventory form (see example shown in Figure 8.1) will certainly suffice for any inventory where the emphasis is on the reduction of space or costs. The first section gives the name and location of the area inventoried, the date, and the name of the contact person in that area. To make things easier, this part can be filled in on one form, and that form photocopied, before beginning the investigation of an area. In the second section the following is required:

- Record series title – The record class or series is that group of documents or files which is always treated together. Examples of these are personnel files, invoices, contract negotiations. They may contain many documents as well as correspondence, but the individual files would not be subdivided and separated.
- Dates – The earliest and latest dates of files in that record series. In some cases, where the series is arranged chronologically, this is easy to determine. In others, as with personnel files, it is necessary to examine a sampling of older files to make a guess. This is especially true of stored files, about which nobody can remember anything.
- Filing inches – Estimate the number of inches (or feet or centimeters) being used, on a shelf or in a drawer, by the files. If on microfilm or microfiche, how many rolls or

---

RECORDS AND INFORMATION INVENTORY FORM

Department: Contact:

Location: Date:

Record series title:

Dates:

Filing inches: of which   %   medium:
                                  inactive

Equipment: Filing/control system:

Documents and content:

Stored elsewhere:

Retention

Office:

Storage:

Legal:

Vital:

Regular purging:

Data Protection

Source of information:

Purpose of holding:

Future purposes:

Released to: Countries:

How is *accuracy* ensured?

How is *security* ensured?

Bureau:

Figure 8.1 A records and information inventory form

sheets. If on diskettes, how many disks, of what size, are used for each series? If on the mainframe, there may be a system that bills each department for its use and storage space. If not, it will be necessary to meet later with the information systems group to discuss departmental use and storage on-line.

● Equipment – Note the type and size of filing equipment, reader printers, terminals, personal computers. Include brand names and model numbers.

- Medium – Is the information stored on paper, microfilm, diskette, hard disk, a mainframe held internally or externally, a video cassette?
- Filing/control system – How are the files arranged: alphabetic, numeric, chronological, terminal digit, alphanumeric, etc? Disk and on-line directories will have to be examined, as will microfilm that is not blip-coded.
- Documents and content – List the type of forms, getting blank copies of each, and documentation within the files of the record series.
- Stored elsewhere – Are other files, including duplicates, from that series stored in any other location? Where?

The third section, 'Retention,' is for gathering information on the use and requirements of the record series. How long is it needed in the office? How long in storage? Does the user know of any legal requirements? Is the information vital to the functioning of the organization? Is the record series regularly purged or weeded? With electronic records, how often is outdated information deleted or archived? Is it done automatically? Who makes the decisions as to deletion?

The fourth section, 'Data protection,' will help to provide the information on personal data necessary for compliance with the various privacy laws. However, for a deeper understanding of information requirements, it would be wise to use it for all record series. The source of the information may be the individual, published articles, supervisors, etc. The purpose of holding the information must be clear, for example in order to perform what task? Any future purpose that the user can imagine for holding the information will help in forward planning. The people to whom the information is released must be listed by name and job title. How the accuracy and security are ensured must be clearly detailed. List any bureaux which handle the information, and any countries to which it is sent.

If there is time, draw a simple diagram or flow chart of these steps. If there is a procedures manual, get a copy, but be aware that most procedures manuals are outdated and are rarely used. Always ask to be shown the procedures and to have them explained. A listing of files and their method of organization is also useful.

The following list gives some possible elements to consider when designing an inventory form:

- record series title
- record series description
- purpose of record series
- documents in record series (component documents)
- record media/format
- report/form numbers/references
- record size/paper/tape/disk/drawings, etc.
- equipment used to store record series
- official copy designation
- official custodian of record series
- archival/historical value
- administrative need
- software/hardware required for machine-readable records
- location/area/building/room
- dates
- record volume (linear ft/cu. ft)
- person conducting inventory
- date of inventory
- record activity
- vital record classification
- department of record

- record range of dates
- sample of folder/item titles
- corporate entity
- physical description
- location of other copies
- record origination
- department's recommended retention

DOING THE INVENTORY

There is little step-by-step instruction that can be given for actually doing the inventory. It requires persistence, alertness, curiosity, a certain thrill at sleuthing, and a great deal of diplomacy. Each department is different, with different procedures, personalities, equipment, needs, histories; and the records manager will have to deploy different techniques to discover the records and information in them all.

One of the typical problems encountered when conducting any type of inventory is that files are not organized by record series. Many departments organize their files in a large alphabetical subject arrangement which contains numerous record series, official and convenience copies, record and non-record material, etc. It is important to take the time to list each record series even though they are buried in the large subject file arrangement. Another problem area is a subseries within large series of case files. Litigation files, personnel jackets, and certain types of project files are good examples where there may be five to ten different record series in one file.

When inventorying inactive files there are often problems with how containers are packed, especially if there has never been a formal records management program in the organization. A typical dilemma is presented in the inventory with containers marked 'Jim's desk drawer contents.' If Jim were the corporate secretary, there may be very valuable historical records in the containers. If he were a middle manager there may be some official records, but the containers probably hold mostly unofficial copies and non-record reference materials.

In an effort to discover everything about the department's records, three criteria may be kept as guides:

1 **Look** at all files in all equipment on all disks, screens, films.
2 **Ask** every question necessary until you truly understand what is in the file, why it is kept, how it is used, where it comes from and goes, and any problems with it.
3 **Find** every storage place with records and information: in cupboards, down the hall, on top of cabinets, shelves, terminals, under desks, at home, in the safe, in another building, at an associate company's office, in commercial storage, in the car. Then go look at that too.

How to approach a physical inventory

1 The first step is to meet with the department manager in whose department the inventory is to take place. In this interview, the inventory method and scope is discussed and the key personnel in the department, most knowledgeable about the records and the flow of information, are identified. Often these key people can be seconded to the inventory project temporarily making the inventory more reflective of the business environment. This arrangement can also develop an ally, who, understanding the effort that has gone into the inventory, is usually supportive of the improvement process.
2 The starting point of the physical inventory is the identification of all places where

records are stored. This can be facilitated by the preparation of a floor plan of each record storage area and the numbering on the plan of every file cabinet.

3 Then all files, manuals, texts, printouts, or reports are recorded manually on the form (and subsequently input on computer), on a dictating machine (and subsequently transcribed), or directly to a notebook computer. A list of all files is compiled identifying titles and inclusive dates of documents within the folders. Any obsolete or duplicate files should be noted, as should the file indexing methods, the space utilization, the context of the files in the departmental work flow, where else in the organization that these files flow, and the present security afforded the records.

4 A hard copy inventory book or compilation of all inventories is created, as is a separate hard copy inventory for each department for its use. These inventories include the floor plan of the departmental file areas and the file listing by cabinet or container. A magnetic disk copy of this inventory should be stored and kept up to date as the inventory proceeds. (This disk copy will be used to load the master file plan database later in the improvement program.)

5 The original of the records inventory is sent to the department manager for review. This includes checking for accuracy and completeness, correcting and including comments, and signing the approved inventory. The department keeps a copy of this final inventory, and the original is kept in the inventory book by the records manager.

6 The approved inventory is then used to begin the analysis of the records and the creation of the indexes.

It is very easy, in all of the information professions, to become obsessed with detail. The catalog number assigned to a book, the correct finding aid in an archive, the best filing system in an office – all can take days of absorbed effort. But it is necessary to remember that this detail must fit well into and support the whole. The occasional exercise in perceiving the whole helps to maintain a balance between the microscopic and the global views. To help in this global view nothing is as useful as the 'all-encompassing gaze around the room.'

The 'all-encompassing gaze around the room'

At some point in each area, simply stop. Stand still in the center of the bustling office, forget the detailed analysis, and try to comprehend the whole.

- Count the people. Are they seated, walking back and forth to files, rushed, relaxed?
- Count the equipment. Is it old, new, mixed?
- Count the heaps of paper. Does everything look messy, cheap, frantic, or clean, expensive, calm? A mixture?

Inventorying computer files

The inventorying of information held on a mainframe computer must be done by interviewing the data processing manager about each of the systems in use, how they work, who controls them, has access to them and what reports are produced. Find out which systems simply receive and process data, and which ones give the user creative freedom to design files and function. Find out how the time using the system and storage are charged, if to the individual workstation, the department, or as a central service. Make friends with the data processing manager. Nearly every records management program will affect or be affected by a data processing program. The two departments must work closely together if the organization is to provide true information resources management.

Where information is entered on to a computer, obtain a blank screen print of each entry record. Obtain a screen print of the list of reports produced from the information, small samples of searches on the files and samples of the reports. Ask how often the information comes in, is processed, and reported on. Where computers are used, it will be necessary, after inventorying each department or, if the organization is small, after the inventory is completed, to talk with the computer group about their understanding of information and procedures used. Note any differences between the two versions.

Observing data as it is collected

An examination of these findings can lead to several observations on the records of the organization, including the total volume, their cost of storage, and their general condition. The total cost of storing records can be estimated on the basis of the number of square feet of floor space occupied. Also, the cost of wasted space and of storing duplicate copies of records can be determined. The need for retention policies and filing system improvements and better security of vital records can be demonstrated. The percentage of documents never or infrequently referenced can be calculated. It should be possible to estimate the outcomes of a lack of uniformity in classification systems, equipment, and supplies standards in terms of wasted time, misfiles, and increased equipment and supplies costs.

Focusing the inventory

Sometimes the inventory is very focused. In these cases a form and methodology appropriate to this scope should be developed. For example, Figure 8.2 shows a typical filing equipment inventory form. It is used to make a quick tally of all the equipment in a room, area, or department. For some people this is one form too many and, rather than use it, they simply write the information on a notepad. What is important is to note:

- type of equipment (for example, four-drawer filing cabinet, 3-ft shelving bays, personal computer, etc.)
- dimensions
- number of drawers or shelves
- model number and make of electronic equipment
- number of pieces of each type and size.

Inventory summary

After the inventory sheets are collected from each area, an inventory summary should be prepared. The inventory summary should contain the following:

- number and types of cabinets in use
- filing depth utilized
- kinds of documents stored
- classification systems employed
- location of all files
- location of secure files.

In a detailed physical inventory, this additional information will be available:

- activity level of all records
- periods covered by records
- periods in active use.

FILING EQUIPMENT INVENTORY FORM

Department:

Date:

Location:

Inventoried by:

Type of equipment	Number of drawers	Number in use	Number empty	Dimensions if abnormal	Remarks (if personal computer or terminal, enter make and model here)

Figure 8.2 A filing equipment inventory form

If the inventory is to be of any use at all, notes must be written up at the end of each day and again as each department, section or group is completed. It is important to include all first and later impressions on weaknesses and strengths in filing, space, systems, and procedures. These impressions have the benefit of being taken while looking at the organization as a whole, and they will necessarily be diluted with time, involvement in specific programs, and in office politics. They will be invaluable when it is time to assess the practicability of any proposed program in any area.

Once the forms have been completed the project manager should review the data collected. There may be two official copies of the same record in different departments when there should be only one official copy. The project manager may be able to identify two record series with different titles that are actually the same record series. The project manager's review will provide the necessary information for the inventory team to make all appropriate modifications or changes. Once these are made the entire inventory should be given to the department to review.

Inventory detail

At the department level, an indepth analysis of the inventory findings must be undertaken as a prelude to developing a streamlined active filing and retrieval system. This evaluation consists of the following tasks:

1   The evaluation of the existing office filing equipment configuration in relation to retrieval activity, space, and security requirements.
2   The factoring in of the estimated growth of the department's programs and personnel and the associated impact on record volumes to maximize effectiveness of filing equipment layouts.
3   The preparation of a flow chart on each record series that shows the movement in and out of the department.
4   The determination of the value of the record and whether it is a record copy or information copy. Then, including due consideration of the activity rates and the archival value, the records should be retained in the active system, transferred to inactive storage, or disposed of.
5   The determination of the vital significance of the record series and the rendering of the appropriate action for protection.
6   The examination of the existing indexes, if they exist, to see if they fit into or need to be redesigned for the new indexing standards of the master file plan being developed organization-wide.
7   The determination of the best medium format and filing system for the record series. This may necessitate the conversion of a hard copy filing system to a more efficient hard copy system, to a microform system, to an imaging system, or, if the material is reference records only, to magnetic media.

Once the records improvement program has reached this step, not only has the organization started to regain control of the records situation, but significant momentum has accrued within the organization. Many employees will have experienced a cleaner, neater, more efficient workplace. More space for people will have been uncovered, and senior management has usually started to show enthusiasm for the overall effort. This is the time to emphasize to all the managers and employees the philosophy of the **continuous improvement** of the management and administration of records. This philosophy embeds a conscious effort by all employees to seek better, more efficient ways to handle and store records.

Part 3

Program elements implementation

INTRODUCTION

Records appraisal is probably the most difficult element of any records management program since it involves the application of values to the records. There are, however, a number of relatively straightforward approaches that can be adopted when conducting an appraisal and these are examined in some detail. Following appraisal is retention scheduling, the basis for all records management programs. Chapter 9 provides guidance for both appraising and scheduling and explains how the two functions interrelate.

Certain records are essential, or vital, to the continued operation of any organization. These must be identified and given particular attention, including classification, appropriate protection, and agreed procedures for handling (Chapter 10). If disasters occur, the organization must be fully prepared to deal with them. Records management will play a key role in the disaster recovery program, and its staff must be aware of the procedures that are to be carried out (Chapter 11).

Until recently records creation, maintenance and use had tended to be forsaken in favor of records disposition. But, with increasing emphasis being placed by government and business on the need for quick and reliable information, records creation, maintenance and use are more and more receiving the attention they deserve. With the increased emphasis on information requirements has come the increased use of forms, the tools which are commonly used to organize, collect, and transmit information. But if the forms themselves are badly designed or used unnecessarily, the quality of the information will suffer. Forms must therefore be properly managed, which includes control, analysis, design, reproduction, stocking, and distribution (Chapter 12).

In much the same way, no organization can operate effectively if it is not sure what it is meant to be doing and how procedures are to be carried out. Policy and procedure statements, or directives, require careful management. They must be part of an established system, classified, indexed, standardized, and controlled in order that everyone in the organization can see that its functions are carried out correctly and with proper authorization (Chapter 13).

Reports are an essential tool for any manager. They are the basis upon which important decisions in any organization are made. Their management, therefore, is a key aspect of the records management program (Chapter 14).

As far as files of correspondence and paper are concerned, recent trends have been towards local filing arrangements for active records and centralized storage for semi and inactive records. Active records are an essential information resource for an organization and as such require effective management. Records managers must provide the expertise necessary to ensure that active records are properly housed and adequately classified for easy retrieval, and that staff are suitably trained to look after them (Chapter 15).

When records are no longer required for the conduct of current business, they should be removed to records centers in order to provide better access to more current records and reduce storage costs. The records centers must provide storage facilities for different media (paper, film, computer tape and disk) and must take account of security of confidential material. In addition an adequate level of service to departments and organizations depositing the records must be provided. Chapter 16 examines these aspects and considers the case for either in-house or commercial storage. It also discusses the use of computerized records management programs in records centers.

When records have ended their useful (active or inactive) lives, they will either be destroyed or transferred to an archival institution. Destruction of records cannot be haphazard. Rather, there are controls and methods, described in Chapter 17, that must be implemented for the protection of the organization.

A great deal has been written on archival storage and archives operations and, while archives administration is essentially a part of records management, it has always been considered in a separate light. Although we see no reason to depart from this tradition, there are a number of aspects of archives without which a records management program would be incomplete. These include archives management, arrangement, classification, listing, and accessioning and are the subject of Chapter 18.

Finally, we come to technology, which is not an 'element' of records management but which has been mentioned throughout this text and deserves further elaboration. Because technology is one of the key factors impacting records management in the 1990s, the opportunities and pitfalls of using technologically advanced equipment and systems are discussed in Chapter 19.

9

Records appraisal and retention scheduling

Records appraisal is often thought of as something that archivists do near the end of the records life cycle to determine which records contain information of enduring value and should therefore be placed in archives. While this is the situation one finds in far too many instances, it is not the best method for adequately documenting history, and additionally it reflects a complete ignorance of the importance of managing recorded information. The practice of determining that a record has value at the end of its life cycle is uneconomical and inefficient. It inevitably results in records with significant value being destroyed and records with little value being retained.

The time to appraise a record is at its creation. By so doing, you are able to accomplish two very important functions:

- You can notify the record users of its value and thereby ensure that it is handled and maintained appropriately.
- You can, when necessary, ensure that the record is created on a lasting medium or provide for future media conversion so that information degradation does not occur.

Appraisal is the basis for retention scheduling, the process of documenting a record's value in terms of the length of time it is to be retained. By establishing a records schedule, an organization ensures that recordkeeping laws are adhered to and that management needs are met, and demonstrates that a systematic program is in place to determine records values prior to destruction of the information.

Records appraisal is not a subject that can be presented in the same way as other records management elements. It should not be based on intuition or arbitrary suppositions of value. It should be based instead on thorough analyses of documentation bearing on the matter to which the records pertain. Since appraisal involves fixing a value on something, it is bound to be immersed in some degree of subjectivity. Nevertheless, an understanding of the various aspects of a record, along with the characteristics of records values, clarifies the appraisal process.

There are a number of key points regarding the function and elements of business records to be considered before embarking on a program of records appraisal.

Function of a record

The three basic functions of a record are its use:

107

1 as **evidence** of a transaction and its terms in case of a dispute
2 as **reference** material for the organization of facts, background, prior actions, and ideas to be used in the decision-making process
3 to **comply** with government or professional regulations for the retention of records.

Evidential records

The term 'evidential' means one thing to an archivist, another to a records manager. The archival meaning is discussed later in this chapter. However, because records management deals with the entire life cycle of records, the fact that a large portion of records in an organization provide evidence (i.e., are evidential) of business operations and safeguard the organization's interests directly impacts on the value placed on these records.

Records created as evidence of a transaction must formally satisfy four elements of a record in order to be accepted in a court of law as an authentic record. In many organizations where singular transactions are being evidenced repetitively, such as is the case with insurance policies, mortgages, or bank loans, it is necessary to implement special records creation methods to standardize input and facilitate output of the records, such as forms and form letters.

The four elements of a record are:

Date of creation. This is an essential element, particularly as it relates to the legal value of a record. The US legal system favors as evidence in a court of law records created at the time of, or immediately following, the transaction in question; in other words, records possessing **contemporaneity**. The more time that elapses between the transaction in question and its documentation, the less force of evidence a record brings to bear on the case.

Definition of limited content. Stated simply, a record should contain no more and no less than is required to identify the parties involved (i.e. the originator and the audience), the place where signed, and the terms of the transaction.

Authentication. The signatures of both parties involved in certain transactions, dated and witnessed when signed, hold the best legal value, and the best witness is a notary public who affixes a seal to the record. For most general business transactions, however, non-witnessed signatures suffice. Internal business records (memos originating from and staying within the organization) sometimes do not actually contain a signature, but through a standardized method of creation and a standard order of recording (i.e., in the normal course of business) they can represent internal policy and procedure records.

Definition of medium. The medium on which a record is captured can affect its value as a record. Paper money and stock certificates are examples of records which, by being captured on special, controlled bank paper, hold special legal status as 'legal tender.' The term 'legal paper' (size 8½ × 14 inches, or 216 × 356mm), was originally coined to describe high-quality paper used by lawyers and the courts to record wills, mortgages, court submissions, and other documents. Tradition, nurtured over the last one hundred years of business, has anchored paper documents as the 'best evidence' preferred by the courts. However, standards and procedures are emerging for recording documents on other media to allow for their admissibility as evidence in a court of law.

The determination of the existence of all of these elements is not always straightforward. Documentation supporting a business transaction is usually, but not always, an evidential record. Statistics gathered to support product pricing strategies are evidential, whereas similar data used to support the development of a marketing plan may serve merely as reference. In either case, these source documents can be subpoenaed and presented in court or in a government proceeding as evidence of the organization's business operations.

Compliance records

Records intended for the purposes of legal or regulatory compliance must be created in the normal course of business and comply in format with the specifications of the government or professional body. Numerous laws from many sources specify how long pertinent business records and documentation must be retained. These bodies often further specify that records must be retained by the organization for a set period of time.

Laws and regulations affecting the use and retention of records and information vary greatly from country to country. The Canadian and US governments have powerful Privacy and Access to Information Acts for public records, while in the UK the Data Protection Act 1984 covers the same subject. Rules of evidence in most countries state what kind of record is acceptable as evidence in court. Public record or archives acts state what government documentation must be retained permanently.

One of the inherent difficulties for businesses in trying to comply with government regulations is the lack of clarity of the legislation as it specifies records. This effort requires a considerable amount of legal research before all of the relevant statutes and laws affecting a business are clearly defined and understood.

Reference records

Records created and received by the organization for the purpose of subject or technical reference material often need not be as formally considered as those in the other two categories. Relational and draft-based information, described below, can be looked at as both evidential and reference records. Certain external information, such as books, manuals, periodicals, video tapes and audio tapes, and audio-visual materials are often included under the general category of reference 'records' even though this material does not formally qualify as a 'record.' All records that are referenced, of course, can be classed as reference records; clearly there can be overlaps with the three functions of records.

Relational information brings together data from various sources for future reference. Computer databases and spreadsheets contain relational information, as do customer lists, price lists, and other compilations. These reference records also serve as evidential records. Other relational information, such as address lists and telephone lists, clearly do not satisfy the elements of a record, and hence are not evidential records.

Another category of information, **draft-based information**, is not so easily distinguishable from a record, yet it too can be treated either as an evidential or a reference record. Draft-based information includes hard copy documents before signing, memos on electronic mail, data or word processed documents in magnetic storage, manuscripts, or other documents that are not in final form. Computer-generated reports also are an excellent example of draft-based information that is classed as reference records. By nature, these records are alterable. This, of course, weakens their force as evidence because the terms of agreement included in the draft could be indistinguishably changed when the agreement is executed.

Although most documents go through this draft stage, draft-based information is not a record. There are exceptions to this. For example, the various drafts of labor union negotiations can be viewed as records with equal value as the final.

APPRAISAL

How the appraisal of records is carried out is largely a matter of organizational preference. There are, however, two basic steps that are usually taken:

Step 1 – *individual assessment*. One person is assigned to do an initial evaluation of what the records retention periods should be. This person may be the records manager or analyst in the organization itself.

Step 2 – *project team decision*. After the initial assessment is made, a more formal appraisal is undertaken by the project team. Records that have been appraised will be reviewed by key officials within an organization. The suggested membership of such a senior level records management project team was discussed in Chapter 4.

Values

Primary values

The most critical aspect of appraisal for retention and disposition purposes is the value of records. Records are created or received by organizations during the course of their normal business operations. This is their primary purpose or value, which can be further sorted into three categories: administrative, fiscal, and legal. The categories themselves can be viewed as those which represent business operations and those which safeguard essential organizational interests.

Administrative value refers to the value a record has to the original creating or receiving office. Its use by the office and its importance relative to performing the organization's assigned functions will determine its administrative value. Records in this category include purchase requisitions, time cards, budgets, and routine correspondence. They have a relatively short life span unless they meet the criterion for some other value. This value is best appraised by the responsible department manager and staff.

Fiscal value refers to the value a record has with regard to documenting the receipt or use of funds. Records possessing fiscal value are related to matters which underlie the day-to-day operations of the organization. They are significant because they summarize operations, set out policy, help in decision making, and explain procedures. The most significant class of records of fiscal value are those records pertaining to the financial transactions of the company such as expenditures, revenues, inventories, manufacturing costs, etc. These include records, such as ledgers which, while in daily use, have administrative value but acquire fiscal value when kept for auditing purposes. Other records in this class include manuals of policy and procedure, annual reports, research and development records.

Legal value refers to the value a record has in documenting business transactions and in providing proof of compliance with regulatory requirements. Included in this class of records are deeds to property, patents, copyrights, contracts, and articles of incorporation. Some seemingly unlikely records such as advertising materials may fall into this class as evidence to validate copyrights, trademarks, and other significant advertising claims. The life span of records in this class often extends beyond that of the previous two classes, to the life of the organization itself.

The latter two categories contain records which safeguard essential organizational interests. Most have lengthy retention periods. Some of the interests and the records that safeguard them are:

- acquisitions/liquidations/mergers
- advertising/marketing
- earnings/liabilities
- employment/personnel
- executive/board/reports
- expansion/relocation
- incorporation/ownership/shareholders
- legal/contracts/agreements/litigation

- patents/copyrights/assignments
- product diversification/development/liability/quality control.

Often, a fourth category is included in the above list – historical value. It is not included here because records are not created for historical purposes. They may be historically significant, but they were not created for that reason. A treaty to end a war, for example, is drafted and signed to end a war, not to provide an interesting archival document for future historians. That the document has archival value can be determined by appraisal, but it is a secondary value, as will be discussed below, not a primary value.

Secondary values

The term secondary value, generally used by archivists, does not imply that the value is less or that the record is unimportant. It is simply a different value category, and one that deals with future record use rather than current use in an active business environment. It should also be understood that value categories are not mutually exclusive and that a record may be valuable for more than one reason.

Records managers who are responsible for their organization's archives will find it necessary to understand secondary value during appraisal. Records are preserved in archival institutions because they have historical values which will exist long after they cease to be of current use, and these secondary values can be ascertained most easily if they are considered in relation to two kinds of value – evidential (not to be confused with previously described evidential records) and informational.

Evidential value covers the organization and functioning of the body that produced the records and is determined by an analysis of the administrative structure of that body and of the functions, activities, and transactions that resulted in the production of the records. From a historical standpoint, evidential value in records is something that cannot easily be gauged until the material is quite old. For public records, the precise age will depend to a large extent on a country's statutory requirements to release material to the public.

Here are three things that the appraiser should know:

- the position of an office in the administrative hierarchy of the organization
- the functions performed by an office
- the activities carried out under a given function.

In addition, all this assumes a knowledge of the general administrative history surrounding the organization's role at the time of the creation of the records. Armed with this, a valid judgment may be made.

The appraiser therefore seeks to explain the activities of the creating organization by preserving records of policy decisions, records which reflect the functions of the organization, and records which are representative of a significant range of institutional or individual activities. Such records might include:

- directives
- organization charts
- annual reports
- official histories
- correspondence
- audit and inspection reports
- statistical summaries
- legal opinions and decisions
- handbooks and manuals
- minutes of meetings.

Informational value characteristics are derived from the factual data that the records contain about persons, corporate bodies, events, problems, conditions, etc. They can be evaluated on the basis of:

- administrative needs
- the uniqueness of the record
- the information it contains
- the importance of the content.

The informational needs of genealogists, historians, economists, sociologists, demographers, etc. have to be taken into account by the records appraiser. Current research interest in quantification analysis requires a concern for informational content.

Because the informational content of case files requires specialized appraisal considerations, guidance for such appraisal is provided in the following pages.

Case files

Records having informational value are generally known as case files, and their appraisal and level of preservation have been the subject of much debate. They are generally large collections of documents, each series being on the same subject but each individual file or paper in a series relates to a different person, organization, event, or whatever. The dilemma for the appraiser is to reconcile the demand for preservation from researchers with the capacity for storage of such large collections.

Examples of these records include census of population returns, ships passenger lists, unemployment returns, criminal case files, schools files, pension records, personnel files and clinical case files. In some instances these series shed light on the activity of the organization (that is, evidential value), but this is so small in proportion to their bulk that this is not an important factor in their selection for preservation.

The same holds true for case files as for general subject files, in that the appraiser must know the background to the organization, how the file/papers fit into the overall functions, the filing system, and the potential for research interest. In the case of case files, the latter requirement takes on added importance. Interest in these types of documents is increasing and shows no signs of slowing down. The shift from the study of administrative history to the study of social history continues.

Administrative needs

Before appraising these collections, there is one major difficulty that must be recognized immediately. On many occasions the records are of long-term administrative use, usually far beyond the normal access retention period given by governments. Records of retirees, for example, must be kept as long as those entitled to receive benefits according to the organization's plan are alive, perhaps as long as 75 years after the employee retires if children are recipients.

Personal files of government workers are also required long after people retire, usually because there are questions of superannuation to be resolved. This category of records presents special problems in that the information on the file that is required for long-term use forms such a small proportion of the file itself, and yet the whole file is generally kept. This means that a disproportionate amount of storage space is being provided for the information. A simple way to reduce this drastically would be to use a system of personal record cards. This card, whose size would be dictated by the amount of information that needs to be preserved, is completed with details of service, qualifications, superannuation, performance, etc. when the person resigns or retires. The card is kept permanently while the file may be destroyed as soon as is convenient.

Uniqueness

The term uniqueness means that the information contained in particular records is not to be found in other documentary sources in as complete and as usable form. Information is obviously unique if it cannot be found elsewhere. But information in public records is seldom completely unique, for generally such records relate to matters that are also dealt with in other documentary sources, and the information they contain may be similar or approximately similar to that contained in other sources.

In applying the test of uniqueness, an appraiser must bring into review all other sources of information on the matter under consideration. These sources should encompass materials produced outside as well as within the organization. The material produced outside may be published or unpublished; it may consist of private manuscripts, newspapers, or books.

Uniqueness also includes the matter of duplication. Records can be duplicated from one administrative level to another, and within an organization several copies of a particular record might exist. It is therefore essential to carefully compare records containing information on any particular matter to avoid retaining more than one copy.

Content

The degree to which the information is concentrated in the records may be in one of three ways:

1 extensive – few facts are presented about many persons, events, etc.
2 intensive – many facts are presented about a few persons, events, etc.
3 diverse – many facts are presented about various matters – persons, events, etc.

For example, census schedules and passenger lists may be said to provide extensive information in that each schedule or list pertains to many people. Pension files may be said to provide intensive information in that each file covers one person and gives a great deal of detail. Reports of consular or diplomatic agents would contain information on diverse matters. Content might also include the physical condition of the records as well as the information within them. Physical condition is important, for if the records are to be preserved in an archival institution, they should be in a form that will enable people, other than those who created them, to use them without difficulty and without resort to expensive mechanical or electronic equipment.

Importance

In applying the test of importance, the appraiser is in the realm of the imponderable. Who can say definitely if a given body of records is important, and for what purpose, and for whom? There is no question that the informational value of case files is high, but the needs of the researcher have to be balanced against the economic necessities of governments and other organizations.

The appraiser should take into account the actual research methods of various groups of people and the likelihood that they would under ordinary circumstances make effective use of archival materials. By and large the scholar can usually rely on the overwhelming mass of published material on recent day-to-day social and economic matters, but, while records appraisers might normally give priority to the needs of the historian and social scientists, they must also preserve records of vital interest to the genealogist and the student of local history. They should not, however, preserve records for very unlikely users, such as persons in highly specialized technical and scientific fields who do not use records extensively in the normal exercise of their professions and are not likely to use archival materials relating to them.

Research values are normally derived from the importance of information in aggregates of records, not from information in single records. Documents are collectively significant if the information they contain is useful for studies of social, economic and political matters, as distinct from matters relating to individual persons or things.

Records relating to persons or things may, of course, have an individual research value. Normally the more important a person is, the more important is the record relating to them. Such records might also have sentimental value because of their association with heroes, dramatic episodes, or places where significant events took place.

Appraisal criteria

Before applying these tests for the appraisal of the informational value in case files, as much background information as possible must be known. One way of doing this is to conduct an inventory of these records (see Chapter 8) and compile a separate index of case files. The index should contain an information sheet for each collection which would show dates covered, creating section/branch, content, references, number of units, whether any formal reports have been produced on the subject-matter, related material, and statutory background. Room should be left on the sheet for appraisal and review comments, and the index should be made available for academic consultation.

When actually applying the tests of informational value, the records can be categorized into three types:

1 records relating to persons
2 records relating to things
3 records relating to events.

Records relating to persons

These records are produced in great quantities by modern governments and other organizations. Certain types of records, like census schedules, are intended to cover all individuals in the country; others, relating to specific classes, often represent large segments of the population (such as laborers, farmers, soldiers, or recipients of welfare services); still others relate to even more specialized classes, such as a group of students taking a particular course at a particular university. As the controls of government over its individual citizens are extended, more records are created in relation to them.

Besides being great in quantity, the records are duplicative in content. If considered singly and solely with reference to the personal information they contain, most records pertaining to persons have little research value. From the point of view of their significance for demographic, sociological or economic studies, they are usually important only in the aggregate. For such studies they have value only if used collectively – because of their information on phenomena that concern a number of persons and not because of their information on single persons.

In addition summarizations of the data they contain are usually available in statistical enumerations and tabulations, either in published or unpublished form.

Records relating to things

When selecting records relating to places, buildings and other material objects, the values to be considered are those that derive from the information they contain on the things themselves, not necessarily from the information on what happens to things.

Among the most fundamental things with which people are concerned is the land on which they live. The kind of material that is likely to be preserved are records on ownership of land, on survey and exploration, on mineral resources, and various other topographical or geological features.

Records on buildings need not be kept to any extensive degree. They are archivally important only if the buildings themselves are important, and buildings acquire an importance because they are identified with important historical persons, with important historical events, or because they are outstanding examples of period buildings.

Records relating to events

The selection of records relating to events or phenomena is largely self-productive. Subjectivity on the part of the appraiser is difficult to avoid. A knowledge of the historical background of the organization and of administrative policy are essential elements in the appraisal process.

Appraisal method

In selecting records for their informational value, two alternative courses are available:

- to select complete series of records that represent concentrations of information, such as census schedules, where single documents provide extensive information in a concentrated form
- to select a limited number of documents that are representative of the whole.

Because of the bulk of these records, there are few that will be selected as a complete collection. Census records are an obvious exception, because experience has shown that they are extremely popular and useful to a particular, fairly large, group of researchers.

When it comes to selecting a limited number of documents from a collection – or sampling, as it is usually called – there are three methods which can be followed:

1. Special selection
2. Random sampling
3. Systematic sampling.

Special selection

This is a method that has little true archival merit and may also be of uncertain value for research purposes. Nevertheless, there are occasions when it can be adopted with some justice. The method simply means the selection from a relatively ephemeral series of papers of one or more specimens to illustrate administrative practice at a particular date. The resultant sample represents a very limited historical or other use since it can only be cited as an indicator and in no way be used for comparative or statistical study.

Special selection is often applied to personal files, where those of eminent persons may be selected for their intrinsic value only.

Random sampling

This method implies that every unit in a series has an equal chance of representing that series, and in this context it is necessary to use a random number table – a list of numbers normally generated by computer and checked in a number of different ways to ensure that they are as random as possible. The table is applied to file reference numbers and documents are selected accordingly.

Systematic sampling

This is the usual method for selection of case files and it is carried out at various degrees of complexity. The most simple way is to decide on the size of the sample required and to select every 5th, 10th, 50th, 100th or whatever file from the series, starting from the beginning of the run on the shelves and continuing until the end is reached. In a collection of regional papers, the system might be to select records for one particular year from region A, for the following year from region B, and so on, in a continuous cycle. In a series with annual cycles, the files from every 10th year might be selected as the sample. In an alphabetical series, all the files with a particular initial letter might be selected for particular years. Whatever selection system is used will depend very much on the characteristics of the whole collection, and, to a certain extent, on the size of the sample required.

For researchers, the problem with systematic sampling is that it depends on a subjective decision of the criteria to be used. Although academic historians are being increasingly consulted before these decisions are made, this sampling method remains the least liked by them.

Problems

Although the scholar can very often rely on the mass of published literature for information on social and economic developments, it can be argued that the existence of published conclusions drawn from a collection of case files is not in itself a valid reason for destroying the raw data. Such data can be used for further research purposes, other than those for which it was originally compiled. In addition, published abstracts often give rise to false, or at least contentious, conclusions which are not supported by original data.

These large collections of papers take up an inordinate amount of space and the general feeling is that as many of them as possible must be destroyed. By doing so, however, researchers are being deprived of valuable sources of study. A number of solutions to these problems has been suggested, including:

- The collections be microfilmed, the film preserved and the original documents destroyed. The main argument against this is one of cost.
- Collections not selected be kept in an intermediate repository and made available to researchers for a specified period, say between five and ten years, so that they can carry out any research on them. After that period they would be destroyed.
- Collections not considered worthy of permanent preservation in a national archive may be offered to other historical institutions and associations, including those privately owned.

RECORDS RETENTION SCHEDULES

In simple terms a records retention schedule is a list of records for which predetermined destruction dates have been established. Such schedules are often referred to as records schedules, disposition schedules, and even retention and disposition schedules. All the terms are interchangeable.

Records scheduling has three broad objectives:

1 prompt disposal of records whose retention period has ended
2 storage of records which must be temporarily retained after they are no longer needed in current business
3 preservation of records which are of long-term value.

Large accumulations of all types of records reflect inadequate management not only on the part of the records manager but also on the part of the organization's overall administration. Some types of records require only one reading or action before disposal, others should be retained for short periods of time; a small number might warrant retention for longer periods; a selected few will be permanently preserved.

While an efficient active filing system is an essential element for the effective and economical management of active records, an equally essential element is an active scheduling program. Retaining too many records will prove expensive in staff, time, space and equipment, and could have adverse legal consequences. The inclusion of as many records as possible on a retention schedule will help to:

- save time by reducing the volume of records which must be searched for information
- avoid legal problems
- promote efficiency by focusing managerial efforts on those records which are most important
- save space by removing from the office records no longer required or no longer in current use
- identify the valuable records for archival preservation.

The results of retention schedules are, therefore, fewer records, better records, more effective records, and more economical records.

The style of the schedule will vary according to individual taste, but certain types of information should be shown:

- the part of the organization responsible for maintaining the record (office of record)
- a schedule reference number (for example, a serial number followed by the year or a revision number)
- file/paper reference(s), if any
- description of series or collection
- prescribed period of retention
- appropriate approval signatures
- date of the schedule.

There are three main categories of records that will appear on the retention schedule:

- those with specific retention periods (that is, 'destroy after x years')
- those which are to be retained and examined again at a later date (that is, 'annual review,' 'while useful,' 'indefinite')
- those which are to be selected for permanent preservation.

Schedule types

Two types of schedule are used by organizations: functional and departmental.

Functional retention schedule

Large organizations, particularly those with several branches or semi-autonomous entities, will often create a functional retention schedule. Generally, it is compiled and maintained by a central organization (such as a national archive or corporate headquarters) and covers records common to all departments or agencies. For example, the separate divisions of a corporation may have their own accounting, personnel, sales and marketing, manufacturing, and information services departments, each creating similar and sometimes identical records. Since it is in the best interests of the corporation for the retention policies to be applied consistently throughout the different divisions, a functional retention schedule is developed. Record series are described in general, functional terms (e.g., 'accounts payable invoices' would include the types of records that support the payment of bills, such as the actual invoice, supporting documentation, check vouchers, computer reports, on-line data, etc.) to accommodate the various terminology,

XYZ CORPORATION   RECORDS RETENTION SCHEDULE - ACCOUNTING DEPARTMENT

NO.	RECORD SERIES TITLE	RETENTION POLICY OFFICIAL	COPY	OFFICE OF RECORD	AUTHORITY FEDERAL	STATE/OTHER	Approval V	A	NOTES
A01	ACCOUNTS PAYABLE								
A01-1	Check Registers	4 years	1	Accounts Payable	26 USC 6501	Statute of Limit.		✓	
A01-2	Daily Receiving Reports	1 month	1 month	Accounts Payable	26 USC 6501	Statute of Limit.			
A01-3	Material Usage	TA or 6 years	1	Accounts Payable	26 USC 6501	Statute of Limit.			
A01-4	Open Receivers Registers	TA or 6 years	1	Accounts Payable	26 USC 6501	Statute of Limit.			
A01-5	Vendor Disbursement Summary	TA or 6 years	1	Accounts Payable	26 USC 6501	Statute of Limit.			
A01-6	Vendor Invoices	TA or 6 years	1	Accounts Payable	26 USC 6501	Statute of Limit.			
B01	BUDGET								
B01-1	Administrative Expense	TA or 6 years	1	Budgets/Financial	26 CFR 1.162-17	Not specified			
B01-2	Budget Forecast	3 years	1	Budgets/Financial	Not specified	Not specified			
C01	COST ACCOUNTING								
C01-1	Absorption (Monthly) Report	TA or 6 years	1	Cost Accounting	26 USC 6501	Statute of Limit.			
C01-2	Cost of Goods Sold	TA or 6 years	1	Cost Accounting	26 USC 6501	Statute of Limit.			
C01-3	Financial Estimates	TA or 6 years	1	Cost Accounting	26 USC 6501	Statute of Limit.			
C01-4	Finished Goods	TA or 6 years	1	Cost Accounting	26 USC 6501	Statute of Limit.			
C01-5	Incentive Audits	TA or 6 years	1	Cost Accounting	26 USC 6501	Statute of Limit.			
C01-6	Intransit Inventory Detail	TA or 6 years	1	Cost Accounting	26 CFR 1.472-2	Not specified			
C01-7	Inventory Valuations/Revaluations	TA or 6 years	1	Cost Accounting	26 CFR 1.472-2	Not specified			
C01-8	Journal Entries	TA or 6 years	1	Cost Accounting	26 USC 6501	Statute of Limit.	✓		
C01-9	Labor Cost Control	TA or 6 years	1	Cost Accounting	26 USC 6501	Statute of Limit.			
C02	CREDIT								
C02-1	Bank Deductions	TA or 6 years	1	Credit	26 USC 6501	Statute of Limit.			
C02-2	Bank Statements	4 years	1	Credit	26 USC 6501	Statute of Limit.			
C02-3	Checks-Accounts Receivable	TA or 6 years	1	Credit	26 USC 6501	Statute of Limit.			
C02-4	Customer Credit Files	TA or 6 years	1	Credit	26 USC 6501	Statute of Limit.			
C02-5	Deposits	TA or 6 years	1	Credit	26 USC 6501	Statute of Limit.			
C02-6	Financial Control Report	TA or 6 years	1	Credit	26 USC 6501	Statute of Limit.			
C02-7	Invoices	TA or 6 years	1	Credit	26 USC 6501	Statute of Limit.	✓		
C02-8	Lockbox Conversion	TA or 6 years	1	Credit	26 USC 6501	Statute of Limit.	✓		
C02-9	Payment Registers	TA or 6 years	1	Credit	26 USC 6501	Statute of Limit.			
G01	GENERAL ACCOUNTING				(Use 48 CFR 4.705-1 for military)				
G01-1	Balance Sheet Accounts	TA or 6 years	1	General Accounting	26 USC 6501	Statute of Limit.			
G01-2	Chart of Accounts	TA or 6 years	SU	General Accounting	26 USC 6501	Statute of Limit.		✓	
G01-3	Closing, Monthly	TA or 6 years	1	General Accounting	26 USC 6501	Statute of Limit.			
G01-4	Financial Statements	TA or 6 years	1	General Accounting	26 USC 6501	Statute of Limit.			
G01-5	Financial Statements Target Report	TA or 6 years	1	General Accounting	26 USC 6501	Statute of Limit.			
G01-6	Fixed Assets Depreciation Register	TA or 6 years	1	General Accounting	26 USC 6501	Statute of Limit.			
G01-7	General Ledger	TA or 6 years	1	General Accounting	26 USC 6501	Statute of Limit.	✓		
G01-8	Journal Entries	TA or 6 years	1	General Accounting	26 USC 6501	Statute of Limit.	✓		

EVENT CODES: F=Final Action; TA=Tax Audit; SU=Superseded
V=Vital Record   A=Archival

SAMPLE ONLY   Schedule effective [Date]

Figure 9.1   A records retention schedule

file and report titles, and methods of handling the records which are unique to each division.

Departmental retention schedule

An adjunct to the functional retention schedule is the departmental retention schedule, which identifies in the department's own language its own records. The functional schedule dictates the retention policy, and the departmental schedule presents that policy to the users of the records. Individual departments and organizations will vary in the style of schedule that they adopt, but the objective must be the same – the prompt disposition of records which do not warrant longer retention.

The departmental retention schedule can also be created to stand alone without a functional retention schedule. The records manager maintains a master list of all department schedules, while each department has its own. An example is shown in Figure 9.1. This particular example lists not only the record series and offices of record; it also identifies statutory and regulatory requirements and which records are vital (V) and suitable for archival preservation (A). Assigning a number to each series aids in quick reference and easy computerized sorting. The steps leading up to the creation of this schedule are described late in this chapter.

The type of records to appear on departmental retention schedules will vary between different organizations. It would be impossible to produce a definitive list of such types, but the contents of those earmarked for destruction after a relatively short period are likely to have a number of common characteristics.

- non-policy making
- low level administration
- low frequency of reference
- clearly of no historical value whatsoever.

Monitoring and implementation

Once a schedule has been developed it must be monitored regularly to see that:

- retention periods are still realistic in the light of experience
- records no longer in existence are removed from the schedule
- new records created are added to the schedule.

The monitoring should be carried out by the records manager and any amendments or additions discussed with a representative of the appropriate department or section.

It is important that all who need to know about the schedule are given a copy and are supplied with amendments. Records managers should keep a complete set of schedules of the organization(s) for which they are responsible and they must ensure that action in accordance with the schedules is carried out.

The production of retention schedules is one of the most important elements of any records management program. Schedules can lead to wide-ranging benefits, not only in the efficient management of an organization as a whole but also in saving expenditure. It is worthwhile, therefore, to take special trouble over their compilation, monitoring, and execution.

Authority to destroy

If a retention schedule is appropriately developed and carefully monitored, and if the schedule users receive regular communication from the records manager, then documents that have been included on the schedule can be destroyed in accordance with the terms of the schedule. Ideally, the records can be destroyed without additional formal authority. The schedule itself is authority enough. This approach should have the blessing of legal counsel and key management. The advantage is that users cannot hang on to records 'just in case' they need them. The risk is that documents will be destroyed that legitimately ought to be kept. For example, an audit may be in process or a special project may be in the works.

Before destroying records, it is appropriate to confirm with legal counsel that there is no pending or existing litigation that may preclude this activity. Often destruction can be carried out by the departmental representative; there is not always a need for records managers to become involved in the actual process of destruction. They should, however, make periodic checks to ensure that the work is being carried out in the prescribed manner commensurate with the sensitivity (confidentiality) of the material. Some records may be simply put in the wastepaper bin whereas others might require shredding, burning or other type of high security disposal (see also Chapter 17).

DEVELOPING RETENTION SCHEDULES

Records cannot be haphazardly scheduled for disposition. They must be grouped into records series and, preferably, further organized according to classification plan. This is because appraisal to determine the retention requirements involves an analysis of the entire information system (indeed, of the entire organization) in which the record is used.

Once the determination has been made as to the value of each record series, a retention period can be established. This retention period may be based on the records manager's or analyst's experience with similar records, knowledge relating to other organization's retention of similar records, original research of government statutes and regulations, or from other sources such as published retention information, as along as such information can be deemed reliable.

Additional factors also influence the determination of retention periods. These factors are organizational, governmental, or archival, and relate to the administrative, fiscal, legal, and historical record values previously described. They should be dealt with by the individual most knowledgeable about the specific area involved. That is, administrative factors should be considered by someone in the originating office, fiscal factors should be considered by the organization's controller or accountant, legal factors should be considered by the legal counsel, and historical factors should be considered by the archivist, historian, or records manager.

Retention schedule development can easily be accomplished in four steps: the regulatory impact report, the regulatory matrix, the master classification plan, and the schedule itself.

Regulatory impact report

The regulatory impact report is an initial listing of all state and federal legislation that may affect records retention at an organization. This guide is created based on knowledge gained from the records inventory and interviews and is used for researching specific citations. Regulations are listed broadly (see Figure 9.2). Once created, it is useful to show this report to the organization's legal counsel prior to beginning the detailed research to see what may have been overlooked or is not relevant. For example, a non-profit organization may have limited reporting requirements to the tax authorities, thus eliminating the need to research state and federal tax codes to the extent one would for a for-profit organization.

REGULATORY IMPACT REPORT

STATUTE, REGULATION, RULES AGENCY OR PROGRAM				
Title	Agency	Chapter/Section #	DESCRIPTION	RESEARCH NOTES
UNITED STATES CODE				
Title 8	Aliens and Nationality	Part 1324A	Unlawful Employment of Aliens	
Title 15	Commerce and Trade	Chapter 15	Toxic substances control	
Title 16	Conservation	Chapter 12	Licenses and public utilities	
		Subchapter III		
Title 18	Crimes and Criminal Procedure			
		Chapter 25	Counterfeiting and forgery	
		Section 495	Contracts, deeds, and powers of attorneys	
Title 26	Internal Revenue Code	Chapter 61	Information and returns	
		Chapter 66	Limitations	
Title 29	Labor	Chapter 8	Fair labor standards	
		Chapter 14	Age discrimination in employment	
		Chapter 15	Occupational safety and health	
		Chapter 16	Rehabilitation services	
		Chapter 18	Employee retirement income security program	
		Subchapter 1	Protection of employee benefits rights	
Title 42	Public Health	Chapter 15B	Air pollution control	
		Chapter 77	Improving energy efficiency	
		Part C	Industrial energy conservation	
		Chapter 91	National energy conservation policy	
FEDERAL REGULATORY AGENCIES				
Title 8	Aliens and Nationality			
	Department of Justice	Immigration and Naturalization		
		Subchapter B	Immigration regulations	
		Part 247	Control of employment of aliens	
Title 10	Energy	Subchapter 3	Energy conservation	
Title 18	Conservation of Power and Water Resources			
		Subchapter B	Regulations under the Federal Power Act	
		Subchapter C	Account, Federal Power Act	

Figure 9.2   A regulatory impact report

NO.	RECORD SERIES TITLE	RETENTION POLICY OFFICIAL	COPY	OFFICE OF RECORD	AUTHORITY FEDERAL	STATE/OTHER	V	A	NOTES
A01	**ACCOUNTS PAYABLE**								
A01-1	Check Registers	4 years	1	Accounts Payable	26 USC 6501	Statute of Limit.	V		
A01-2	Daily Receiving Reports	1 month	1 month	Accounts Payable	26 USC 6501	Statute of Limit.			
A01-3	Material Usage	TA or 6 years	1	Accounts Payable	26 USC 6501	Statute of Limit.			
A01-4	Open Receivers Registers	TA or 6 years	1	Accounts Payable	26 USC 6501	Statute of Limit.			
A01-5	Vendor Disbursement Summary	TA or 6 years	1	Accounts Payable	26 USC 6501	Statute of Limit.			
A01-6	Vendor Invoices	TA or 6 years	1	Accounts Payable	26 USC 6501	Statute of Limit.			
B01	**BUDGET**								
B01-1	Administrative Expense	TA or 6 years	1	Budgets/Financial	26 CFR 1.162-17	Not specified			
B01-2	Budget Forecast	3 years	1	Budgets/Financial	Not specified	Not specified			
C01	**COST ACCOUNTING**								
C01-1	Absorption (Monthly) Report	TA or 6 years	1	Cost Accounting	26 USC 6501	Statute of Limit.			
C01-2	Cost of Goods Sold	TA or 6 years	1	Cost Accounting	26 USC 6501	Statute of Limit.			
C01-3	Financial Estimates	TA or 6 years	1	Cost Accounting	26 USC 6501	Statute of Limit.			
C01-4	Finished Goods	TA or 6 years	1	Cost Accounting	26 USC 6501	Statute of Limit.			
C01-5	Incentive Audits	TA or 6 years	1	Cost Accounting	26 USC 6501	Statute of Limit.			
C01-6	Intransit Inventory Detail	TA or 6 years	1	Cost Accounting	26 CFR 1.472-2	Not specified			
C01-7	Inventory Valuations/Revaluations	TA or 6 years	1	Cost Accounting	26 CFR 1.472-2	Not specified			
C01-8	Journal Entries	TA or 6 years	1	Cost Accounting	26 USC 6501	Statute of Limit.	V		
C01-9	Labor Cost Control	TA or 6 years	1	Cost Accounting	26 USC 6501	Statute of Limit.			
C02	**CREDIT**								
C02-1	Bank Deductions	TA or 6 years	1	Credit	26 USC 6501	Statute of Limit.			
C02-2	Bank Statements	4 years	1	Credit	26 USC 6501	Statute of Limit.			
C02-3	Checks-Accounts Receivable	TA or 6 years	1	Credit	26 USC 6501	Statute of Limit.			
C02-4	Customer Credit Files	TA or 6 years	1	Credit	26 USC 6501	Statute of Limit.			
C02-5	Deposits	TA or 6 years	1	Credit	26 USC 6501	Statute of Limit.			
C02-6	Financial Control Report	TA or 6 years	1	Credit	26 USC 6501	Statute of Limit.	V		
C02-7	Invoices	TA or 6 years	1	Credit	26 USC 6501	Statute of Limit.	V		
C02-8	Lockbox Conversion	TA or 6 years	1	Credit	26 USC 6501	Statute of Limit.			
C02-9	Payment Registers	TA or 6 years	1	Credit	26 USC 6501	Statute of Limit.			
G01	**GENERAL ACCOUNTING**				(Use 48 CFR 4.705-1 for military)				
G01-1	Balance Sheet Accounts	TA or 6 years	1	General Accounting	26 USC 6501	Statute of Limit.			
G01-2	Chart of Accounts	TA or 6 years	SU	General Accounting	26 USC 6501	Statute of Limit.	V		
G01-3	Closing, Monthly	TA or 6 years	1	General Accounting	26 USC 6501	Statute of Limit.			
G01-4	Financial Statements	TA or 6 years	1	General Accounting	26 USC 6501	Statute of Limit.			
G01-5	Financial Statements Target Report	TA or 6 years	1	General Accounting	26 USC 6501	Statute of Limit.			
G01-6	Fixed Assets Depreciation Register	TA or 6 years	1	General Accounting	26 USC 6501	Statute of Limit.			
G01-7	General Ledger	TA or 6 years	1	General Accounting	26 USC 6501	Statute of Limit.	V		
G01-8	Journal Entries	TA or 6 years	1	General Accounting	26 USC 6501	Statute of Limit.	V		

EVENT CODES: FI=Final Action; TA=Tax Audit; SU=Superseded
V=Vital Record A=Archival

SAMPLE ONLY

Schedule effective [Date]

Figure 9.3 A regulatory matrix

REGULATORY MATRIX

STATUTE, REGULATION, RULES AGENCY OR PROGRAM — Description	CITATION CODE (Title & Section #)	IMPACTED RECORDS	RETENTION POLICY	RESEARCH NOTES
UNITED STATES CODE				
ALIENS AND NATIONALITY				
Unlawful Employment of Aliens	8 USC 1324A	Verification form	3 years	
COMMERCE AND TRADE				
Toxic substances control	15 USC 2607	Adverse Reaction to Health	30 years	
		Adverse Reaction to Environment	30 years	
CONSERVATION				
Licensees and public utilities, procedural and	16 USC 825	Accounts	See FERC rules and regulations	
administrative provisions		Cost accounting procedures	See FERC rules and regulations	
		Correspondence, memoranda	See FERC rules and regulations	
		Papers, books	See FERC rules and regulations	
INTERNAL REVENUE CODE				
Records, statements, & special returns	26 USC 6001	Tax returns and supporting records (e.g., invoices, journal entries)	Not specified	
Limitations on assessments	26 USC 6501	Books of Account	3 years from filing date	
Limitations on collections	26 USC 6502	Books of Account	6 years from assessment	
LABOR				
Fair Labor Standards Act	29 USC 211c	Records of:		
		Employee Wages	Not Specified	
		Hours & Other Conditions	Not Specified	
		Practices of Employment	Not Specified	
		Time Sheets	Not Specified	
Employee Retirement Income Security Program	29 USC 1021	Employee Benefit Plans	Not Specified	
	29 USC 1022	Employee Benefit Summary Plan	Not Specified	
	29 USC 1023	Annual Report - Benefit Plan	Not Specified	
	29 USC 1027	Records Related to Benefit Plans	6 years	
Participation and Vesting	29 USC 1059	Employee Benefit Reports	1 year	
PUBLIC HEALTH				
Air pollution control	42 USC 1857f-b	Records and reports	No stipulated retention period	

MANAGEMENT/LEGAL Review Draft   SAMPLE ONLY   Date

Figure 9.4 A master classification plan

Regulatory matrix

Once the regulatory impact report is developed, the next step is to create the regulatory matrix. This is a compilation of the specific research of relevant legislation, including the actual citations and record series specifically mentioned in the text (see Figure 9.3). The matrix should also have legal counsel review for the reasons mentioned above.

Not every citation referenced in the matrix necessarily applies to the organization, but it is better to err on the side of too much research than not enough. In the sample, which represents the research and development division of a public utilities company, citation 15 USC 2607 is included because during the inventory interviews it was revealed that, while they do not now, certain future R&D projects may involve toxic substances.

Master classification plan

The master classification plan of an organization categorizes all records into record series that can be filed together as a block, used as a block, and which can be evaluated as a block for retention purposes. Each of these record series should have:

- a primary classification, representing a generic category of records groups
- a secondary classification, representing more specific records in the series
- the length of time that the files within the record series should be retained by the organization
- the department responsible for maintaining the 'official record' of the files in this record series.

Figure 9.4 illustrates the master classification plan that results in the retention schedule, Figure 9.1. In this case, the primary classification coincides with the department name. The accounting department is divided into several smaller departments that coincide with accounting functions, thus creating ready-made primary classifications. The record series under each department/function are the secondary classifications.

What about individual files? File folder titles, not listed on either the master classification plan nor on the retention schedule, are tertiary classifications that meet specific user needs and may or may not be standardized. The master classification plan provides a high level classification scheme for ensuring that records are properly categorized for retention purposes. You might consider each secondary classification as a 'bucket' in which several files or types of records may be categorized. Let's take engineering project files as an example. Every project is likely to be different and demand unique documentation, yet there are common elements (e.g., drawings, design specifications, change orders, contracts, etc.) that can be identified as record series on the master classification plan and consequently can provide a certain amount of standardization when trying to define retention requirements. The remaining records that tend to be project-specific can be classified under a generic record series 'bucket' called 'Project Support Documentation.' Thus, a combination of standardization and flexibility is built in to accommodate a variety of files and yet still meet retention needs.

Designation of official record and information copy within the master classification plan

One of the major costs for organizations is duplicating and storing duplicate information copies of a record. This practice can be significantly reduced in an organization by the designation of an official record (sometimes referred to as the record copy) when a record is created. It would be the designated responsibility of an individual or department of the organization to store and maintain records for the evidential and compliance functions. Then any copy of the record created and distributed for the reference needs of other employees of the organization could be destroyed as soon as their reference requirements run out.

Records creation within the master classification plan

The master classification plan should include all records on all media. It is a centrally controlled policy index which specifies the framework for recordkeeping within the organization. When a record is created internally or received from an external source it is classified within the context of the master classification plan. Fortunately, over 90 percent of records creation and receipt is repetitive in nature. This means that a decision about which record series for each document being created is not constantly required. Most employees create or receive a very small subset of the organization's records in the performance of their jobs. They are able then to become knowledgeable about the types of records series for which they are responsible. In the event that they require records they haven't created, a quick reference to the master classification plan will tell them which department has that information. If they find they require constant reference to these records they may have to create information copies for themselves.

Active or inactive record

Once it is determined that a document is an official record rather than an information copy, the decision needs to be made as to whether or not it is active or inactive. An **active record** is one which has high administrative value, or to put it another way, is required to carry on current operations. This frequently means that the record has been referred to in the last six-month period or that it is not over a year old. Active records need to be stored where they can be quickly accessed, which usually means in prime office space.

   Inactive records, which are not necessary for current operations, but have some value in protecting organizational interests, can safely be stored in secondary office space, in a warehouse, or in some other low-cost holding area.

Retention schedule

The final piece is the retention schedule, which has been discussed in detail at the beginning of this chapter. Record series identified during the records inventory are matched to the citations in the regulatory matrix and appropriate retention periods are assigned. Operational and administrative retention periods are given to those records not covered by legislation. The latter is often negotiated with the users.

   The information on a retention schedule should always include the length of time the official record (sometimes known as the record copy) is kept and who is the office of record. The schedule should also indicate how long reference or information copies are kept – *never* longer than the official record retention period.

   Some organizations like to include the length of time the records are to remain in the originating office, the length of time they are to be retained in a storage facility, and the date of scheduled destruction or transfer to an archives. This tends to work better in theory than in practice, as users transfer records to storage when they run out of space, not when the schedule tells them to. On the other hand, such information can serve as a reminder to people that they have an alternative to purchasing more filing cabinets, and may give the records manager more leverage in administering the records management program.

   As a general rule, records should be retained in the originating office as long as they are active (referred to once per file drawer per month). When records become inactive they should be transferred to a storage facility. For those records which will have no archival value, disposition should occur at the earliest possible time after retention requirements have been met.

Scheduling machine-readable records

The main elements involved in the appraisal and scheduling of data processing records are essentially no different from those involved in dealing with paper records. But because of the format in which they are held and because of the technical problems involved in handling them, certain considerations have to be taken into account.

In some organizations the records manager has the authority for establishing integrated retention and disposal schedules for all records regardless of their physical form, hard copy or computerized. Often the reality is that the records manager is organizationally removed from the data processing systems area which may be responsible for a considerable volume of the organization's information holdings. Ideally, a rapport has been established between the records manager and the head of the management information systems (MIS) department during the preparation of the organizational strategic information plan. The plan would relate the data processing records to the applicable source documents and other supporting records. A consistency of retention periods could then be applied to data and documents, being careful not to keep duplicate records beyond administrative needs.

However, often this rapport, let alone this plan, does not exist in an organization, and the records manager is left with the responsibility of scheduling these data processing records. The first task, then, is to understand how data processing records are administered.

Administration of data records

Data managers would much rather view the scheduling issue from the point of view of systems supporting the delivery of programs rather than thousands of tapes overcrowding a tape library. This generic approach is also much more appealing to systems analysts who tend to view their world in a systems (i.e., data and processes) rather than media context. In order to understand this world, it is helpful to look at exactly what data records are and how they are logically organized.

A discussion of data records includes data on magnetic tape, paper/mylar tape, disk packs, diskettes, mass storage cartridges and optical disks used in conjunction with data processing systems. It should be noted that recorded information stored in machine-readable media is uniquely valuable because it can readily be processed, modified, or updated. The ability to easily sort, aggregate, tabulate, and summarize machine-readable media records adds a dimension and a value not to be found in paper records or computer output microfilm (COM) files.

These data records are organized in major units called **data sets**. Data sets are a collection of data laid out in a prescribed arrangement depending on the application. A descriptive term or phrase is assigned to each data set which is used to identify it. Data sets, or files as they are sometimes called, can be further broken down into 'master files' and 'processing files.' The master file is the complete authoritative source of the information. Processing files on the other hand are used to create or update a master file and are therefore not normally retained after production and validation of the master file. These master files can also be output to other media such as COM or paper (computer printouts).

The records manager then, must be concerned with the retention of the source documents, the master files and processing files, and any output reports. The key here is to eliminate unnecessary duplication. This involves determining the appropriate and most efficient storage media (e.g., disk, tape, paper, film) considering the nature and volume of retrievals, cost and admissibility requirements.

Once the records manager understands how data are administered, the next step is to establish a rapport with a sympathetic individual in the systems area, preferably at a senior level. Based on this rapport, efforts should be made to develop a proposal to senior management for the establishment of a pilot project to address issues which are common to both MIS and the records manager, but which are elevated to a level which addresses the organization's ability to continue generating the information products it requires to do business properly. This is usually a prelude to a truly organizational strategic information plan.

Determination of specific data retention periods

The determination of specific retention and disposal provisions should be undertaken in consultation with users and information systems specialists. The user would be responsible for the overall administrative requirements, and the information system specialist would recommend retention periods for the various records as appropriate based on the life cycles established by the systems specifications. Based on this approach, the individual stages and their associated retention periods should be described generally in the order that they are created within the system. Consistency should be achieved with respect to the retention periods established for related hard copy documents controlled by records management. Of course, the organizational specialists in legal, tax, audit, and such would be involved in this process as appropriate just as in the case of hard copy records.

The success of the data scheduling function from a records management perspective is dependent upon the degree to which a records manager is willing to share in the responsibility for the proper management of data processed by automated systems. If records managers are to obtain the support of users and systems personnel, then they must be prepared to take an active role, first of all, in sharing the accountability for carrying out the scheduling process and, secondly, in providing some form of service which would make the scheduling function worthwhile. This could involve a range of activities from sharing in the responsibility for the establishment of an archival management function in the organization's tape library to arranging for off-site tape storage facilities.

Other supporting functions could include accepting responsibility for researching archival standards for the preservation of data on magnetic media and providing efficiently managed storage systems for the masses of documentation which are often associated with automated systems. In this latter context, and given the significant lack of documentation which can be associated with some systems, the records manager could even assume responsibility for sharing in the development of corporate documentation standards for automated systems.

Scheduling of the electronic records of personal computers

In the past few years retention scheduling for personal computers has usually meant 'buying a bigger hard disk.' Of course this approach causes a number of problems:

- It leaves potentially destructive information in revisions to documents, should there be a court case where these records can be ordered into evidence by your prosecuting attorney. (Electronic records are not evidential records for the plaintiff but are often admissible for the prosecutor.)
- If there is no backup, and the hard disk has become the primary storage for documents, it could mean losing essential information, either through inadvertent revision or complete hard disk failure.
- As the amount of documents kept on the hard disk multiplies, so do the classification and indexing problems. Many organizations have sophisticated hard copy systems, but have left important electronic document systems to the whim of the user, and then are surprised when they can't find anything.

These are but a few of the potential problems that electronic records in the hands of employees who have little skill or experience in either computers or records management can wreak on an organization. The best way to handle these records is to include their creation within the confines of the organizational master classification plan which has the built in retention for each record series. Two other corporate policy decisions should also be made. First, there should be a policy and procedure for the regular backup of all personal computers in the organization. Second there should be a directive from the legal counsel of the organization about the admissibility of electronic records and a policy and procedure for the alternative storage of any electronic records that are required for iegislative/regulatory compliance or that could become evidential in the future.

10

Vital records

A private airplane carrying a bank's daily volume of canceled checks and non-negotiable securities crashes, killing the pilot and destroying all documents beyond recovery. An explosion renders a building unsafe to enter, resulting in delays in retrieving the records stored inside. A disgruntled employee erases all the data on an organization's payroll system. A business is burned to the ground during urban riots, leaving nothing intact. A fire burns inside a vault damaging many engineering drawings before it can be extinguished. The water poured onto the fire causes further damage as the documents become soaked.

What do all of these incidents have in common? They represent disasters that can strike an organization at any time and severely damage or destroy its records.

Businesses suffer a myriad of computer disasters every year, leading to serious monetary losses. These are only a small part of the many business disasters, nearly 40 percent of which have been due to fire or explosion. In other countries, disasters caused by floods, vandalism, and warfare are also numerous, leading to the financial and operational crippling or even collapse of organizations.

The kind of disasters that can affect an organization's records are many:

- power fluctuations causing corruption or loss of data on computers
- rats eating through wiring causing shorts and fires
- air conditioners breaking down causing computer failures
- explosions in neighboring buildings causing fires and damage
- leaking pipes dripping water onto files
- flash floods taking away whole file rooms
- transport vehicles crashing or being stolen causing loss of files, letters and tapes
- military or airport radar equipment causing computer data corruption
- employee negligence or malice causing security leaks
- vermin nesting in and devouring files
- a cup of hot coffee tipping over and into a personal computer causing a breakdown
- computer viruses causing widespread destruction of data
- vandals causing any damage that is fairly easy to inflict.

The possibilities for disaster are endless and the means of protection against it limited. A vital records protection program can be expected to use the limited means to protect against some disasters and to lessen the damage in the case of their occurrence, but it cannot be expected to serve as an absolute and sure defense against any and all disasters. Even so, whether the disaster is natural or man-made, the results can be devastating to an organization unless it has implemented policies and procedures which assure the protection of its vital records.

**General Classifications of
Vital Corporate Records**

Accounting
        Accounts Payable/Accounts Receivable
        Check Registers
        Data Processing Operational Manuals, Systems Analyses
        General Ledgers
        Journal Entries
        Loans, Lines of Credit

Engineering/Manufacturing
        Designs, Drawings, Reports, Specifications
        Inventory Summaries
        Laboratory Reports and Notebooks
        Product Specifications/Formulas
        Quality Control Reports

Executive/Administrative
        Acquisitions, Mergers, Reorganizations, Liquidations
        Agreements, Contracts, Leases, Licenses
        Articles of Incorporation (optional)
        Board of Directors Minutes, Reports
        By-Laws
        Deeds, Mortgages
        Insurance Policies
        Litigation, Claims (optional)
        Patents/Copyrights/Trademarks
        Stockholders Registers, Transfers

Marketing
        Mailing Lists
        Plans and Strategies
        Price Lists
        Product Development
        Sales and Marketing Forecasts

Personnel
        Payroll Registers, Earnings Records
        Pension/Profit Sharing/Insurance Plans
        Personnel Histories, Medical Histories

Figure 10.1   A list of vital records

WHAT ARE VITAL RECORDS?

Vital records are those records essential to the continued functioning of an organization during and after an emergency and those records which protect the rights and interests of the organization, employees, stockholders, customers and the public. Vital records include such records as would protect material and human resources, the maintenance of public health, safety and order, and the conduct of civil defense. They can also include records relating to employee compensation and benefits, insurance, valuable research findings, proof of ownership, financial interests, and legal proceedings and decisions. A sample list of vital records is found in Figure 10.1.

While commercial organizations view vital records protection from the aspect of survival of the enterprise, governments must have a larger view. A government's vital records protection program must attempt to ensure not only the survival of the government but of its ability to govern. A full governmental disaster contingency plan will coordinate a large number of departments or agencies. Records management, through its vital records protection program, must be a strong component of this plan, and must liaise closely with the government information and communications departments. Vital records protection plans must include the following:

1   records which will be necessary and usable during the disaster (these may have to be paper if electricity and the presence of computer operators cannot be guaranteed)
2   records necessary to reconstruct the government when the disaster is over
3   records necessary to protect the rights of individual citizens.

With few exceptions, vital records should not be the original records of an organization. They should be duplicates, located away from the area where the original records are kept.

As with any records management program, vital records protection requires careful planning and implementation. The objectives for a vital records program are to:

- define vital records
- assign program responsibility
- identify potential hazards
- analyze and classify vital records
- designate appropriate protection methods
- select appropriate vital records storage facility or facilities
- develop operating procedures
- audit and test program procedures.

VITAL RECORDS PROTECTION IS INSURANCE

Protecting vital records and designing and testing a disaster recovery plan is costly and brings no profits or cost savings. Consequently, some organizations are slow to authorize such a program; but at their great peril. Not all organizations burn to the ground, but all have fire insurance, and those that need it are grateful. Similarly, not all organizations lose all of their records and systems overnight, but all should be protected against such a loss. Over 40 percent of all companies that suffer a serious disaster fail.

To encourage full management awareness of the organization's vulnerability to the loss of records, data, and information, a few measures may be worth considering:

- Submit a preliminary report on weaknesses and vulnerabilities discovered during the survey, for example no backup for information on personal computers; no procedural manuals exist to explain processing and inputting procedures; payment systems are protected but without a supply of the necessary blank checks or remittance advices; there are 17 copies of keys to the management central file room but only ten keys can be located; etc.
- Contact the organization's auditors, legal and financial advisors, and insurers to find out their recommendations, requirements and possible reductions in premiums for disaster planning.
- Ask senior managers to attend a sales briefing by a disaster planning consultant.
- Ask to attend a seminar or course on disaster planning and/or vital records protection.

The vital records program should be regarded as essential to the organization's contingency planning effort. Management must be cognizant of the rights and interests that the organization is responsible for protecting and of what records are necessary to protect them. It must also recognize what the essential functions of the organization are under normal circumstances and what records are necessary to continue to perform those functions both during and after an emergency.

For this reason, the authority for the vital records program should be spelled out in a program directive which clearly outlines the policy, objectives, and responsibilities for the management of the program and which provides procedures and guidelines for maintaining the organization's vital records. The records manager should be responsible for the establishment and coordination of the program.

In addition to the basic authorities and responsibilities, all operating and auditing procedures should be incorporated into a directive, either as part of the basic records management directive or as a separate vital records/disaster recovery document. The directive should also include a designation of individuals authorized to access the records, sample forms, and all pertinent standards, specifications, and procedures.

EVALUATING POTENTIAL HAZARDS

The extent of the vital records program depends largely on the potential hazards to the organization and its records. A clear evaluation of the type of disasters likely to happen will indicate what kind of protective measures need to be taken. Generally, disasters are either natural, via the weather, or man-made, accidental or intentional. The following should be considered.

Environment. What problems are common in a given area? Tornadoes, floods, bush fires, earthquakes, electrical storms, heavy snowfalls, insect invasions, power failures, regular warfare or invasions, high winds, tidal waves, etc. By far the most common hazards to records safety in most places are fire and the water or chemicals used to extinguish it.

Enticing vulnerability. What, by the very nature of the organization, would make it particularly vulnerable to attack or sabotage? A bank in an area where people are starving, a military installation, an innovative research facility whose secrets would be valuable if stolen, a political organization, a key national utility or communications installation, a high publicity or glamour business, etc.

Unpopularity. (This is closely related to the above.) What organizations might be particularly unpopular to some people? The police, the tax collection agency, the courts, companies that have just made many people (or only one vengeful or desperate character) redundant.

Technical vulnerability. What part of the organization's equipment and technology is both vital and so highly sensitive that a minute occurrence could cause a major disaster? (For example, one human hair in a computer disk causing a total crash.)

Specific steps taken to protect against fire and the damage caused by fire extinguishing agents will be discussed in the next chapter. Vital records facilities should be inspected regularly by local fire departments for the adequacy of alarms and detection systems and the condition of fire deterrents. Plumbers and electricians can assist in identifying other potential sources of damage to records.

The geographic location of an organization must be considered when establishing a vital records program. Records in places with high humidity must be protected against mold and mildew. Insects and vermin are more prone to attack records in some environments than in others. Vandalism and theft may be more of a threat in an urban area than in a rural one.

Potential hazards and their risk to vital information can be identified and evaluated by answering the following questions:

1   Have the following hazards been identified as potential threats to the organization's vital records?
    • fire and fire containment materials

- water (due to flooding, bad plumbing, or high humidity)
- impact damage (resulting directly or indirectly from fire, flood, earthquake, violent wind, or bombing
- infestation by insects or vermin
- theft, vandalism, or loss

2 Have the frequency and severity of these hazards been assessed?
3 Has the dispersal of duplicate vital records to a location not subject to these hazards been considered?
4 Does the existence of these hazards influence the choice of an appropriate vital records storage facility?

VITAL RECORDS APPRAISAL AND CLASSIFICATION

Only a small portion – roughly two to six percent – of an organization's records can be legitimately classified as 'vital.' To determine which records actually fall into this category, all records, that is, both active and inactive records from all functional areas, should be appraised for their vital record value to provide the required depth for a meaningful program. Such appraisal is begun during the records inventory.

Appraisal

In the appraisal of vital records, consideration must be given to:

- the type of information needed during an emergency
- the specific rights and interests that require protection
- the value of the records which meet this need
- the availability of the information elsewhere.

In addition, these questions must be asked:

- Do these records include records of debts owed *to* the organization but not of those owed *by* it?
- Do these records exclude those which support legal rights that can be re-established through affidavit and are well known to the affected individuals?
- Do these records exclude those which are routinely duplicated by another organization or entity?
- Does the organization classify as 'vital' only the minimum volume of records in accordance with the program's objectives?

Vital records are generally active, reflecting the ongoing operations of the organization, although some inactive records are also protected. Certain original documents, such as deeds, contracts, or articles of incorporation, may require vital records protection if they alone will satisfy legal requirements.

Many types of records are of great importance but not of vital importance. Such records require much effort and expense to reconstruct if lost, or they may have intrinsic historical value. They could also include source records used to reconstruct vital information. The vital records program does not involve these important records, although the standards and methods of protection associated with the program may well be applied to them to the degree that the value, risks, and available resources for their protection are appropriate.

Classification

A useful guideline for the classification of records might be:

- Operational or functional records/systems – those without which the organization would collapse, unable to function. Such systems would include the general ledger and production systems; such records would include licenses to operate, project drawings, procedures manuals.
- Costly records systems – those that may be of secondary importance but that, if lost, the time and money necessary to replace them would alone constitute a disaster. Such systems would include corporate budget and planning, and full personnel systems; such records might include reports that were the products of expensive studies.
- Legal records/systems – those which are necessary for the organization to operate legally, to protect itself or individuals, or which, if lost, would leave the organization open to crippling litigation. Such systems would include data protection monitoring and safety controls; such records might be the articles of incorporation, a constitution, contracts, insurance policies, union agreements, trademarks, deeds.
- Emergency records/systems – those which are not vital except in the case of an emergency. Such systems would include all automatic building, door, safe, sprinkler, alarm systems; such records would include personnel lists, building plans, security clearances.
- Vital objects – those which satisfy any of the above criteria and which are necessary for the use of those records, but are not considered hardware. Such objects would be building keys and government seals.

Identifying vital records is a judgmental process and is best accomplished by relying on the originators' or users' understanding of the function of the record. The classification must be realistic. The 'two to six percent' rule of thumb applies to the organization as a whole. A specific department may have no vital records at all, or it may find that as many as 50 percent of its records holdings are vital. It is essential to capture only those records which fit the vital records definition, or the protection program will become unwieldy, diluted and will not be taken seriously.

PROTECTION METHODS

Several methods are suitable for protecting vital records. The most important selection factor is the ratio of protection from hazards to the cost of that protection. Since relative security is all that can possibly be attained, the best choice is that which brings the cost of security most closely in line with the degree of risk. Beyond the evaluation of actual risks of loss for vital records, three other factors influence the selection of protection methods:

1 *Need for accessibility* – in the event of an emergency, vital records would be needed immediately. Paper records are preferable to avoid reliance on special equipment, but if it is necessary for the information to be on another medium, both the required equipment and its power source must be dependable under emergency conditions. Vital records which must be readily available for reference may require different methods of protection from those records infrequently used.
2 *Length of retention* – vital records of a short-term nature may require different methods of protection from long-term or permanent records.
3 *Physical qualities of records* – vital records are susceptible to destruction from heat, water, chemicals, and aging depending upon the record medium and the duration of retention. Magnetic tape or microfilm require different protection from that needed for paper documents, and paper itself varies greatly in its ability to withstand aging.

One or more of the following methods can be used to protect a vital record series.

Dispersal

The least expensive protection method is built in or routine dispersal of vital records, wherein the information is routinely distributed to other departments, individuals or organizations located elsewhere. The assumption is that the same disaster is unlikely to strike two different locations, although to ensure protection of the dispersed copies, they should be located at least 50 miles (80 km) apart.

Branch offices, subsidiaries, government agencies, and the like are apt to receive the dispersed records. If the organization is depending upon dispersed copies in the event of the disaster, the copyholders should be informed of this and of any retention and protection requirements. In the event of a disaster, this information must be promptly retrievable and with no restrictions.

Improvised or planned dispersal modifies a routine dispersal procedure by creating an additional copy specifically for protection purposes. The copy is then sent to the vital records repository or some other location. This is a fairly economical and easy approach, since copies are already being created and the cost and effort of making and distributing another is minimal.

Dispersal is equally effective for long and short-term retention, durable or fragile records, and high or low-reference requirements.

Computer backup of vital data, either separate from or part of routine, system-wide backup, is a form of protection by dispersal. (See also the section at the end of this chapter.)

Duplication

Duplication is an effective protection method where the conditions for dispersal do not exist. While dispersal automatically creates a current vital record copy, duplication involves reproducing the record specifically for its protection. Protection by duplication is as effective in all ways as is dispersal.

The reproduction may be on the same medium, as in microfilm to microfilm or paper to paper. This approach is often less costly and complicated than changing the medium. However, such duplication methods as microfilming source documents, putting computer data directly onto microfiche (COM) or optical disk (COLD), or storing data off magnetic disk onto tape or optical disk, is justifiable under certain circumstances.

If a vital record is stored on any medium other than paper, there must be equipment readily available to retrieve, read, and reproduce the information. This means a reader printer for microfilm or microfiche, data processing equipment for magnetic tapes or disks, and optical disk equipment for optical disks. In addition, the proper storage environment is more critical for these media than for paper. Machine-readable media require that the correct hardware, software, and operating system be available.

Uninterruptible power supplies should be installed to ensure that a short electrical outage does not destroy electronic records. Security precautions must be in place against unauthorized personnel or other outside 'eavesdroppers' gaining access to information simply by calling for it at their computer terminals or 'listening' to the transmission of confidential information over public communications lines. Procedures should be established to ensure that the duplicate is actually made, whether this takes place when the record is created or at some other stage in its life cycle.

The frequency of required updates dictates the frequency of duplication. Some records have an annual cycle, such as annual reports or shareholders' meeting minutes. Others are updated monthly or more often, such as various accounting records. Still others, such as engineering drawings or contracts and agreements, are updated at irregular intervals.

The duplication of an original record raises the question of its acceptability as a legal document should the original be destroyed. A copy may be better than nothing, but if its legal value is nil, an alternative protection method should be considered.

Selection criteria

In analyzing whether to rely on dispersal or duplication for vital records protection, the following selection criteria should be considered:

1   What is the cost and effectiveness of the following?
    Using existing duplicates located elsewhere
    Creating a duplicate at the same time as the original for storage at another location
    Reproducing existing records either on the same or different media for storage at another location
    Removing inactive original records to an off-site location.
2   In determining the duplication medium, what considerations have been given to the following?
    The availability of equipment needed to retrieve, read, and reproduce micro-images or machine-readable data
    The environmental controls of the storage facility (temperature, humidity, air filtration).
3   Can the dispersed or duplicated record be used for vital records purposes rather than the original? If not, is it because the copy does not have the same legal value as the original?

Three other methods offer some degree of protection, although should a major disaster occur in the building, or devastate the immediate geographic area, such methods would be of little or no use.

Special storage equipment

Original and unique records can be protected from most hazards through the use of special storage equipment such as vaults, fire resistant cabinets, or safes. The relative effectiveness of this method is less than dispersal or duplication, particularly if this does not physically remove the records from the organization. This method is usually the most costly and should be considered only when other methods are physically not feasible.

Removal of hazardous conditions

The effectiveness of this and the next method is low and should be considered only when other methods are not economically feasible. By removing unnecessary hazards, such as combustible materials and steam or water pipes, from the storage area, and by eliminating undesirable conditions, such as airborne chemicals and extremes of heat or humidity, a relative improvement in the protection of vital records can be achieved.

Relocation of records

The effectiveness of relocating vital records to a less hazardous area within the organization is the same as, or slightly better than, removing the hazards, while the cost is as low or slightly lower. However, the feasibility of this protection method is further affected by the accessibility requirements for the records.

SELECTING A STORAGE FACILITY

An adjunct to selecting the best protection methods is the selection of the appropriate storage equipment or facility. Storage can either be off-site, that is, remote from its home location, or on-site, usually within the building or plant perimeter of the organization. Optimum protection comes from remote storage of the information; on-site storage of vital records compromises the program, but may be the only feasible alternative, economically or physically.

Off-site storage

Off-site storage facilities can provide extra security and protection to original vital records and economical storage for those that have very little reference. Off-site facilities are usually located in low-rent areas, and some are underground in caves, mines (abandoned or active), former railroad tunnels, missile sites, and the like. Underground storage of certain vital records may be advisable if the risks associated with the destruction of the information are high.

Whether the off-site facility is owned and operated independently by the organization itself, or by a group of organizations, certain factors influence the choice of storing the vital records in a remote location. The facility should be located away from high-risk areas, such as rivers, geological faults, coasts, and volcanoes or away from man-made structures that might pose a threat. It must be accessible to the organization's officials both in emergency and in non-emergency situations.

Fire safety, atmospheric conditions, pest control, security, and technical services of the vital records facility must be carefully evaluated. The communication link between the organization and the storage facility must be reliable in the event of an emergency.

On-site storage

Vaults, file rooms, safes, and fire-resistant cabinets and containers provide some degree of protection for vital records.

Underwriters' Laboratories in the US have produced standards that rate the temperature and humidity levels records can undergo before deterioration. Paper can withstand 50°C (122°F) while magnetic and photographic media can only withstand 15°C (59°F) and 85 percent relative humidity, and diskettes 10°C (52°F) and 80 percent relative humidity.

Vaults are very expensive to construct, but can be justified if the volume of records is high or the needs of the organization dictate this type of protection. In buildings with a high fire risk, a vault may be the only recourse to protect records against this hazard. Vaults should be constructed of fireproof materials not only to resist a severe fire, but also to insulate against high temperatures. Vault doors come with 2, 4, or 6-hour ratings.

Although the likelihood of a fire starting within a vault is low, this has been known to happen, and a decision must be made regarding the installation of interior automatic fire protection. Certainly, precautions must be taken to ensure that no flammable or combustible materials are stored within, no smoking is allowed, wiring and electrical equipment is in accordance with the code, and no other conditions exist that could start a fire.

Vaults resist fire. However, they are not immune to water damage. Underground or basement vaults are susceptible to water leakage from faulty pipes or from flooding, and water used to extinguish a fire can get inside a vault and damage the records.

While fireproof safes do not provide as high a degree of fire protection as that of vaults, they will resist fire for up to four hours. Safes are useful for smaller volumes of records and for locating the records close to the point of use. It should also be remembered that fireproof safes are built to resist fire, not theft.

File rooms and fire-resistant cabinets and containers naturally provide less protection than the heavily insulated walls and doors of vaults and safes. They are also less expensive. The risk associated with the loss of the information being stored must be evaluated before investing in any of these on-site storage facilities or containers.

OPERATING PROCEDURES

Once the protection methods and storage facilities have been selected, procedures for operating and auditing the vital records protection program must be established. These procedures should cover the following.

Vital records inventory

Much information about vital records and information would have been revealed in the original inventory. The inventory forms, or the database compiled from them, will yield a preliminary list of vital records, what storage media they are on, where they originate and are sent, what systems process them, etc. This provides an excellent starting point from which to begin questioning people in departments.

This questioning must be in greater detail than that of the original inventory, and will involve more immediate evaluation to determine which steps in a series of procedures are vital or where, should a system break down completely, old manual procedures could be resurrected and used. Trying to protect information and simultaneously prepare plans for the emergency use of information will be costly and, eventually, detrimental to the program. In a true emergency, people will have neither the time nor the inclination to maintain secondary records and systems.

Vital records information can be collected during the records inventory, identifying vital records and systems during that process or using the completed inventory as a basis for subsequent determination. Once the inventory is taken, the list of vital records and systems should be divided into two groups: those which will be needed immediately; and those which will be needed when the disaster has ended and recovery can begin. Within these two groups, records and systems should be listed by department, then by function. For example:

> Immediate records and systems
>> Finance:
>>> general ledger system
>>> invoices
>>> printed checks
>> Production:
>>> robotic assembly system
>>> backup procedures and tools for manual assembly
>>> inventory records
> Recovery records and systems
>> Finance:
>>> expenditure analysis system

This information is collected during the analysis process and can be documented manually on the form or keyed into a computer database. The database can be programed to print the resulting inventory list directly onto the form or as a report. A number of commercially available database management software packages are suitable for creating a vital records database on a microcomputer. If a database has already been established for retention scheduling, the vital records data can easily be linked to it through one or more elements, for example records series, department name or number, or the retention schedule item.

The inventory list should be reviewed regularly, based on the volume of records and frequency of change in the organization. Usually the records identified as vital remain fairly constant, but the departmental responsibility or protection method may fluctuate, requiring more frequent updating of the list. The records manager and repository operating personnel should maintain a complete and up-to-date set of inventory lists, and each department should have a copy of its own list.

Transfer instructions

Instructions for transferring vital records to storage are essential procedures. A transmittal label, with minimum information of record series number, transfer date, and originating department, should be placed on each box, tape, or container being transferred.

If vital records are being transferred by a commercial transportation service, adequate provision should be made for their security en route. The value of the records will dictate whether they should be carried in locked pouches which can be concealed from view, or if regular storage boxes or other containers are sufficient. Only bonded carriers should be used.

Receiving instructions

When records are received, the date of receipt, location of the material in the repository, date of disposition of previously stored records in that series, disposition instructions, and other remarks are noted on a form containing this information or in the database. A link or cross reference is made to the inventory by way of any of the data elements in the form's header so that the frequency of transfer and the retention of the record can be monitored.

Instructions regarding the disposition of superseded records must be clear. For instance, once new records are received, the superseded ones may be destroyed, returned to the department, or transferred to inactive storage because their usefulness as a vital record has ended.

MAINTAINING VITAL RECORDS

Security procedures

To ensure that only authorized personnel are able to gain access to vital records, there are a number of precautions that may be taken. These should be in place at all times even when, in accordance with standard procedures, the records are destroyed.

Personnel who are authorized to enter secure areas should wear identification badges that include the employee's name, photograph, and the organization's name or logo. Doors can be fitted with magnetic contacts wired to a security service. Windows should be eliminated, or where this is not possible, they should be protected against breakage. Motion detection devices and television cameras can be installed for monitoring activity both inside and outside the building.

Locks require special attention, as well. They should be of the coded type in which the code can be changed as desired. Automatic locking of inside doors should occur as outside doors are opened. If these locking devices are not used, then keyed locks may be used, but the names of those who possess keys must be recorded and keys retrieved when employment is terminated.

Procedures should be put into effect incorporating the appropriate approval forms which assure the persons releasing vital records that those receiving them have the required authority to receive them. Receipts should be retained by persons releasing vital records. Persons receiving vital records must retain an inventory of vital records, showing the description and location of records in their possession. This is particularly critical in the vital records center. Such procedures provide an audit trail for determining who has which documents, where they have taken them, and the time during which they borrow them.

When vital documents are being transmitted from active to inactive storage facilities, adequate provision should be made for their security en route. They should be carried in locked pouches which can be concealed from view, or if visible, attached to the carrier by means of a locked chain. Only bonded carriers should be used.

Keeping vital records up to date

Vital records can become dated very quickly. To maintain the value of these records and to ensure their integrity, it is necessary to make sure that any administrative updates to records stored in the vital records center are carried out. Amendments to vital records should be transferred to the vital records center on a regular basis. Where the amending records supplement vital records already in storage, they should be placed with these. Where the amending records replace existing vital records, the old records should be extracted and the procedures for records destruction initiated. In either case, the date of compilation of the amended vital records should be readily visible on the records. Also, copies of vital records should indicate that they are copies and when the copies were prepared. In this way, the user knows that the original has been properly secured.

Vital records destruction

Outdated vital records should be destroyed only in accordance with the records retention schedule and established, approved procedures. Normally, when vital records are transferred to the vital records center, their destruction date is shown on a transfer form. One of the copies of the form is filed chronologically by date of destruction, so that as destruction dates arise, the records can be systematically released. If a database is used, regular reports, sorted by destruction date, will provide guidance.

Emergency procedures

The protection of vital records must go beyond just the provision of physical facilities and maintenance procedures for the storage of vital documents to the point of determining in advance of a disaster what the organization will do and who is responsible for executing the various emergency tasks. Emergency recovery procedures should be tested at least annually by all departments owning vital records. (Specific disaster recovery procedures are discussed in Chapter 11.)

A vital records recovery checklist should include the following:

- Each department has practiced responding to a simulated disaster in which all its records are lost. The response outlines what steps it takes to make itself operational again and what records it needs to recover.
- Variations in the recovery plan have been developed to account for the effects that different types of emergencies, such as flood, fire, sabotage, and so on, have on the plan.
- Further variations include an examination of the effects of different office or plant locations being struck by disaster.
- Key individuals are identified for roles during an emergency. Their roles need to be defined and communicated to them. In some cases, this may include actively removing vital records to another site or placing them in a fire-resistant vault. Other individuals will be expected to make their way to a remote storage location to retrieve copies of vital documents.

The vital records recovery plan should be incorporated into the organization's disaster recovery manual. Employee orientation should include training in what to do in the event of a disaster. Evacuation drills should be incorporated into the organization's routines.

Some organizations maintain active poster campaigns to keep employees aware of the potential for disaster and the importance of security procedures.

The procedures for dealing with emergencies require constant review for a number of reasons. Buildings are renovated, old facilities are torn down, additions are made. Escape routes practical in former buildings no longer exist. The nature of jobs and personnel change. Employees who were responsible for vital records change jobs, while others become responsible for vital records without realizing it.

Many organizations perform disaster simulations to test their organizational preparedness. These simulations are taken seriously by large corporations and governments. Often they are surprise simulations where the operating manager is held directly responsible for failure to reconstruct the business under the simulation. The seriousness of the repercussions is understandable given the potential of seeing one's business totally destroyed.

COMPUTER BACKUP

The systematic backup of computer data that resides on mainframe or other centralized systems is a standard procedure usually administered by an organization's management information systems (MIS) department. While this is not generally a records management function, the records manager should be aware of these procedures, particularly in the context of protecting vital records in electronic format.

For example, where is the tape library housed? In the same building? In a climate-controlled room? Is there any connection between the length of time data is stored on tapes and the approved retention periods for such information?

In addition to the tape library, there is often a provision for the recovery of data at a remote location in case of disaster. The organization may have a 'hot site,' where data is sent regularly to a location that has a working duplicate of all systems and equipment, or a 'cold site,' where compatible equipment and systems are available to read and process backup tapes.

Another type of backup is electronic vaulting, wherein data is transmitted electronically off-site to a storage center and stored onto a hard disk and then onto tape. Any of these provisions may be managed by the organization itself, particularly if it has operations spread over a geographical area, or by a commercial vendor.

The proliferation of personal computers (PCs) in the office increases the likelihood that important records are being created without enough thought given to backup. This situation offers the records manager a good opportunity to work closely with MIS to ensure protection of important information. Computers that are networked and have a network manager, are often wisely set up for automatic tape backup at night, with a weekly tape sent off-site. But the network manager may need to be educated about vital records to ensure that information on the network deemed vital is in fact being backed up.

Educating PC users who are not connected to a network to back up their important data regularly is likely the responsibility of MIS, but it may also fall to the records manager, particularly if the records inventory identifies vital electronic information. Backup onto diskettes or a tape drive is essential for any PC application, but vital information may be best protected by printing it out rather than trying to store it on magnetic media.

11

Disaster planning and recovery

Contrary to popular belief, a disaster is not something that always happens to someone else. Disaster can strike anywhere, at any time. Nature deals its blows with no respect for person, place, or thing; accidents, by definition, are unpredictable; sabotage or terrorism is not necessarily somebody else's problem.

Protecting against the consequences of losing vital records has been discussed in the previous chapter. The broader issue of responding to a disaster that affects any and all information in an organization, not to mention its employees, is the focus of a disaster recovery program which is designed to:

- minimize disruption of normal business operations
- prevent further escalation of this disruption
- minimize the economic impact of the disaster
- establish alternative operating procedures
- train personnel with emergency procedures
- recover/salvage organizational assets
- provide for rapid and smooth restoration of service.

A disaster recovery program should consist of three parts: prevention, preparation, and recovery. Establishment of a program begins with the formation of a disaster team which is responsible for:

- ensuring that efforts are made to prevent potential disasters
- providing documentation of the organization's readiness to respond to a disaster
- possessing knowledge of salvage procedures, costs, and results to the extent necessary to ensure competent, timely response.

Members of the disaster team should represent the records management, facilities, security, data processing, library, and archives departments. If the size of the organization warrants, the team may be divided into two committees: a pre-disaster committee, responsible for the prevention and preparation stages of the program, and a post-disaster committee, responsible for the actual salvage operations. Since recovery operations demand quick response and emergency expenditures of money, one member of the team should have overall responsibility for the program and complete authority to make decisions in the event of a disaster.

The basis of a disaster recovery program is the disaster recovery plan. Because a disaster team should be concerned with all aspects of the organization, from damaged buildings to damaged information, the disaster plan should be comprehensive. This chapter concentrates on that portion of the plan dealing with the organization's records.

DISASTER PREVENTION

Common sense dictates taking steps to protect against fire in the records center, hacking in the computer center, and vermin in the vital records vault. As part of a disaster recovery program, all the various prevention techniques are spelled out in one plan, wherein the protection of the organization's records are cast in the same light as the protection of its other assets and of its employees.

It would be unrealistic to suggest that all disasters can be prevented from ever happening. However, their threat can be minimized to some extent. One method of minimizing the problems that might occur is to identify potential hazards by regularly conducting a facility and security inspection of records storage areas, including off-site inactive and vital records facilities. The records manager should coordinate this inspection with the accommodation and security departments, which should already be including records storage areas in their regular inspection procedures. Figure 11.1 provides an example of a disaster prevention checklist.

Disaster Prevention Checklist

Building or Location:

Inspected by: Date:

Check each item to indicate that it has been inspected. Describe any problems.
Fire or smoke alarms – functional?
Sprinkler systems – functional?
Fire extinguishers inspection date in accordance with local or state code?
Flashlights – at designated locations? Fresh batteries?
Hazards?
Emergency packets – complete? At designated locations?
Staff familiar with locations of last three items?

Figure 11.1   A disaster prevention checklist

The facility inspection should document:

- the general construction and condition of the records storage site or sites.
- the area in which the facility is located, specifically its susceptibility to disasters (flooding, high winds, etc.).
- the location and condition of the plumbing, electrical wiring, heating and air conditioning, drainpipes, steam and water pipes, roof, and mechanical equipment.
- any past problems with leaks, seepage, faulty wiring, broken pipes, or similar problems.

The security inspection should cover active files areas, inactive and vital records storage, vaults and buildings, magnetic tape libraries and computer operations areas, and should identify:

- who has authorization to access the records
- how this access is controlled
- what security devices are in place to prevent or detect unauthorized access.

Basic precautions to consider fall into three categories: accommodation protection, security, and staff awareness.

Facilities protection

This requires that all parts of all buildings have the best possible protection against fires, floods, collapse, etc. While some areas, such as basements or storerooms, may not seem worth the expense of full fire protection, they must not be neglected to the point that they become hazardous. There should be full compliance with local fire and safety codes and with the environmental requirements for information technology and equipment.

Facilities and storage equipment requirements should include the following:

- the use of strong, non-inflammable, structurally sound filing shelves and cabinets (buckled shelves, broken drawers, and rusted equipment should be replaced)
- floors strong enough to take the weight of equipment and hardware
- roofs strong enough to take the weight of support equipment, particularly air conditioners and generators
- bottom shelves on the ground floor should be 6 inches (152 mm) above the floor, in case of flooding.

Be aware of all areas that surround a records storage area. For example, could a faulty air conditioning system result in water leaking through the ceiling onto filing cabinets and workstations? Or does the room across the hall from the basement records room house the main water pump for the building's sprinkler system, or worse, the drums of waste from the manufacturing area?

Fire protection should begin with a discussion with the local fire prevention officers as to the most appropriate fire prevention and fire fighting precautions and equipment to have, and as to the problems that the water used in fighting fires can cause. Many records that survive a fire do not survive the fire hose. Fire precautions should include:

- the discouragement of smoking within any buildings and the complete ban on smoking in filing areas
- general tidiness and removal of hazardous clutter such as piles of files, papers, boxes, rubbish
- the timely destruction of all useless records and the transferral of all semi-current or inactive records to storage
- the removal of all inflammable liquids
- a clearly marked, and regularly tested, fire alarm system with triggers in every room
- fire extinguishers, which are checked regularly, in all rooms
- regular safety checks of all electrical wiring and rodent traps
- clearly posted fire escapes, exits, and procedures, with regular fire drills on their use.

Water damage and flood prevention is more important than many realize, especially in tropical climates where rainstorms regularly carry off whole buildings and towns. Water destroys tapes and disks, washes ink from paper, turns microfilm to a congealed mass. Even a little water for a short time will cause sufficient humidity to allow mold to grow on paper and microfilm. Water damage and flood precautions should include the following:

- The records and systems are placed far from water mains and drainage pipes.
- Roofs should not be flat or leaking.
- All possible sources of water leaks are checked and repaired regularly (for example, air conditioners, washrooms, water tanks, windows, drain pipes, gutters).

Animals and insects cause major disasters particularly by chewing through wiring, but also by shedding fur into computers, nesting in or eating paper, swarming into computer rooms, even bringing diseases that wipe out the records staff. Precautions against animal and insect invasion should include the following:

- a full building inspection to discover and block all points of animal or bird entry
- strong, fine mesh screening over all necessary openings, such as windows, skylights, ventilators, chimneys; and screened doors for all external doorways
- a total ban on all eating and food storage in records and systems areas
- regular fumigation
- regular and thorough cleaning of ceilings, walls, floors, underfloors, and of all furniture
- the humidity level kept as stable, if not as near the ideal, as possible.

It should be noted that, too often, where ideals of structure, equipment, protection, and environment cannot be obtained, records managers despair. While it is true that some buildings seem too ghastly ever to be made safe, an attitude of ingenious common sense must prevail. Where screening is not available, what is there that will serve as well? Where fumigants are out of supply, what is available that might keep insects and molds away? Whatever is necessary to create a safe environment for records, systems, and their users should be done.

Security

Theft and sabotage are not natural disasters as are fires and floods, but they are disastrous acts to the organization that has had its records purloined or destroyed. While no one would deny that security is important, some organizations tend to consider it as the sole function of records management. This is a slightly obsessive approach which must be tempered by common sense. Security violations are of two types, intentional or negligent, and both are generally easy to prevent. (It is often argued that the best security is complete lack of records management, on the assumption that no intruder could sift through the disorder. The authors do not share this view.) Negligence can be combated with a strong awareness program (see below) coupled with a certain amount of vetting. Intentional security violations can be combated with vetting of staff and with the standard forms of protection devices. However, it must be accepted that truly valuable and sensitive information will always be at risk and will require a permanent war of wits between the security and the thieving experts.

One of the most important aspects of any security plan is the clear identification of what is most at risk, and of what truly merits full protection. Far too many innocuous records and systems are labeled secret or even confidential, putting a strain on the whole security team to protect the oversized mass. This is a consequence of the obsession with security taking precedence over common sense. If the confidential and secret classifications were used more wisely, the result would be greater security for the information that truly merits it. A full review and, if necessary, restructuring of classification criteria may be necessary before implementing any new security procedures.

Electronic records and systems, especially those on personal computers, are much more vulnerable to negligence and crime, and the consequences much more severe than with paper records. It takes time and hard work to break into a system, but it takes only moments for a user to leave a screen or printout visible to the wrong person, or to mistakenly enter data, or to leave a disk in an unsafe place, such as a car. The increasing concern over the security of electronic records and systems has often been distorted into a concern for the safety of the computer, when it is much more often the software, the records, and the information that are at risk. Thus, security measures must seek to protect the most important records and systems; and, while it is true that electronic systems are more vulnerable than paper, it must be remembered that it is the systems and the records that are to be protected, and not just the machine that houses them.

Security precautions for buildings, equipment, and personnel, should include the following:

- staff responsibility for locking windows and doors at closing time
- automatic security alarms
- locks on all doors and windows
- strict control of all building keys, with locks changed when keys are lost
- strict supervision of non-staff who enter the building, especially of cleaners and maintenance workers
- bars or toughened glass on ground floor windows (but ensuring bars or grills can be opened in case of a fire)
- nightly locking of all rooms which contain mainframe or personal computers
- limited access to systems, either by the use of passwords or, with personal computers, power locks
- confidential destruction of classified records, such as by shredding or burning
- data encryption
- auxiliary generators and surge protectors for computers
- control of static electricity near computers
- extreme care should be taken when handling any floppy or hard disks, or magnetic tapes.

Staff awareness

The best disaster prevention will always come from the staff. If they are trained to look for trouble spots, irregularities, and to report them, then, because of their daily familiarity with their records, systems and environment, they will be the first to notice anything problematic or suspicious. In preliminary discussions and interviews to identify vital records and systems, staff should also be encouraged to contribute opinions about risks and how to prevent them. In prevention plans, staff should be given responsibilities for specific areas, records, and systems, and encouraged to work together as a team to protect them. They should be fully trained in all disaster plan phases and drilled at regular intervals in them. At least annually, there should be a staff meeting to discuss any changes in the plans, any new risks or problems, or any new training in protection required. This kind of teamwork will enhance the vital records protection program by boosting staff understanding and support of it and by reducing the tacit tolerance of internal theft.

Staff awareness programs should include the following:

- the formation of department or area teams, with appointed team leaders
- visits and talks from police and fire prevention officers, and from those who design the vital records protection plan
- training and drills in following the plan, using fire extinguishers, testing auxiliary equipment, etc.
- the placement of copies of the vital records protection plan manual with each team
- a certain amount of internal publicity to keep awareness high, for example, posters, articles in internal publications, refresher training programs, etc.

Common sense must prevail in disaster prevention. Thoughtful planning by architects and by those responsible for records can avoid some problems before new construction or space utilization plans become final. For example, the floor on which a mobile shelving unit is placed must meet certain stress requirements so as not to end up on the floor below. An archives collection should not be housed directly below the air conditioning equipment, which is a potential water hazard. In fact, no records collections should be stored in areas which are especially vulnerable to water. That includes washrooms, water pipes, and even fish tanks!

Basements are another area of potential hazards that should be avoided if at all possible. If a basement must be used, however, the records should be stored several inches off the floor. A water sensing alarm that is wired to an outside monitor should be installed to detect any flooding when the area is unattended. Basements also tend to be 'catch alls' for miscellaneous equipment or supplies. If the supplies happen to be chemicals, they should be stored as far away from the records as possible. A liquid chemical spill could not only damage any records it contacts, but also make the area inaccessible, so that by the time the records can be retrieved they may be beyond recovery. Fire prevention is virtually achievable. The installation and testing of modern fire detection and extinguishing equipment, correction of defective heating systems, installation of heavy-duty wiring to prevent electrical overloading, storage of flammable liquids in proper containers and cabinets, and good housekeeping and maintenance are effective prevention measures.

Protecting against loss of data or damage to data processing equipment or the operations site is another element of disaster prevention. Usually this falls under the auspices of the data processing manager, but the records manager should be knowledgeable of the type of disasters that can occur in a computer operation and be ready to cooperate with the data processing manager in all stages of the disaster recovery program.

PREPARATION

Because an organization must respond very quickly to a disaster, recovery operation procedures must be spelled out clearly. A written plan developed by the disaster team is the key to preparing for such an emergency. It should define the scope of authority of the person in charge of recovery operations, list emergency personnel, equipment, sources, and supplies, and outline specific salvaging procedures. The plan should be in the hands of each member of the team and of those who will be instrumental in recovery efforts.

Authority

Usually, one member of the disaster team, designated as the disaster recovery director, is assigned complete authority to direct everyone when disaster strikes. This individual consults with other members of the team or with outside experts and is the final decision maker during recovery operations. He/she may delegate some authority to the various team members, such as designating the records manager to handle the records salvaging process. In any event, the records manager should provide whatever guidelines are needed to ensure that the director will respond quickly and properly to the disaster.

Equipment, sources, and supplies

Equipment and supplies for salvaging records are relatively easy to stock. Although some supplies may be quickly purchased in an emergency, one cannot count on stores being open at three o'clock in the morning! The telephone directory can supply sources of equipment and supplies that will not be kept on hand and for lists of companies that will provide refrigerated trucks and freezer facilities, freeze, vacuum, or air drying space and services, and conservation services. Agreements for provision of services in times of emergency should be established with these companies. This is especially important, since there may be certain times of the year that facilities may not be available. For example, freezer space during the Christmas holidays may be quite limited.

A telephone listing of all disaster team members to be contacted should be arranged in call priority order. This list should also include police, fire, other emergency numbers and individuals having particular skills or expertise, such as electricians, plumbers, chemists, pest controllers, building maintenance service, etc. Both this list and the list of necessary equipment and supplies must be kept current and distributed to all team members.

The following checklists will be of assistance.

Equipment and supplies checklist

Plastic milk crates
Plastic trash bags
Plastic sheeting
Garbage cans
Records storage boxes
Unprinted newsprint
Paper towels
Freezer wrap
Neoprene gloves (1 pair per worker)
Protective clothing
Portable fans
Dehumidifiers
Hygrothermograph or thermohygrometer
Flashlights
Floodlights
Portable generators
Portable electric pumps
Heavy duty extension cords (3-wire grounded, 50-foot cords)
Walkie-talkies
Pallets
Hand tools
Flatbed carts
Hand trucks
Forklift trucks

Sources/services checklist

Drying space
Refrigerator trucks
Frozen food lockers
Freeze drying facilities
Document conservation services
Emergency telephone numbers
    Fire
    Police
    Ambulance
    Electrician
    Plumber
    Pest Control

Reproduction equipment must be available for recovery of vital records and information on magnetic and microfilm media. Service bureaus and vendors can be lined up in advance to provide equipment on short notice. Reciprocal backup agreements may be made with other nearby companies that have compatible data processing or micrographics equipment.

Preparation also includes providing system support in case of loss of data processing programs and procedures, as well as the data itself. Backup tapes and disks of program and data and the necessary application documentation should be stored off-site. The primary problems in maintaining backup information are ensuring that changes made to the master program files are also made to the backup copy and ensuring that the tapes do not deteriorate.

Insurance coverage

Sometimes overlooked is the adequacy of insurance coverage for disaster situations. The insurance policy may specifically provide for salvage and restoration of records and information after any disaster, or this type of provision may be assumed under a general contents policy for equipment and materials. If the latter is the case, there must be adequate coverage, or alternatively, additional contracts with insurance companies specializing in recovery of damaged records after fire or flood should be considered.

RECOVERY

When writing recovery procedures, a list should be developed of records which should be salvaged first following a disaster. Keep in mind the following considerations when setting priorities:

- Can the information be replaced? At what cost?
- How important is the record? Is it a vital record?
- Is the record itself of intrinsic value? If so, can it be replaced, and at what cost?
- Would the cost of replacement be less or more than the cost of restoring the record?
- Is the information available elsewhere?

Once priorities are established, the specific steps for responding to the various types of disasters and for salvaging the various types of media are outlined as follows.

Damage assessment

The first step immediately following a disaster is to assess the type and extent of the damage. Once an accurate assessment has been made, salvaging operations may proceed based on the priorities and procedures already outlined in the disaster plan. A word of caution despite this careful planning, salvage estimates and final decisions must be made at the time the extent of the damage has been determined. The basic objectives of any salvage operation are:

1 to stabilize the condition of the records before and after removing them from the disaster area by creating the necessary environment to prevent further damage
2 to salvage the maximum amount of damaged records in a manner that will minimize restoration requirements and costs.

Water and fire are the most likely disasters to affect records, and there are specific salvaging techniques for water and fire damage. Other disasters, such as bombing, earthquakes, chemical contamination, and severe storms, can wreak havoc in a records area, but the actual damage to the records may be no more than tears and disarray and may allow for a deliberate recovery pace. This is not to minimize the effect of these disasters, since buildings and lives may be affected, only to concentrate on the more common water and fire-related disasters, since their recovery procedures are precise and demand swift action.

Weather will greatly influence what course to take after any flood or fire in which records are damaged. When it is hot and humid, salvaging operations must begin with minimum delay to prevent or control the growth of mold. Cold weather allows for more time to be taken to plan salvage operations and experiment with various drying procedures. In addition, the selection of the proper salvaging technique for damaged records is influenced by the record media as well as the type of disaster.

Enter into a disaster area with caution. Because water-damaged records demand the quickest response, you will need a timely decision from fire and safety officials as to when the area is safe to enter. The building may be structurally damaged; the water may be concealing hazards such as sharp objects or broken live wires; a fire-ravaged area may require a number of days to cool off before being safe to enter. These types of problems require contingency planning for salvaging procedures.

Salvage procedures

Paper

Fire. If paper records are charred or damaged by soot and smoke, there is no need to take care of them immediately. Fire-damaged paper is stable and can be successfully treated after many years have passed. About 70 years went by before conservators began treating documents damaged during the great New York State Library fire of 1911. Documents may only need trimming around the edges to be usable once again, or they can be photocopied and then destroyed if the duplicate is an acceptable substitute for the original. What frequently happens is that fire damage to records is usually compounded by water damage resulting from extinguishing the fire.

Water. Water damage is likely to occur during most disasters, not just during a fire. Flooding is a problem in many locations. Pipes can easily burst during a bad freeze, a storm, or an earthquake. In fact, air conditioning systems and water pipes have been known to leak under the most benign climates, causing severe damage to the records.

Speedy reaction to water damage can happen only if the disaster plan has comprehensive steps for handling this situation. Supplementary publications on salvaging water-damaged materials can be a useful adjunct to the plan.

The age, condition and composition of paper determines the rate at which it will absorb water. Where large volumes of paper records are at stake, the approximate amount of water which will have to be extracted in the drying process must be calculated in advance, and there must be some understanding of the length of time each type of paper can be submerged in water before serious deterioration begins.

Paper manufactured later than 1840 absorbs water to an average of 60 percent of its original weight. Thus, by estimating the original weight of a records storage box at 25 lb, drying techniques must be set up to remove 15 lb of water. That is approximately 75,000 lb of water to be removed if 5,000 boxes of papers are affected.

Paper that is dated earlier than 1840 will absorb water to an average of 80 percent. Older papers are especially vulnerable to mold because of their receptivity to water and because of the highly proteinaceous nature of the leather or vellum with which they are frequently bound. However, they are able to withstand longer periods of time submerged in water than can modern papers and books.

Bound volumes incur their greatest damage due to swelling during the first eight hours after they have been soaked. The paper in the text block and the cardboard cores of book covers have a greater capacity for swelling than the covering materials used for the bindings, resulting in the expansion of the text block such that the spine becomes concave and the fore-edge convex. These very wet volumes will need to be rebound after they have been thoroughly dried. Those that have absorbed less water may retain their normal shape and dry without distortion.

In the event of water damage the environment of flooded areas should be stabilized and controlled both before and during the removal of the damaged records. During the winter, all heat in the building should be turned off. During the summer, every effort should be made to reduce the heat and humidity as rapidly as possible and circulate the air. Mold growth may appear within 48 hours if the weather is hot and humid or in an unventilated area made warm and humid from a nearby fire. The object is to avoid pockets of stagnant, moist air.

The temperature should not be raised in an attempt to lower humidity, as this will only hasten the growth of mold. Hygrometers, hygroscopes, thermohygrometers, and the like can be used to measure and record temperature and humidity, and the results should be monitored regularly. Open doors and windows to create maximum air flow. Dehumidifiers and fans may be needed. If there is no electricity, portable generators should be brought in. If electricity is available, all electrical lines should be waterproofed and grounded.

Before and during removal and packing operations, a constant watch should be kept for signs of mold development. If access has not been permitted for several days, it may be necessary to use fungicidal fogging, a procedure that should be attempted only under supervision of a competent chemist or conservator.

Prior to removing water-soaked records, it should be determined whether freeze drying, vacuum drying, or air drying will be the recovery method. If the materials are to be frozen, arrangements should be made immediately to ship the packed materials to the freezing facilities within a few hours of being removed from the site. This may mean a number of trips to the facility, but packed material allowed to remain on or near the site for too long is subject to mold development.

When beginning the removal operations, it is best to cover all work surfaces with polyethylene sheeting. All unnecessary equipment and furniture should be removed from the area. Lighting, fans, dehumidifiers, and all possible venting should be operational.

The aisles and passageways in the records storage area will probably be strewn with sodden materials. These materials should be removed first in the exact condition in which they are found. By dividing the salvage team into two groups for removal and packing operations, with the removal team forming a human conveyor chain to move the material along to the packing team, it is possible to avoid bottlenecks and the need to stack records on the floor to await packing.

If records have been scattered about the area, an indication of the approximate location in which they are found during the salvage operation may be very helpful at a later date. Do not remove these items in large batches or leave them piled on top of each other, since excessive weight is very damaging.

Starting from the nearest point of access, pack the wettest records first. This will bring down the humidity level in the area. Then follow with removal of the very damp or partially wet records. Only then should the balance of the material be inspected. Records that are damaged beyond salvaging or not worth saving should be discarded and a record kept of this disposition. Time wasted salvaging records which can be replaced easily or for less money than they could be restored might result in the loss of other valuable records and information.

The contents of records storage boxes probably will not be saturated with water if they were previously positioned close together. Boxes with a corrugated inside layer may be very wet, however, even though the major portion of the contents is only damp. In such cases, it is best to repack the contents in new boxes. This will help the drying in addition to making the box lighter to lift and preventing the collapse of a wet box. Be sure to identify the contents of the new boxes properly when repacking.

Even though closely packed materials are unlikely to develop mold internally, since they have been in a very humid atmosphere for several days, their external parts may have been exposed to a far greater quantity of mold spores than is usual under ordinary circumstances. These drier records should not be left in place but moved to a controlled environment during clean up of the area. They should be stacked with sufficient space between them to allow for good circulation of air.

If mold has already begun to develop, and the original paper may be replaced with a photocopy, try to obtain a copier dedicated for this purpose only. Have non-linty paper towels available to clean and dry the pages, and also to clean any mold that gets onto the photocopier glass.

After all materials have been removed from the area, it may be necessary to sterilize the shelves, walls, floors, and ceilings to prevent further mold growth, and to take care of any maintenance work to return the site to its former condition.

Freezing

Freezing and storing records at low temperature is the most generally accepted and proven method of stabilizing water-damaged paper records. This technique buys time for determining the best drying method and for carefully coordinating and controlling the drying operation. It makes it possible to assess the value of the damaged material, determine which items can or cannot be replaced, estimate recovery costs, prepare adequate environmental storage conditions, and restore the affected buildings. Cold storage facilities provide accessible and inexpensive space in which large volumes of records can be stabilized in the condition in which they were found to prevent further deterioration.

Freezing will not dry the records nor will it kill mold spores, although it controls mold growth by causing the spores to become dormant. It will stabilize water-soluble materials, such as inks, dyes, watercolors, tempera, and the like, which may diffuse during conventional drying.

Before freezing, wash off accumulated mud and filth only if there is time within the 48 hours to do so without delaying the freezing of the bulk of the material. Washing should be done by a trained person so as to prevent further damage. Washing records containing water-soluble components should not be attempted in any circumstances.

Wet, coated papers should be frozen immediately. If permitted to dry, they will bond together. In fact, it may be desirable to leave them under water until a few hours before they are to be frozen, since the period between pumping out the water and beginning the salvage operation is critical. Freeze or vacuum drying is the only successful method for salvaging this type of paper.

Loose, single-sheet materials with no soluble components may be washed under clean, cold running water by trained personnel prior to freezing. If the single sheets are in masses, it is best not to try to separate them, but to freeze them as they are. They will easily separate during the freeze or vacuum drying process.

Groups of loose records may be wrapped in freezer paper, wax paper, or silicone paper to prevent them sticking together during the freezing process. Each package should be no more than two inches thick and marked to indicate the type of material, its previous location, and its priority. If it is known that the damaged material will be vacuum or freeze dried after freezing, the wrapping step may be avoided and the materials packed in plastic cartons or cardboard boxes to about three-quarters capacity. Never pack or wrap the records tightly.

Boxes and their contents should be frozen as found. Try not to turn boxes of records upside down. The wet contents may stick to the bottom and be torn if upended.

Records should be moved directly from the storage area to the freezing facility, preferably in refrigerated trucks. Small volumes of records can be packed in dry ice and transported in unrefrigerated trucks to the facility. If freezing space is limited, priority should be given to items which have already developed mold, important original documents that are irreplaceable or expensive to replace, art on paper, materials on coated stock, and artefacts with water-soluble components.

Freeze drying

Once the records have been transferred to freezing facilities, the drying method must be selected. The most successful method for drying large collections is vacuum and/or freeze drying. Freeze drying involves removing the water, which is now in solid form, from the records through the process of sublimation. The ice transforms directly to vapor without passing through an intermediary liquid stage. The result is that individual documents will not stick together as they would if heat-dried.

The costs of freeze drying will be a factor to consider when determining the volume of records to be dried. In some instances, the cost is for the freeze drying chamber, not for the number of records going into it, and it is more economical to fill the chamber as near to capacity as possible. Other companies charge by the volume of records. Two elements combine to aid in the freeze drying process: low pressure and extreme cold.

Typically, records are placed in a chamber designed to keep them frozen during processing. A vacuum system reduces the air pressure in the chamber to a near-absolute vacuum. This permits ice to vaporize without becoming liquid. A condenser, positioned in the direct path of the migrating vapors, collects and holds ice molecules removed from the material. Efficient rates of sublimation are obtained by maintaining a vapor pressure differential between the material and the condenser.

Freeze drying reduces stains and reduces odor caused by smoke. It also virtually prevents the feathering of inks.

Vacuum drying

Vacuum drying offers many advantages when large quantities of material are involved. Records may be put in plastic milk carton containers and placed in the drying chamber. At this time, the material is at room temperature. Air is evacuated from the chamber until the temperature reaches freezing point. The chamber is then filled with hot dry air and purged with this air until the wet material is warmed to 10°C (50°F). The number of cycles required depends on the initial wetness of the material. The effectiveness of this process is illustrated by the fact that a typical loading of one chamber with approximately 2,000 milk container cases can result in the removal of approximately 8 lbs of water per case or 8 tons per chamber load.

Air drying

Air drying is ideally suited for emergencies involving a small volume of records, when temperature and humidity are relatively low and conducive to drying (between 10° and 17°C (50°–63°F) and 25 to 35 percent relative humidity). If weather conditions are not suitable, or if a large volume of records is involved, freezing followed by freeze or vacuum drying is the safer way to proceed.

Under proper environmental conditions, wet paper can be air dried. Damp paper can easily be dried if spread about in a space with cool and dry air and good air circulation. Very wet papers can be treated similarly but interleaved with absorbent paper such as unprinted newsprint or a good grade of paper toweling. The toweling is more effective than newsprint but significantly more expensive, especially if used with a large collection. The interleaving material should be frequently removed from the working area so that humidity will not increase or mold set in.

Some conservators recommend interleaving sheets, impregnated with a fungicide such as thymol dissolved in alcohol, between the documents so as to reduce the possibility of mold damage. However, working with large amounts of these chemicals is hazardous – the solution gives off toxic and flammable vapors – and such operations should be directed by trained personnel.

Bound volumes can be similarly air dried by interleaving the absorbent sheets at intervals of 50 pages (25 leaves). Care should be taken not to interleave too much, because the spine will become concave and the volume distorted. As with loose documents, frequent changing of the interleaving material is much more effective than allowing large numbers of sheets to remain in place for extended periods, and it should not be left in the volumes after the drying is complete. If the humidity is high, it might be necessary to interleave every 10 pages (5 leaves) and to change the sheets every two to three hours to hasten the drying and discourage mold growth.

Bound volumes weighing less than 6 lb, that have distorted spines as a result of the interleaving process can be hung, when partially dry, on thin, monofilament nylon lines to help return the spine to its original shape as it dries. The lines should be about 6 ft (1.82m) long and spaced approximately an inch apart. Volumes of up to 1½ inches (38mm) thickness can be hung on three lines; thicker volumes will require more lines. Bound volumes should never be hung when saturated with water. Not only can this damage the spines, it can also cause spine adhesives, particularly those made of gelatin, to migrate through the volume, staining the leaves and even gluing them together.

It may be necessary to separate a wet mass of single items for immediate hand drying. The safest method is one which takes advantage of the special properties of polyester non-woven fabric and film. A damp sheet of polyester film is laid on top of the wet pile. The surface energy of water makes it possible to ease away several sheets at the corner of the pile and roll or peel these back with the polyester. Transfer this material and the attached sheets, polyester side down, to a work surface covered with a polyethylene sheet.

Place another polyester film on top of the transferred batch of papers. Repeat the process until you are able to roll the film back with a single wet sheet attached. As each single sheet is removed and placed, polyester side down, on the work surface, a dry polyester web is placed on top of the wet sheet. Then the sandwich is turned over, the polyester film removed, and a second piece of dry polyester web is placed on top. (The final interleaving should be done only with web.) This process is repeated for each sheet. The items may be safely frozen or air dried at this stage.

If the volume is small enough, place each 'sandwich' separately on tables or closely spaced on nylon lines to dry. After 100 or so have been processed, the first sheets will be dry. Fans may be used but should not blow directly on the material. Gentle, warm air and good ventilation will remove excess moisture. Air conditioners or dehumidifiers may also help the drying process.

Microfilm, negatives, and photographs

If microfilm has been soaked, it should be kept wet at all times. Large, clean containers filled with fresh water can be used to submerge the film and transfer it to a nearby mirofilm processing center for reprocessing. If possible, the film should be kept in its original package for future identification.

Freezing may damage the images on any film media. Photographic materials should not be frozen unless professional help is delayed longer than 48 hours, since the formation of ice crystals may rupture the emulsion layer and leave marks on the film. Wet, muddy black-and-white negative film and prints can be sealed, for emergency stabilization, in polyethylene bags and placed in plastic (not metal) rubbish bins under clean, cold running water and left under these conditions for no longer than three days before the emulsion will separate from the film backing.

The colored layers of color slides and color negatives and positive film will separate, and the dyes will become weak or completely lost unless professionally treated within 48 hours. After this time, freezing the collection is the best way to save it until special arrangements can be made.

Diazo or vesicular films should be salvaged last since they are almost impervious to water damage and can be easily washed with liquid detergent, rinsed, and laid out to dry on absorbent paper.

Magnetic media

Fire. Fire is most destructive to computer magnetic tapes. A live cigarette ash which lands on a tape surface can cause instant tape damage and data loss. Direct contact with open flames or an extremely hot environment reduces the chances of recovering data to virtually nothing. The damaging effects of heat are primarily in the form of physical and chemical media changes rather than magnetic data loss. Excessive heat affects the mechanical integrity of the tapes and the reels through warping, distortion, layer-to-layer adhesion (blocking), loss of durability, and binder breakdown and softening. Also, the chemistry of the binder (the compound used to bind the oxide particles to the base material) will be altered due to the volatile losses of its components.

Magnetic tape is a poor heat conductor. A properly wound reel with a very smooth pack offers more resistance to fire and water damage than a loose or uneven pack. The latter will allow more water to seep between windings and cause tape cupping and other distortions.

Tapes that have been subjected to extremely low temperatures for long periods of time should be relaxed and dried, if necessary, for a number of days at gradually increasing temperatures in order to relieve the stresses which may have developed with time. Tape shrinkage due to exposure to extreme cold can produce layer-to-layer adhesion, which can cause tape tearing and surface coating damage in portions of the reel.

Carbon dioxide, halon, and water can be used for direct fire fighting in a computer tape installation. Carbon dioxide and halon are clean and do not leave a residue. Tapes which have become wet during the fire-fighting effort can be salvaged.

If recorded computer tapes have been subjected to fire and heat, separate out those reels which appear to have sustained the least amount of physical damage as soon as possible and try to recover these first. All fire debris, ash, and smoke residue should be cleaned from the canisters, wrap-arounds, and flange surfaces before opening the canisters or wrap-arounds. Using the slowest speed transport available, perform at least two wind/rewind passes, inspecting the tapes as they are being wound. If they are badly warped or display layer-to-layer adhesion which is damaging the coating, or are shedding large amounts of coating debris, the chances for data recovery are poor. The transport should be cleaned after each tape is run. Then give the tapes two full cleaning passes on a tape cleaner/winder, preferably constant tension type, and rewind them on to clean or new reels and make new labels.

Relax these tapes for 24 to 48 hours in the normal operating environment. Then perform a read and recopying pass. If the tapes will not load on to the transport at this time, store them in a low humidity environment and retry at intervals. This process should be repeated for the next least damaged group of tapes until all tapes have been examined.

Water. Magnetic tapes that have been inundated by or immersed in water are likely to respond to data recovery as long as high temperatures did not exist at the time to produce steam or very high humidity in the tape pack. Temperature and humidity in excess of 60°C (140°F) and 85 percent relative humidity can lead to significant tape damage. The hygroscopic effects of the extreme humidity can also produce binder breakdown.

Inundated tapes should be quickly separated into wet and dry groups; also vital records should be separated from less important ones. This organizes the salvage operation and permits a more rapid media recovery.

Move all tapes quickly out of standing water areas. If possible, move the smallest group (either the wet or the dry tapes) out of the storage area. Check all wet tape labels to be sure they are legible. Replace or make existing labels legible, but do not paste new labels over the wet original.

Begin a general drying of the entire storage area, including shelves, floors, canisters, safes, and vaults. Quickly open, check, and drain any water which may have entered the tape canisters. Since tape reel hubs are often capable of trapping and holding water, check for this, and shake and rotate the reel to empty the water. A wet-dry vacuum cleaner may be used to absorb any standing water that is accessible.

The air drying process should begin immediately. Wet tapes should not be replaced into their canisters. Hand dry all external wet surfaces. Do not force dry the wet tape pack with a heated airflow. This can cause high internal humidity which can lead to binder damage and layer-to-layer adhesion. Gently separate the reel flanges with spacers such as rubber grommets to allow airflow through the tape pack-flange interface. This reduces the probability of tape-to-flange sticking damage when the tapes are first run. It will also permit additional water run-off from the vertically standing tapes. If possible, maintain a forced, room temperature airflow through this tape-to-reel configuration.

The drying process begins most effectively when the individual tapes are run reel-to-reel on a device such as tape cleaner or winder. Wet tapes should never be run on a regular tape drive. They will not perform correctly in the vacuum columns, and they are likely to adhere to the column walls or on to the capstan, resulting in tape tearing or other damage. The tapes should be run over cleaning tissues only, not over the blades.

Recorded tapes have been successfully reactivated after being totally submerged for a period of time in unclean river water and in salt water. First, all accessible surfaces were hand dried as described above. Then the tapes stored in the normally recommended temperature and humidity environment for 48 hours.

Next the tapes were run for six or seven passes on a tape dry cleaner unit over tissue cleaners only. When they were reasonably dry, two cleaning passes were performed over tissues and cleaning blades. The tapes were then immediately read and recopied on to new reels. Recopying was important because of the potential for binder degradation to occur due to the water absorption.

This recovery process can also be applied to tapes which have been subjected to clean water inundation. In this case, it would probably be sufficient to recopy only the key tapes. Also, the two blade cleaning passes may be omitted.

12

Forms management

If four people were asked to supply their name, address, telephone number, and date of birth on a card, the likely results would be the following:

1   John Jacob Jones
    123 Anystreet
    Anytown, USA 54321
    (109) 876–5432
    January 1, 1950

2   John Jones   1/1/50
    123 Anystreet
    Anytown, USA
    876–5432

3   J.J. Jones
    123 Anystreet
    Anytown, USA 54321
    (109) 876–5432
    January 1

4   Jones, John J.
    123 Anystreet
    Anytown, USA
    876–5432
    1/1/50

Of the four responses, only number one provides complete information in the order in which it was requested. At the risk of oversimplifying, that is why forms management is necessary.

Forms are tools which may be used to organize, collect, and transmit information. When properly analyzed and designed from a systems perspective, forms can:

- enhance the flow of work through an office or an entire organization
- increase operational efficiency and effectiveness
- reduce costs.

A form is a fixed arrangement of captioned spaces designed for entering and extracting prescribed information. Traditionally, these captioned spaces were preprinted on paper and the person supplying the information would merely fill in the blanks with a pencil or typewriter. Today there are other options. For example, with computer technology, a form can be stored in memory and called up as needed onto a visual display unit so that data may be entered into the system through the terminal keyboard. A form may also be stored in memory and produced via a high-speed laser printer as output with the rest of the processed data.

Additionally, a form may be photographically placed on a glass slide and optically enlarged on film along with the processed data as a simultaneous exposure for computer output microfilming (COM) generation.

Regardless of the type of form, however, it must always be carefully analyzed and designed if it is to be effective, and available in the proper place if it is to be used. Because the various forms management functions require knowledge that most people do not have, forms management programs are established and staffed with specialists who are able to use their expertise to organization-wide advantage.

The specific objectives of a forms management program are to:

- determine that forms are necessary and up to date
- design forms to enhance information processing
- ensure that instructions for use are adequate
- specify the most economical method of reproduction
- ensure that forms are available when and where needed.

There are three aspects to a forms management program which, when combined, enable the objectives to be met. These are forms control; forms analysis, design and composition; and forms reproduction, stocking, and distribution. These are similar to aspects of the reports management program (Chapter 14), and, in many respects, forms and reports management programs function almost identically. The basic difference between the two is that forms management personnel must have the highly specialized forms design knowledge and an understanding of the printing, stocking and distribution functions in addition to the more general analytical expertise which is a basic requirement for all records management professionals.

It would be reasonable to assume that the forms and reports programs could be combined. Their functions are often inextricably intertwined and there is a great deal of overlap. As a practical matter, the primary vehicle for transmitting reported information is a form. However, since there are many information processing systems which use forms and which are not reporting systems, and since there is the requirement for the specialized knowledge, the programs are usually established as separate entities. Nevertheless, there is no question that the staff of both must work together and continuously coordinate their efforts.

For a forms management program to be effective, all of the functions must be performed. If there is good control and no analysis, then the program is controlling nonsense. If there is good design and no distribution and stocking plan, then the well-designed form will not be available to the people who need it. A complete program is an absolute necessity.

FORMS CONTROL

Control over the proliferation of forms in an organization is one of the major aspects of a forms management program. When people feel the need to create a form, there is usually little hesitation about doing so. This willingness to create, combined with the readily available means to create (all that is needed is a piece of paper, a pencil, and a copying machine) means that the unauthorized or 'bootleg' form is a fact of life in most offices.

Theoretically, all forms should be subject to control and all forms should be analyzed, designed, inventoried, etc. but that principle is unpractical. If an individual working on a project creates a worksheet that only he (and maybe a few other people also working on the project) will use, and if the total number of those worksheets will probably not exceed 25, and if the life of those 25 copies will be four months, and if the cost of the entire thing is $43.00, a real question exists as to the necessity for the forms management staff to become involved.

Forms managers who insist on absolute control over everything that fits the form definition without regard to the practicality of the situation, quickly become people to be avoided in organizations, and are seen as obstacles to progress rather than facilitators of it. Obviously, dismissal of the control responsibility is not being advocated; merely a pragmatic approach to its implementation.

A forms management program should have an authorizing directive that spells out the various authorities and responsibilities, and clearly outlines the procedures to be followed for creating a new form or modifying an existing one.

Generally, unauthorized forms should not exist. An effective way to inhibit their creation is to establish the policy (in cooperation with both the print unit and the procurement authority) that no form will be produced or purchased until it has been approved by the forms management staff. Simply initialing the printing or procurement requisition is a convenient way to indicate approval.

Control is also necessary so that forms are subjected to periodic review. Each time a form is reprinted it should be reviewed to ensure that it is still necessary and adequate for the purpose for which it was created. By coordinating the periodic review schedule with the reprint schedule, necessary changes can be made in a timely manner so that stock shortages are prevented.

The tools available to make the forms control job easier are the history file, the functional file, the control number, and the catalog. In order to create these tools, a forms inventory must first be undertaken.

Inventory

To conduct a forms inventory a letter or memorandum should go to all organizational units requesting copies of *all* forms currently being used and the estimated annual usage for each. It is helpful to include the definition of a form and an explanation of the collection effort in the letter, along with a due date for the submissions.

The result of this request will be lots of forms, indeed, more forms than are needed. However, only by incurring this one-off duplication can a complete picture be drawn regarding organization-wide forms usage. As the forms are received, copies should be filed both numerically by control number and alphabetically by subject. If the forms do not contain control numbers, assign numbers sequentially even if only as a temporary measure. The numerical file will become the basis for the forms history file and the subject file will be the basis of the functional file used for control purposes.

History file

The forms history file contains historical information on each form including:

- copies of the current and previous editions
- working papers showing stages of development
- a copy of, or reference to, the prescribing directive
- the original request for approval and subsequent requests for revisions
- documents containing specifications and showing reproduction/procurement action
- documents relating to stocking and distribution.

The history file is organized numerically by forms control number.

Functional file

The forms functional file is a subject classification file used in the analysis process for comparing forms in the same functional area in order to avoid duplication. The file should be arranged alphabetically by function (subject) which, of course, necessitates that a comprehensive list of organizational functions (that is, apply, authorize, certify, order, request, etc.) be developed. The following is a basic list of functional file categories:

- acknowledge
- agree
- apply
- assign
- attest
- authorize
- bill
- cancel

- certify
- claim
- estimate
- follow up
- identify
- instruct
- layout
- list
- notify

- offer
- order
- record
- report
- request
- route
- schedule
- transmit
- verify

Use of the functional file allows the forms analyst to:

1 avoid creating a new form that duplicates an existing one
2 identify existing forms that can be eliminated or consolidated
3 identify forms that can be standardized throughout the organization.

Control number

The forms control number is a number assigned to an approved form and, preferably, printed on its face for identification purposes. Each form subject to the control system should have a number and, ideally, the numbers will all be part of the same sequential scheme. When modifying an existing forms control system, however, it may be necessary to have forms with different numbering schemes or to have two numbers assigned (new and old) for some period of time.

The simpler the numbering scheme the better. For example, a number such as 123–PRO–85 would indicate that the form was the 123rd in the system, that it originated in the PROcurement department, and that it was created (or revised) in 1985. That is sufficient information for identification purposes. Attempting to include data such as functional file codes and retention periods into the form numbers will only confuse the users.

A simple log should be kept of form numbers issued and the titles corresponding to them. Although that information is obtainable by looking in the history file, a log provides a much more convenient reference.

Catalog

A forms catalog is not an absolute necessity for a control program (as are history and functional files) but it is often helpful to have for quick reference purposes. Catalogs vary greatly in both size and format. In some instances they consist of hundreds or thousands of pages, each containing a facsimile of a particular form and instructions for its use. In other (more frequent) instances, a catalog is merely a listing of forms and contains only basic information such as title and number. The development and use of a forms catalog is dependent on the number of forms in the system. Generally, for a small organization, a catalog is not required.

Automated control

So far, all of the control tools described have been manual. These paper-based systems are entirely adequate for most organizations. While automated control systems have been developed for some extremely large organizations, they are generally not cost-effective for use in a less expansive environment.

The developmental costs alone for a computerized functional file system could well exceed $150,000, and, even with the most advanced system, there will still be substantial

REQUEST FOR APPROVAL AND DEVELOPMENT OF FORM
(If more space is needed, use reverse and identify by Item No.)

To: *(forms management office symbol)*	From: *(office symbol)*	Project officer: *(typed name and phone no.)*

1 Type of form ☐ New ☐ Revised	2 Form title		

3 Form designation and no. *(Leave blank if new)*	4 Form update	5 Report control symbol	6 Controlled forms ☐ Accountable ☐ Safeguard

7 Use | **8 Used within** | **9 Method of completion** | **10 Recommended size**

Perma-nent	Test	One time	One office	One area	One region	Nation-wide	Type-writer	Hand	Machine *(see item 21)*	

11 Type of file | **12 Date form must be available/implemented** *(line one out)* | **13 Prescribing directive**

Visible	Vertical	Folder	Ledger	3-ring binder	Other *(specify)*		

14 Explain purpose for which form will be used (if proposed form replaces an existing higher level form prescribed for the same purpose, attach a written waiver from the originator)

15 Type(s) of using activities	16 Frequency of preparation *(daily, weekly, monthly, etc)*

17 No. of copies filled in at one writing	18 Distribution of original and each copy indicated in item 17	19 Initial issue quantity	20 Estimated monthly use

22 Superseded forms ☐ Yes ☐ No *(if yes complete A and B. Complete C if stock is to be destroyed)*

A Number(s)	Date(s)	B Existing stock		C Justification for destroying stock *(explain why superseded form(s) cannot be used)*
		Use	Destroy	

23 Concurrences *(office symbol, name and extension of individual outside the immediate organization who concurred in accepting the workload this procedure will impose on his/her organization)*

24 Date of approval	25 Typed name, grade, and title of approving official	26 Signature

For use of Forms Management Office

27 Unit of Rqn	28 Const/Pkg	29 Trim size	30 Carbon interleaved sets			31 Carbonless paper	
			No. of parts	Color of carbon	Carbon coverage	No. of parts	Color of paper

32 Punching | | | | | **33 Binding**

No. holes	Diameter	C to C	Kind	Position	☐ Staple	☐ Glue	Other *(specify)*

34 Paper | | | **35 Print** | | | | | **36 Forms stocked by** *(if other than publications distr. center)*

Basis weight	Grade	Color	Color ink	One side	Head to				
					Head	Foot	Left side	Right side	

37 Additional specifications attached ☐ Yes ☐ No	38 Total quantity to print	

39 Functional code(s)	40 Date processed	41 Forms management office approval *(signature)*

Figure 12.1   A request for approval and development of form

work required of the forms management staff to determine if consolidation or elimination of forms is desirable and to decide how such actions should be accomplished.

Forms control process

The forms management directive should contain the procedures for establishing a new form or revising an existing one. Basically, the control process should operate in the following manner.

A request for a new or revised form (shown in Figure 12.1) should be completed and submitted to the forms management staff along with a rough draft or sketch of what the requestor thinks the form should look like. Associated documents such as instructions and a draft of the requiring directive should also accompany the request form. If necessary, the forms management staff should assist the requestor in completing the request form and in producing the associated materials.

The forms management staff should review the request and analyze the proposed form for necessity, adequacy, usefulness, and economy (see following sections). Approval should come only after it has been determined that:

- all items on the form are needed
- all copies of the form are needed
- the design is functional
- clear and complete instructions have been developed
- stock levels have been determined
- distribution patterns have been established
- printing and construction specifications have been developed
- the form is cost-effective.

When the form is approved it should be assigned a control number and sent for composition. No further control is necessary until the form reaches a reprint point at which time the periodic review should take place. It should be noted that the forms management staff initiates the periodic review, not the form originator. The originator, however, must be contacted during the review process.

ANALYSIS AND DESIGN

The analysis and design of forms is, by far, the most important part of the forms management process. If all forms were going to be analyzed and designed properly by their originators, the rest of the management and control process would be almost unnecessary, inasmuch as the primary reason for controlling is to achieve efficiency and effectiveness – precisely what properly analyzed and designed forms do.

Analysis

The general subject of analysis is covered in some detail in Chapters 6 and 7. Specifically regarding forms, however, analysis seeks to answer the following questions:

- What is the work that creates a need for the form?
- How is the work done or how will it be done?
- Why is the work done or why will it be done in a particular way?
- Who does the work?
- What are the processes, operations and documents involved?
- What are the purposes of the form?

- In which operations and in what procedures is the form used?
- Are there related organizational activities that should be considered?

By answering these questions, the forms management staff will be able to determine the following points:

- Is a new form really needed? The form may be the wrong tool for the purpose. Perhaps an existing form can be used.
- Can the form be used in a different way? Perhaps a form can be designed to serve several purposes and meet the needs of various users throughout the organization.
- Does the form meet the needs of those who will have to supply the requested information? For example, the users might be handicapped or speak a different language.
- Have the working conditions under which the form will be completed, processed and used been considered? Handling can be facilitated by simplified or improved design and construction.
- Have special features such as automated use been considered?

Quantitative data should also be collected. The following information will help in developing a complete picture of the form and what needs to be done with it.

- number of forms completed in a given period
- time required to complete and process the form
- costs of activities involved in completing and processing the form.

Design

Forms design is such a specialized area that entire books could be written about it. Indeed, several books have been written and are readily available in the market. Although no attempt will be made here to cover the vast and detailed subject of forms design, no book on records management would be complete without at least including a discussion of the concept.

Part of the reason forms analysis is so important is because a form is designed around the answers to the analytical questions asked. The phrase, 'form follows function' is literally true in this instance.

The work process should dictate the design of the form. In that regard, a designer must have an understanding of those processes so that the form can be designed to fit them. For example, if a form is required to be completed by typing, the designer must know that a standard typewriter spaces vertically in sixth-of-an-inch increments. If this basic consideration is ignored, and the form is designed for one-quarter-inch vertical spacing (as would be used for handwritten entry), the typist will constantly have to realign the platen in order to get the information lined up properly on the form. This is extremely frustrating for the typist and, obviously, inefficient.

Should it be acceptable to cither type or hand-enter the information at the user's discretion, the form might be designed with two-sixths-of-an-inch vertical spacing. This allows sufficient room for hand entry (two-sixths being larger than one-quarter) and also provides for efficient typewriter operation in that the typist need only set the machine to double space.

The forms designer must also understand the kind of information that the form will be used to obtain. Almost everyone has had the sad experience of trying to complete a form which has insufficient space allocated for the information requested. A 'phone number' block that can hold seven digits will not do in locations where an area code is required to dial a number. A 'zip code' block that can hold five digits is inadequate if the address is in Canada or England where six digit codes are used. One inch of horizontal space for 'city' is far from adequate if the person lives in San Francisco or Oklahoma City.

The above are relatively basic forms design considerations. There is significant potential for easing the information supply burden using good design techniques. The more involved a process is, the greater the possibility that a well-designed form can enhance it. Various types of specialty forms, such as self-mailers, spot carbons, optical character recognition, etc., can save thousands of hours of employee time.

Commercial forms design software packages are now available for personal computers (PCs). This software allows anyone with a PC to perform both the design (and composition – see below) functions. In the hands of a competent forms designer, the tool may be put to good use. In the hands of someone who knows nothing about forms design, it is a disaster waiting to happen. Good-looking forms that don't work are not an improvement!

Composition

Forms composition, which is the process of preparing a form for printing, is a technical

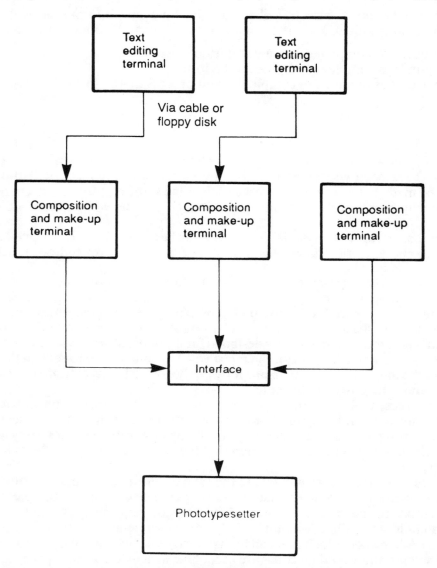

Figure 12.2   An electronic composition equipment configuration

PRINTING SPECIFICATION WORKSHEET
(Cross out items in left columns which do not apply)

1 Form no. and title	Form no.		Title		
2 Size	Specify width first				

	Kind	Grade	Substance	Color	Color of ink
3 Paper and ink					

4 Grain	Direction ☐ Parallel to top of form		☐ Parallel to left of form		
5 Print	☐ One side ☐ Two sides	If two sides, print ☐ Head to head ☐ Head to foot		Head of front to ☐ left of back	Head of front to ☐ right of back
6 Margins	Front Top Left		Back Top Left		
7 Register	☐ All sheets ☐ In sets ☐ In pads		☐ With form no.		
8 Number	Singly, in duplicate, etc.	Starting no.	Ending no.	Skips ☐ Not acceptable	Acceptable ☐ if listed
9 Perforate	No. of perforations	Direction ☐ Horizontal ☐ Vertical	Location Inches from top	Inches from left	
10 Score	No. of scores	Direction ☐ Horizontal ☐ Vertical	Location Inches from top	Inches from left	
11 Fold	No. of folds	Direction ☐ Horizontal ☐ Vertical	Location Inches from top	Inches from left	
	After folding the following should be on the outside				
12 Punch	No. holes	Diameter	Kind	Location (top left)	Inches center to center	Inches center of hold to edge of sheet
13 Round corner	Radius	No. corners	Location Top ☐ right	Top ☐ left	Bottom ☐ right	Bottom ☐ left
14 Collate	No. sheets to set	In order shown ☐ Under paper	☐ Other (specify)		
15 Pad	No. sheets to pad	No. sets to pad	Location of padding ☐ Top ☐ Bottom ☐ Left ☐ Right		Reinforce with ☐ Chipboard back
16 Dummy attached	☐ Fold	☐ Punch	☐ Other (Specify)		
17 Wrap	No. sheets per package	No. sets per package	No. pads per package	No. cards per package	Best ☐ method
18 Label	Label each package on one end showing form no., title, quantity in package, special nos if any				
19 Special	*(Information not specifically provided for on worksheet, such as make and model of machine on which form is written)*				
20 Prepared by and date	Name			Date	

Figure 12.3   A printing specification worksheet

area of specialization closely aligned to the graphic arts function of camera artwork production and the printing function of typesetting. In fact, many organizations have found it more cost-effective to contract out the highly labor-intensive composition work to graphic arts or typesetting firms rather than to develop and maintain the capability in-house.

With rapidly expanding computer technology, however, forms composition is virtually becoming a completely automated process that can be performed with much less technical knowledge and in much less time than was previously required. Using an equipment configuration consisting of a text entry and editing terminal, a composition and make-up terminal, a phototypesetter, and a processor as shown in Figure 12.2, an analyst can completely design a form on a visual display screen and reproduce camera-ready artwork in up to two-thirds less time than would be required by the manual composition method. Although such equipment is still relatively expensive, larger organizations with a substantial number of forms might easily be able to justify the investment.

The forms management staff is responsible for production (or procurement) of camera-ready artwork and for proofreading to ensure accuracy prior to printing.

Reproduction

If an organization has a printing facility, many forms will probably be reproduced in-house. If there is no such facility, or if the form is such that it requires a special manufacturing process (such as marginally punched continuous forms or carbon-inter-leaved sets), the reproduction job will be contracted out.

The key to success, whether dealing with an internal printer or a contracted manufacturer, is to provide complete, written specifications so that there is no question as to exactly how the form is supposed to be produced. While specification writing can be somewhat complex, it can be greatly simplified by using a printing specification worksheet as shown in Figure 12.3. By entering all the appropriate data and submitting the worksheet along with the printing requisition, chances of error due to misunderstanding are greatly reduced.

It is not possible to provide too much information to a printer. For forms with unusual construction, a printer's dummy (shown in Figure 12.4) may also be submitted. A printer's dummy is a mock-up version of the form, clearly indicating the exact placement of folds, perforations, margins, etc.

If a specialized form is to be manufactured by a contractor, it is possible that the composition will be included as part of the contract. If this is the case, the forms management staff will be responsible for proofreading the camera artwork received as well as for following up to ensure that the job is produced and delivered in a timely manner.

STOCKING AND DISTRIBUTION

If a form is not where it is supposed to be, it might as well not exist at all. To the person who needs to use a form, the fact that there are 13,000 of them on order is irrelevant. Proper stocking and distribution, therefore, are key elements of a successful forms management program.

If all supply cabinets, stockrooms, and warehouses contained twice the number of forms that were needed, shortages of stock would virtually be eliminated. That, however, would be an expensive type of security blanket to maintain. All storage space costs money and, obviously, the forms cost money as well. Additionally, there is always the possibility of a form revision rendering the costly inventory obsolete.

The question, then, is 'How many forms are enough?' The answer may be determined

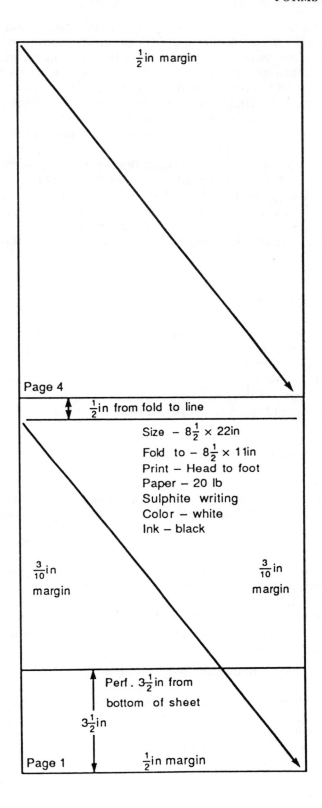

Figure 12.4   A printer's dummy

by considering the cost per order, the holding cost of inventory, and the value of the annual number of forms used. Additional factors, such as unit-price discounts and transportation quantity discounts may also need to be taken into consideration. If the determination is made that a form needs to be ordered more than once a year, the periodic review should be scheduled to coincide with the yearly cycle.

The amount and time of ordering is only one aspect of stocking and distribution. Arrangements must be made with supply personnel to receive the stock and make it available through organizational distribution channels. This may involve setting limits on the quantities available to each customer, and most certainly will involve timely notification to the forms management staff when the reprint level is reached.

In larger organizations, forms purchased from manufacturers or printing contractors may be shipped to multiple geographical locations for distribution to local offices. In some instances, the entire ordering and stocking function may be decentralized. When operating in a decentralized environment, extra care must be taken to ensure that the overall forms control responsibilities remain centralized – at least for those forms used on an organization-wide basis.

On-demand forms printing

The foregoing deals with the traditional methods of reproducing, stocking, and distributing forms. Modern computer technology, however, has provided new alternatives. By composing forms electronically and transmitting the digitized images to a remote processor hooked into a laser printer, it is possible for users to reproduce forms as required and thereby eliminate the processes of bulk printing, stocking, and distributing.

One way in which a demand system can operate is shown in Figure 12.5. The key steps in the process are:

1   forms design – through the use of a graphic workstation or electronic composition terminal
2   image transmission – through telecommunications to remote user sites
3   image storage – on floppy disks until a hard (paper) copy is needed
4   reproduction – via low-speed laser printer hooked up to a user's computer.

The system described is only one possible configuration. There are many others. For example, camera artwork could be created and optically scanned into the system to produce the digitized image; a high-speed laser printer could be used at a regional center for decentralized reproduction on a larger scale; or an integrated offset press could be used instead of the laser printer.

While demand printing can eliminate the problems of bulk reproduction, stocking, and distributing, it can also create problems of a managerial nature which are not present with the traditional methods. Among the problems are:

1   control of the print image – to ensure that the design is not modified at the remote site and that the latest version is the one being used
2   allocation of printer time between various functions (forms printing, word processing, convenience copying) – since a laser printer dedicated to forms production would probably not be justifiable
3   additional staff training – so that forms can be produced by users on demand.

ELECTRONIC FORMS

When we speak of electronic forms, we do not mean forms that are simply stored in some sort of electronic format and then reproduced on paper for use as described in the 'on

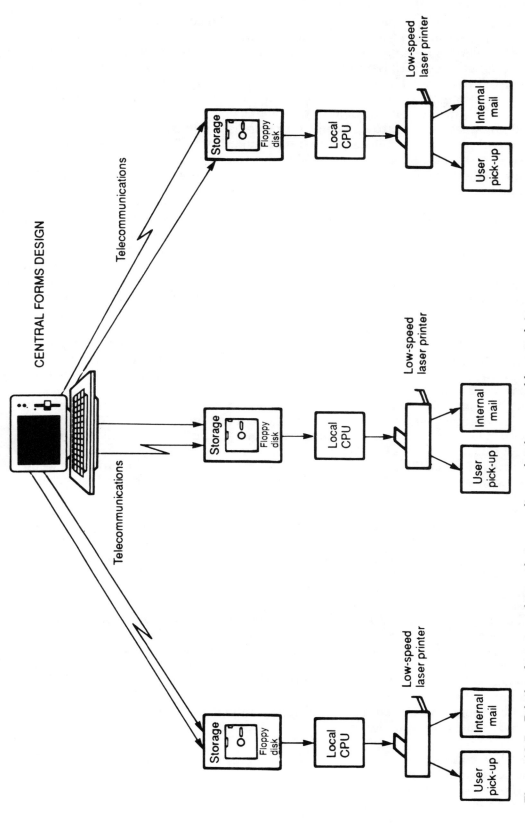

Figure 12.5   Printing forms on demand at user sites using low-speed laser printers

169

demand' section above. An electronic form is one that resides in electronic format and is also used electronically, that is, completed by the user on a computer.

An example of how electronic forms may be used to good advantage is the PC software available to assist persons in filing US income tax returns. Each year, US residents with incomes over a certain dollar amount are required to file an income tax return with the federal government. A return is a form or series of forms used to determine the amount of tax a person must pay. The returns are quite complex, require many mathematical calculations, and might consist of anywhere from one form to over a dozen forms, depending on how the person's income was obtained.

The traditional way to prepare an income tax return is to obtain all the necessary paper forms from the agency that collects income taxes, the Internal Revenue Service, (not always an easy task); gather all one's personal financial data so that the information can be properly entered on the forms; and start making the calculations and entering the data. For a complex return, three days of effort would not be unusual.

Enter electronic forms. The paper forms gathering step is now eliminated because income tax software packages contain all the forms that are necessary. Once the financial data is in order, a person simply needs to enter the data into the computer using the worksheets that appear on the screen in the order that they are required. (The computer asks questions about an individual's financial situation and brings the appropriate form to the screen depending on the answer supplied.) When the job is done, the forms with all the information entered are printed out and sent to the Internal Revenue Service. In some cases, the entire return can be filed electronically (see below). The three-day job has been reduced to perhaps three hours.

How is this possible? Because the electronic forms in the computer are not merely being used for information collection. They are not merely blank forms hooked to a printer. The electronic forms are part of a system built into the software package that does all the calculations, cross-referencing, and checking. No longer, for example, does a person have to calculate the subtotals for each of the individual deduction areas on one form (Schedule A), total the subtotals, and then transfer the total to a line on an entirely different form (Form 1040). Once the data is entered into Schedule A, it is automatically subtotaled, totaled, and transferred – without error!

The one area in which the use of an electronic form does not simplify a process is when an original signature is required. Electronic forms are limited to electronic code signatures or signature facsimiles generated by the computer.

In some cases, there is no eliminating the paper. With the previously mentioned tax return, for example, the Internal Revenue Service requires that persons filing electronically sign and mail a signature card to verify that the forms were filed. In other cases, however, trading partnerships are established and the parties execute written, paper contracts agreeing to the use of certain electronic data interchange methods. Such systems often operate in a high security environment and involve the use of passwords, personal identification numbers, and data encryption.

A familiar example is the Automatic Teller Machine (ATM) at your bank. Before you were able to use it, you and the bank made a written agreement. The bank gave you an access card and a personal identification number (PIN), both of which you agreed to be responsible for. With that agreement in place, you have 24-hour access to your accounts which you access by entering the secure information PIN into the electronic form that is shown on the ATM screen.

Significant benefits, both quantifiable and non-quantifiable, can accrue through the use of electronic forms. For example:

- faster data entry
- more accurate data entry
- less repetitious data entry
- reduction in errors

- faster forms design and revision
- elimination of printing and distribution requirements
- more efficient filing and retrieval
- elimination of 'out of stock' conditions
- assurance that the most recent version is being used.

These benefits, however, will only accrue if the electronic form is used as an information capturing vehicle for a system that will then automatically process that information in some manner. If electronic data entry is merely a substitute for manual data entry, not only will savings not accrue, but the entire information gathering process might well cost more than it did originally.

The forms analysis and design process for electronic forms is essentially the same as it would be for paper forms. The difference is that the electronic forms analyst/designer must have knowledge of automatic data processing systems as well.

13

Directives management

The word 'directives' has been used here to describe policy and procedure statements issued by an organization. They have different titles in different countries, sometimes even within countries. Essentially, what is covered in this chapter are office notices, bulletins, board notices, management statements, circulars, etc., all comprising the policies and procedures of a particular organization. In many offices these are consolidated into a manual or staff handbook, which can itself be described as a directive.

In the absence of written guidance, people will perform an operation in the manner they think is best – or at least the easiest. Few of the methods, if any, will be identical. Some will be efficient and some will be inefficient. With written guidance, the 'approved' way of operating (which hopefully is efficient) is clearly spelled out so that people know exactly what to do and how to do it.

What a person should do is called policy. How it should be done is called procedure. Policies and procedures originate at practically all levels within an organization. What usually happens is that the various entities at each level – and sometimes even within a level – develop their own methods for disseminating policy and procedural information. This way of operating is both the easiest and the hardest. It is easiest on the policy and procedure originators because they can sit in a vacuum and think up instructions and have them printed. It is hardest on the organization as a whole, because inevitably this sort of non-system leads to duplication, conflict, increased workload, and poor decision making.

Policies and procedures are types of directives. Directives guide, instruct, or inform people in an organization about their work. It is important to have procedures documented in directives to achieve consistency of decision making and uniformity of operations. It is also important to have the directives themselves organized in a logical manner so that the people who originate guidance and instructional information have a way of disseminating it, and so that those in the organization who need to refer to the information can easily obtain it.

Because most people within an organization are generally unaware of how to design and operate directives systems, directives management programs are established.

To establish a directives management program an authorizing document is prepared outlining objectives, responsibilities, and authorities for the program, and procedures for operating the directives system.

There are two aspects to a directives management program: establishment and operation of the directives system; directives analysis and control.

DIRECTIVES SYSTEMS

The basic types of directives systems are:

- Single-level – where one system exists for an entire organization and all issuances must conform to one standard;
- Multi-level – where a principal system is established at the highest administrative level and individual systems are allowed at lower levels, but with a standard subject classification scheme.

The single-level system is generally used in a small to medium-sized organization and the multi-level system is most appropriate in a larger organization, especially one that is highly decentralized.

Regardless of the system used, there should be two types of directives: permanent and temporary. Permanent directives have continuing reference value and long-term significance, whereas temporary directives are of a transitory nature. The distinction between permanent and temporary directives is made to reduce the volume of material retained in the overall directives system.

Permanent directives

Permanent, in a directives context, does not have the same meaning as the term permanent in an archival context. Archival permanence means forever. Directives permanence, however, means until specifically canceled or superseded. It is the use of a directive that is the determining factor in deciding on its permanence.

A directive should be issued as permanent if it:

- establishes or changes the organizational structure
- delegates authority or assigns responsibility
- establishes or revises policy
- prescribes a method or procedure
- establishes standards of operation
- revises or cancels other directives
- promulgates a form or report.

Directives containing information to be retained for reference and guidance should be issued as permanent directives, as should handbooks and manuals which are part of the directives system.

Specific names should be given to permanent directives so that they are easily distinguished from the temporary type. Among the most common names used for permanent directives are orders, instructions, and regulations.

Temporary directives

Temporary policies and procedures have no continuing reference value. They are used to establish short-term programs, to test or establish interim procedures, and to make announcements. Temporary directives remain in effect for a fixed period of time, usually not exceeding one year. They are self-canceling in that they are assigned an expiration date when they are issued, and they should be destroyed upon expiration or cancellation. Only in emergencies should a temporary directive be used to modify a permanent directive, and in such cases a revised permanent directive should be issued as soon as possible thereafter.

A variety of names can be used to identify temporary directives. The most widely used terms are notice, bulletin, and circular.

ESTABLISHING A SYSTEM

The development and establishment of a new directives system requires the review and updating of all policies and procedures that have been issued regardless of form. The existing methods of communicating policy and procedure should be evaluated, and any deficiencies remedied.

All organizations should ensure that there are particular staff responsible for the management of directives. These staff should be an operational unit of the records management program. In addition, copies of directives must be placed in files. There are two main types of directives files:

History file. A permanent, continuous record of directives that have been issued by an organization. This file provides an easy reference source to past directives that have been cancelled, revised, or superseded, and can provide the means for tracing the development of a policy or procedure on specific subjects. History files are generally organized by subject classification code. Essential documents to be included in them are the original copy of the directive, each draft version sent out for clearance, significant working papers, the document containing signatures of officials who concurred during the clearance process, notations regarding regulatory source materials, and the signed original of the authorization for cancellation.

Master reference file. A copy of each directive should be filed by subject classification code. When a directive is canceled, it should be marked as such with the cancellation date and cross-reference to the cancellation notice indicated. When a directive or page is revised, the new material should be filed in front of the superseded portion, plainly marked as revised.

Directives indexes

Indexes serve as finding aids for users and help the directives management staff locate all issues in the system. There may be two basic indexes – a numerical index and a subject index.

A numerical index is a list of all current directives arranged by control number, and is often referred to as a checklist or inventory. This index supplies information on the most recent version of each directive and on each revised page or change. The numerical index should be issued periodically and should contain the control number, date, and title of each directive. It may also include the originating office symbol, the distribution code, and the review date.

A subject index contains an alphabetical list of keyword subjects with corresponding control numbers for the directives in which those subjects are discussed. A subject index should be issued as a user finding aid when there is a sizeable amount of related material in the directives system.

Classification

In addition to the general category names (that is, notices, orders, bulletins), directives are more specifically identified by a subject and classification code. The development of a subject classification scheme provides a uniform, systematic method of identifying and locating directives and ensures that all directives on a given subject are in one place. By grouping directives by subject, all existing policies and procedures can be evaluated in order to prevent duplication, conflict, procedural weaknesses, or gaps in coverage. A classification scheme should be:

- *Complete* – containing a category for all existing directives
- *Flexible* – allowing for expansion or reduction of subject areas

- *Logical* – grouped so that the reasons for the arrangement will be obvious
- *Restrictive* – with subject titles mutually exclusive of each other
- *Precise* – so that each subject is clearly identifiable.

The complexities of an organization must be understood before a directives subject classification scheme is proposed. Regulations, organizational changes, functional statements, delegations of authority, and position descriptions are possible sources for gaining knowledge of organizational operations. A detailed analysis of administrative and program files should be completed to identify the subjects on which an organization would be preparing directives. Conceptually, the classification scheme should follow the major functions of the organization.

When the subjects have been identified, a subject classification table should be developed. This hierarchical classification listing divides broad groups of interrelated subjects into primary categories, and subdivides the primary categories into successive levels of subordinate categories as shown in Figure 13.1. Subordinate subjects must logically relate to each appropriate primary subject, and some primary categories will, of necessity, have more subordinate categories than others. In preparing a subject classification table there are a few factors to be considered.

ENERGY POLICY AND EVALUATION
RESOURCE APPLICATIONS

    Petroleum

        Natural gas
        Coal
        Uranium
        Shale

    Power marketing

    Geothermal

ENERGY CONSERVATION
SOLAR APPLICATIONS
CONSTRUCTION AND ENGINEERING

    Construction

    Engineering

    Design criteria

Figure 13.1 Part of subject classification table

Various organizational entities may want separate sections/subdivisions to cover their particular operation, even though their functional responsibilities fit quite well within one primary subject. If a classification scheme is devised according to the wishes of each organization, the results will be an organizational classification scheme, not a subject classification scheme. Splitting primary subjects increases the chance for overlap and conflict.

In a similar vein, an effective subject grouping cannot be achieved if portions of the subject classification table are reserved for the exclusive use of one organizational unit. Each directive must be classified and assigned to the most appropriate subject area. In any directives system the requirements of the user should always be given preference over the convenience of the originator.

Coding

Coding consists of assigning symbols or abbreviations (numbers, letters, alphanumeric combinations) to the subjects listed in the subject classification table. Prime considerations in selecting a codification pattern are concise identification, easy retrieval, expansion, indexing, uniform reference sequence, and control.

There are many patterns for numbering the subjects in the classification table. The most common are numeric, alphabetic, duplex numeric, alphanumeric, subject numeric, and decimal. Examples of these six types are shown in Table 13.1.

Table 13.1
Codification of directives

	Numeric	Alpha	Duplex numeric	Alphanumeric	Subject numeric	Decimal
Personnel	100	A	3	A	PERS	1.
Employment	110	Aa	3–1	A/1	PERS–1	1.1
Recruitment	111	AaA	3–1–1	A/11	PERS–1–1	1.1.1
Appointment	112	AaB	3–1–2	A/12	PERS–1–2	1.1.2
Promotion	113	AaC	3–1–3	A/13	PERS–1–3	1.1.3
Demotion	114	AaD	3–1–4	A/14	PERS–1–4	1.1.4
Separation	115	AaE	3–1–5	A/15	PERS–1–5	1.1.5
Veteran	116	AaF	3–1–6	A/16	PERS–1–6	1.1.6
Special	117	AaG	3–1–7	A/17	PERS–1–7	1.1.7

When coding a classification scheme, a determination should be made about the number of code characters necessary to provide complete coverage and room for expansion. While three characters may adequately cover some arrangements, four characters may be necessary to completely pinpoint identification and allow for future expansion. Using one of the examples in Table 13.1 the secondary subject, Employment, may need to be further broken down into tertiary and quarternary categories as follows:

Personnel	3000 (Primary)
Employment	3100 (Secondary)
Recruitment	3110 (Tertiary)
College program	3111 (Quarternary)
Special program	3112 (Quarternary)

The numbering pattern should provide for specific identification of different directives in the same subject area. Procedural practices may dictate that several directives are required to implement various segments of a particular operation.

Revised directives

A common method for identifying a revised directive (a complete rewrite of an existing directive) is to add an alphabetical suffix to the originally assigned subject classification code. For example, OA-144.1A would indicate the first revision of OA-144.1. The next revision would be indicated as OA-144.1B.

Another method used to identify directives which are periodically revised is the addition of a hyphen or similar mark to the original assigned classification code along with a sequence number. Using this method, the first revision to the original OA-144.1 would be designated as OA-144.1–1 or OA-144.1/1.

Manuals

Some organizations incorporate directives on specific subjects into sets of manuals. In the administrative areas, for example, there may be manuals on such subjects as accounting, office services, and personnel. A different approach would be to combine these functional directives into one manual called the administrative manual. Where directives are collected in a manual arrangement, identification is usually accomplished by manual title and sequential numbering, with each manual assigned the appropriate primary subject classification number for the specific functional area it covers.

Temporary directives

Temporary directives are usually identified by sequential numbers. A common method used is a series of consecutive numbers preceded by the originator's symbol and a reference to the calendar or fiscal year (for example, PER-88–2).

Documentation

A complete outline and explanation of the directives system must be prepared and issued so that users can understand and utilize the system effectively. One possible method is to incorporate the material into the original program document. However, the following information should be included:

1 the complete subject classification table (titles and numbers)
2 a listing of organizational symbols for those entities authorized to originate directives
3 an illustration showing how to completely identify a directive by its code, for example:

OA	. . . .	originator's symbol
2010	. . . .	subject classification number
.2	. . . .	consecutive number
B	. . . .	revision designation
Chg 1	. . . .	change number.

FORMAT AND STANDARDIZATION

The adoption of standards for the format and contents of directives is essential to ensure their economical production and effective use. The most basic question is whether the system will be manual or automated.

Automation technology has provided many options that were formerly unavailable. Although the basic manual system consisting of looseleaf papers filed in three-ring binders is still the most popular format for directives issue, there are now alternative methods such as micropublishing using computer output microfilm (COM), electronic publishing on optical disks (CD-ROM), and complete on-line systems wherein the text of all directives is centrally stored in electronic form and may be instantaneously accessed through remote terminals.

A frequently seen hybrid system is the issue of directives text in hard copy manual format combined with a corresponding automated keyword index. The automated index greatly speeds up the referencing process which is the most time-consuming aspect of directives utilization.

The advantages of automated directives systems are many and varied. Whether the technology utilized is micrographics, computer, optical disk, or a combination, the result can be substantial increases in the timeliness of the information issued (a key factor in any directives system) along with commensurate decreases in document storage space, system maintenance, user reference time, and overall costs.

An automated system must be carefully planned and designed. There is a risk in stating this because the interpretation could be made that a manual system, in contrast, might be thrown together haphazardly. This is not true. All systems require great thought and intensive analysis if they are to function effectively, efficiently, and economically. Yet there are definite differences between automated and manual systems. Because a directives system is organization-wide in scope, if there is the slightest doubt as to whether an organization is ready to automate, in terms of capital investment, user acceptance, managerial support, or a host of other areas, automation should not be undertaken. Any system which is only half-finished or half-used is a mess. And an automated mess is worse than a manual mess.

Regardless of whether the system is automated or manual, a basic format for presenting the information must be developed. All directive material should be organized and arranged in a logical manner to enable the user to locate the desired information quickly. There are a variety of formats which have been developed to present directive material. The most commonly used are the outline format and the playscript format.

Outline format

As its name implies, the outline format arranges information in outline form within an alphabetic and numeric hierarchy. The outline is a highly structured format and is useful where a policy or procedure must be broken down into its component parts with each part individually described.

The outline could be considered the all-purpose format. Policies, procedures, instructions, etc. can all be presented in outline form. It is described in some detail, but one must keep in mind that structure and consistency are key elements of an effective directives system. Whether the system is manual or automated, the manner in which the information is presented is critical. (See Figure 13.2).

A directive page heading should be brief and simple in order to give maximum space for text. The appearance of the heading should be different from the organization's letterhead in order to avoid the possibility of confusing directives with correspondence.

The head of the first page should include the identification items listed and described below. This information enables the users to quickly determine if the directive applies to them.

1   *Issuing point/organization*. Identification of the issuing organization is essential for organizational management purposes, for directive users who may need to contact the originator, and for archival reasons. The name and short address of the issuing organization should be shown in the heading of the first page of a directive. This name should also be shown on each succeeding page.
2   *Directive identifier*. When developing or revising a directive, the originating office must consider all related directives on the subject and should know how and where its directive will fit into the overall system. Originators should be responsible for assigning a subject classification code to each directive issued. This code will:

*   make it easier to locate
*   establish uniformity of sequence
*   provide an automatic grouping of subjects
*   simplify control.

Because directives are filed by subject classification code it is important that the

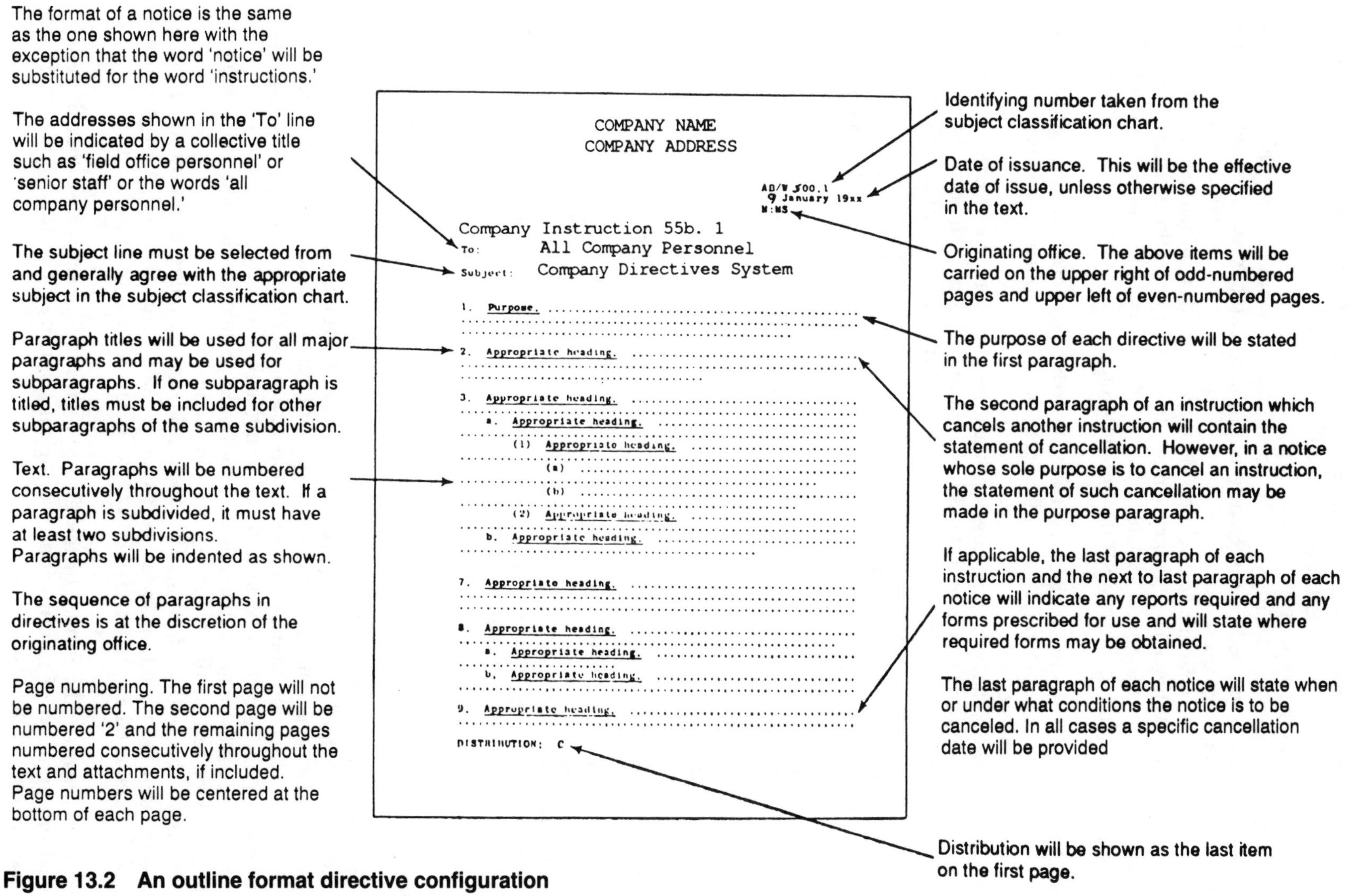
The format of a notice is the same as the one shown here with the exception that the word 'notice' will be substituted for the word 'instructions.'
The addresses shown in the 'To' line will be indicated by a collective title such as 'field office personnel' or 'senior staff' or the words 'all company personnel.'
The subject line must be selected from and generally agree with the appropriate subject in the subject classification chart.
Paragraph titles will be used for all major paragraphs and may be used for subparagraphs. If one subparagraph is titled, titles must be included for other subparagraphs of the same subdivision.
Text. Paragraphs will be numbered consecutively throughout the text. If a paragraph is subdivided, it must have at least two subdivisions.
Paragraphs will be indented as shown.
The sequence of paragraphs in directives is at the discretion of the originating office.
Page numbering. The first page will not be numbered. The second page will be numbered '2' and the remaining pages numbered consecutively throughout the text and attachments, if included.
Page numbers will be centered at the bottom of each page.
COMPANY NAME
COMPANY ADDRESS
AD/W 500.1
9 January 19xx
M:MS
Company Instruction 55b. 1
To: All Company Personnel
Subject: Company Directives System
1. Purpose.
2. Appropriate heading.
3. Appropriate heading.
a. Appropriate heading.
(1) Appropriate heading.
(a)
(b)
(2) Appropriate heading.
b. Appropriate heading.
7. Appropriate heading.
8. Appropriate heading.
a. Appropriate heading.
b. Appropriate heading.
9. Appropriate heading.
DISTRIBUTION: C
Identifying number taken from the subject classification chart.
Date of issuance. This will be the effective date of issue, unless otherwise specified in the text.
Originating office. The above items will be carried on the upper right of odd-numbered pages and upper left of even-numbered pages.
The purpose of each directive will be stated in the first paragraph.
The second paragraph of an instruction which cancels another instruction will contain the statement of cancellation. However, in a notice whose sole purpose is to cancel an instruction, the statement of such cancellation may be made in the purpose paragraph.
If applicable, the last paragraph of each instruction and the next to last paragraph of each notice will indicate any reports required and any forms prescribed for use and will state where required forms may be obtained.
The last paragraph of each notice will state when or under what conditions the notice is to be canceled. In all cases a specific cancellation date will be provided
Distribution will be shown as the last item on the first page.

Figure 13.2 An outline format directive configuration

code appear in the upper corner of each page. On even-numbered (left side) pages the code should be in the upper left corner. On odd-numbered (right side) pages, the code should appear in the upper right corner.

3 *Originating office code*. Identifying the specific office within an organization that originates policy or procedure can greatly assist the researcher. A code, abbreviation or short name may be used.

4 *Date of approval or effective date*. Unless otherwise stated, a directive is effective on its approval date. When it is necessary to make the provisions of the directive effective on a date other than the approval date, a paragraph headed 'Effective date' should be included. When dating directives, take into account the time needed for printing and distribution.

5 *Subject line*. Each directive is given a subject line to briefly identify the area addressed. The subject identified should generally agree with the appropriate subject in the classification scheme.

6 *Distribution code*. The office that develops the directive should know exactly who will carry out the required action and should, therefore, determine the distribution. The distribution code is usually placed at the bottom of the first page of the directive.

7 *Subsequent page identification*. Not all identifying items included on the first page of a directive are needed on subsequent pages. It is usually sufficient to include only the name of the issuing organization, the subject classification code and the date of the directive.

8 *Approval or signature block*. Each directive must be approved or signed by an authorizing official. The most common area for indicating this approval is on the first page.

Playscript format

The playscript format is entirely different from the outline format. It is modeled like the script of a play with the names of the characters (responsible persons) on the left side of the page and the corresponding lines (actions) listed down the right side of the page. The format is simple to write and easy to use because it goes through an entire operation from beginning to end. It is very useful for detailing procedures. The disadvantages of a playscript format is that it is not hierarchical and does not break down a function into routines and subroutines as would an outline format.

Organization of directives

The basic unit of text in a directive is the paragraph. All paragraphs require a number or letter designation. Each main paragraph should have a brief description heading to assist the reader in identifying the subject matter. Subparagraphs should be used to divide long paragraphs or to list conditions, exceptions, or procedures. Headings may also be used for subparagraphs, and they may be underlined to highlight the text.

Lengthy directives such as manuals or handbooks should be divided into chapters. Chapters may be further divided into parts and sections.

When using the outline format, the basic rule for outlining is followed. That is, whenever a unit is divided, at least two subunits must be established. Paragraphs are alternately numbered and lettered at each level of subordination.

Paragraph sequence. The format of the directive must be prescribed so that there is a standard presentation of information in a logical sequence. The following paragraph headings are commonly used:

- Purpose (should be stated in the first paragraph)

- Scope/applicability
- Cancellation (other directives, related forms and reports)
- Authority/background
- References (other directives or documents)
- Policy
- Objectives
- Definitions
- Responsibilities
- Substance paragraphs
    Information
    Instructions
    Procedures
- Effective date (if other than approval date)
- Forms prescribed
- Reports required
- Expiration date (for temporary directives).

Margins/indentations. The margins and indentations for each page should be established to provide maximum readability. These format specifications may be quite different depending on whether the system is manual or automated.

Page numbering. The first page of a directive should not be numbered. The second page (left-hand page) should be numbered '2,' and the remaining pages numbered consecutively. All left-hand pages should contain even numbers and all right-hand pages should contain odd numbers. If chapters are used, pages should be numbered consecutively within each chapter. Numbers should be centered at the bottom of each page so that they will not be confused with the identifying subject classification code. Directives material is usually referenced by paragraph number rather than by page number. Page numbers are primarily used for inserting revised pages or removing obsolete ones.

Supplementary materials. Materials such as appendices, attachments, and exhibits should be placed at the end of the chapter to which they relate or at the end of the directive, whichever will be most convenient to the user. Each page of the supplementary material should be identified clearly showing the subject title, classification number, and issue date.

Figures. Figure numbers may be used to identify illustrations, charts, and tables placed within the text of a directive. If figures are small (one page or less) place them as close as possible to the paragraph to which they relate or where they were first mentioned. Place longer illustrative materials at the end of the appropriate chapter. All figures should be captioned and numbered consecutively.

References. These are used when the material being referenced relates directly to the subject-matter, makes a significant contribution to understanding the text, or eliminates the need for repeating lengthy material. Although references can be useful, they should be used sparingly. When first cited, the complete designated title and identification number should be included, and the reader should be told why the referenced information is needed.

Transmittal sheets. Transmittal sheets may be used to forward directives to users. Directives can be self-transmitting, however, by supplying the pertinent information on the first page. Directives having fewer than five pages are usually issued without a transmittal sheet. The transmittal sheet is used to give a summary of the contents of a directive or to outline the changes that have occurred in a revision. It can also be used as a canceling device, to cancel directives, forms, or reports.

Revisions. The process for making revisions should be standardized to prevent confusion. Revisions and changes should be given exactly the same distribution as the directives they amend. If extensive changes are required, the entire directive may be revised and reissued. If only minor changes are necessary, issuing a few revised pages may suffice.

Revised pages should carry the change number and the revision date. This information should be placed at the top of the page near the subject classification number. Time may be saved by the users in comparing an old directive page with a new one if a distinguishing mark is placed in the margin opposite the changed portion of the text, or at the beginning and end of the changed sections.

If an additional page is needed to incorporate a revision to the body of a directive, the page numbering scheme may be adjusted by adding a letter to the applicable page number (for example, 14, 14a, 14b). At such time as the directive is completely revised or reissued, however, the pages should be renumbered consecutively to conform to the original pattern.

Often, minor typographical errors can be corrected by instructing the directives' recipients to make pen and ink changes to the printed text. Substantive changes, however, should not be made in this manner.

Supplements. Supplements to directives are often allowed in order to enhance managerial flexibility by enabling managers to issue specific instructions on procedures or to interpret policies for their particular organization entities. Such guidance usually applies only to a specific area within the organization and should only be issued within that area. All supplemental issuances should be numbered with the same subject classification code as the basic directive, and should complement the basic directive, not conflict with it.

REPRODUCTION, DISTRIBUTION AND STOCK

The most comprehensive and well-organized directives are of little value if they are not available to the persons who need to use them. Therefore, reproduction and distribution of the directives material is considered to be an integral part of the directives management system.

Reproduction

The method of reproduction will depend on the type of directives system which is being used. For the common looseleaf manual type of system, original, camera-ready copy must be prepared for printing. Many organizations use specially designed format sheets, preprinted with non-photographic blue ink, for preparing reproducible directive material.

Although it is not uncommon to find the original copy is prepared by the directives management staff, this is not necessarily the most efficient way of operating. As long as the material is prepared using consistent formats and type styles, it can be prepared satisfactorily by the originating office.

When an automated system is involved, the situation is somewhat different. In order to maintain control and guard against errors, directives text should only be entered into the system by the directives management staff. This is not to say that the material could not be typed by another unit and electronically transmitted to the directives staff, or that a floppy disk could not be transferred to achieve the same purpose. If the organization has a sizeable directives system, but without organization-wide automation, there is also the possibility of having directives material keyboarded on standard electric typewriters and optically scanned into an automated directives system by the directives management staff.

Once the information has been entered into the system, it can be electronically photocomposed and prepared for printing; it can be output in a microform through use of a COM system; it can be 'electronically published' on CD-ROM; or it can be stored for electronic access by users through remote terminals.

Distribution

A good directives system provides timely distribution of the required number of copies of directives on a 'need to know' and 'need to use' basis. In establishing or revising a distribution system, the following principles should be considered:

- Distribute selectively – send directives only to those who require them.
- Distribute directly – send directives directly to the organization level that uses them rather than through 'official channels.'
- Distribute consistently – send revised directives or notices of cancellation to the same organizations that received the originals.
- Distribute to titles – distribution lists that use organization or position titles are easier to keep current and are less subject to change than those using individual's names.

A directives distribution system is usually based on the structure of the organization. This framework is familiar to most employees within the organization and the hierarchical terminology used (that is, office, division, branch, section, unit) remains fairly constant over time. Further refinements of distribution patterns could be made based on factors such as geographical locations, functions, employee titles, or combinations of the above.

Even with a manual directives system, the distribution function is one that can probably be automated. Mail (distribution) lists seem to naturally lend themselves to computer applications. A microcomputer with basic, commercially available file management software can handle most smaller distribution systems, and many larger, more complex systems can be handled by using commercially available database management software programs. It is more than likely that the productivity increase and resultant cost savings from automating the directives distribution function alone would be sufficient to justify the purchase of both the hardware and the software necessary, and the equipment would then be available for automating other functions as well.

The orderly operation of a distribution system requires a uniform way of requesting changes in distribution lists. The method of requesting and approving changes and a description of the operation of the system should be documented in the basic directive and made available to users and originators.

Stocking directives

With a manual directives system, additional copies must be available for users. The number and location of the stocking points will vary with the size of the organization. Generally, extra copies to be stocked should be a part of the initial reproduction order, although stocking reproducible masters may be more convenient and economical in some instances. The cost of stocking reproducible masters should be compared with that of stocking extra copies. The availability of reproduction equipment, the length of time required to reproduce extra copies, and the possible savings in space and personnel costs should also be considered.

Where central stocking occurs, the initial stocking levels may be recommended by the directives originators. Replenishment of the stock would be determined by the stocking unit and by the directives management staff based on requisition experience, frequency of revision, cost, and the time needed to print additional copies.

DIRECTIVES ANALYSIS AND CONTROL

The directives analysis and control process includes analysis of the directive's content, editorial assistance for directives originators, coordination of proposed new or revised directives with various organizational entities, assignment of control numbers, and maintenance of the entire directives system.

Directives analysis

A proposed new or revised directive should be analyzed by the directives management staff for timeliness, readability, format consistency, and accuracy. While most of these factors are self-explanatory, the accuracy factor requires some explanation.

The responsibility for writing a directive belongs to the directives originator. Therefore, the responsibility for the accuracy of a directive belongs to the originator as well. The directives management staff can review the directive's content to determine if forms or reports referenced are still current, if organizational references are up to date, and if there is a conflict between the proposed material and that contained in a directive already in existence on a related subject. It is unrealistic, however, to expect the directives management staff to know every procedure for every system in the entire organization. The accuracy review, therefore, is done for much the same reason as the editorial review – to assist the originator, not to do his/her work.

Editorial assistance

To ensure that all organizational directives can be understood by those who must use them, the directives management staff should provide editorial assistance to originators as required. Often directives originators know exactly what they want to say, but have a great deal of difficulty in determining exactly how to say it. Help from persons who are skilled in the art of simple writing is usually welcomed.

Coordination

Each proposed new or revised directive should be cleared with all organizational entities that will be affected by it or that have a functional interest in its content. Insufficient clearances may result in inadequate directives which have to be prematurely revised and reissued. When the proposed directive prescribes forms and/or imposes reporting requirements, coordination with the units managing those functions should be included in the clearance process.

To facilitate the clearance process, a directive clearance form such as that shown in Figure 13.3 may be used to obtain concurrence or comments from the reviewers. The directives management staff should forward the draft directive and the clearance form together to each reviewing office. Routing copies to several clearance offices simultaneously speeds up the clearance process while allowing more time for thorough review and analysis. A reasonable deadline for the completion of each review should be provided.

After receipt of the reviewing offices' comments and concurrences, the directives management staff and the originator should jointly consider the comments and determine their impact on the proposed directive. Where the comments or recommendations will improve the directive, changes reflecting these comments should be made. Where they are not considered essential for improving the directive, an explanation should be given to the office(s) concerned. If differences between the originator and the reviewers persist,

DIRECTIVE CLEARANCE RECORD	Kind of document	Identification (if any)

Subject	Person most familiar with attached		
	Name	Routing symbol	Extension

Reason for attached: what does it do? (Continue on reverse)

Proposed distribution (Spell out – do not use code)

ORIGINATING OFFICE CLEARANCE

Routing symbol	Init	Routing symbol	Date	Signature and routing symbol	Date	Office forms approval	Office reports approval

CLEARANCE ROUTING

Deadline date

Routing symbol	Internal clearance			Signature and routing symbol	Date	Concur substance and distribution		Non-concur	Comment accepted
	Init	Routing symbol	Date			No comment	Comment attached	Comment attached	Changes made
	Final administrative clearance								
	Final approval (authorizing release)				Date approved				

After approval send to:

Figure 13.3   A directive clearance form

the problem should be taken to the next higher authority for resolution. Directives should ordinarily not be transmitted for final signatory review without reconciliation of the comments. If the differences cannot be reconciled at the program level, the directive should be forwarded to the approving official with a written staff analysis outlining the nature of the dispute.

Control numbers/issue dates

Assignment of a directives control number that is consistent with the subject classification scheme should be done after all clearances have been obtained. The official date of issue should be assigned with the control number.

14

Reports management

Organizations are usually in existence for specific purposes. The way organizations accomplish their purposes is by dividing the necessary work among various departments or sections and by establishing a corresponding managerial hierarchy to run those organizational entities. The managers of the different departments have goals and objectives to meet to help the organization achieve its overall purpose, and they are given a variety of resources (people, facilities, equipment, etc.) to use in order to meet them.

One of the primary tools managers use to manage their resources is the report. Reports are used to convey information. In order for the information to be useful, it must go to the right person at the right time. In order for information to be economical, the cost of obtaining, formatting, and transmitting it should be less than the value received from its use.

Although this chapter is called Reports Management, we are really dealing with the management of reporting systems. No report exists in a vacuum. Even the most basic report, consisting of a single sheet of paper containing only a few items of information, is part of a system which has been developed to help someone obtain, process, and use that information for a specific purpose. If the same information were transmitted electronically, using electronic mail or networked computers with visual display screens instead of typewriters and paper, that arrangement would be neither more nor less of a reporting system. It would merely be an automated system as opposed to a manual one.

All reporting systems cost money. Because of this, and because managers who want information are not always cognizant of the most efficient and effective method of obtaining it, reports management programs are established.

The goal of a reports management program is to improve the quality and economy of reporting systems on an organization-wide basis. Specific objectives of a program include:

- identification of the information needs of managers at all levels
- collection, transmission, processing, and storage of information through the most economic use of personnel, funds, and equipment
- prevention, and/or elimination of invalid, inefficient, or unnecessary reporting
- coordination of reports management with other records management functions
- evaluation of reports and reporting systems on a continuous basis to ensure economy, efficiency, and effectiveness
- reduction of reporting costs.

There are two aspects of reports management: reports control, and reports analysis and design. Both are of equal importance. While the system improvements and resultant cost savings primarily come from the analysis and design functions, as a practical matter, when the control function is inoperative, the analysis and design work rarely gets done. An effective program is one in which all functions are being performed.

REPORTS INVENTORY

Prepared by:
Name:
Organization:
Tel:

Date:

Instructions

Submit an original and one copy for each report required or prepared by your office. All offices complete Section A. Complete Section B if report is required by your office. Complete Section C if report is prepared by your office. Attach sample copy of report and send to the reports management office

Section A – Identification Data

1 Report title	2 Report control symbol or number (if any)	3 Form no. or format (e.g. memo, tabulation narrative, etc.)
4 Requiring directive or instructions	5 Frequency (monthly, quarterly, etc.)	6 Due date
		7 Expiration date

Section B – Requiring Office Data

1 Purpose and use of report (identify other reports for which this report is used as a feeder report)

2 Offices required to submit report		3 Sources of information used by preparing offices to complete report (form no., report, file, etc.)	4 No. of copies required
Type	Number		5 Distribution

6 Date report originated	7 No. of revisions since origination	8 Date of last revision

9 Estimated cost of developing report	10 Estimated annual cost of using report

11 Current appraisal

		yes	no			yes	no			yes	no
Need	a Is this report still needed?			**Data Instructions**	h Is data best for the purpose?			**Possible improvements**	o Combining with others?		
	b Is every item still needed?				i Is comparative data needed?				p Making easier to complete?		
	c Is the report needed as often?				j Is report clear and easy to use?				q Using a form if not used?		
	d Is every copy still needed?				k Are there written instructions?				r Stopping negative reports?		
	e Is there another source?				l Are they clear, concise, complete, current?				s Using summary?		
Value	f Is it worth its probable cost?				m Are they issued in a formal directive?				t Using sampling?		
Date	g Does the due date give enough time?				n Are illustrations needed?				u Reporting by exception?		
									v Changing source?		
									w Changing sequence?		

Section C – Preparing Office Data

1 Sources of information for completing report	2 No. of copies prepared	3 Distribution (original and copies)
4 Estimated annual cost to prepare report	5 Estimated annual cost for collecting and maintaining information needed for report	

Figure 14.1 A reports inventory form

REPORTS CONTROL

As with all records management programs, reports management should have an authorizing directive which spells out the various authorities and responsibilities, and also clearly outlines the procedure to be followed when establishing a new reporting requirement or revising an existing one. This control mechanism ensures that no reporting requirements will get promulgated in an organization without first having been reviewed and approved. An effective way to ensure that no unauthorized reports exist is to establish the policy that a reporting requirement which has not been approved does not have to be responded to.

Another reason for the control mechanism is for periodic review. Although a report is static, the organization in which it exists is dynamic. Therefore, changing goals, objectives, and even organizational structures can reduce the need for and value of information which was once considered important. It does not necessarily follow that when a need for information is diminished, the requirement for supplying it is proportionately curtailed. Generally nothing is done about such a requirement unless a specific challenge to it is raised. The periodic review provides an automatic challenge mechanism.

At the time a report is evaluated and approved it should be assigned an expiration date. Some time (perhaps 60–90 days) prior to that expiration date the report should again be evaluated to ensure that the requirement is still valid. If it is valid, the report may be renewed. If not, action should be taken to correct the problem or the requirement may be allowed to expire on schedule.

Several tools can make the reports control job easier: an inventory (or catalog); a history (or case) file; a functional (or analysis) file; and reports control symbols.

Inventory

To establish the inventory, a form such as the one shown in Figure 14.1 may be used. The form should be distributed to all organizational units with an explanation of its purpose and with instructions for its completion and submission. A copy of each report, the prescribing directive (or a reference to the directive), and any associated forms should also be requested for use in the history file. All organizational units requiring a report from other offices, and all offices preparing a report should complete the appropriate parts of the form and submit the requested materials.

This second factor is quite significant. Although it is somewhat duplicative to have respondents as well as requirers complete the inventory forms, the effort, for the initial inventory, will ultimately prove to be worthwhile. Inevitably, the information received from the two sources will not match. The discrepancies can alert the reports management staff to problems regarding those particular systems.

Once the information is obtained, a temporary inventory listing of all reporting requirements should be created. The listing should include the:

- title
- control symbol
- associated form numbers
- frequency
- due dates
- requiring directive
- requiring organization
- respondent organization
- expiration date
- cost.

When all the reports have been analyzed, those that remain should be listed in a final inventory which should be selectively distributed throughout the organization. For ease of use, the final inventory should be organized alphabetically by report title and also cross-indexed numerically by report control symbol.

History files

The history file should contain complete, historical documentation on each report, including:

- the original reports request approval
- associated forms and instructions for completion
- correspondence, worksheets, and other documents relating to the report
- a reference to, or a copy of, the prescribing directive
- a reference to feeder reports, if any.

A file should be created for each report when it is established and for existing reports identified in an inventory. History files may be arranged alphabetically by the report title, or numerically by the report control symbol.

Functional files

Functional files (which are really subject classification files) are used for comparing reports on the same subject or functional area, for identifying duplicate reporting requirements, and for eliminating unnecessary reports. Functional files assist analysts in understanding relationships between reports and reporting systems and in streamlining systems and procedures. The files contain report request approval forms or inventory forms and are organized by broad functional categories (personnel, budget, procurement). If the volume warrants it, functional files may be subdivided by subordinate subject headings.

For larger systems, a functional file may be automated by establishing an integrated subject classification database which can then be used to identify reports in the same functional category along with associated directives, forms, and files.

Reports control symbols

A reports control symbol is a coded series of numbers and/or letters assigned to an approved report and which is usually printed on the report form or, at a minimum, contained within the prescribing directive. The symbol serves two major purposes: it indicates to respondents that the report is authorized, and it may also be used as a unique identifier.

The extent to which a reports control symbol is used as an identifier depends on how the coding system is structured. For example, the control symbol 63-PER-Q might indicate that the report was the sixty-third authorized report in the control system; that the personnel department was the requiring office; and that the response was due quarterly. A symbol such as the one just described could be used with an automated database functional file.

The expiration date of the report may be incorporated into the control symbol if desired. In fact, almost any type of identifying information might be included. It does not matter how lengthy a control symbol becomes as long as those using it can understand the coding.

REQUEST FOR CLEARANCE AND EVALUATION OF REPORTING REQUIREMENT

1 Submit to	2 Report (*check applicable boxes*)
	Action ☐ New ☐ Revise ☐ Exempt ☐ Cancel ☐ Continue

INSTRUCTIONS Complete and submit an original and two copies of this form to request the clearance and evaluation of all new or revised reporting requirements that are subject to the reports management program. Attach a supporting statement that fully justifies the need for the requested information, a listing of responding offices, copies of worksheets used in costing the report, a sample of the report form or format, copies of the prescribing directive or instructions that would be available to respondents, and copies of the cost/benefit evaluation. This form will be used for the annual review of reports.

3 Office symbol of the originator/user	4A Person to be contacted for information	4B Corres. symbol	4C Telephone no.
5A Title of report		5B Current approval no.	

6 Frequency of submission of report (*check*)

Annually	Quarterly	Weekly	On occasion	Other (*specify*)
Semi-annual	Monthly	Daily	Contingent	

7 List canceled or modified reports or forms

A Title	B Report approval no

8 Summary of estimated reporting workload

A Number of respondents	
B Number of times this report submitted annually by each respondent	
C Total number of reports submitted annually (*A X B*)	

9 Summary of estimated reporting costs (*attach worksheets used in cost report*)

Description (a)	Development costs (b)	Annual operational costs (c)	Annual user (d)
A Requiring office	£		£
B Responding agencies/offices	£	£	
C Totals	£	£	£

10 Name and title of requesting office approving official

11A Signature of approving official	11B Date	12A Signature of reports control officer	12B Date

Below for use of clearance and evaluation office

13 Clearance and evaluation results

☐ Approved (*see below*) ☐ Recommend disapproval (*see attached*) ☐ Exempted (*see attached*) ☐ Canceled (*see attached*)

14 Assigned report title	15 Assigned report approval no
	16 Expiration of approval (*date*)

17A Signature of approving official	17B Date

Figure 14.2   A request for clearance and evaluation of reporting requirement form

Reports control process

The procedures for establishing new reporting requirements or revising existing ones should be part of the overall reports management directive. Basically, the control process operates as follows.

Whenever a report is initiated or revised, a report approval form, such as the request for clearance and evaluation of reporting requirement, shown in Figure 14.2, should be completed and submitted to the reports management staff. The form should provide a description of the proposed report and a justification for its creation, including its estimated costs and expected benefits. Associated documents, such as the requiring directive, additional forms, and a copy of the proposed report format should accompany the request. The reports management staff should provide any necessary assistance to the report initiator in completing the form and in obtaining the required information.

Having received the request, the reports management staff should coordinate with other organizational units having an interest in the information being requested and with those that will be required to respond. The proposed report should be reviewed by the reports management staff for adequacy, necessity, usefulness, and economy (see analysis and design section following), and should be approved only if:

- a valid need exists for the information required by the proposed report
- the information requested is limited to items needed to satisfy the report's purpose
- the information is not available elsewhere through an already existing reporting system
- the value of the information exceeds the cost of obtaining it
- the reporting frequency is consistent with the time by which the information is needed
- clear and complete instructions for reporting have been developed and are contained in the prescribing directive.

Assuming that the reporting requirement meets *all* of the criteria for approval, it should then be assigned an expiration date and a reports control symbol and entered into the inventory. This is the entire control process until there is a request for modification or the periodic review takes place.

REPORTS ANALYSIS AND DESIGN

Proper analysis and design of reporting systems are basic functional requirements for effective reports management programs. Unfortunately, these functions are often only given lip-service or are overlooked entirely in many organizations. Without the critical analysis and design functions, a reports management program manages nothing. The control function in such a deficient program is diminished because it, of necessity, becomes a 'rubber stamp' authorizing process, and the reports management staff personnel are little more than number assignment clerks.

Adequate reports analysis and design requires a significant investment of resources. This investment, however, is paid back substantially through the development of improved and more economical reporting systems. The methodology which may be used to achieve that payback has already been outlined in Chapters 6 and 7. The following additional information, however, is specifically oriented to analyzing reporting systems.

Needs assessment

The first step in the development of a report or a reporting system is to assess information needs. There are two ways of approaching this task. One is to determine the information needs on an organization-wide basis by identifying the needs at each level of the organization from the top down. The objective is to develop an overall understanding of the organization's information needs and to construct a set of interrelated systems to meet those needs. This approach is basic for the creation of an overall information management system. Although talked about a great deal, such systems are usually not established because of the time and effort involved in their development.

Another way to assess information needs is to focus on the requirements of individual managers and to develop systems to meet those requirements. Simultaneously, the possibilities for integrating those systems with other organizational systems are considered. When comprehensive systems design and integration is done at all, this second approach is usually the one taken.

Assessing information needs requires the involvement of persons possessing several different skills, including:

- reports management analysts to coordinate the collection, analysis and synthesis of data into specific information requirements for affected organizational units
- program managers and specialists to provide firsthand knowledge of the information needs and operations of their programs
- senior managers to formulate policies
- automated data processing specialists to provide the necessary expertise in the formulation of, and possible integration of, automated systems and processes.

In assessing information needs, certain sources should also be reviewed to determine information requirements that are imposed by law or directive. These sources consist of legislation, regulations, orders and directives. Additionally, survey and audit reports should be examined to ascertain if information management problems have been previously identified.

Individual reports analysis

Each prospective report in a reporting system should be subjected to a comprehensive analysis. The analysis should ensure that each requirement:

- is necessary, meaningful, and useful
- does not duplicate other reports
- is designed to obtain information from the best source and in the simplest manner
- has a frequency consistent with the time when the information is needed
- is cost-effective.

There is a myriad of questions to be asked when analyzing a report or a reporting system. While some information should be available from reports history and functional files, most information for a new requirement will have to be obtained from the persons who require, prepare, process and use the particular report being reviewed. The facilitate the review process, a reports evaluation checklist, as shown in Figure 14.3, has been developed. The checklist is a summarization of the following 144 questions which must be answered for a complete reports review.

The report as a whole

- What information does the report provide?
- What is the stated purpose of the report?
- Who required the report?
- Who established the report?
- How is the report used? Is it used to take specific action, or to make plans and decisions?

REPORTS EVALUATION CHECKLIST			
Report title			Review date
Section 1 – Need			
Instructions. (Check either column (b) or (c). If questionable, show changes in column (d)) (a)	Questionable (b)	Satisfactory (c)	Proposed changes (attach additional sheets, if needed) (d)
1 The report as a whole: Who uses it? How? What is its purpose? Should it be continued?			
2 Use of each item: Is every item used? Any missing items to be added?			
3 Use of each copy: Are all copies used to good advantage?			
4 Functional relationship: Is the information within the scope of the office functions?			
5 Misapplication: Does the report try to solve a problem which should be solved by other means?			
6 Stand-by data: Is the data obtained for 'just in case' use?			
7 Sources: Is the data available in another report or office?			
8 By products: Is it possible to get the data by some other process?			
9 Direct use of records: Could actual records or 'last copy' of record be used instead of a report?			
10 Sampling: Would a sampling of a few offices give reliable data?			
11 Exception reporting: Would it be appropriate to report conditions only when other than normal?			
12 Combination: Could the report be combined with another report?			
13 Non-related material: Are non-related subjects included in the same report?			
14 Adequacy and suitability: Is scope or content tailored to meet needs?			
15 Value versus cost: Is the report worth its cost?			
Section 2 – Timing			
16 Reporting periods: Are reporting periods properly stated?			
17 Frequency: Is the present frequency suitable, excessive or inadequate?			
18 Due date: Is the due date specifically stated?			
19 Preparing office workload: Has this been considered? Can due dates be changed to avoid peak workloads?			

Figure 14.3   A reports evaluation checklist

REPORTS EVALUATION CHECKLIST (page 2)			
Report title			Review date
Section 3 – Style			
Instructions. (Check either column (b) or (c). If questionable, show changes in column (d)) (a)	Questionable (b)	Satisfactory (c)	Proposed changes (attach additional sheets, if needed) (d)
20 Report title: Is it the same as, or listed in the directive?			
21 Purpose of report: Is it clearly stated?			
22 Reporting instructions: Are reporting instructions clear and adequate?			
23 Integrated reporting: Are data needs of other levels included?			
24 Feeder reports: Are procedures for feeder reports provided to assure uniformity and simplicity?			
25 Reporting units: Are reporting units shown? Are there too many, too few?			
26 Negative reports: Are negative reports required? What use is made of them?			
27 Number of copies: Are number of copies specified?			
28 Routing: Are correct mailing addresses given?			
29 Format: Is the best format for this report used?			
30 Arrangement and size: Are items sequenced according to user need? Is spacing adequate? Are item captions clear? Is size adequate and practical?			
31 Standardization: Do all offices use the same forms or format?			
32 Summary information: Would a summary of information rather than statistics or a narrative be better?			
33 Cumulative data: Can data be maintained on a cumulative basis to eliminate last minute workloads?			
34 Comparisons: Are comparisons made against goals, past performance or current performance of others?			
35 Graphics: Are graphics used to good advantage?			
36 Authentication: Are verifying or approving officials' signatures used only when necessary?			
37 Data sources: Are records from which reports are to be prepared identified?			
38 Arrangement of records: Should records be rearranged to simplify reporting?			
39 Report symbol: Is it shown after title of report?			
40 Style of presentation: Does the overall report provide clarity and simplicity?			

Figure 14.3 (cont.)

- What specific plans and decisions are based on the report?
- What would happen if the report was discontinued?
- Would a program function be impossible to perform or severely hampered without the report?

Use of each item

- Are all the items used?
- How is each item of information used?
- Does each item fill a specific information need?
- Do any items fall into the 'nice-to-know' category?
- Are all items consistently reported by all preparing offices?
- Is the information being reported valid?

Use of each copy

- How many copies of the report are prepared?
- What is the distribution of the report?
- Which copies are actually used (action copies)?
- Which copies are information copies, and are they necessary?
- Should any recipient be removed from the distribution?
- Would broader distribution eliminate the need for other or summary reports?
- How is distribution accomplished? Is it adequate for the distribution volume?
- When was the last time the accuracy of the distribution list was checked?

Functional relationship

- Is the report within the scope of the recipient's functions?
- Have the recipient's interests or responsibilities change?
- Have other offices acquired related functions or responsibilities?

Misapplication

- Is the report a substitute for taking action to improve a situation?
- Does the report attempt to solve problems that actually require administrative or other action? (It is possible that direct or better supervision would considerably improve a situation.)
- Is the real purpose of the report to create delay in the hope that a problem will solve itself?

Standby data

- Is data obtained just for standby or 'just-in-case' use?
- How often has it been used?
- Was the need critical at the time?
- Was the information up to date?
- Did it answer all the questions or was additional information required?
- Is it worth the cost to prepare and maintain this information just in case the need arises?
- Would a one-off situation report serve the purpose?

Sources

- Is another source of information available that will satisfy the reporting requirement?

- Is it possible to obtain the information from other available reports or records?
- If another office has the information available in a different form or format (for example, computer printout), can it be used or modified to provide acceptable information?

By-products of other activities

- Will the need for a report be eliminated by using by-products of existing operations?
- Can routine office procedures at the source of needed information be modified to provide by-product data during the normal work process?
- Can information be extracted from existing systems, procedures, or products by modifying existing forms, recordkeeping, or accounting systems?
- Can existing operating procedures be modified to meet information needs without requiring a new report?

Direct use of records

- If the information is obtained from a record or form, could it (or a copy) be used directly instead of creating a separate report?
- Could records photographed or otherwise copied quickly at the source be used instead of a new report?

Sampling

- Is complete coverage essential rather than a scientific sample?
- Would a sample of offices or persons provide sufficient data?
- If sampling is used, are the present respondents representative enough to provide accurate data when projected to the whole?

Exception reporting

- Is exception reporting feasible? (Can reports be made only when conditions are other than normal?)
- If exception reporting is being used, are instructions on timing and procedures well defined?

Combination

- Are there possibilities for combining the report with other records? (Use a recurring data analysis chart to identify duplicative information.)

Non-related material

- Does the report contain items of information unrelated to the primary purpose of the report?
- Can this information be included in other related reports or a separate report? (In contemplating changes, consider the effects on work patterns at the source of the information.)

Adequacy and suitability

- Is the scope or content of the report too broad or too narrow for its intended purpose?
- Does the data match the specific needs of the using offices?

Value versus cost

- Has a cost/benefit analysis been performed on the report?
- What are the developmental, operational, and user costs?
- Has the value been quantified?
- Does the cost exceed the value?
- Can the data be obtained in a less costly manner?

Reporting periods

- How long is the information needed?
- Indefinitely or only for a few weeks or months?
- Has the report been assigned an expiration date consistent with this need?
- Are reporting periods, such as work-days as opposed to calendar-days, properly stated in the instructions?

Frequency

- Is the frequency (monthly, quarterly, annually, etc.) of the report prescribed in the requiring directive?
- Does the directive state when the first report is due?
- Does the frequency fit the users' needs?
- Is it possible to lower the frequency without hurting operations? (The lower the frequency, the more economical the report.)

Due date

- Does the requiring directive indicate the date when the report should be received at its destination?
- Are the most distant preparing offices and the method of transmittal taken into account when assigning due dates?

Preparing office workload

- Has the workload of preparing offices been taken into consideration?
- Is there adequate preparation time?
- Are deadlines realistic?
- Have the heaviest workload periods, such as the end of months or quarters, been avoided wherever possible?

Report title

- Is the title brief and descriptive?
- If the directive concerns only the report, is the title of the report similar to the subject of the directive?

Purpose of report

- Is the purpose of the report clearly stated in the requiring directive?
- Is it clear to preparing offices what use should be made of the data?

Reporting instructions

- Are the reporting instructions sufficiently detailed and clear so they can be readily understood?

- Is a completed sample report included to clarify complex reporting?
- Do the instructions provide for uniformity of reporting?
- Do the instructions provide a clear picture of who is to report what, when, how, to whom and why?
- Is the directive organized so that it can be conveniently used by all those involved with the report?

Integrated reporting

- Where more than one organizational level uses the reported information, have the needs of all levels been tied into the reporting system?
- Is the pyramid principle applied? Is the information less detailed as it goes up the organizational ladder?
- Do the reporting instructions include specific data requirements for each organizational level?

Feeder reports

- Is the report a feeder report – does it provide information to be included in another report?
- What is the extent of feeder reporting?
- Would it be feasible to bypass intermediate feeder reports and furnish lower level data to the requiring office?
- Would additional feeder reports improve operations and the quality of information?

Reporting units

- Are specific offices required to prepare the report identified in the reporting directive?
- Are these offices in the best position to furnish the information?
- Are there more or fewer reporting units than needed?
- Is the existing number of reporting units sufficient for data comparison?

Negative report

- Is this a negative report?
- What use is made of it?
- Is it necessary?
- Is the requiring directive specific about the necessity of submitting negative reports?
- Where negative reports are required, what percentage of the total reports do they represent?
- Are the reporting units continually submitting negative reports?
- Can exception reporting be substituted?

Number of copies

- Is the number of copies to be prepared and distributed specified in the requiring directive?

Routing

- Does the requiring directive contain the correct address of each recipient?
- Can the report be transmitted without a covering transmittal letter or memorandum?
- Is the method for distributing the report adequate?

- Is a copy of the report sent to everyone who needs and uses the information?
- Has the accuracy of the distribution list been verified in the last year?
- Have those who do not use the information been removed from the distribution list?

Format

- Is the format of the report prescribed in the requiring directive?
- Is the format suitable for the way the report is used?
- Is the report easy to prepare?
- If the report were changed to a form, would it lose its effectiveness?
- Do users have to search through the text to find the information they need?
- Does the report contain information which is repeated in successive reports? Could a code word, symbol, or number be substituted for this information?
- After identifying possibilities for converting narrative reports to forms, have the forms management staff been consulted?
- If a form is prescribed, has it been cleared with the forms management staff?

Arrangement and size

- Has the reporting form been designed according to established standards?

Standardization

- Do all preparing offices use the same form or format?
- Is the terminology used in presenting information standardized as much as possible?

Summary information

- Does the report require a time-consuming review by users to obtain essential data?
- Can selective or summarized highlighting of certain elements be used to advantage?

Cumulative data

- Can last minute workloads be eliminated by maintaining cumulative statistical data at the source?

Comparisons

- Should the report contain comparisons of data? (Reports that include comparative data are more useful than raw data or statistics.)
- Have production or performance goals been established to compare data against?
- Are the most meaningful comparative bases used, such as established standards, past performance, time spans, trends, financial or production goals, and correlation with other schedules, programs, or events?

Graphics

- Are graphics used in the report?
- Would graphics enable users to comprehend data faster?
- If illustrations, photographs, charts, graphs, and symbols are used, are they used to good advantage?

Authentication

- Are the signatures of verifying and approving officials required only when absolutely necessary?

- Are these signatures at the appropriate level of authority?
- Does each approval add to the information's reliability?
- Are these signatures collected merely for prestige?

Data sources

- Does the requiring directive specify the records from which reported data should be extracted?
- If no source records exist, or if they cannot be specified, does the directive prescribe how to develop or obtain the information?

Arrangement of records

- Are files or other sources maintained so that data can be easily extracted?
- Can records be arranged in the same sequence or order as the report format?
- If not, can the report format be adjusted to match the data sequence of records?
- Can file headings be matched with the report headings?
- Does the arrangement meet the needs of both the report and file users?

Report symbol

- Is the report symbol in the prescribed location?
- Is the symbol in a conspicuous place on the report?
- If the report title is the subject of the requiring directive, is the report symbol included in the directive title?

Style of presentation

- Is the report style suitable for its intended users (executives, technicians, the general public)?
- Is the tone of the report and the detailed statistics appropriate to the users' levels of knowledge and responsibility?
- Does the complete report reflect as much simplicity and utility as possible for the intended users?

An additional tool that analysts often find useful for reports review is the recurring data analysis chart, shown in Figure 14.4. This chart can be used to evaluate the possibilities of consolidating or eliminating duplicate reports and is particularly helpful in identifying repetitive data by functional category. Use of the chart involves selecting a functional category of reports, such as personnel, and listing the reports in sequence across the top, starting with the report having the greatest usage. Each information item required by each report is then listed down the left-hand column and checked off in the appropriate right-hand column whenever the item appears. When completed, the chart identifies information items that are common to various reports in the group, and provides the basis for reducing the number of reports or information items.

COSTING REPORTS

It hardly seems necessary to state that a comparison of two factors is not easily made if one of the factors is unknown. Yet, when managers are determining the value of a report or a reporting system, that truism is often forgotten. In organizations of all types and sizes reports are routinely considered to be justifiable in the complete absence of any knowledge as to how much they cost.

To ensure effective and economic reports management, organizations should

Page   of   pages

RECURRING DATA ANALYSIS CHART	Title, description, or source							
Subject of analysis or activity	Report X	Report Y	Report Z					
Personnel Reports								
Analysed by: Ann ALIST Date: 4/88								Total
Item	No.	No.	No.	No.	No.	No.	No.	
1 Name	✓	✓	✓					3
2 Address	✓	✓						2
3 Phone No.		✓	✓					2
4 Birth Date	✓	✓						2
5 National Insurance No.		✓						1
6 Employee No.		✓						1
7 Organization Code		✓	✓					2
8								
9								
10								

Figure 14.4   A recurring data analysis chart

determine the costs for all reporting requirements. Lest this be considered overkill, it should also be pointed out that the effort involved in developing a cost estimate for a particular report should be related to its probable expense. In determining the amount of effort to be expended in estimating reporting costs and the degree of accuracy needed, two factors should be considered. One is the probable cost of the report: the higher the cost, the more accurate should be the cost estimate. The second is the cost-benefit ratio, which can be used to determine the degree of accuracy needed by comparing the cost of a report against its value. The value can be expressed in either quantitative or qualitative terms. If the benefits of a report clearly outweigh its costs, it may not be necessary to achieve as high a degree of accuracy as when the costs and benefits appear to be more evenly balanced. When benefits are not clearly and substantially higher than probable costs, greater precision in cost estimates will permit a more valid evaluation of a report's cost effectiveness. The use of costing short cuts, such as sampling or averaging, should be consistent with this general guideline.

Cost segments

The total cost of a report may be divided up into three distinct segments:

1 *Developmental costs* which stem from activities involving the establishment of a new report or the modification of an existing one
2 *Operational costs* which are a factor of ongoing activities such as data collection, processing, and transmitting
3 *User costs* which result from activities performed by the office which imposes the reporting requirement.

All segments exist whether the report is manual or automated, the only difference being the type of activities which are included in the reporting process.

Although, ideally, all segments should be considered, it may not be possible to obtain all the data or to obtain it in the detail required for a complete costing effort. As always, common sense should be applied. It is usually difficult, for example, to determine developmental costs for systems that have been in operation for several years when records had not been maintained during the developmental process. Operational and user costs, however, are available for an active reporting system, and should be recorded and updated periodically. Conversely, developmental costs are available for new systems while operational and user costs may not be, and only a projection or estimate of the latter costs may be possible. In these instances, estimates should be made as accurately as possible under the circumstances, and later revised to show actual costs when the information becomes available.

It may also be difficult to delineate reporting activities precisely. For example, the analysis of a reporting requirement and the design of a reporting system may overlap. Separating the costs of these two activities may be purely arbitrary, and, in such cases, the costs may need to be combined under a more general category. The following guidelines may be used to determine the various segments into which activities may be categorized for costing purposes.

Developmental costs

Specification of reporting requirements including:

● identifying the need for certain information
● determining the objectives and scope of the reporting system that could provide this information
● identifying the benefits of the system

- appraising the impact on existing and planned operations and systems
- conducting feasibility studies.

Analysis of the reporting requirements including:

- determining the specific data that should be provided
- identifying alternative methods for obtaining the data
- identifying data sources, processing requirements, and equipment
- describing inputs, reports, major functions, and the limitations of each alternative
- selecting the best alternative for providing the needed information.

Design of the reporting system, including development of system descriptions (specifications), including input and output documents, data collection procedures, data and document processing, contents of files, interfaces with other systems, and output distribution. For automated systems, this includes the development of technical specifications for the programmer and the writing of the computer program.

Installation of the reporting system encompassing:

- testing the new system procedures
- acquiring and installing new equipment or modifying existing equipment
- developing and issuing implementing instructions, users' guides, operations manuals, and forms
- converting existing methods and procedures to the new system
- scheduling and conducting orientation and training
- preparing the site (for large automated systems).

Operational Costs

Data collection activities which include:

- obtaining, assembling, and recording source data by the preparing units
- controlling the accuracy of source data
- forwarding the source data to the processing unit
- storing source data for future reference.

Data processing activities which include:

- receiving and controlling source data documents at the processing unit
- preparing data for data entry – logging and batching input forms, transcribing data, manually editing data, correcting errors
- translating data to machine-readable form
- resolving data errors and obtaining missing data
- updating files and databases
- performing system maintenance tasks – updating and upgrading system software.

Data transmission activities which include:

- reproducing copies of reports
- delivering reports (mail, electronically, by hand, etc.).

User costs

- interpreting and analyzing the reported information
- reading, reviewing, and discussing the reported information
- using the information for the intended.

Basic costing requirements

In the development of a reporting system, estimates of reporting costs should include the resources expended on each of the three basic cost segments – developmental, operational, and user. For each segment, the direct personnel costs; direct equipment, materials, and supplies costs; other direct costs; and overhead costs should be developed as described in Chapter 7 and included in the calculations.

Costs to be excluded

There are two types of costs to exclude when estimating the costs of a reporting system – independent reporting costs and non-reporting costs. If a reporting system uses a feeder report as input and if the feeder report is an independent report that would continue if the reporting system did not exist, the cost of the feeder report should be excluded from the estimated costs of the reporting system. Likewise, costs that constitute and integral part of an organization's functions and would continue if the reporting did not exist are non-reporting costs that should be excluded from the estimates even though the reporting relies heavily upon, or could not exist without, such operations. For example, a reporting system that uses payroll data should not be charged with the cost of the data needed to produce the payroll or with the by-products of the payroll system such as payroll control registers, time and attendance cards, etc.

Alternative data gathering methods

There are various methods for gathering data. The method used should be appropriate to the degree of accuracy required to evaluate a reporting system for cost-effectiveness. The following alternatives should be considered:

- *Pilot testing* – This method provides actual costs and may be worthwhile in high-cost reporting networks with fully mechanized systems including data banks, a large number of data elements, or a new data collection system. Pilot testing may also be useful if respondent costs are needed for budget purposes.
- *Factoring* – A comparison may be made with a similar report or reporting system for which costs have already been established. Assuming that the estimator is experienced, this method can provide data at a medium to low cost with a high degree of accuracy.
- *Sampling* – This method is best applied when the report is new in concept and will have a large number of respondents. Obtaining a representative sample is the key to success, and care must be taken to ensure sample accuracy. Costs may be low to high.
- *Technical estimates* – A low-cost method of data gathering based entirely on the estimator's experience and judgment. Best applied only to low-cost reporting systems such as those with few respondents or a short life.

Data summarization

To simplify the summarization of data, the summary worksheet for estimating reporting costs has been developed. This worksheet, shown in Figure 14.5, aids in summarizing and presenting information in a clear and systematic manner, and helps to ensure that all pertinent information is collected and that no significant reporting activity or cost items are overlooked. Summary worksheets should be supported by working papers showing detailed computations and including the source and basis for the data used. This material

SUMMARY WORKSHEET FOR ESTIMATING REPORTING COSTS

Report symbol: Report title: Estimate prepared by: Date:

| Factors | | Costs (£) | | | | | |
Reporting categories	Reporting activities	Direct personnel (a)	Overhead (% of column (a)) (b)	Direct equipment (c)	Direct material (d)	Other direct costs (e)	Total (a + b + c + d + e) (f)
Developmental costs	1 Specification of reporting requirement						
	2 Analysis of reporting requirement						
	3 Design of reporting system						
	4 Installation of reporting system						
	5 Developmental costs (add totals in column (f))						
Operational costs	6 Data collection						
	7 Data processing						
	8 Data transmission						
	9 Operational costs for one report (add totals in column (f))						
	10 Annual operational costs (cost for one report multiplied by frequency per year)						
User costs	11 Refining, interpreting and analyzing information received						
	12 Reading, reviewing, discussing and documenting information presented						
	13 User costs for one report (add totals in column (f))						
	14 Annual user costs (cost for one report multiplied by frequency per year)						

Figure 14.5   A summary worksheet for estimating reporting costs

should be retained until the cost of a reporting system is again estimated, which should be done whenever a major change occurs in the system, or (in an abbreviated manner) during the periodic review.

15

Management of active records systems

Traditionally, records managers have spent an inordinate amount of their time organizing and managing the *inactive* records of the organization. Because these records require special handling in order to safeguard crucial organizational interests, the nature of these interests tend to necessitate long-term storage. Hence the incurrence of long-term storage costs. When these storage costs are managed carefully, significant savings are accrued for the organization. Nevertheless, we will see in this chapter that the best records management investment is in the improvement of *active* record systems.

The reason why active records systems provide the best opportunity for return on investment is quite simple. Studies by the major filing equipment vendors have revealed that over 75 percent of every dollar spent on filing expenditures is spent on salaries, benefits, and other related personnel costs. Since this represents by far the largest pool of expenditures, even small increases in the productivity of those involved in making records available, yield substantial savings for the organization.

In fact, the most significant savings opportunity is usually in the improvement of active records systems. Active records are called such, because they are constantly referenced in the daily performance of office work. Since over 60 percent of people are employed in office work, this improvement has a direct impact on increasing the productivity of the majority of workers in today's organizations. A positive increase in records availability, when required for reference, produces a positive effect on the productivity of the worker requiring the information. An improvement in active records systems directly and positively affects productivity by providing the right information, to the right place, at the right time. In this chapter we will explore the strategies and tactics that will significantly improve the quality, availability, and cost effectiveness of active records systems.

PREPARING FOR THE IMPROVEMENT OF ACTIVE RECORDS SYSTEMS

Preparation for the improvement of active records systems is as important to the process of improvement as stretching is an important preparation for exercise. The recordkeeping practices at most organizations have taken many years to become cumbersome and unproductive. They must be improved slowly and methodically or, just as the muscles become stiff and sore without proper stretching, so too the users of the records become inflexible and irritable without proper preparation.

Why does this phenomenon usually not occur when addressing the inactive records?

And why don't people in the organization care as much about how the inactive records are organized or stored, so long as this storage cost is minimized? The answers lie in the value of active records in assisting employees on a day-to-day basis to run the business. A problem in finding these records directly and immediately affects the performance of their jobs. Most users aren't interested in taking a chance that some 'outsider' can better organize their records than they can. Too many users of records confuse the value and importance of records to their work with ownership.

Ownership of the records

This may seem to be a theoretical topic but it is crucial to the information professions. The conflict over ownership of information stems from very natural impulses and assumptions that we are only now, because of technology, being forced to clarify and articulate. It is appropriate to discuss here the problems and confusion surrounding the ownership of information because it is with the active records that individuals use, process, and store to do their work, that the issue of ownership arises constantly.

At its very foundation, the whole concept of records and information management rests on the premise that the information collected and created by employees during the course of their work for an organization belongs to that organization. The records manager's function is to manage all of that information in its recorded forms for the benefit of the organization as a whole. However, it is natural for people to consider that the products of their mind, coming from the very private source of their identity, belong to them. The information that they glean from publications or surveys and compile in an original way, the ideas of their own that they develop on a scratch pad or on a computer, the documentation of their work, the reports and studies they write, all quite naturally seem to them to be their personal property.

Active records are often looked upon as the property of an individual, or at the very least, of the department. Outsiders, (even if they are part of the organization) are not welcome to be poking around and presenting new ideas that just might complicate the lives of the users of the information. Often, users who might like some help, are just too embarrassed to have anyone see what a mess their records are in. The last thing that management wants is any internal squabbles or any time put in that is not moving the business ahead, particularly on something as nebulous, in their minds, as records management.

Many records managers have been too intimidated by the complex organizational culture issues inherent in addressing the active records, to risk their cozy niche of tending the inactive records. After all, they are safeguarding the crucial interests of the organization. But senior management routinely takes this kind of tending for granted. They soon want to know what their administrative managers have done lately to seek out new ways to increase the productivity of the workforce. It is up to the records managers then, if they hope to have a dynamic role in managing the future information systems of the organization, to put the emphasis on providing assistance to the users of the active records.

Realistically dealing with improving the active records systems of any organization is realistically preparing all involved parties for the change. Management must be convinced that there is a strategic business opportunity in active records improvement. The users of the records will want to see the retrieval benefits for them, before putting up with the disruption and inconvenience of a major change. And even the file staff, involved in making records more available, must see the new system as one which will help them do their job more effectively, or they won't be eager to deal with the daily wrath of the users during the period of change. Once these groups are prepared and approached with professional management analysis techniques as discussed in Part II, records managers can get on with the most important aspect of their job – the improvement of active records systems.

THE IMPROVEMENT OF ACTIVE SYSTEMS

Streamlining the existing system

As the records inventory discussed in Chapter 8 is completed and analyzed, a clearer picture of the records holdings of the organization begins to develop. The records with value isolated in protecting the long-term crucial organizational interests are moved off-site to less expensive (but suitable) storage and the records with significant value for administrative reference remain in the active office close to their users. The nature and scope of any problem areas with these active files usually come to the surface during the inventory. The most chronic situation occurs when users of the active records cannot get access to these records within a reasonable amount of time whenever they require them to perform their jobs. This delay not only wastes their valuable time, but it also compromises the service and integrity of the organization in carrying out its commitments and responsibilities.

Addressing this serious records availability deficiency requires the development of a standard approach to file organization, one that will ensure that information is available when required. In addition, this system should ensure that any active records series created to safeguard the crucial interests of the organization are identified, and that a person or department is designated responsible for their storage protection. This standard approach is called an active filing system.

The development of an active filing system

Once the inventory findings have been analyzed, a summary sheet should be prepared which recaps all pertinent data by department or by filing area. From this recap a records manager can develop a standard approach to filing systems in the organization. It is very important to note that 'standard approach' does not mean that every record series in the organization will have the same filing arrangement or labeling system. What it does mean, however, is that these systems will be set up under a master file plan (described later in this chapter) for classification and retention purposes and that there may be a limited number of standard filing models applied to these series. In other words, where necessary a 'standard system' is implemented that requires strict adherence. In other cases a 'standard flexible approach' allows for compromise without sacrificing system controls. Standards are also developed for filing equipment and labeling supplies, and a standard set of alphabetical rules and daily filing activities are implemented. A simple three-point plan is an effective guide to the improvement of active filing systems.

The three-point plan to improve active filing systems

1 *Space planning* – minimize space utilization without impeding access to records.
2 *Filing and retrieval* – develop a system based on the needs of the users of the files.
3 *File control and security* – ensure system is in line with corporate and government requirements.

Space Planning

Once the inventory is complete, and the record values of each of the record series established, there is a rule of thumb formula for what will be left to organize. This rule of thumb is a result from the study of hundreds of inventories in many different industries. It holds that of the records found in an active system before a records management program is in place, approximately one third of them can be disposed of, because they no longer have any value; another one third can be sent to inactive storage because they have little administrative value, but still retain some long-term safeguarding value; leaving only one third of the original files that are actually administratively active, to be organized into an efficient active filing system.

This point deals with minimizing the use of floor space for storing these active files. This can be done by using lateral filing equipment for paper files, or miniaturizing the files through the use of microforms or optical memory systems. We will deal with the traditional filing equipment in this chapter.

Planning the utilization of space and the placement of equipment requires careful attention to a number of factors. The number of workers to be accommodated and the lines of communication must be considered. The prime function of the work area affects the relative importance of particular features. The flow of work and worker comfort and efficiency should be improved where possible. Also to be considered is the nature of the equipment that must be made available for work to proceed (for example, will sorting equipment be required, or will shelving need to be allotted for the staging of the inflow of new records and the outflow of obsolete or inactive records). Space planning needs to take into account anticipated expansion, as well as extra space required at peak work levels.

The number of people who will want access to stored records and how they will use them, must also be taken into account. For example, almost any type of filing cabinet can be attached to mobile carriages which rest on tracks. The cabinets can then be moved back and forth on the tracks. This can increase space utilization by over 50 percent but if more than one person is accessing files regularly it may slow retrieval rates to a point where the space savings are overshadowed by added personnel costs.

Medium height cabinets may double as counter space while providing convenient records storage. They also permit workers to see other workers as they walk past. Two-compartment cabinets may be used by seated workers as well as giving additional working surface and full visibility of other seated workers.

Many of the new work spaces that have been developed for office workers do not provide enough room for any filing cabinets in an individual workstation. There is some space provided for filing in overhead shelves and desk side drawers. This set-up makes it imperative that individuals only keep what they need to do their work daily in their workstations. Cabinets can be more efficiently grouped in departmental files convenient for reference if further immediate access is required. An efficient records retention schedule is one that ensures records can be disposed of promptly or moved to departmental or off-site storage as indicated by reference activity requirements.

A step-by-step approach to space planning

1 Prepare an accurate sketch plan of the floor area. (A scale of 1/8 inch = 1 foot is appropriate.)
2 Mark in the size and location of all windows, doors, and the space required to open them, electrical outlets, lighting, heating sources, telephone lines, and support columns.
3 If the plan is for an area through which office traffic flows, the paths should be indicated based upon entrance ways, exits, washrooms, elevators and escalators.
4 Plot what activities can be performed where, bearing in mind the flow of work and lines of communication.
5 Calculate the amount of space required to accommodate the personnel, their equipment and machines. Include in the calculation the amount of aisle space needed to permit movement about the office. For example, a worker requires at least 3 1/2 feet to be able to push a chair from the desk and exit. Side aisles between rows of desks should provide approximately 3 1/2 feet, whereas main aisles may require 5 feet. Aisle widths between rows of filing cabinets will vary depending upon the style of cabinets

used and their arrangement. Vertical cabinets with pull-out drawers require the depth of the drawer plus 30 inches if the cabinets face in the same direction. If they face one another, they require the depth of two drawers plus another 3 1/2 feet. Lateral cabinets require approximately 30 inches if they face the same direction and 36 inches if they face one another.

6 Prepare templates of the equipment, furnishings, and machinery to scale. Use them to approximate the best layout for the space, adjusting them as required. Check to see that adequate aisle space is provided and work flow and communication lines are facilitated.

7 Mark in required electricity and telephone lines and identify which worker is to be located at each desk or workstation.

8 Verify layout with management and personnel affected. Remember cleaning personnel in your consultation. Remember to consider special requirements for disabled persons. Make required adjustments.

Recommendation of centralized vs. decentralized records management system

An active filing system can consist simply of a cabinet beside a desk or be standardized organization-wide. However, even if a filing system is set out for the whole organization, the records manager normally addresses the physical areas where files are housed one at a time. These physical areas can be broken down into three categories:

* the central file
* the departmental file
* the individual workstation.

The central file

For many years records managers debated over the respective advantages of *centralized filing* and *decentralized filing*. These terms refer to the physical location of files in an organization. In centralized filing, all departments put their files in one large filing area, much like the books in a library. The advantages include:

* standardization of filing policies and procedures
* more efficient utilization of filing staff
* maximum floor space utilization (particularly if done in a basement or off-site area, on a lower cost per square foot basis)
* standardization of equipment and supplies
* improved file security and control.

However, if departmental file users must wait an inordinate amount of time to have files delivered or must walk a considerable distance to pick up files, centralized filing systems soon break down. Departmental file users start to open up their own files, promoting duplication and incomplete records. The rule is to err on the side of locating the active files as close to the users as possible. However, centralized filing might be indicated in an organization where there is one or more of the following:

* security is the major issue
* computer systems at the organization are so sophisticated that actual hard copy file reference is the exception rather than the rule and paper files are kept only for legal or legislative compliance
* only semi-active and/or inactive files are allowed in central files
* there is no room for files in the active office areas and for a variety of reasons an expansion or relocation is not possible.

The departmental file

Departmental files can either be configured as mini-central files for one whole department or consist of pockets of cabinets positioned functionally throughout the department. The former configuration tends to have the same advantages and disadvantages as centralized files except that they are usually closer to most departmental users. The latter configuration promotes the best file accessibility but requires a central control over equipment and supplies selection and filing procedures. Usually, this configuration is most welcomed by file users who like to feel some ownership of their files, to access them when they want, and to quickly retrieve them.

An efficient departmental filing system can be designed using an organizational standard but tailored to the reference needs of the department. Filing equipment should esthetically match workstations and facility colors and layouts. However, this latter issue should be the secondary issue to the efficiency of the filing system.

The individual workstation

Files at individual workstations should be the files that are in use (being referenced) by a particular person. If a central or even a departmental filing system is inefficient, file users tend to keep more and more files at their workstations fearing that they will never see them again if they are returned to their 'homes.' In an efficient filing system scenario, any given user should have no more files at the workstation than can be worked on that day. This can significantly increase file availability to other potential users in the organization, as the hardest files to find are those at someone else's workstation (even given the unusual case of knowing which workstation to search).

Workstation filing systems are usually not controlled by the records manager as they tend to reflect the paperwork habits of the individual. However, the temporary file holding equipment provided to a user should match the type of files the individual uses (i.e., drawer files would not be practical if end-tab files are being used). Records management discipline at this level will become more important, some argue essential, in the future with the handling of electronic records particularly from PCs.

Most organizations use all three types of filing system configurations. As a rule of thumb the records being worked on today are at the workstation, the records for the past year (or possibly two) are in departmental files, and the semi-active files (over two years old) are transferred to central files. Files that are seldom referenced but must be kept in order to comply with certain legal and legislative demands are moved off site to cheaper storage.

Filing and retrieval

Filing and retrieval is a broad catch-all subject that covers the development of the master file plan, the development of filing arrangements, and the development and implementation of filing systems.

The master file plan

The list of an organization's record series, the description of their content, and the length of time that records within these series must be kept is often referred to as the master file plan. *The master file plan of an organization categorizes all records into record series that can be filed together as a block, used as a block, and which can be evaluated as a block for retention purposes.* Each of these record series should have:

1   a definitive name
2   the specific documents or at least the specific nature of documents that should be included in the series

3 the length of time that the files within the record series should be retained by the organization
4 the department responsible for maintaining the 'record copy' of the files in this record series. One of the major costs for organizations is duplicating and storing duplicate copies of a record.

The practice of needless storage of duplicates can be significantly reduced by the designation of a record copy (or more precisely the official copy of a record) when a record is created. It would be the designated responsibility of an individual or department of the organization to store and maintain records for the evidential and compliance functions. Then any copy of the record created and distributed for the reference needs of other employees of the organization could be destroyed as soon as their reference requirements run out.

Once it is determined that a document is a record copy rather than an information copy, the decision needs to be made as to whether or not it is active or inactive. An active record is one which has high administrative value, or to put it another way, is required to carry on current operations. This frequently means that the record has been referred to in the last six-month period, or that it is not over a year old. Active records need to be stored where they can be quickly accessed, which usually means in prime office space. Inactive records, which are not necessary for current operating, but have some value in protecting organizational interests, can safely be stored in secondary office space, in a warehouse, or in some other low-cost holding area.

The master file plan should include all records on all media. It is a centrally controlled policy index which specifies the framework for recordkeeping within the organization. When a record is created internally or received from an external source it is classified within the context of the master file plan. Fortunately, over 90 percent of records creation and receipt is repetitive in nature. This means that confusing decisions about where each document being created should be classified are not constantly required. Most employees create or receive a very small subset of the organization's records in the performance of their jobs. They are soon knowledgeable about the types of records series that they are responsible for. In the event that they require records they haven't created, a quick reference to the master file plan will tell them which department has that information. If they find they require constant reference to these records they may have to create information copies for themselves.

In order for the master file plan to be used, it needs to be ordered or arranged in some logical order. Typically records series are arranged by subject and then by file name. Case files tend to be arranged by one level of subject reference and a file name. Subject files, on the other hand, usually have two levels of subject reference and a file name. The following section on filing arrangements will deal with these differences and their impact in detail.

Filing arrangements

The predetermined ordering of a series of documents or files is referred to as its filing arrangement. Although we will be discussing many different filing arrangements, three means of organization form the basis for all the rest – organization by date, by alphabet, and by number. The reason is quite simple – the order of the calendar, the order of the alphabet, and the order of numbers are very widely understood by people. The reasons for choosing a particular filing arrangement or developing a variation of it depend exclusively on how and why the records will be requested. These arrangements, then, can best be discussed in the context of documents, and case files and subject (including project files) because these categories have evolved compatibly with organizational reference requirements.

Arrangements for documents

The most common arrangement for documents is by date. A filing arrangement by date is called a **chronological file**. This arrangement is almost exclusively used for documents, especially correspondence. The date used is either the date the document was created or the date the document was received by the organization. This aids in the search for a letter, for example, when all that is known is that a letter pertaining to a particular subject was sent out or received around a particular date. Sometimes a copy of the document is filed chronologically and another copy is filed alphabetically or numerically. This is often the case for purchase orders, invoices, and shipping papers. This type of arrangement helps an organization to respond to vague inquiries from its customers. Most effective document filing systems also employ computer systems to aid in the search for a particular author, subject, or recipient.

Arrangements for files

File folders are almost exclusively ordered by alphabet or by number (or some variation of the two). Whether an alphabetic or a numeric filing arrangement is used, the individual or individuals establishing and maintaining the system have a number of factors to consider. The decision must be made as to where to divide and subdivide the files. This will aid in later searching for a file by limiting the search to a specific part of the overall file series. Whether filed by letters of the alphabet, colors, numbers, or a combination of these alternatives, occurring in a simple filing system or a large, complex one, the system must possess some form of **division guides** which organize the filing task into manageable parts.

An individual file folder must be assigned a name or title – called a **caption** or **key title** – where all documents pertaining to that caption are unitized. Before a document can be placed (or filed) in the folder the file clerk or employee responsible for filing the record must determine the caption under which the record is to be filed. Selecting the caption is called **indexing**. Any listing of these captions is called an **index**. The process of marking the record with the caption under which it is to be filed is called **coding**. The coded record then can be placed in the file folder bearing the same caption on its label. If it is possible that a record could be sought under more than one caption, a notation must be made in a file or in the index indicating that the record is stored elsewhere. This is called a **cross-reference**.

There are many types of files such as working paper files, research files, and administrative files. However, all types of files can be broken down into three categories – case files, subject files, and project files.

Arrangements for case files

Case files, as the name implies, are files that pertain to particular sets of circumstances. They often document a specific transaction or are related to a particular person or organization. Good examples of case files would be mortgage files, medical records, personnel records, insurance policy files, workers' compensation files, and income tax files. These types of records can be filed in a series, are usually unitized, and have a common denominator for arrangement such as the name of an individual or organization or a specially assigned number. Case files generally account for the majority of the organization's records. Because of the volume of these records, their uniform nature, their high reference rates, and the fast retrieval turnaround usually required, special file arrangements have been developed. However, the main arrangements are still simple alphabetic and simple numeric.

Simple alphabetic arrangement. Probably the most widely used source of business information that is arranged alphabetically is the telephone directory. It lists surnames of telephone subscribers in alphabetic order. Many offices use the same approach to arrange lists of names and to file records. It is the most popular system, because it is easy to use. Usually with this type of system large, stiff cards displaying the letters of the alphabet form the division guides that separate the file folders that begin with one letter from those that begin with another. Thus, ahead of all the folders bearing a caption beginning with *A* is a card that prominently displays an *A*, and so on.

By way of explaining how the alphabetic arrangement works, let us try a simple application. Suppose we want to prepare an alphabetic list of our clients. We can readily see that a surname such as *Black* beginning with the letter *B* comes before *Suzuki*. And it does not take much to see that if we have two surnames, each starting with an *S* we can use the second letter of the surname as a basis for determining that *Stavraky* with *t* as the second letter in the surname should precede *Suzuki*. However, if we have two *Stavrakys*, let us say *Freda* and *Walter*, we must find some other basis upon which to arrange the names. So it is that we move to considering the given names as the basis of further arranging. Therefore, it seems logical to place the name *Stavraky, Freda* ahead of *Stavraky, Walter*.

As you can see, it is necessary with the many variations in names to apply a set of consistent rules that everyone uses, so that when the time comes to retrieve a record from the files, it can be found expeditiously. For an alphabetic system, these rules are referred to as the **alphabetic indexing rules**. A comprehensive set of standards for alphabetizing filing systems, the **alphabetic filing rules**, has been developed by the Association of Records Managers and Administrators, Inc. (ARMA International) and can be ordered from their headquarters in Prairie Village, KS.

When an employee requests a record filed in an alphabetic arrangement, the file clerk must know the caption under which it is filed in order to search the files for the label displaying that caption. It is at this point that problems associated with simple alphabetic arrangement begin to emerge. A major problem arises from the number of file folders that may be contained in a system. As a filing system grows in size, more and more folders are placed behind each division guide. In fact, it is conceivable that in some systems several file drawers could be filled with folders all displaying the same first letter on their labels. The file clerk must then scan through several drawers, inspecting hundreds of labels, to arrive at the file folder displaying the correct caption. To overcome this problem and others, manufacturers of filing supplies have devised variations of the simple alphabetic arrangement.

Subdividing the alphabet. The first example of a variation of the alphabetic arrangement simply adds more divisions to the alphabet. Lettered division guides displaying single letters of the alphabet are used but supplemented by division guides placed between the single letters. These industry-standard divisions have been refined following the study of thousands of alphabetic filing systems. For example, the *B* may be subdivided by guides as follows:

B, Bar, Be, Ben, Bi, Bl, Bo, Br, Bro

This system provides for files with captions starting with *B* to *Baq* to be placed behind the first guide. Thus, *Bacon, Alistair* is placed in this subdivision. Similarly, *Barsford Limited* and *Barstead & Daughters* are placed in the next division, and so on.

Combining alphabetics and numbers. In an attempt to further simplify alphabetic filing, some systems assign numbers to each alphabetic subdivision. In this case, the division guides *A*, *B*, and so on serve as primary guides and division guides labeled *Aa-Al 1, Am-Ar 2*, and *As-Az 3*, for example, become secondary guides. The proper location for a file folder is then determined by using a chart comparing alphabetic subdivisions to numbers. Although cumbersome for the occasional user, this system can be very effective for full-time file clerks who quickly memorize which numeric guide goes with which alphabetic string. This type of system is being replaced by effective color coding of letters (see 'Alphabetics and Color Coding').

Geographic arrangement is essentially a variation of alphabetic arrangement. The file folders are arranged alphabetically on the basis of geographic location rather than the names of correspondents. In one such system, states are arranged alphabetically and divided by division guides. Then the states are subdivided by additional division guides bearing the names of cities or towns within each state arranged alphabetically within the primary division. File folders are set up for individual correspondents where the volume of records warrants. These are arranged alphabetically by the names of the correspondents. At the beginning of each subdivision, a miscellaneous file folder for the city or town is set up to hold the records for correspondents who do not warrant an individual folder. An index, cross-referencing an alphabetic list of the names of the correspondents to their locations, is necessary with this system because the person retrieving the records may not know the correspondent's location.

Alphabetics and color coding. Alphabetic systems, as well as others, often incorporate color to aid in filing and retrieval to avoid misfiling. Color is used to enhance or replace the division guides. As a simple illustration, the first division of our file, say *B* to *Bar*, orange division guides and labels with an orange bar across the visible edge of the file folders are used. For the next division, *Bar* to *Be*, yellow division guides and labels with a yellow bar are used. Now the file clerk replacing a file folder into the files can quickly scan the labels and guides for the matching color. It is easy to see at a glance if a folder is misfiled.

Modern filing systems utilize shelves instead of drawers to house folders. This way the ends of the folders are visible instead of being hidden. To understand how effective this transition has been, imagine how difficult it would be to find a book in a library if the collection were hidden in drawers rather than on shelves. This relatively recent change in equipment has substantially increased the use of color coding.

A simple method of color coding uses colored file folder labels. Thirteen colors are used twice. Each color identifies a letter in the first half of the alphabet and a repeat of the colors identifies the letters of the last half of the alphabet. Misfiles of the first letter of a name are singled out in this way. Another method using colored file folder labels with alphabetics is based on the theory that most misfiles are made by the second letter of the name. In this method of color coding, the alphabet is divided into groups by the vowels *A*, *E*, *I*, and *O*, and the letter *R*. These are the five groups: *ABCD, EFGH, IJKLMN, OPQ, RSTUVWXYZ*. A different colored file folder label is used for each group. Misfiles are seen as unmatched colors. When using file folder labels with color bars, a decision must be made to use the color bars to identify either the first or the second letter of the name. Its effectiveness would relate directly to the size of the filing application and the care and attention given to its operation.

An innovation in color coding provided color identification of the first two or three letters of the caption. This is accomplished by assigning each letter of the alphabet with a distinctive color representation. The colored labels are placed on a special end tab style of file folder thus making every folder a division guide. Thirteen distinctive colors are used twice, the second time with a distinctive white block. Every color representation for each letter is unique. One letter cannot be mistaken for another.

When only one letter is identified, the file is divided into 26 segments, one for each letter. When the first two letters are color coded, the search for a misfile is limited to a smaller segment of the file. By identifying two letters, the file is divided into about 300 or 400 segments. (The possible total is 26 x 26 or 676 segments, but all combinations of letters do not occur in names.) This increased precision adds another dimension to the color coding of alphabetic filing. By adopting this method of color coding it is practical to convert numeric filing systems with their cross-reference indexes (a name is cross-referenced to a number) of up to 10,000 names to an alphabetic filing system. This permits direct access to records without the clerk having to use the cross-reference. Naturally, when this is done there is substantial savings both in the time it takes to locate a file and also in the number of staff needed to operate the system.

Simple Numeric Arrangement. Many case files used by offices bear numbers. These files, when kept in numeric order, may be divided by thousands and subdivided by hundreds and tens, using division guides to mark off the divisions and subdivisions. Common examples of numbered records are invoices, checks, and purchase orders, which are numbered consecutively when they are printed. It is easy to understand why such records are often filed in numeric order. However, numeric arrangement is also used in other instances.

Large organizations which process and retain substantial volumes of records may assign numbers to their clients. One reason for this is that a simple alphabetic arrangement does not permit easy expansion, since in order to accommodate additional files, succeeding files must be displaced. For example, if it becomes necessary to expand accommodation for files in *B* division, all succeeding file divisions, *C* to *Z*, may have to be moved or 'backshifted.' Another reason is that the names of individuals are often similar and sometimes identical. To prevent confusion, a unique number can be assigned to each individual. This leads to speedier and more accurate filing and retrieval. Organizations such as banks, insurance companies, oil companies, and department stores frequently use this approach when they file by policy or account number.

The simple or straight numeric arrangement described above is used when records are prenumbered. In hospitals, insurance companies, government agencies, and legal offices, the client is assigned a number for reference purposes. The number is drawn from an **accession book** containing a series of consecutive numbers which are predetermined and not duplicated. The client's name is entered beside the assigned number. That number is placed on the file caption for the client, often together with the client's name. Any record that pertains to that client is coded with the number for filing purposes. Filing in such a system is generally an easy task. But how does one file a record that does not show the client's number or retrieve a record when the client is known only by name? In order for the numeric system to be effective in these odd cases when the file number is not known, it must include an index that contains the names of the clients arranged in alphabetic order with their assigned numbers. This index consists of a drawer or series of drawers containing cards referred to as the **card control file index**.

When a document that has been released for filing is processed, it is coded with the number shown with the name or title on the card control index card. If it is necessary to retrieve a document (or the entire file for that matter), the file clerk can determine the file's number by referring to the same cross-reference index file. More recently, the accession book and card control file index have been replaced by a computer file. Computerization allows faster editing and cross-referencing as well as having the capacity to keep a limited amount of other frequently accessed information about the client. In most filing operations, the most recent records are usually in the highest demand. In fact a general rule of thumb is that 90 percent of references are made to a file in the first year of its life. With a simple numeric arrangement, all the active files could be at the end of the file system. This can cause a serious congestion problem as clerks attempt to work in one particular area. To overcome the problem, variations of the simple numeric arrangement have been devised: terminal digit arrangement, middle digit arrangement and phonetic numeric arrangement.

Terminal digit arrangement. As numbers increase in length, the chances become greater that file clerks will confuse the order of the numbers and misfile records. In addition, there is the need to maintain an even work distribution, and hence an even distribution of the volume of current documents throughout the files. To accomplish this and to gain greater accuracy in filing, the terminal digit arrangement is used, particularly in systems with over fifty thousand files. Terminal digit filing is simply a different arrangement of file numbers originally developed in the general insurance industry to file policies in drawer files. Rather than arranging them by units, tens, hundreds, thousands, etc. as in a straight numeric system, the number of a record is broken into small groups of two or three digits and arranged by them. For example, 236517 might be divided by the file clerk, using two-digit groupings, into 23 65 17. This would be interpreted by the file clerk as:

Place the record in this sequence in the folder:	File the record in the folder bearing:	Look for the folder in this drawer:
23	65	17

Thus, the file clerk would go to drawer number 17, look for the file folder 65, and place the record in the folder as the 23rd record. The next record in the series, 236518, would therefore be filed in drawer number 18, in file folder number 65, as the 23rd record in the folder. The last two digits, in these cases 17 and 18, are called the **terminal grouping**. There are one hundred of these groupings, 00 to 99. If the number does not contain six digits, sufficient zeroes are added to the left to bring the number of digits to six.

The terminal digit system is very successful at distributing currently active files throughout the system. Inactive records being pulled for transfer or disposal are also evenly distributed. Work distribution is the major advantage of terminal digit filing. Five file clerks might each be assigned twenty terminal groupings. This would give each clerk almost exactly the same number of files to service, with an equal number of active and inactive files. On the other hand, this system requires more space because expansion must be allowed for at the end of each terminal grouping. However, there isn't the constant, time-consuming back-shifting of files inherent in a straight numeric system where usually the older files (hence lower numbers) are being disposed of.

This system can pose a problem, particularly if it is necessary to retrieve a large block of a record series for further processing. Let us suppose a file clerk wishes to retrieve records from number 236518 to number 236617. That would mean going first to drawer number 18, to look for folder 65, to retrieve record number 23 from the folder; then to retrieve record number 236519, going first to drawer number 19, to look for folder 65, to retrieve record number 23. In short, the search would require going to one hundred different places to retrieve one hundred consecutive records.

Middle digit arrangement. If it is likely that large blocks of records will be retrieved in consecutive sequence, and work distribution is still a concern, the middle digit arrangement might be used for filing. This system was also designed in insurance companies that issued blocks of numbers to agents and then might have to retrieve all of a particular agent's files for an audit. In middle digit filing, a six-digit record number can be broken into three two-digit groupings, as above. The groupings, however, are considered in a different sequence than they are in the terminal digit arrangement. Using a record bearing the number 147803 as an example, the file clerk would interpret the number as:

File the record in the folder bearing:	Look for the file folder in this drawer:	Place the record in this sequence in the folder:
14	78	03

Thus, the file clerk would go to drawer number 78, look for file folder number 14, and place the record in the folder as the 3rd record. The next record in the series, 147804, would therefore be placed in the same drawer, 78, and in the same file folder 14, but as the 4th record in the sequence. With this arrangement, placing records in consecutive order requires less movement from drawer to drawer and from folder to folder. Similarly, retrieving records in consecutive order requires far less movement.

Let us suppose the same clerk now wants to retrieve one hundred records bearing the numbers 236518 to 236617. All the records can be found in the two drawers 65 and 66 in two file folders, each marked 23. Unfortunately, this compromise arrangement does not provide as great a work distribution advantage as terminal digit filing and hence is not as widely used as either of the other two types of numeric arrangement.

Phonetic numeric arrangement. Because many names sound alike yet are spelled differently, it is difficult to know just where to look in a filing system for a correspondent's file folder. In a telephone directory, you may find a note at the beginning of a section referring you to alternative spellings; for example, *Schwartz – see also Swartz* or *Smith – see also Smyth*. These cross-references refer you to another source of information you desire. Such an arrangement is acceptable in smaller filing systems. However, in very large systems which file by names of correspondents, a name may be filed according to its sound.

A system that files by sound is called a phonetic system. With the advent of computer indexing it is now more likely for files to be physically arranged in simple alphabetic or simple numeric order with a search capability in the computerized index that will pick up multiple spellings of words that sound alike.

Numbers and color coding. Color coding is not a filing system, but is a method of identifying the file folders within a filing system and preventing misfiles. Terminal digit filing is often thought of synonymously with color coding. Although the two don't necessarily have to occur together, their historical use connects them. We already mentioned that as shelf filing replaced drawer filing, color coding became more and more popular. Early color-coded systems concentrated on color coding only the last two digits – the terminal grouping.

Two methods of color coding with terminal digits were developed. One involves the matching of stripes on different colors of folders. Here the side of the folder, or more correctly part of it, is divided into eleven equal parts. The parts, beginning at the top, are assigned to the ten digits 0 through 9. The bottom position identifies a repeat of a number. Each element of a terminal digit is represented on the folder by a black band, thus creating two black bands on each folder for each terminal digit. Additionally, if the first digit is lower than the second, such as in the case of the terminal digit 57, the section of the files will be green and if the second digit is lower than the first, such as in the case of terminal digit 62, the files are printed in orange. If the two digits are the same, such as in the case of terminal digit 55, a black band is put on the 5 and on the repeat position. If a folder is misfiled the stripes will not line up, in either the green or the orange segments of the file.

The second method of color coding with terminal digits is to use ten different colors assigned to the digits 0 to 9. Each terminal digit, then, is represented by two color bars on the edge of the folder. Whenever the color bars for a specific folder do not match, a misfile is indicated.

Thus, with both of these variations of color coding, any search for a specific file folder is limited to a specific group or segment of the system. With two terminal digits color coded, any search for a file is limited to about one-hundredth part of the system. Sometimes three terminal digits are identified with color bands. When this is done the file is divided into a thousand segments. A search for a file location or a misfile is thus limited to about one-thousandth part of the system.

For a time, most color-coded filing systems were restricted to two or three labels because of the labor-intensive job of affixing more labels than this to a folder. With a technical breakthrough in the manufacture of color-coded folders, at little additional cost the whole file reference number, or at least five or six digits of it, could be color coded. The only requirement was that the numbers form a consecutive series. Hospital patient numbers, for example, suit this arrangement perfectly. There has been a marked increase in filing efficiency with this breakthrough as a specific file can be located by simply matching the colors at the extreme edge of the file folder to their corresponding numbers. The very thin lines of color at the edge of the end tab are 'read' as numbers.

There has since been additional technical breakthroughs in the manufacture of color-coded folders. One was the automatic application under computer control of single-digit, self-adhesive labels to any type of folder. This 'automatic labeler' enables color-coded folders to be manufactured at great speeds in any sequence or at random. Another is the automatic color printing by a laser printer of a strip label directed by a computer system. These labels can also be printed in any sequence or at random. The colors of these labels are not always consistent, however. Both of these inventions answer the problems inherent in file conversions of supplying folders to meet any reasonable filing changeover schedule.

It is easy to see how color coding with numerics makes filing faster and more accurate for groups of case files that are in their filing equipment. However, outside the file room is where the advantages of fully color-coded filing are most striking. At any one time up to 20 percent of the active files may be in circulation throughout the office. Fully color-coded files, even when they are in piles on desks, can be easily located by examining the color on the edge of the folder. This significantly enhances search time in the office area where arrangement is determined by workload rather than by file name or number.

Guidelines for using color-coding in filing systems. The use of color coding to limit the search for files has gained widespread popularity. There are several proven rules of thumb to keep in mind when developing an effective color-coding system:

1 **Color should be used only if it is significant**. Usually no more than six color-coded labels should be used with one system. Beyond this, the colors can be more a distraction than an aid to filing. The key is to find the significant letters or numbers to code. For instance, there is little value in coding more than the first three letters of a surname in a personnel file. A common name like *Smith* will receive no more breakdown with four letters than with three. In an alpha file of up to 2,000 folders, two letters should be sufficient. In an alpha file of 2,000–15,000, three letters should be used. If you have an alpha file of over 20,000 files, strong consideration should be given to a numeric system.

   In a simple numeric file, coding one number breaks the system into 10 parts, two numbers into 100 parts, three numbers into 1,000 parts, four numbers into 10,000 parts, and five numbers into 100,000 parts. In a file of 65,000 folders, then, an individual folder can be selected by color by coding five significant digits. How do you find the significant digits? Let's use as an example 65,000 insurance policies issued sequentially with eight-digit policy numbers. If we color code the first five digits, there could be up to 1,000 policies with this number. However, if we color code the last five digits we will likely have no more than two policies with this coding. The first three numbers can be printed in black on the folder. The folders would then be filed first by the last five digits then by the first three digits. Finding five or six significant numbers is not always easy. However, since most file indexes are on computer, they can be sorted in various orders to find the most efficient ordering and hence the obvious candidates for color coding.

   It is important to remember that color coding is used to find the file. Using color to designate information contained in the file will often slow file retrieval, soon become outdated and lose all significance.

2 **Large enough labels should be used to give a bar effect**. Often in an attempt to code ten or more numbers or letters on a folder because there has been no attempt to find the significant characters, there is temptation to use labels 1/2 inch high or less. Because folders contain unequal thicknesses of documents there tends to be an unevenness of up to 1/8 inch up or down, which translates to a possible 1/4 inch jog from folder to folder.

   The success of color coding in a file system depends on the creation of bars at each coding level that the eye can follow. These bars do not develop well with the smaller labels because of this jogging. Labels 1 inch in height provide this barring effect well, yet easily allow six labels to be positioned on an end tab.

3 **Color coding should be used on end tabs only**. Often a lot of time and effort goes into color coding top-tab folders in drawers. By and large this is wasted effort. Once the drawer has been located, the search has been limited to 25 inches of filing. The key to an effective filing system is the visibility of all files so that the search can begin as soon as a clerk steps into an aisle of files.

4   **Color coding should be standardized in an organization**. Different manufacturers provide different approaches to alphabetic color coding, and have different colors for their numbers. Staff from one department are immediately familiar with the filing system in another department if the same colors represent the same numbers and letters.

A brand should be chosen that provides letters, numbers, year labels, month labels, and other specialty labels. The label graphics should be crisp and readable from at least 6 feet (2 meters) away as new people and infrequent users will use the actual numbers and letters like division guides if they are not familiar with the colors. Plastic-coated labels resist oil from fingers as they are being handled and last much longer. Print consistency and fade resistance are also important factors. Colors that vary from one print run to the next or fade under ultraviolet office lights could be mistaken for another color and cause misfiles.

5   **Machine application instead of hand application should be considered**. Applying color-coded labels to file folders by hand is a tedious and time-consuming process. Sometimes in alphabetic, alphanumeric, or even some numeric systems the coding for the next file is not known until it is created and hand labeling is unavoidable.

However, mass file conversions of back files and ongoing systems where numbers are issued sequentially can be done by a manufacturer who is supplied with a handwritten list, a computer printout, or a magnetic tape of file numbers. The three most common color-coding application methods are:

- hand application of individual labels
- hand application of machine-printed strips with individual color blocks printed on the strips
- machine application of individual labels.

Arrangements for subject files

As we have pointed out, case files are often arranged according to names of correspondents or in some logical numeric order. Within any case file series the significant attribute by which a file is most likely to be asked for and hence by which it is indexed is uniform and repetitious. This is rarely the situation for subject files. The reasons for opening a subject file tend to relate to the needs of a specific department or even an individual, as problems arise or research is done. This disparate collection of information is anything but uniform or repetitious and certainly does not diminish the importance of subject files to an organization.

Filing by subject brings together all records on a given topic, issue, or problem. As such, it is an indispensable tool to management for effective decision making. Subject files often include memos to and from senior or middle management. These are the files that reveal the organization's basic objectives, policies, and procedures. This is one area where managers should understand that being able to reference this information efficiently is critical. Unfortunately these files are often stuffed into desk drawers or so casually organized that their reference is difficult, if possible at all. This presents a real opportunity for the records manager to show that although their volume is not as large as the case files, they are very significant to the organization and particularly to the managers that run it. And, of course, that a records management program that deals effectively with the problems unique to this type of file is the only way to ensure this availability.

Setting up subject filing systems is no easy task. Their very nature promotes personal arrangement or perceived 'personal files.' There are two parts of this nature that makes setting up a standard arrangement for subject files difficult:

1   It is difficult to convince individual managers that these files are part of the organization's information resource and not their personal possessions.
2   It is difficult to decide under what single significant attribute a record should be

indexed. In fact the nature of the records going into a subject file make it conceivable that the record could be filed under more than one key title.

The dictionary alphabetic subject arrangement. Because it is the easiest to set up and the easiest to learn and remember without an index, most personal arrangements naturally gravitate to simple alphabetic arrangement by subject names. This allows direct access to any file as they are all given equal weight, disregarding any relationships between them. Because alphabetic order is maintained throughout, this system is sometimes called the dictionary method of arrangement.

Major reference problems begin to develop with this approach, however, once the volume of subject files gets much beyond one cabinet. Key titles begin to overlap as it becomes more and more difficult to keep track of subtle differences in the way in which subject-matter can be interpreted. This tends to defeat the major reason for subject filing (which is to keep all subject-matters that are closely related in the same folder) by dispersing records that should be filed together throughout a variety of key titles with similar but not identical meanings.

The encyclopedic alphabetic subject arrangement. Once a subject system gets beyond one cabinet a more sophisticated system than the dictionary method is required. A further refinement brings broad classifications of records under major subject areas. The organization of the records is by department or more often by function performed. All records associated with each of these major headings are accordingly divided into related secondary and tertiary headings – hence the name 'encyclopedic.' As an example, the division guides of a hotel's encyclopedic alphabetic subject arrangement might be labeled in part as follows:

AUDITING	*primary or functional heading*
Cash receipts	*secondary heading*
Disbursements	*secondary heading*
Food and beverage control	*secondary heading*
Management statements	*secondary heading*
January–March	*tertiary heading*
April–June	*tertiary heading*
July–September	*tertiary heading*
October–December	*tertiary heading*
Payroll	*secondary heading*
CATERING	*primary or functional heading*
Beverages	*secondary heading*
Preparation	*tertiary heading*
Purchasing	*tertiary heading*
Service	*tertiary heading*
Storage	*tertiary heading*
Food	*secondary heading*

etc.

Subject classification index. Once an encyclopedic arrangement like the one partially shown above is set up its use becomes obvious. However, choosing the original headings is painstaking. Even once they are chosen, as in this example, one could conceivably file a record pertaining to the cost of beverage storage under one of three headings; either:

AUDITING	
Disbursements	or
AUDITING	
Food and beverage control	or
CATERING	
Beverages	
Storage.	

Hopefully, the record would be specific enough to choose the appropriate folder. However, if confusion arose a cross-reference pointing to the appropriate file from the other suitable files should be prepared. This can either be a note which is physically inserted into the suitable files or a cross-reference entry on a subject classification index. A subject classification index is almost always required in an encyclopedic subject arrangement. (The exception is a small desk-side system with limited primary subjects. Often these small systems (up to two cabinets) are simply modified dictionary arrangements.) In fact, a subject classification index is the key to the original indexing of records, the coding of the records, the filing of the folders and, most importantly, the retrieval of the records at a later date.

It is important to understand the relationship between the subject classification index and the physical file folders holding the records. In a subject classification index, the primary heading level is always a subject heading only, with no file folders being made up with this heading alone. The tertiary level is always a file folder level. (There can be an exception if there is a four-level arrangement where the tertiary level can be a subject level. However, the majority of encyclopedic subject arrangements can effectively be structured with three levels.) The secondary level can be a subject level (when it acts as a miniprimary) or a file folder level (when there are not enough records under this heading to warrant separate tertiary breakdowns).

In organization-wide subject classification systems the headings chosen for the primary and secondary headings are usually centrally controlled by the records manager, but individuals can create their own file folder captions at the tertiary level under the standard primary and secondary subjects. Some organizations attempt to centrally control the subject classification system down to the file folder but this usually proves unwieldy. It is effective to break down an organizational subject classification system into two sections before assigning primary, secondary, and tertiary headings. These sections are administrative and operational.

Administrative subject files. Administrative subject files are sometimes called 'housekeeping records' because they are as basic to running a business organization as the routine household chores such as washing, ironing, doing dishes, cleaning, etc. are to maintaining an efficient home. They serve to document the routine tasks that an organization undertakes to make it an ongoing, effective, viable entity. These records include annual tasks such as budgeting and auditing, monthly activities such as management reporting, and daily activities involved in such tasks as the management of human resources (hiring, training, benefits, vacation scheduling, etc.).

Separating these housekeeping records allows an organization to develop an organizational standard approach for administrative tasks for all departments and branches. A standard classification index for these records, then, would be used across the organization. This facilitates management reporting, auditing, and training. It also allows a blanket retention schedule to be developed for all administrative records for an organization so that each organizational unit does not have to reinvent the wheel.

Operational subject files. Each department in an organization exists to carry out a specific mandate. The purchasing department procures goods and services, the finance department receives and disburses funds, the manufacturing department produces the goods or services for sale, the sales and marketing department is responsible for the distribution of the goods or services for profit. It is obvious that in addition to their administrative files, each department of an organization requires files specific to its operating mandate.

Some of these operational files will be transactional (case) files such as the invoice files, personnel files, or in the bank example, the mortgage files. However, specific to the needs of a particular department or function are general subject files that document issues related to the operation of that department. A purchasing department may have a file on the purchasing practices of other organizations, or on laws governing legal purchasing practices. A sales and marketing department may have files on competitors or competitive products and pricing, or on general subjects relating to the sale of their product, sales training, or advertising. A manufacturing department may have general files on different manufacturing processes, and research into the use of certain materials or relative to safety in the workplace. These general operational reference files help managers in these departments make decisions regarding how best to run their area of responsibility. These files would contain newspaper and magazine clippings, research papers, correspondence, charts, brochures, literature, and case studies.

The nature of these operational subject files requires a classification system unique to a particular department or function. The organizational master classification system, then, would be the administrative subject classifications (standard for all departments) and a compilation of all operational classifications (which are unique to a department or function).

Standard classification systems. Most numeric subject arrangements have their roots in a widely known decimal system called the **Dewey decimal system**, originated by Melville Dewey in the 1870s for classifying books in a library. The system is based on the number ten. All books are divided into ten main classes, such as general works, philosophy, religion, etc. Each of the ten classes is subdivided into ten groups; then each group is divided into ten subgroups, and so on. Below is an excerpt from the main class, applied science:

```
600    Applied science
       600–609  General works
                        608  Inventions
       610–620  Medicine
                        613  Personal hygiene
       620–630  Engineering
                        629.1  Aeronautics
                        629.2  Automobiles
```

Numeric subject filing arrangements. A more refined system of standard subject classifications is published in a two-volume list by the US Library of Congress and is now in widespread use in North American libraries. Unfortunately, the library approach, which requires the classifying of all human knowledge, is not very practical for business or even government organizations. However, many companies and government departments that have embarked on a comprehensive records management program have installed an organization-wide alphanumeric subject system.

To assist in the coding, filing, and retrieval of records, large subject arrangements can sometimes be improved by assigning numbers, letters, or combinations of numbers and letters to the primary, secondary, and tertiary headings. The numbers or letters must, of course, indicate the interrelations between the headings. The previous hotel subject file example might be recorded as follows:

```
100    Auditing
110       Cash Receipts
120       Disbursements
130       Food and beverage control
140       Management statements
141          January–March
142          April–June
143          July–September
144          October–December
150       Payroll
200    Catering
```

210	Beverages
211	Preparation
212	Purchasing
213	Service
214	Storage
220	Food

In this system, instead of having to code a record as CATERING, Beverages, Storage, it could be coded as 214 and filed in folder number 214.

Businesses have been slower to adopt organization-wide subject systems because of the tremendous cost in human resources of originally developing a system. Then by nature, a subject file is in constant transition requiring updating, editing, and more descriptive indexing and cross-referencing. The inclusion of an organizational standard subject filing system into a comprehensive records management program has increased as computer maintenance of such systems has recently become viable.

Both mainframe computers and personal computers have been used effectively to create and maintain on-line indexes to subject files.

Arrangements for project files

Project files are a special type of file because they usually relate to a fixed time frame, bracketed by the start and end of the project. Though project records can be in the form of individual documents, most are unitized by subject. In fact, they resemble subject files enough to be appropriately called a subset of subject files. However, they are generally filed physically separate from subject files and grouped as projects so that when a project is complete they can be evaluated as a unit for retention purposes. An individual's daily working papers often fall into this category as many office tasks are really miniprojects.

Organizing project files is particularly sensitive to users because these files really are thought to be personal files by the users. Engineers, for instance, feel professionally liable for their projects and therefore do not want anyone except themselves involved in the recordkeeping. Scientists often feel the same way as they do not relish the thought of having to repeat certain tests if, in fact, they can be repeated at all. An analyst needs to realize that these users do not see organizational standardization of a filing system as a high priority. They often view their physical control of the records as the most important filing criteria to protect themselves and their projects. This, of course, leaves the organization very exposed if any of the records are lost or if the project manager leaves and takes the records.

A solution to this chronic records management problem is certainly not exact but it can give each group most of what they want. The steps to this program would be as follows:

Step One: Separate the project files into two groups. Project files are grouped as either 'open' projects that reside with the project manager or 'closed' projects that usually reside in a more centralized filing room or off-site if they are older. This is usually non-threatening to the users as their greatest interest is in the open projects and at least gets control of the records of completed projects.

Step Two: Develop a project records close-out procedure. This should include organizing the information into common groups to facilitate future reference. It should also include a certain period of time that the records should be in the central facility after the project has closed.

Step Three: Make sure that the centralized facility provides a high level of service. This is the only opportunity to gain the confidence of the project managers. Work with a records improvement project team of project managers to discuss ways that service can be improved.

Step Four: Utilize the records improvement team to develop a list of about ten to twenty categories that are common to every project. Promote the use of these categories by all project managers. It is not necessary to limit the type of equipment or supplies they are using unless you have a senior management mandate to do so. Whether they keep their files in folders in their desks, in ring-binders, or even neat stacks is not as important as using a common approach to the organization of their project material. Examples of these common categories could be:

Project plan	including:	schedule and milestones
Formal authorization	including:	contract task agreements, job estimate
Contracts	including:	scope of work, budget, rate, travel & expenses, invoices, cofunding, and bids/cost proposals
Correspondence	including:	incoming, outgoing, mailing list
Project status	including:	cost tracking (included in quarterly status/year-end expenditure reports). project schedule technical accomplishments (or issues)
Results	including:	reports, systems, etc.
Reference material	including:	subject files, journals, clippings, etc.

File control and security

Once we isolate what we have to organize, set up a system in the minimum of space, with the maximum availability when required, we need to set up some controls on who accesses the records, and where they travel to in (or out of), the organization. We need to adequately secure confidential records and protect vital records on an ongoing basis.

The information that an organization acquires in the course of its activities is a valuable resource. Without some records, the organization cannot carry on such operations as the collection of outstanding accounts or the control of inventory. Other records contain confidential information. Some types of file equipment do not provide their own security. In an investigation of equipment and systems, then, the records manager must consider security or ascertain how well the company's records must be protected from theft or invasion of privacy. Records filed in such equipment might be centralized in a lockable room. Enclosed lockable cabinets are preferable for this type of records in a decentralized filing area.

Provision for adherence to company policies and government requirements must be made when selecting appropriate storage equipment and systems. The policies and practices for efficient storage of records are determined by senior records personnel in consultation with senior management. It is also the responsibility of senior records personnel to ensure that storage practices conform to government regulations and legal requirements. For example, the length of time original records are maintained in readily accessible areas before they are destroyed or transferred to less expensive sites must be set out in the **records retention schedule** which conforms to both company and government requirements.

Machine-readable labeling systems

While color coding is most helpful for filing and retrieval purposes, **bar coding** may be used for tracking file folders which have been charged out to users. The code used is similar to that found on packaged products in grocery stores and supermarkets. The bar code forms part of the label, on the file folder tab, so that part of the label is readable by the records clerk and part of the label is readable by machine. A device which resembles a pen light, called a 'wand,' is used to read the bar code into a computer terminal. The operator may then enter the name (or more usually the number) of the person or department charging out the folder. This information is recorded as part of an automated records management system so the recorded information is accessible by the operator at any time.

The advantages of bar coding are speed and accuracy of input. Just as shoppers are impatient in a checkout line, so too people removing files from a file room are anxious to get on with their work. A fast scan of their security badge (if bar coded) and the bar code on the file lets them carry on quickly and usually elicits more cooperation in the important job of keeping track of folders that are out of the file.

Summary

Although many different filing configurations are required in a modern business enterprise, the need for centrally controlled policy and procedures is the cornerstone of an effective records management program. Senior management must support the program as corporate policy. The operations managers must feel so comfortable with the way that the program is helping them accomplish the business of the organization that they support the program daily. And everyone involved in the creation, control, maintenance and storage of records must feel confident that they have clear direction in how to accomplish this essential organizational task.

Organizing active hard copy records is the most important step in getting control of all records in an organization. It can be the most significant opportunity for records managers to obtain a visible payback on their program. And it can be an opportunity to work with most of the individuals in the organization and to show them the merits of effective records management.

The future use of computers and microimagery for the storage and retrieval of records also depends on first streamlining the hard copy records system. Since conversion of hard copy records to digital or photographic images is slow and expensive, an organization must pare its records to only 'must have' documents to reduce these conversion costs. Further, even if it makes economic sense for a wholesale conversion, a messy hard copy system will be a messy computer or microform system.

Once the active records of the organization are under control, it is time to focus on the inactive records which are usually held off-site. In the next chapter we will discuss how to establish an inactive records storage program that will be a complement to the storage and retrieval systems developed for the active records.

16

Records storage

Records 'storage' refers to the housing of records when they are semi-active or inactive, but must still be retained. Those records that are rarely used but that must be retained for occasional reference, for auditing, or for legal or archival reasons are less expensively stored outside the office area. For this simple economy alone, records centers were created. Experience shows that the need to consult a closed file or other document no longer required for the conduct of current business evaporates rapidly after the first 18 months. Removal should therefore be carried out two years after closure of the record.

The objectives in creating and operating a records center are to:

● achieve economy and efficiency in the storage, retrieval and disposition of semi-active and inactive records
● secure against both unauthorized access to and destruction of these records in keeping with its obligations to its customers
● protect stored records against the risk of natural disaster such as fire, flood, earthquake, etc.

The economic advantages of storing semi-active and inactive records somewhere other than the office is clear. While floor space costs per square foot vary (offices in large cities undoubtedly command a higher rate than those in small towns), they are still greater than warehouse space. Add to that the volume space savings from storing records to near-ceiling height in the center as against inactive filing equipment, and the records center storage costs drop dramatically.

Records centers are of great importance in the management of records because they enable significant savings in space and equipment costs:

● Records center space is better utilized – five times as many records can be stored per square foot as in equivalent office space through the use of compact high-density equipment.
● Records center storage space away from city centers costs less – on average there is a saving of between 750 and 1,500 percent.
● Staff costs are less away from city center locations.
● Records center storage equipment costs less – high-density equipment can cost on average 25 percent of traditional office storage equipment.

It should be noted that while cost saving has been traditionally the primary reason for, and function of, records storage, there is a growing trend toward requiring more reference services from records centers.

Whether on a minimal or full basis, the records center is a service operation. While, initially, senior management in an organization may agree to the establishment of a records storage program because it will save costs, the only points that will interest the users of the records are security and reference. If there is no guarantee that the records they surrender will be protected from damage or loss, people will not surrender them. If there is no guarantee that they can quickly get back the record or information they need, they will not release it. Thus, a records storage facility may be established to save money, but it will survive only if it provides a faultless service.

Though the records storage program manages records during the latter part of their life cycle, it is usually one of the first programs the records manager must establish after doing the initial inventory. The inventory will have revealed numerous problems, for example, confused filing systems, inappropriate software, lack of backup or protection procedures, antiquated or inefficient filing equipment. While all of these problems need to be addressed and improvements made, it would be a great waste of time and money to make any improvements on semi-active or even dead records. Before writing new filing systems or software, ordering new equipment or folders, and transferring anything to computers, the mess of old records must be cleared out and put into records storage.

Ideally, a records storage program would be able to handle all records of all media, to provide the appropriate environment for all media, to ensure complete security, and to provide a full reference service. However, limitations of funds, space, personnel, equipment, or expertise often require that a less than ideal records storage program be established. Even so, as with all records management endeavors, it is always better to start with the less than ideal and to work to improve it, than to wait for the highly unlikely event of all necessary conditions for the perfect program being satisfied.

ESTABLISHING A RECORDS STORAGE PROGRAM

In establishing a records storage program, four things must be determined:

1   What is to be stored: what media of records? what levels of secrecy or confidentiality? what is the volume?
2   How it must be stored: special environment, humidity, temperature? extra security?
3   What level of service will be provided?
4   Where it will be stored? purpose-built records center? the archives? commercial storage? the basement?

What is to be stored

The records inventory will have revealed those records that are semi-active. Those papers, files and disks that are referred to or used less than once a month are semi-active. A decision must be made as to what records or collection of information elements will be accepted into records storage. Paper but not books? Engineering drawings but not photographs? Tapes but not floppy disks? Each requires special containers, environments, or equipment for maintenance. Can all of these be obtained, maintained, and operated? Can full confidentiality and secrecy be assured? Will the budget permit the higher salaries of vetted, or security-cleared, staff?

The records inventory will have revealed an approximation of the volume of semi-active or inactive records. To estimate the volume of records expected to become semi-active in future years, take one-third of the total from the inventory, per year. Thus, if there were 12,000 linear filing feet of semi-active and inactive records in the inventory, then an estimated 4,000 more will become semi-active each year. (However, where major changes in systems or equipment are planned, the media and volume of records can change dramatically. To estimate the rate of production of semi-active records here, the records manager must work closely with the planners.)

How it must be stored

Most non-paper records require a strictly controlled environment for long-term storage. While many records in storage may be destroyed after a very short time, others may be transferred to the archives, so the archival conditions should prevail in the records storage area. However, according to the medium of the records, these environmental requirements vary widely and are, at times, incompatible:

- *Paper* should be stored in a steady temperature between 55°F to 68°F (13°C–18°C), with the relative humidity between 55 and 65 percent.
- *Microfilm (silver)* must be stored in a temperature between 59°F to 68°F (15°C–20°C), with a relative humidity between 20 and 40 percent. It must also be free of dust and exposure to the gases exuded from most filing cabinets and from diazo and vesicular duplicate films.
- *Color slides* require complete dark, a steady temperature of 64°F (18°C) and a relative humidity between 30 and 35 percent.
- *Magnetic tapes and disks* require a steady temperature of 68°F (20°C) with a relative humidity of 50 percent, and a dust-free atmosphere.
- *Optical media* ideal storage conditions have not yet been established. It has been suggested, however, that a temperature range of 50°F to 140°F (10°C–60°C) and a relative humidity of 10 to 80 percent would be adequate.

Thus, separate rooms or storage facilities must have different environments for different media. It is not advisable to try to store all media together in a sort of 'average environment.'

Security is another issue to be considered. Whether or not confidential or secret records are in the storage area, all users will expect their records and information to be fully protected against damage, destruction, or loss. Security against theft of information from a magnetic tape is much easier to guarantee than that of files, because a thief would have to know the precise software and hardware with which to run the tape, whereas files are easily read. Yet the destruction of the same tape would be a much greater loss than that of a single file.

What level of service will be provided

The storage facility can be as simple or as elaborate as needs require and costs allow. It is here, in the differences in service to users of stored, semi-active records, that the difference between records warehousing and information management can most clearly be seen. Of the two extremes described below, the simplest storage service treats only the objects, the records, on which information is stored. A box of files, a file, a tape, a floppy disk, are all so many objects. The information they may contain is of no interest to the managed records center, the center being little more than a warehouse. The much more elaborate service – one that provides a full reference capability – is less concerned with the object than with the information stored on it. Information on capital gains taxes may be on many objects, a file and a floppy disk for example. The reference service would not simply return the objects, but would extract and compile the information for the user.

A storage facility can be simply a secure and environmentally controlled building, in which departments of organizations are allotted a certain amount of space. This space is divided, and each department holds the key to its own area. The department sends its own personnel to deposit, retrieve, and maintain all of its records. The records manager does nothing more than to maintain the building's environment and security. The advantage of this is that it is very inexpensive, requiring almost no staff or administration. The disadvantage is that while providing physical storage, it is an inefficient use of the space, and the records manager is not, in any way, providing assistance with the management of records. However, it does provide slightly more control than if the departments had no storage, or contracted individually with commercial storage facilities.

The most elaborate records center will provide a full information reference and storage service. In this, the entire facility is secure and is operated wholly by records management staff. The delivery, accessioning, storage, protection, retrieval, destruction, and transferring are all done by the records management staff. A full reference department will retrieve files, documents, or tapes on request; or will search information on tape or disk, or run reports. The advantages of this are greater security for the information and, in managing it as a resource, a much greater exploitation of it, to the benefit of the organization. The disadvantage is that, in requiring large numbers of qualified staff, vehicles, computer hardware and software, it is expensive.

Most organizations are forced to settle for something between the two extremes. The criteria on which to base the decision as to the level of service are those that reflect the needs and abilities of the organization:

- *The users' information needs.* Do the users need to access their semi-active information regularly? Is their information retained simply for legal requirements, as with most accounts records, or because its information is still useful and is used, though not daily, as with studies? Where the information has a consistent and long-term value, a full reference service would be of real benefit to the users. Where the records and information are simply retained but rarely referenced, a supervised storage with a simple reference service may be adequate.

  The inventory will have revealed most of the answers to these questions, but it will be necessary to discuss them further with those departments most likely to benefit from such a service. This will heighten their awareness of new possibilities for exploitation of their information, and will gain their support.

- *The benefits of information sharing.* From the inventory, the records manager will have discovered which sections or departments are duplicating one another's efforts in obtaining and producing information. If there is a large amount of duplication, work in these departments could be greatly reduced through controlled sharing of semi-active information services. A full reference service could ensure the security of all information, while facilitating the work-saving by sharing of some of it.

  The security, when sharing is discussed with users, must be stressed. They must be assured that sharing will be limited to only the information that may legally be shared and that no sharing will be without the creating department head's consent.

- *Cost.* While cost is always a consideration in every program, it is particularly so with reference services. A full reference service, whether done by the records management or commercial storage staff, is extremely expensive. The service must clearly benefit users if the cost is to be justified.

- *Availability of qualified people.* While a simple service will require staff who are literate, do not transpose numbers or letters, and have an understanding of the importance of security, a full service will require a number of highly qualified people. A computer systems staff and trained archivists and/or reference librarians will be needed to access, understand, and analyze the information. If such people are not available in an area (and it is unlikely that they will all be in the commercial storage companies), then a full reference service cannot be considered.

The choice of the level of service to be provided by records storage is not a final but an open-ended decision. The best service that the organization truly needs and can afford will, naturally, be selected; and it can and should always be improved.

Where it will be stored

Where can the records be stored is a deceptively simple question. 'They must be stored wherever there is space,' is the usual answer. That is entirely possible, if that space is brought up to the very stringent archival standards necessary. In the United States, a number of records storage facilities, both commercial and private, are in caves, abandoned mines, old missile silos and dockyard warehouses. The history of records centers represents one of the great stories of industrial reclamation.

Most records managers are not, however, in the business of commercial storage, and most have to decide not where to build a records center, but if to build one. After it has been determined what records and how much of them must be stored, what their requirements are, and what services are to be offered, the question then is: Is this to be done by the organization itself or is it to be contracted out to a commercial storage company? In some areas or countries there are no commercial storage companies. On the other hand, for some organizations it would be out of the question to purchase land, construct a building, and staff a records center. Restraints such as these, of availability, of cost, of policy, may make a records manager's decision for him. Indeed, most records managers use existing space as best they can.

Yet, all things being possible, the choice still requires much consideration. The results of the earlier questions must be ranked according to importance.

- Media – must the facility be able to accept all kinds of records?
- Volume – is the most important thing simply to find a place big enough to take all the records?
- Security – is security more important than anything?
- Environment – or is the proper environment, to ensure the survival of the records, more important?
- Service – finally, is the quality and amount of reference service the primary consideration?

There is no rule as to how the above criteria should be ordered in importance. Each situation is different. Each organization has its own structure, policy, finances, plans, opportunities, records, and information. While records managers will want to work towards providing the best protection and service, in the beginning they will have to weigh all of the circumstances and influences in order to choose the best solution possible. Once this is done, they can then compare the facilities available with those they might create to see which would best satisfy their requirements.

Commercial storage centers

An organization may wish to use the services of a commercial records center if:

- it has too few inactive records to justify operating its own facility
- it is important to store records more than 50 miles away (for vital records, disaster planning, or other reasons)
- it has no available low-cost space for records storage
- it has exceeded the capacity of its own records center
- it has employment ceiling restrictions precluding the hiring of staff
- it has an organization-wide structuring policy
- it is simply not inclined to run its own operation.

Perhaps the biggest concern for an organization considering a commercial facility is the security of its information. The management of the records center must take the utmost precautions to ensure the integrity and protection of its customers' records. Many centers require that their staff be bonded. Strict procedures should be in effect at all times to ensure that only authorized records center personnel have access to the storage area and to any information (inventory, billing, circulation) that the records center maintains on its customers' records, and that only authorized customer personnel are permitted to retrieve their organization's records.

Commercial storage centers are a big business and many people have set up storage centers of extremely poor quality in order to make quick money. There is currently no inspectorate for, or certification of, commercial storage facilities and there is no single standard to cover all aspects of such facilities and their services. This means that records managers must educate themselves about the relevant standards, demand their own certification, and make their own inspections. The checklist provided at the end of this chapter should help with this effort.

In addition, steps for the selection and contracting of a service are generally outlined in the Appendix and should be followed when choosing a commercial storage facility. Points to look for in a good commercial storage facility are:

1   *Sound construction.* The storage center should be in a sound, modern (or well-modernized) building that fully complies with all local building codes and specifications. There should be proper drainage to prevent a build up of water, and there should be no exposed pipes. Temperature and humidity controls should be working at all times. There should be a room where clients can work with their records in privacy.
2   *Full fire protection facilities.* These include sprinkler systems, heat and smoke detectors, and fire extinguishers where tapes and disks are stored. All of these should have labels showing that they are checked and tested regularly. There should be no exposed wires, and no smoking within the building.
3   *Cleanliness.* The appearance should be neat, orderly, and dust free. There should be no evidence of insects or rodents; and no piles of files on the floor that 'will be destroyed this afternoon.'
4   *Security.* Where electrical security systems are unreliable, the building must have round-the-clock security guards on duty. There should be no windows, and access limited to employees only. All personnel, including drivers, must be fully bonded.
5   *Convenience.* The facility should be near enough to allow for regular deliveries within two hours, and accessible to the records manager for occasional inspections.
6   *Deliveries.* There should be at least one fully operational and insured vehicle, and a guarantee that, if it breaks down, deliveries will still be made, on time, at no extra charge to the client. Delivery service should be regular and reliable. There should be a round-the-clock service for emergency deliveries. Ask:

How quickly does the center respond to requests, that is get the information to the customer?

How are 'rush' requests handled, or those which are placed outside normal working hours?

Can specific files from boxes or information from within files be requested, or must entire boxes be returned to the organization?

Can the customer's staff access the records at the facility at any time?
7   *Insurance.* This should cover the full value of the information, not the object on which it is stored, and the cost of recreation. It should cover the records from the moment they are picked up and signed for by the delivery person to the moment they are returned to the owning organization. Such comprehensive coverage would be expensive and the cost would, of course, have to be weighed against the risks.
8   *Destruction.* There should be an established program for notification when records are due for destruction, and an adequate facility for the destruction of both confidential and non-confidential records.
9   *Containers.* Many storage centers will provide, at a cost, boxes or cartons as well as tape canisters. Ensure that these are made according to standards, and that using this service will truly be less costly than purchasing the containers from another source.
10 *Knowledge and attitude.* Finally, the management and supervisory staff should have

a thorough knowledge of all applicable standards, and of the principles of records storage, retention, and destruction. They should show a general willingness to provide the best possible service, and to constantly improve on that service.

Cost, of course, influences an organization's decision to use or not use a commercial facility. Not only is there a charge for storage (usually based on one cubic foot per year), there are various charges for the services – accessioning new boxes, generating customer-specific reports, etc. These charges may be built into one overall charge per box or calculated individually.

The more adaptable the commercial facility is to the needs of the customer, the better. As a prospective customer, an organization should learn firsthand from the center's other customers of the quality of service.

In the final analysis, a number of factors should be considered which encompass security, retrievability, and cost:

1   Does the facility have sufficient space to store the customers' records, including room for growth?
2   What type of security procedures and systems are in place, and how well are they followed?
3   What reputation does this facility have among the business community?
4   What type of contract or agreement is required? What is built into the standard charge? What additional charges are to be expected?
5   What inventory and circulation systems do the center have?
6   Are the staff well trained, courteous, accommodating?
7   Are proper environmental controls in effect?
8   What record media can be stored?
9   What destruction procedures and methods are used?
10 Is there proper fire protection?
11 How far is it located from the organization?
12 How accessible are the records to the organization?
13 Is the facility clean and neat?
14 Insurance:
      What type of insurance cover does the center have?
      Is it necessary for the organization to obtain additional cover?
15 Security:
      Are there adequate physical security controls inside and outside the facility?
      Are there adequate controls for limiting access to your records?
      Are there special areas for storing classified or sensitive information?
16 Communications:
      Is the communication link between your organization and the storage facility reliable?
17 Technical services:
      What is the level of records management expertise among operating personnel?
      Does the facility offer inventory control
      Does it provide microfilming, duplication, reproduction, reference and other services?

Records managers must take the time to visit each facility, to discuss services and standards with the manager, and to interview other clients. During contract negotiations, they should insist on a certificate of compliance, stable prices for a reasonable period of time, and full insurance coverage. Any commercial storage company that will not include these as part of its contract has an obvious reason for not doing so and should not be considered. After the contract is signed and the records stored, the service should be monitored closely as to:

●   the prompt notification when records are due for destruction

- the reliability of the delivery/pick-up service
- the clarity of labeling
- the appearance and order of records or information retrieved
- the timeliness and correctness of invoices
- the general attitude and willingness to provide a service to all personnel who come in contact with the organization.

At least once a year, a surprise visit to the facility should be made. A schedule should be established for periodic review of the service. If it is unsatisfactory, a warning should be given to the company, with a three-month probation period. If the service is not substantially improved in that time, the contract should be terminated and the records transferred to a better facility.

In-house storage centers

Two key reasons for maintaining an in-house records center are security and cost. Many organizations simply prefer their records to be controlled by their own employees. This does not preclude the need for security procedures, however. Cost, of course, is a major determinant in choosing in-house over commercial storage. Another factor that may require an organization to operate its own records center is its distance from a commercial facility, although some commercial storage centers are able to serve distant customers.

Planning an in-house facility requires the same evaluation effort as that made when selecting a commercial facility, in addition to evaluating staffing, equipment, systems, and layout requirements.

Facility. The records center building should be within easy access of the users, either in the same building as the users (if economically practical) or in a nearby building. The more distant the facility, the more difficult it is to service the users quickly. The building should also be located in an area that is not subject to flooding or other hazards.

The center should preferably be the sole occupant of the building, and if possible, a stand-alone facility. This adds to the protection against fire and external hazards. The building must have adequate space for office, reference, and processing areas as well as for the stacks.

For the stack area, the ceiling height has a direct relationship to the cubic foot capacity of the center. Fourteen feet high ceilings generally provide a 5 to 1 square foot to cubic foot ratio. This height is easily accessible by safety ladders. Higher shelving may require scissor-lift type picking equipment, special ladders, or mezzanines. Aisles must be wide enough to allow easy movement of ladders and other equipment, taking into consideration that boxes hang over the edge of the shelves by a few inches.

Floor strength requirements are based on the ceiling heights. A standard records center carton (12 x 15 x 10 inches) can weigh 25 to 30 lbs. If the center is on the ground floor with no basement, floor strength is probably not of concern. The records manager should work with the facilities engineer to determine the requirements for the building based on current and future storage requirements.

Protection. The protection of the records is of utmost importance. Precautions must be taken to guard against fire, water, pests, and vandals and to ensure that proper environmental controls are in place and functioning. The building itself should be fire resistive, and fire prevention procedures should be established in addition to the installation of fire control systems. Local fire standards and controls should be followed.

Most older buildings and many new ones have sprinkler systems, but such deterrents can pose a problem for records since water can inflict more damage than fire. Nevertheless, an automatic wet-pipe sprinkler system is the most effective fire protection element and the most economical automatic fire control system for the protection of records.

Alternative fire control systems are high-expansion foam, and carbon dioxide. High expansion foam inundates the entire volume of the storage space, quickly extinguishing a fire. However, the foam contains a small amount of water, and records exposed to foam would need to be put through a drying process. A fire can also be extinguished by flooding the area with carbon dioxide followed by a soaking period. The danger is that carbon dioxide is fatal, and the design and proper installation of such a system is critical.

In addition to fire protection systems, the roof and drains of the facility should be periodically inspected and repaired, replaced, or cleaned as needed. Some older buildings have roofs that drain through iron pipes within the building walls. These pipes are susceptible to deterioration and can expose records to water damage. Bad plumbing and defective heating and air conditioning systems are also avoidable potential hazards.

PHYSICAL ARRANGEMENT

Floor plan

The floor plan of the records center should include office, reference, shipping and receiving space, as well as the stack area. Each non-stack area should be designed to serve the volume of records flowing in and out of the center, the number and responsibilities of the records center staff, and the number and frequency of customers visiting the center. Ceiling height, fire and building codes, floor strength, and existing wiring and pipes will influence the specific layout of the shelves in the stack area.

Shelving

The most common shelving units are open shelf arrangement with 42 inches wide by 30 to 32 inches deep shelves. This allows for six boxes – three abreast and two deep – to be stored on a single level or twelve boxes when stacked two high. In the former case, the shelves are placed 12 inches apart; in the latter, 23 inches apart. The 32-inch depth is preferable to 30 inches to avoid having the boxes hang over the edge and obstruct the aisle. Shelving is also available in 69-inch wide by 30 to 32 inches deep dimensions. Shelving material usually consists of steel frame, posts, and shelves, although wood shelves are sometimes used.

Shelving units can be set up in single banks with aisles on each side. Boxes are easily accessible from either aisle, but this arrangement does not provide maximum use of floor space. Placing the units back to back results in a more efficient layout, which more than compensates for the increased effort in handling the boxes. Triple units can also be set up if space requirements warrant, but access to the boxes in the center unit is awkward, making this arrangement difficult to justify. A better alternative, if space is a critical factor, may be mobile shelving, if floor loading requirements allow. Single units, of course, are the logical choice for placement along a wall.

From a practical standpoint, it is best to provide a break in any row of shelving that exceeds 50 feet in length for employees to pass through the next aisle. Long rows should also end no closer than 36 inches to the wall to allow for faster access to other aisles.

Aisles

Aisle space is determined by the height of the shelving, the wheelbase clearance requirements of material handling equipment, the needs of the employees, as well as any local fire or building code specifications. A shelf height of 8 feet or less can easily be accessed with small platform ladders, so aisle space of 30 to 36 inches is adequate. Anything less than 30 inches is difficult for the operator to pull out boxes. Some platform ladders and mechanical material handling equipment that are needed to access higher shelving will fit within 36 inch or wider aisles.

In 1992, the Americans with Disabilities Act (PL 101–336) was passed in the United States. While it does not mention 'records center' or 'records storage' shelving aisle requirements, it does reference 'library' shelving, prescribing a minimum aisle width of 36 inches.

Main aisles, such as would be found in larger records centers, should be at least 48 inches wide to allow for movement of bulk shipments and for employees and standard equipment to pass freely.

Lighting

A critical part of the layout of any records center is the placement and method of lighting. Lights should be centered lengthwise over the aisles and over the shelves. Most areas have local fire codes that fix the minimum distance between the lights and the highest cartons. Lights should also be high enough so as not to interfere with handling the highest cartons. Fluorescent lighting is preferred to incandescent because it minimizes glare and shadows. However, fluorescent light is harmful to paper over the long term, so archival documents should not be stored where they will be exposed to this kind of light.

Wiring and piping

In addition to lighting, wiring and pipes of any sort should not be installed over the shelving but over the aisles and other work space.

Bracing

Bracing the shelving units is a good safety practice, and in some areas it is a building code requirement. Anchoring the units to the floor provides stability. Structurally tying the shelving at the top across the aisle is advised when the height to the top of the highest load exceeds six times the depth of the shelving. For example, a standard 42-inch wide by 32-inch deep unit may warrant tying if the height to the top of the highest carton approaches or exceeds 15 feet.

Space numbering systems

Once the shelving has been installed, a system for identifying the location or address of each container must be established. Rows, units or sections, shelves, and spaces, or any combination of these can be numbered and used for the address. This allows for many variations to what is essentially one basic system: row-space. Information on determining an appropriate arrangement of records on the shelves, and ways to identify available shelf space, are discussed further in this chapter under 'Records center operations.'

Row-space

This basic method simply assigns a number to each row and a number to each container space in that row. For example, a box stored in row 5, space 47 could be numbered 0547 (or 5–47, or 05-47, or 05/47, etc.). The advantage to this system is its simplicity; there are only two elements within the code to interpret. The disadvantage lies in learning the order in which the space numbers are assigned from unit to unit and on each shelf. The longer the row and higher the unit, the more spaces available, and the more space numbers to keep track of. For instance, a row made up of 25 units with 7 shelves each containing 12 boxes, would require spaces numbered 1 through 2100.

Row-unit-space

An improvement on the simple row-space system is to add a third element to the address: the unit or section. Within each row, the units are assigned sequential numbers, and within each unit the space numbers are assigned. Using the example of a 7-shelf unit storing 12 containers per shelf, the space number would run 1 through 84. Thus, a container on row 5, unit 12, space 47 could be written 051247 (or 5–12–47, or 5/12/47 etc.). Although this third element lengthens the address, it does allow for faster locating of the containers, and therefore faster retrieval. On the other hand, there is still the problem of remembering where each space is.

Row-unit-shelf-space

By adding a fourth element to the address, the shelf number, the process of identifying the location of the container becomes more exact. Thus, a container on row 5, unit 12, shelf 4, would have a space number of only 1 through 12 and could be written something like this: 05120407 (or 5–12–4–7, or 05/12/04/07, or 5/12/4/7, etc.). An advantage of naming the shelf number is that the records center operator can know whether or not special equipment is necessary to retrieve or shelve the container. The disadvantage of this identifier is the length of the number and the possible difficulty of remembering the order and meaning of each element.

Row-unit-shelf

It is possible to ignore the particular space in which the container is placed on the shelf and limit the address to the three elements: row, unit, and shelf. Thus, a container with the address, 051204 (or whatever variation is used), is one of up to twelve containers found on row 5, unit 12, shelf 4 (if they are stored twelve to a shelf). The greatest advantage to this method is not having to worry about exact placement of the container on the shelf; it can go in any of twelve spaces. A three-element address is easier to read than a four-element one. The disadvantage is that the operator may handle the containers more with this method because the exact space is not known. However, this loss of time may be no greater than that spent remembering a space number.

EQUIPMENT AND SUPPLIES

Ladders

Since records center shelving takes advantage of height to gain maximum storage, equipment is needed to handle the containers that are out of reach when standing on the floor. Ladders of various heights are the most common equipment used, and platform ladders offer the most utility. The number required depends upon the number of operators and level of activity.

Any ladder should meet safety standards, regardless of height. The platform should measure the width of the ladder, be at least 10 to 12 inches deep, and securely fastened to the top of the ladder to carry the weight of the operator and a few containers. At least one side of the ladder, and preferably both, should be equipped with a safety handrail. The platform should also be surrounded by a safety handrail.

The width and depth of the steps must allow ease of ascent and descent while handling containers; the standard step size is 8 inches deep. Waffle, ribbed plate, rubber-covered, and open grid treads are available. Open grid is preferable since it is anti-skid and self-cleaning; rubber treads tend to loosen about the edges and deteriorate with use. The number of steps depends upon the height to be reached and the height of the persons using the ladder. Five steps is generally adequate to service shelving nine feet high, while ladders with seven or nine steps can be used with shelving that exceeds nine feet. A two or three-step platform ladder is useful for servicing lower shelves.

The ladder should be equipped with rubber-tipped legs or casters that lock into place when weight is placed on the steps. Rolling casters will allow ease of movement. Steel construction is recommended being durable, lightweight, and maneuverable.

Carts

Rolling, tabletop carts with one or two shelves are useful for handling containers, folders, and individual documents. The height should be approximately 32 inches high for ease of use and to prevent back strain. A small platform ladder can serve a dual role as cart and ladder.

Catwalks

Catwalks are used in some very large records centers where the ceiling height allows for tall shelving. Either for safety or practical purposes, access to the highest shelves is easier by catwalk than by ladder or lift. The catwalks should meet safety standards and should be open grid construction so as to allow maximum lighting to reach the lower shelves.

Other equipment

Hydraulic lifts can be used instead of, or in addition to, ladders. These usually have larger platform space, can accommodate more weight than ladders, and eliminate climbing up and down; however, they are quite expensive. As with ladders, health and safety standards will provide safety guidance when purchasing a lift.

A forklift truck is necessary if pallets are used for moving large quantities of containers. Records center operators should be properly trained in forklift operation.

Conveyors can be used to move containers a short distance, such as inside a truck, or over a long or elevated distance, such as to a second level of shelving.

Floor guides or rails, post protectors, and other aids and buffers can be installed to prevent any of the equipment from hitting the shelving or containers.

Containers

The most common type of records center container is the standard carton measuring 10 inches high by 12 inches wide by 15 inches deep. This carton, approximately one cubic foot in volume, easily stores letter size (8 1/2 x 11 inch), legal size (8 1/2 x 14 inch), and computer printout (8 1/2 x 12 inch or 11 x 14 inch) documents.

Containers should be constructed of at least 200 lb test corrugated fiberboard. This is standard for most manufacturers. Containers may be either single or double-wall construction. For short-term storage single-wall containers may be satisfactory, although they do not hold up as well as double-wall containers under the stress of stacking and frequent handling. Some organizations offset the higher cost of double-wall containers by reusing them after the contents have been destroyed.

Useful features of a records center container include handholes on the ends, a shoebox-type lid, and custom printing or markings on the side. Handholes are placed below the lip of the lid on the 12-inch wide ends. Their placement is critical to hand fatigue. If placed too far (more than 3 inches) down from the top, an operator with small hands could find this puts too much strain on the thumbs. Placing the handholes too close to the top, however, could cause the cardboard to weaken and tear. Lid lips are usually 1 1/2 to 3 inches. The shorter the lip, the more likely it is to pop off the top of the container.

'Acid-free,' that is, alkaline-buffered, containers are available for storing archival documents. These come in standard size or a smaller manuscript size.

Containers are available in other ready-made sizes to fit various needs. Invoices, checks, microfilm and microfiche are accommodated by smaller boxes. Large (approximately two cubic feet) cartons, also referred to as transfer cases, are available, but are very heavy when filled and may require special handling. Long, narrow tubes or containers hold various sizes of rolled documents, such as engineering drawings. In addition, custom-size containers may be ordered from most corrugated box manufacturers.

RECORDS CENTER OPERATIONS

The primary goal of all records center operations is 100 percent accuracy in maintaining control over the records entrusted to the records center. The procedures for achieving this goal are critical to the success of the operation. These procedures, outlined below, should be followed with the utmost care.

Responsibilities

In most organizations, the customer (department, office, or individual) who transfers records to inactive storage retains ownership responsibility. That is, the customer has the authority to designate the time of transfer to storage and the destruction of the records at the appropriate time. The customer also has the authority to withdraw its records from the center either on a permanent or a temporary basis at any time and to rearrange the contents of the container.

Under these circumstances, the records center is simply the custodian of the records, responsible for protecting them, tracking their movement within and without the center, and ensuring their proper destruction. (This holds true for both in-house and commercial facilities.)

In a few cases, the records center becomes the owner of the records upon transfer from the user. In these instances, it may be responsible for maintaining the integrity of the container contents and for authorizing the destruction of the records.

Clarity of responsibility is important from both a legal and a customer satisfaction standpoint. A well-run operation in which the customer receives timely, accurate, and cooperative service will do more to instill trust and encourage the use of the center than one or two instances of negligence. Negligence can haunt both the customer and the records center. The absence of records because of their premature destruction, loss, or misplacement (essentially lost), regardless of the offending party, is not acceptable during a tax audit, lawsuit, or other required review of the information. Missing records could result in monetary damage to the organization and, perhaps, in the dismissal of those responsible for the protection of the records. A commercial records center may have certain liabilities, depending upon the terms of the contract with the customer.

Accessioning

Records center operations begin with the transfer of semi-active or inactive records from the office to the center. Records should be transferred on a regular basis to avoid overloading the records center staff with incoming shipments. Records should not be accepted for transfer unless listed on the retention schedule.

Some organizations prefer to indicate the timing of the transfer of records from the office area to the records center on the retention schedule. During the records inventory

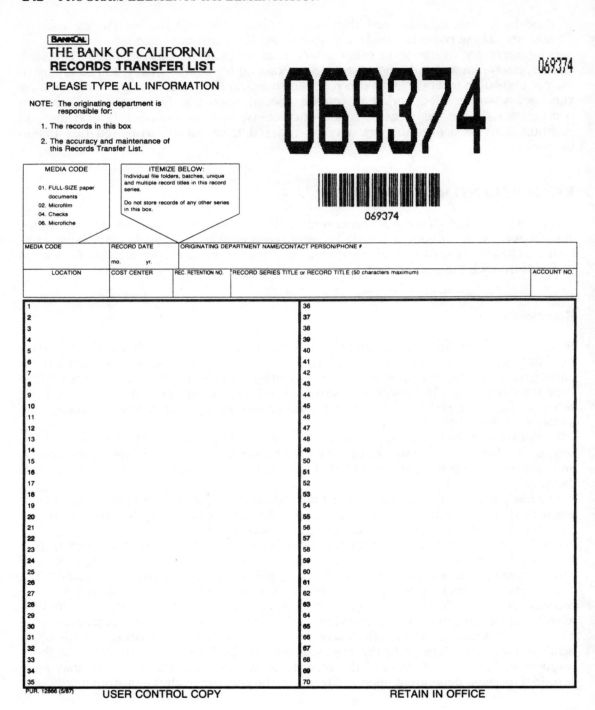

Figure 16.1   A records transmittal list (Courtesy of The Bank of California)

and retention scheduling process, customers may indicate the length of time records are to be stored in the office, based on reference activity, and their subsequent transfer to the records center. With this indication, the retention schedule can act as a control point for notifying departments to review records for transfer and for ensuring that all stored records are listed on the schedule. The disadvantage of this approach is that usually people ignore this guideline and transfer records when convenient.

The key steps in transferring records – transmittal, container packaging, and disposition date – are described below. Control over the transfer of records is best achieved when one person on the records management staff is designated the central contact for coordinating box transfers and retrievals with the records center. The records management contact then inspects each box to ascertain that the transfer forms are correct and the records are packed appropriately.

A few selected users are authorized to represent their respective departments in dealing directly with the records management contact. These department representatives are trained in how to use the retention schedule as their transfer guide, and how to fill out the transmittal form and pack the boxes properly. They should receive written guidelines, preferable as part of a records management manual. This will eliminate boxes of 'Joe's stuff' or personal effects going to storage for an undetermined length of time.

Transmittal

It is essential for there to be evidence of what has been transferred to the records center, however that may be described. All accessions, therefore, must be accompanied by a transmittal list (see Figure 16.1).

Networks and modems make it possible to substitute electronic for the paper forms described in this section. The exchange and content requirements of the information do not change; only the medium. Many commercial records centers offer on-line access to their clients that eliminate the need for some, if not all, paper forms. Records management software packages purchased by an organization, or similar computer systems developed in-house, may also be capable of transmitting required information on-line to and from the records center.

The form should have a unique identifier which links it with its box and with no other. This identifier could be a sequential number or a combination of codes such as retention schedule number/date/department box number, department code/record series number/ date, etc. The sequential number is advantageous in that it is simple to understand and incorporate into an automated control system, it provides an easy way to file the forms, and it can serve as the actual box number. The other types of identifier are just as capable of providing control, but can be cumbersome if used as access points to an automated database.

The transmittal list should be completed by the transferring section/department. It need not be of archival standard; it is, after all, merely an inventory and will only be used internally. The form of the list should, however, be uniform.

Information on the transmittal may include record series number, record title, transfer date, record date, destruction date, media type, department code, department name, retention schedule number, and box contents description. The organization should determine which information is relevant and will ensure the highest control for the protection, retrieval, and disposition of the records.

The transmittal should be at least a two-part form. A three-part form in which one part is the box label itself is useful. (Figure 16.1 has a removable label in the upper right corner.) One part is the original, which should be retained by the customer as owner of the records. The second part is the copy, which is submitted with the box to the records center (see Figure 16.2).

If an intermediary prepares the forms and transfers the records on behalf of the customer, that person may also keep a copy. As an example, the accounting department

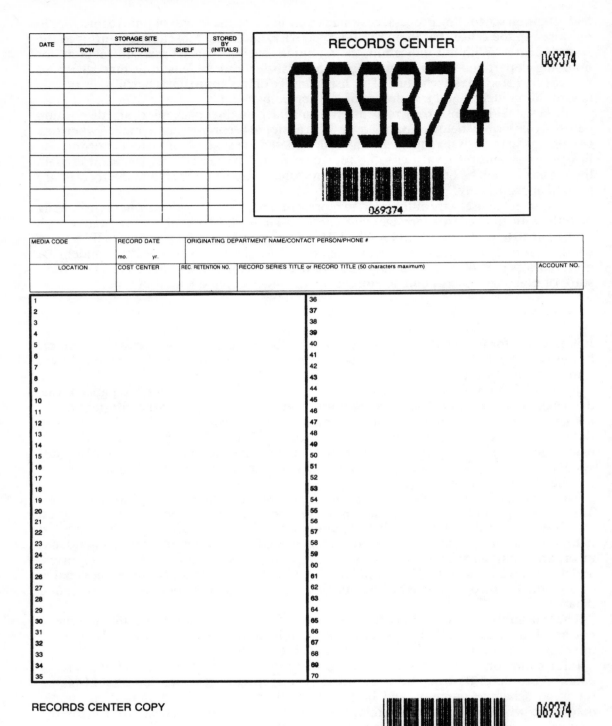

Figure 16.2 The records center copy of transmittal list (Courtesy of The Bank of California)

(the customer) fills out a transmittal, keeps one copy, sends one copy to the records management department, and sends one copy with the box to the records center. Accounting uses its copy to request the records and keeps it until the records are destroyed. Records management uses its copy to update the inventory database and then disposes of it. The records center uses its copy as part of the inventory control process.

The transmittal must contain clear and concise instructions for filling it out and dispersing the multiple copies. The customer is responsible for filling out the form with accuracy and describing the box contents to the extent necessary to retrieve the information at a much later date. Common errors in filling out these forms are misstating the record date and inadequately describing the contents. The records manager or designated person should educate customers as to the importance of the various fields on the forms.

Container packing

Procedures for packing storage containers should be clearly communicated to customers. Suggested guidelines are in Figure 16.3. Records should first be removed from binders or hanging folders and placed loose or in file folders in the boxes. This avoids injury from the metal edges to those handling the boxes and the high cost of replacing these supplies in the department. Boxes should be packed loosely to allow for additions, interfiling, and easy retrieval of the records.

Guidelines for Preparing Records for Transfer

- Remove files from hanging folders and three-ring binders.

- Eliminate duplicate copies of documents and files before transferring them to storage.

- Place one record series with one disposition date in a box. Records will later be disposed of by box, not by removing individual files from boxes.

- Pack the files in the same sequence in the cartons as they are arranged in the file drawer, using the same filing system as that used in the department.

- Do not overpack boxes.

- Prepare a records transfer list showing the description of the first and last file in each box.

- For security, do not identify the contents of the box on the outside.

- Retain a copy of the records transfer list as proof that records have been forwarded.

- (Optional) Number each box in an accession sequentially. This is the temporary box number. The records center will assign a final location number.

Figure 16.3   Guidelines for preparing records for transfer

One records series per box is the best procedure for packing boxes, even if multiple records series have the same retention period. This ensures that retention changes to any record series will not result in needing to remove records from a box. It is also advisable to pack records with the same disposition date in one box to avoid the premature destruction of some records or the elongated retention of others. If one record series with one disposition date fills up less than one-third of a box, and even with this small volume there is simply no room to keep it in the office area, it is better to add another year rather than another record series. This means that the earlier records will be retained for an extra year, which is generally of little consequence, particularly for small-volume records.

Disposition date

Documents stored in records centers must indicate on the transmittal form (or on-line equivalent), at the least, and on the container itself (if not a security issue) a date when the records are to be reviewed or destroyed. Without that date, material languishes on the shelves indefinitely and thereby defeats the whole object of why it was put there in the first place. Records managers will check these dates annually in order to identify those records which are due for review or destruction in the current year and will arrange for the appropriate action to be carried out. This exercise is made simpler by ensuring that documents with a common review or destruction date are packed in the same box. The contents should not be described on the outside of the box, but on the transmittal form. This provides another level of security as does using a code, rather than the name of the department. The record date, indicated either on the box or in the computer database, is essential.

Records center services

Records centers should provide the maximum service given the available resources. Services may include accessioning new containers, loaning out containers and later picking them up, looking up information in containers, pulling files to be loaned out, refiling returned files, interfiling new files into existing containers, providing specific turn-around time, disposing of containers, providing management reports, and charging back costs to the customer.

There are three levels of records storage service:

1 Minimal storage
2 Standard inventory control storage
3 Full reference storage.

Minimal storage

This type of center, also known as an intermediate repository, is used simply for the storage of material that is awaiting review or destruction. Little or no servicing is carried out on the records, other than to produce files and papers required for consultation. There are usually no lists or indexes of the material, other than those originally produced when the records were active. Boxes are normally marked only with the references of the contents and the date of destruction/review.

Some intermediate repositories are large enough to hold material from a number of organizations. These will usually be administered by central staff, but the records themselves will be serviced by staff from the organizations to which the records belong. Minimal storage records centers which remain an integral part of the creating organization will be under the control of that organization.

Standard inventory control storage

Standard inventory control is the traditional form of records center management. Its sole objective is to account for the whereabouts of each container at all times. Inventory control procedures may be manual, automated, or a combination of the two. There is no best way; the procedures simply must meet the objective.

Once the records are accessioned they are placed in a staging of processing area. If they have not already been checked against the transmittal at the pick-up point, this should be done. The containers are now ready to be placed on the shelves. The procedures may call for assigning the space number/location either prior to or at the time of actual placement on the shelf. If containers are given a permanent location, so that they are always returned to the same place after being on loan, the space number assignment should be marked on the front-facing end. If the containers are randomly shelved and reshelved, the number may be omitted. The records center should be solely responsible for assigning space numbers and maintaining this information. Reliance on the customer for this information is risky.

The space number assignment, along with the date of receipt and the initials of the records center operator handling the box, should be indicated on control card or form, such as the actual transmittal if it is designed to include this information. Control data may also be recorded on-line, if operations are automated. The control card or database fields may also be used to note the movement of containers in and out of the records center.

Full reference storage

Many centers of this type are run by private commercial organizations supplying a comprehensive storage and referencing service to their clients. A number of countries, notably Canada and the United States, also operate their government centers by providing this service.

Detailed requirements have to be met before the center will accept records for storage. These include the completion of a transmittal and receipt form, a document information schedule (to enable lists and indexes to be compiled), the use of standard containers, and reference to a records control schedule.

The centers provide a full reference service, including loan or return of records to the agency of origin, preparation of authenticated reproductions of documents, and furnishing of information from records. They will have a high degree of computerization and will provide facilities for the storage of records in various media – microfilm, microfiche, computer tape and disk, photographs, etc.

Procedures for requisition services are established to ensure consistency in responding to each request and in documenting the movement of requested material. Procedures may require that all requests be in writing, sent via interoffice or electronic mail; or they may allow for telephone requests. The latter can provide unproductive if records center personnel are frequently interrupted by telephone calls for services. However, the use of a telephone answering machine on which customers identify themselves and state the nature of their requests allows the staff to respond to the calls at their own convenience. A drawback to verbal requests of any sort is the speaker's difficulty in enunciating clearly, resulting in time wasted by the staff in tracking down inaccurate information.

All requests should be recorded on a service or work order form. If customers are required to submit all requests in writing, a preprinted form should be available to them. This ensures consistent information is provided by all requestors. If customers submit verbal requests, the records center staff should record the information on the form. If this information is to go into the database, the data should be arranged on the form in the order that it is to be keyed in. The service order form should indicate the following:

- requestor
- requesting department
- telephone number
- requestor's location
- type of service requested
- container number(s) involved
- billing and other information, as appropriate.

Collection

Accession procedures have already been covered. As a service, new containers should be collected in the office. Transmittals should be readily available for the customers. It is preferable that only one or two persons in a department be responsible for preparing containers for transfer to ensure consistency and competence in this step, otherwise the records center personnel may spend unnecessary time advising others of the proper procedures. All containers in a department should be collected from a central point in the office, again, to save time and effort. If it is not practical to pick up from individual departments, pick-up points may be strategically located throughout the organization. Access to any pick-up point should be unrestricted, enabling the necessary material-handling equipment to be moved throughout the building.

Some records centers require the use of outside personnel for the transportation of containers. Procedures for using in-house or commercial carriers should be established with the organization's traffic management operation.

Retrieval

Only authorized personnel should have access to material in the records center. Retrieval of containers or files should be done by the records center staff so as to control the documentation of the movement of the records in and out of the center. Requestors should be verified as authorized to call for and receive the records. Records should be given only to the organizing department unless that department has given written permission to another to receive the records. Some records, such as employee related information, may be sensitive enough to require only authorized individuals within the department to request and receive them.

In some instances it may be expedient for customers to visit the records center in order to review material or search for specific records within containers. A service area should be provided for this, away from the incoming and outgoing staging area, so that customers can have uninterrupted, private access to records, and their material will not inadvertently be mixed with others. All visitors should be required to sign a visitors' log to document the presence of non-records center personnel on the premises.

Records center staff should be prepared to respond to after-hours or emergency requests. Supervisory personnel are usually 'on-call' at all hours, but it may be necessary to schedule one or more staff members on 'stand-by' on a rotating basis.

Delivery of containers and files should be directly to the requestor or to a central point in the requesting department. From a cost standpoint, centralized delivery points servicing more than one department may be more advantageous, but the personal touch does more to enhance the image of the records center from a customer satisfaction standpoint.

Turnaround time for responding to requests depends on available resources, including personnel and transportation. A 24-hour response, with exceptions allowed for emergency requests, is adequate for most operations.

If records are delivered by non-records center personnel, verification of receipt should be obtained from the requestor and returned to the records center. Containers should be handled in such a manner as to ensure the contents remain intact. Files should be placed in an envelope to ensure that the contents do not spill out. Interoffice mail may be used for files instead of personal delivery, assuming the turnaround time is met. Confidential records should be placed in a sealed envelope, marked 'To be opened by addressee only.'

Records that are on loan should be noted in such a way as to allow for follow-up, for example on the database, in a tickler card file. Notices should be sent to customers on a regular basis, reminding them to return the records to storage. All too often, without notifying the records center, a container is dismantled, and the records destroyed by the customer or reboxed and shipped to the records center as a 'new item.' Customers should be given the option of returning the records, extending the loan period, or permanently withdrawing the material from the records center, but these actions should always be communicated to the records center.

Storage arrangement

There are three main ways in which the records can be stored at a records center:

1 In box number order
2 in review/destruction date order
3 in file/document reference order.

Box number order

When files and papers are ready to be sent to the records center, they are boxed up and the boxes labeled simply with a box number and other information, as needed. A master list of box numbers may be kept by the records manager who issues the numbers. It is important to keep files and papers with the same destruction/review date (year) in the same box. The transmittal form is then completed, as previously described. The records manager keeps the master set of forms, and copies of their own deposits will go to the originating sections. In Figure 16.1, for example, the user keeps the top copy and the records center keeps the bottom copy.

If a file is required for consultation, the person requesting it has to quote the box number. It is then a simple operation to locate the box and extract the file.

With this arrangement, the review/destruction exercise is normally carried out annually (towards the end of a year). It is straightforward to remove all boxes marked with the year in question in order to carry out the necessary action. However, while this means that gaps in the run of boxes on the shelves will appear each year, there are a number of ways to identify space availability to ensure optimum use of the shelving (see section on Space availability).

Review/destruction date order

All files, papers, etc. are kept on the shelves in strict chronological order (month/year) of the date of review or destruction. Within this arrangement, files may, as far as possible, be kept in reference number order although there are bound to be large gaps in the sequence, since all files in a series are not likely to have the same review/destruction date. It will be seen that a series of records will be dissipated among a number of boxes and that an efficient index is necessary in order to locate particular files or papers. As an aid to finding requisitioned documents, boxes need to be numbered.

With this arrangement, it is a straightforward operation to carry out review and destruction and, because sections of the shelving are emptied in one exercise, optimum use is made of the storage facilities.

File/document reference order

All files, papers etc. are kept on the shelves in strict numerical order within their series, that is in the same order as that in the active records office. This arrangement makes it very straightforward to locate files and documents that may be required for consultation, without the need for a special list or index.

It will be seen, however, that dates of destruction and review will be spread quite randomly round the series, making it necessary to examine each box when carrying out the monthly or annual exercise of destruction or review. This can be made a little simpler by marking the index of files with the destruction/review date, and, if the index is in a suitable form (for example, docket sheets), by keeping a duplicate set of index slips in chronological order of destruction/review date.

Space availability

Space availability is handled in a number of ways. A chart may be created of all spaces, with each occupied space marked with an *x* and each available space left blank. While this may be practical for a small center, the disadvantage is readily apparent when hundreds, or even thousands, of boxes are being stored. The size of the chart, not to mention the erasures when hundreds of containers are destroyed, points to the need for a more efficient method.

Another procedure is to maintain a card file of vacant spaces, arranged in space number order. As each space is filled, the card is attached to the container. When the container is destroyed or returned to the customer, the card is returned to the file. This file represents vacant spaces only.

Colored magnets may be used on the shelves to designate empty spaces. A plastic-coated magnet placed on each shelf has written on it the number of available spaces. This number can easily be erased and rewritten as the spaces are filled. Another color may be used, in addition, to note the number of empty spaces caused by boxes on loan. An alternative to writing on the magnets is to use one magnet for each empty space.

If the inventory information is maintained in a computer database, the space number assignment should be part of that information. Computerization of the inventory control process should allow for the reporting of available spaces for new boxes in addition to the unavailable, empty spaces of boxes on loan.

Once a box has been assigned a location, it should not be moved to another. From a practical standpoint, the more active boxes (that is, the ones that are recalled most frequently by the departments) should be stored on the most accessible shelves, usually those between knee and eye level of the operator, while the more inactive ones should be placed on the upper shelves, the very bottom shelf, or in rear positions. When a box is returned to the records center after being borrowed by the department, it should be placed in the same space from which it was removed. Placing it in a new location would require changing the space number written on the box and on the control card or in the database.

It is a good practice to store boxes randomly on the shelves regardless of box identification number or originating department. Likewise, it is advisable to mark each box with the minimum amount of identifying information, such as box number and space number only. The resulting anonymity of box content and ownership contributes to the security of the records, and those two numbers are the only elements necessary to locate a box on the shelf because the properly filled out transfer list or control card has pointed the way to it.

If the inventory control procedure is to assign a unique number to each box, it is best to avoid assigning blocks of numbers to each department. Rather, distribute the transfer lists randomly, in quantities needed by the customers. This proves useful when the forms are updated.

Physical inventory

A physical inventory of boxes should be taken periodically, preferably annually. This activity provides an audit trail of the inventory activity and assists in determining if any procedures need improvement.

The inventory process should identify four conditions:

- *Matched* – container on the shelf is in the correct/assigned location.
- *Away* – container is away from its assigned location, properly checked out.
- *Missing* – container should be in its assigned location but is not.
- *Found* – container is found in a location where not assigned.

The physical inventory is easier to accomplish when the inventory information is on-line. A report which sorts the containers in space number order can be divided among the operators who would be responsible for specific rows. Pairing off sometimes expedites the process, with one person handling the boxes while the other calls out the number.

Regardless of whether the physical inventory is a manual or an automated process and whether it is performed as an ongoing or an annual activity, the exceptions ('missing' and 'found' above) must be reconciled immediately. Otherwise, the 'snapshot' of the collection at the completion of the inventory becomes less accurate with each passing day because of the constant movement of boxes in and out of the records center.

Bar code

The use of bar coding in conjunction with a computerized database can be very useful in records center inventory control. It provides for error-free data entry of box numbers, space assignments, and other data. Applications include circulation control and physical inventory support. Bar code applications require bar code labels using a standard format, bar code scanning equipment (wand), a portable or hand-held data collection device, and if necessary, a cable interface and software program to upload data to the records center database. Bar code labels representing each box number are placed on each box. Certain computer printouts are capable of generating bar code labels, or the bar code can be designed as part of the box label form and printed by the forms manufacturer (see Figure 16.1). Bar code labels should also be created for space locations and if desired, for each customer, using a numeric code. If the row-section-shelf space numbering system is used, only one label is affixed to each shelf. If the specific space on each shelf is designated, a label must be created for every space.

When a container is received into the records center, its number is scanned by the bar code wand which is connected to the data terminal. If customers have been assigned numeric codes, these can be listed on a large sheet of heavy paper stock with the corresponding bar code labels next to each one. The appropriate customer code is then scanned. Additional container information is then keyed into the database. When the container is assigned its location or placed on the shelf, the space number label is scanned. This procedure avoids transposition and other data entry errors that affect the integrity of the database.

The circulation of containers loaned back to and returned from customers can be tracked using bar codes. Once again, the container, space, and customer codes are scanned by the bar code wand. The software has been programed to interpret this data as charge out or return information rather than accession information.

Bar codes can speed the physical inventory process. Rather than checking off each container on the inventory report, writing down the exceptions, and then manually comparing the results against the database, the container and space numbers are quickly scanned, the data is uploaded into the computer and matched against the database.

Storage conditions

With increased diversity in the size and type of records, a corresponding diversity in storage equipment and conditions has evolved. The basic concept of any records center, however, must be to provide as much storage capacity as possible in as little space as possible. By definition the records in the center are not going to be used or requisitioned by the public and the call on them by the originating organizations and agencies is likely to be minimal. Access to the records, therefore, is less important than the conditions under which they are stored.

Although a minority of the records in a center will eventually find their way into the archives, it is necessary to provide an environment that will guard against excessive deterioration. In this respect, air conditioning is the best system. In its absence, heating and ventilation must be kept within tolerable limits. In addition, centers must be protected from fire by sprinklers or smoke detectors or both, and must be secure against unauthorized intrusion. By their very nature, a great many of the records will be sensitive.

If the records center staff themselves are authorized to carry out the disposition of material, there needs to be some kind of chronological 'trigger' to indicate which boxes are due to be destroyed in any particular month or year. By keeping a copy of the transmittal form in chronological order of disposition dates, it is a simple matter to extract from this file each month, or each year, those forms for records due for destruction or archival review at that particular time and to locate the boxes accordingly. Such a system can be used however the boxes are stored and whether the documentation at the center is computerized or not.

If a file is required for consultation and is removed from its box at the records center, two essential pieces of documentation are required:

- A slip or note must be left in place of the file in the box to indicate its reference, to whom it was sent, and when it was sent. This will enable any further request for the file in the period before it is returned to be met (if only to explain that the file is in use), and will guard against files going astray.
- An indication must be made on the file of the box number or location reference at the records center so that it can be replaced properly when it is returned. This indicator might be a label or it might be written on the file itself.

Often, specific chargeout forms are developed to meet both of the above requirements.

Specialized records centers

A number of countries have introduced records centers for special categories of records, particularly personnel records of government employees, both military and civilian. The operations of such centers need not be different from other records centers but it is inevitable that they will have to provide a very full reference service. Normally, this is the main reason why they have been set up in the first place, especially in countries (such as Canada and the US) where there is freedom of information legislation.

PROMOTING USE OF RECORDS STORAGE

As any records manager knows, a large part of the job entails the publicity and promotion of records management services, especially the records storage services. Because the facility is out of sight it is out of the users' and the potential users' minds. They must constantly be reminded of the benefits of records storage, or they will forget to use it, and it is the records manager who must do the reminding. While some may find this sales aspect of records management distasteful, it is vital to the success of a records storage program.

In promoting records storage services, it is necessary to make contact with potential users, explain the services to them, and to encourage them to try the services.

- *Contact* can be as simple as strolling into an office, noticing piles of records on the floor, and striking up a discussion with the manager about how best to remove them, or it can be as complex as a full user orientation program. Publicity is a key to contact. Simple memos, printed leaflets, booklets, posters, or a full video can all be used to describe and encourage use of records storage services. Consider also a photographic display about the facility, articles in the internal press and tours of the facility.

- *Explain* in publicity, briefing sessions, or in conversation, the services offered through records storage, emphasizing security, cost savings, quick retrieval, time and space released in users' offices. When possible, arrange a meeting between those who use the storage and those who do not, to have a full discussion of the benefits.
- *Encourage* users to test the services, to ask for trial retrievals, to deposit records for trial periods of time. This not only gives them the chance to approve the services, but it keeps records storage staff in practice.

Promotion is a constant in records management, and a good storage promotion program will increase use of the facility and thus, an appreciation of records management.

RECORDS CENTER SELECTION CRITERIA CHECKLIST

Location	Must	Avoid	Not an issue
1 Proximity to offices			
• same site			
• no further than *x* miles/kilometers			
2 Adjacent properties/tenants			
• records center is sole tenant of building			
• building is shared with another department			
• building is shared with another company			
• building located away from fields or food storage (potential rodent problem)			
• records are stored away from heat-generating equipment			
• records are stored away from hazardous materials			

Facility

1 Ownership
   - company-owned
   - leased
2 Fire safety
   - fire-resistive
   - meets NFPA (National Fire Protection Association) standards
   - fire protection system
        – sprinkler
        – halon
   - 'No smoking' signs posted
   - no smoking policy strictly enforced
   - regular fire inspections
   - fire extinguishers strategically located and properly identified
   - staff trained in fire prevention
3 Water safety
   - sprinkler system has manual shut-off safeguards
   - no overhead pipes

| | **Must** | **Avoid** | **Not an issue** |

- records are stored above ground (above flood level)
4 Environmental controls
  - natural environment
  - man-made environment
  - temperature between 64 to 72°F (18–22°C)
  - relative humidity 50 to 60 percent
  - reliable power source
  - backup power source available
  - controls monitored regularly
5 Lighting
  - incandescent
  - fluorescent
6 Shelving
  - meets local building code(s)
  - braced and/or reinforced for safety
  - open-type units
  - mobile units
  - construction
      – steel only
      – steel and wood
7 Other
  - building constructed to withstand high winds, storms, floods, earthquakes, etc.
  - pest control procedures followed
  - available space for growth
    (*x* percent growth per year required)
  - signs conspicuously posted (for example, 'No eating,' 'No drinking,' 'Authorized personnel only,' etc.)

Security

1 Access to records
  - company personnel only
  - one person per department only
  - one person per company (when using a commercial facility)
  - security clearance required
2 Confidential/classified records
  - government classified records storage capability
  - separate area for company-confidential records

Vault

1 Location
  - same site
  - company-owned building
  - same criteria as for records center
2 Construction
  - *x*-hour fire constructed vault
  - *x*-hour door

	Must	**Avoid**	**Not an issue**

Services

1 Turn around time
   - *x*-hours for container pick-up
   - *x*-hours for container/file retrieval and delivery
   - 24-hour emergency retrieval available
2 Reports to customer
   - inventory listing
   - billing detail
        - by cost center
        - by service type
        - other
   - frequency of report distribution
        - monthly
        - on demand
        - other
3 Destruction
   - methods used for non-sensitive records
        - recycle
        - skip (dumpster)
        - shred or render unreconstructable
   - methods used for sensitive records
        - shred
        - render unreconstructable
4 Transportation
   - provided by records center staff
   - provided by company employees
   - provided by
5 Allocation of expenses
   - charge back to departments or cost centers
   - charge to overhead account
   - consolidate storage and service charges

Commercial storage facility (unique issues)

1 Contract provisions
   - future cost increases
   - cost of permanently removing records
   - contract termination clause
2 Employees
   - bonded
   - labor union(s) involved
   - access to customer offices
        - unlimited
        - limited to central drop-off point
3 Other
   - procedures compatible with company policy
   - comparisons with in-house facility
        - storage and service rates
        - remaining lease costs if company-owned
          building is being vacated
        - available services.

17

Records disposition

Records disposition occurs in two forms: the physical destruction of the records or their transfer to an archives for historical, permanent preservation. This chapter discussed physical destruction, while the next looks at archives management.

Records are authorized for disposal in accordance with a records retention schedule, whether the records are stored in the office area or in a records center. Ideally, the retention schedule provides all the authority needed to carry out the disposition of records. Rather than going back to a department to obtain permission to dispose of the records, thereby leaving the door open for someone to say no and setting a procedure that may be construed as 'selective destruction,' the records manager can notify the department that the records will be disposed of in, say, 30 days, unless it can show legitimate reason why such disposition should not take place. Examples of legitimate reasons are legal actions, described later in this chapter, and substantial organizational changes. Such reasons should be well documented and approved by the individuals who approve other changes to the retention schedule.

An automated records management system that captures the disposition date makes the identification of records eligible for disposition a simple task. The easiest way to determine which records are eligible is to run reports off the database, sorted as needed. For example, select records with disposition dates 'less than' today's date, then sort the report by shelf location for a 'pick list;' or sort it by department, then by disposition date. If files and boxes are tracked manually, filing one copy of the records transfer list chronologically by disposal date will serve the same purpose, although creating a handwritten pick list will take some time.

Active records that are eligible for destruction should be pulled from the filing area and disposed of at once. Some organizations have an annual 'purge day' to clean out their files. The advantage is that everyone is involved, and employees feel more comfortable about spending valuable time in the activity. The disadvantage is that people often see the records management function as 'trash disposal.' If a 'purge day' is to be held, the records manager should advertise the event well in advance so that managers are supportive and people have little excuse not to participate. Line up an 'advocate,' that is, someone in authority and with credibility among the employees who can vouch for the importance and necessity of this activity. Arrange for plenty of trash receptacles and for staff (perhaps from the maintenance department) to be readily available to remove the trash as the receptacles fill up. Also, arrange for the destruction of confidential records by one of the methods described later in this chapter. If the organization is small enough, provide refreshments for all employees throughout the day.

Inactive records in the records center should also be destroyed immediately upon receiving notification to do so. If there are many boxes, however, it may be more economical or convenient to place them in a holding area until all are pulled and destruction can take place as a single event. Sometimes it is also convenient to indicate in the database or, if a manual system, on the inventory record, that the box has been destroyed. This will prevent users from asking for the records, since they believe them actually to be destroyed.

Three instances will halt the destruction of eligible records: litigation, government investigation, or audit. If one of these legal actions against the organization has been filed, or if there is forehand knowledge that such action will take place, no relevant material may be destroyed. This includes pertinent records that are normally scheduled for destruction under the retention policy or are still awaiting destruction in the holding area. Failure to provide records that exist, even though they could have been destroyed but have not, can prove detrimental to the organization as in the assessment of severe fines and penalties, or prosecution of contempt of court or obstruction or justice. Paper source documents, relevant to the action, which have been filmed or scanned and then sent to storage rather than being destroyed, cannot be destroyed once litigation is known, even though they duplicate what is on microfilm or disk. This is because the paper is generally considered 'best evidence' by the courts or government agencies.

Records transferred to the archives, of course, are not marked as destroyed, and users can retrieve them. Because the archives is now the owner of the records, users will have different procedures to follow (see Chapter 18).

PHYSICAL DESTRUCTION

In-house destruction

There are several methods of records destruction. For non-sensitive records, the trash bin or dumpster is satisfactory, but perhaps not environmentally sound. From an environmental standpoint, recycling is preferred. Linking inactive records destruction with a paper recycling program for the office areas (usually handled by an organization's facilities management department) not only saves landfill space, it also means revenue generated through the sale of the paper. Recycling usually requires sorting the paper into white bond, computer printouts, colored and copier paper, etc. Silver halide film may be sold to a vendor who will recycle the silver.

Sensitive records should be shredded at the very least. A shredder that turns the paper or film into confetti is better than one that slices in one direction. A very persistent individual could reconstruct records that are shredded into thin strips only.

Alternatives to shredding are pulverizing, pulping or macerating, burying, or incinerating the records. Some organizations use 'security bins,' others use 'burn bags.' These are storage containers in which the documents are deposited whole for later sensitive destruction by any of the above methods. The containers are locked so that once the documents are put into them, they cannot be retrieved. An authorized individual is responsible for removing the documents and ensuring their proper destruction.

If a recycling program is in place, sensitive paper records can be shredded first, then recycled.

The purchase of appropriate shredders can be quite costly if the volume of records to be destroyed is quite large. Small, portable models can handle modest quantities of records, such as in an office area. For a records center, something like a conveyor-fed model would be more appropriate. Because of the cost, many organizations choose a commercial records disposition firm.

Commercial records disposition firms

Using a commercial records disposition firm often proves to be the most efficient, if not cost-effective, way to destroy large quantities of records, particularly sensitive records.

For example, the cost of purchasing equipment is eliminated. Or in the case of recycling, the firm has the labor and time available to sort through the destroyable records.

Be sure to inspect the commercial firm periodically to ensure the secure destruction of the records. In particular:

- Are the records housed in a secure staging area from their arrival at the firm until their destruction?
- Does the destruction occur as contracted? (In other words, if pulverizing is specified in the contract, is that the actual method used?)
- Is the firm bonded as a protection to your organization if it fails to destroy the records properly?
- Does the firm provide a written confirmation of records destroyed, and does that match what was sent to them for destruction?

Destruction of electronic records

As the use of electronic records grows in an organization, with the proliferation of networked computers and the telecommunication of records over telephone and fiber optic lines, a records center may find itself storing inactive electronic records that were once stored in paper form. **Such records are still subject to retention policy and must be destroyed at some point!**

Electronic records stored on magnetic media and rewritable optical media are obviously destroyed if the tape or disk is physically destroyed. They are also destroyed when a disk is reformatted and, for all intents and purposes, when written over. But electronic records are not destroyed when merely deleted from tape or disk. 'Delete' removes the index pointer to the data, not the data itself.

Electronic records stored on write-once optical media also disappear with their physical destruction. Otherwise, the image remains intact, and the only way to lose it is to eliminate the index to that image, which is on the computer, not on the disk.

DISPOSITION CERTIFICATION

Once records have been disposed of, proof that such disposition in fact has occurred is important. The archives can provide a receipt showing that records have now been accessioned by them. Commercial disposition firms can provide proof of physical destruction; indeed, it should be required of them. For in-house destruction of boxes in the records center, a certificate such as Figure 17.1, signed by the individual who performed or witnessed the destruction, validates the operation.

XYZ CORPORATION

CERTIFICATE OF RECORDS DISPOSAL

Department:

Disposal Date:

Records Series Title	*Dates/Range*

Disposition Method:

☐ Nonconfidential   ☐ Confidential   ☐ Archives

I certify that the above records were disposed in the regular course of business per XYZ Corporation Records Retention Schedule date _____

_____
Signature

Figure 17.1   A disposition certificate

18

Archives records management

While file maintenance and appraisal are two of the basic functions of records management, the communication and description of records which are finally transferred to an archive for permanent preservation is an essential operation if the information in them is to be properly made available for research.

It is not our intention to describe in detail the functions and procedures of an archival institution – a great many works have been produced on that subject alone – but rather to outline those elements of archiving which follow naturally from the appraisal and scheduling processes, namely archives management, arrangement, classification, listing, accessioning, finding aids, access and security, and storage and preservation techniques.

MANAGEMENT

Archives are established to preserve history for the benefit of those who would learn from it. An archives is a memory book. It may house collections on specific subjects or represent the life of its parent organization. It may contain artifacts and be a showplace. But its fundamental purpose is to preserve and make available for research, information of enduring value.

Archives traditionally refers to the agency or department responsible for preserving the records of its parent organization. The National Archives, for example, is the federal agency for preserving the records of the government of the US. In addition there may be archives for local public administrations, and some corporations and smaller companies have established their own business archives. The definition has evolved over time to include organizations such as documentation centers, universities and museums that collect the records and papers of others. Archives has also come to mean the collection itself.

Since the advent of formal records management, the administration of archives has generally been looked upon as a separate profession. Being the last phase of the information cycle, however, archives administration is really part of the overall records management function, albeit a specialized element. An archivist may not necessarily be a records manager or even a historian. The records manager, whose primary concern is with the controlled creation, maintenance and final disposition of records, may not have the training for pure archival work, although in some organizations may have the responsibility.

There are enough similar issues and concerns to support the close working, if not the actual reporting, relationship between the records manager and the archivist. Both are concerned with proper appraisal, arrangement, and access and retrieval of information. Both want to protect information in appropriate equipment and environmentally suitable storage areas. Both are concerned with security issues, with disaster recovery planning, and with standardization. Both are aware of the impact of technology on storage, access, and retrieval, of different media, and of the use of technology to support each program.

The archivist receives a large body of material into a collection and must identify and locate distinct items while not losing sight of generic relationships. The records manager similarly receives a large body of material but may not be concerned with describing the content of the records for future research, however historical they may be. Records transferred to a records center remain the property of the entity that transferred them, while records transferred to an archives become the property of the archives.

Historical information goes into any of three types of archives: public archives, historical manuscript repositories, and business archives.

Public archives

Official records created by federal, state, central or local governments fall into two categories:

- Records filed with or by a government agency as proof of private ownership of a commodity or privilege, or which establish citizenship or other rights (deeds, wills, licenses, birth records, naturalization papers, etc.).
- Records of the administration of governmental functions (policies, methods, results, etc., affecting society).

A public archives is the repository of those records whose enduring value may be primarily legal, but which may become historical over time. Legislation frequently designates the officer and agency responsible for public records, as well as which records have permanent archival value. The integrity of these records must be protected in such a manner that their value to the individual and to the government will not be impaired.

Historical manuscript repositories

Some organizations, particularly universities, maintain archives comprising records other than their own and not necessarily related to their own functions and activities. Collections in manuscript repositories are usually acquired by gift or purchase under a written collections policy. Donors of papers sometimes impose restrictions upon the use of all or parts of their gift.

Business archives

Nongovernmental records preserve the history of corporations, companies, and similar enterprises, bodies which create and own their records. There is usually no legislation to govern preservation and availability for research – such functions being mainly a matter of company policy.

Preserving the corporate memory – business archives

Managers generally are not as aware as they should be of the importance of company archives. Historical material is frequently viewed as little more than a handy resource for celebrating a significant anniversary and for little else. The contents of the past are given more emphasis than the historical process of which the present is part. But corporate history should be a way of thinking about the company, a way of understanding why the present is what it is and what might be possible for the future.

Managers must recognize the potentially high value-added uses of the organization's history and need to consider how to preserve high-quality data for future use. Organizations have aptly mastered quantitative recording in the finance and accounting area, but are lagging in their understanding of the importance of maintaining good records on the processes of management and decision making. Because the electronic age has made the task of preserving the corporate memory more difficult, it is imperative that methods of recording and preserving important facts be developed.

The retention schedule can be used to designate records that should be transferred to the archives as their final disposition. The appraisal process described in Chapter 9 is used to identify appropriate record series. Some series may have only selected records actually accessioned by the archives, but that final determination should be the archivist's, not the user's. For example, subject correspondence files from a departing senior manager may or may not have historical relevance. The series on the schedule that represents those records is marked for archival review, but the archivist decides their ultimate disposition. Figure 18.1 lists several record series that one organization has chosen for archival preservation.

The first consideration in establishing the business archives is the nature and purpose of the archival function. Before any action is taken, these questions must be resolved.

**RECORD SERIES CONSIDERED
FOR ARCHIVAL REVIEW**

Annual reports/financial statements
Artifacts (product labels, containers, etc.)
Articles of Incorporation
Biographical data (board of directors, executives, senior managers)
By-laws
Company publications
Consumer affairs correspondence
Correspondence files (executives, senior managers)
Director and stockholder meetings (minutes, reports, resolutions, etc.)
Employee benefit plans (company-produced booklets)
Engineering drawings
External audit reports
Facilities plans/specifications/architectural models
Labor relations (contracts, negotiations)
Laboratory notebooks/formulas
Legal decisions
Maps
Marketing and sales subject files
Mergers and acquisitions
Official history
Organization charts
Patents/trademarks/copyrights
Photographs/slides/tapes/presentations
Plans (strategic, marketing, business development, etc.)
Policies and procedures manuals
Product publicity/advertising/promotions
Sales kits
Specifications (processing, packaging)
Speeches (executives, senior managers)
Statistical summaries
Stock certificates/ledgers

Figure 18.1   A list of record series considered for archival review

- What is the state of the corporate memory?
- What does the organization expect from the archives?
- What departments are or will be using the historical material most frequently?
- What records management policies pertain to the archives?
- Will it be part of the records management program or, if not, how will the functions be integrated?
- Will only the organization's records be collected, or will materials documenting the role of the organization in the community be preserved as well?
- Will the archives collect the personal papers of the organization's officials?

The placement of the business archives in the organizational structure is critical. The directive authorizing its establishment should provide the archivist with the right to seek out, collect, and preserve inactive office files of enduring value.

The business archives should logically be part of the records management function with the archivist reporting directly to the records manager. If this is not the case, there should be a very close working relationship between the two. Because of the complexity and specialized nature of archival organization and methodology and the difficulty of dealing with the past, it is important that a qualified professional be responsible for the business archives. Organizations too small to cost-justify an archivist should seek professional archival advice.

Programs that use corporate history

An organization can develop programs that use a well-researched history. Some useful questions managers can ask are:

- How does the organization communicate its history to new employees? What is the historical content of training programs or ongoing management seminars?
- Would it be useful for the organization to have ongoing public relations activities based on its history? Should it create a museum or open a library? Should it create ties to universities, museums, historical societies, or other community agencies that might have an interest in its history?
- When major policy changes are debated at the senior level, does the history of existing policy inform that debate? Should histories of policies be prepared for ready access?
- Should histories of organization strategies and other decisions be developed to assess the past performance of the organization in qualitative as well as quantitative terms?
- Should histories of the organization's experience with social and government pressures be prepared to aid responses to public policy debates?

General principles and techniques

Although archives are records, there are methodologies for managing them which differ from records management activities. Records techniques relating to active files management, to the design and control of forms, and to the development of a directives or reporting system are very dissimilar from archival techniques. Even when they relate to activities that parallel those of archives, records management techniques have a different emphasis. For example, the activity of classifying and filing current records differs from the arrangement of archival material. Finding aids produced for current records are not the same as those developed for the archives collection.

Generally, archivists must give careful and analytical attention to records while arranging, describing and servicing them. They may be concerned with the management of current records, especially in a small archival program, just as they may be concerned with the management of books and museum objects. But if they are engaged in both kinds, the techniques of one would not necessarily apply to the other.

ARRANGEMENT

There are two main objectives in the arrangement of records selected for permanent preservation: to preserve their evidential/informational value, and to make them accessible for use.

Two basic principles of archival arrangement have been used:

By provenance. This means that the records are maintained in the order in which they were transferred to the archives, which is not necessarily the order in which they were created. With frequent changes in organizations, the principle has come to mean the order of institution that transferred the records rather than that which created them. When large organizations are created by merger, for example, they often take over the records from smaller organizations. In addition records within an organization are often rearranged after they have served their current uses.

Original order. With this principle, records are maintained in the order in which they were kept when in current use in file reference order, case number sequence, committee paper number order, etc. When arranging by provenance more than one series may be grouped together, but when preserving by original order, records series are kept apart.

Original order may present difficulties where a series of records is the subject of a succession of separate but overlapping transfers. In such cases it is generally preferable to keep the records of each transfer in their own proper sequence and to draw the user's attention to the overlap by means of an introductory note or a contents list.

In general, records will have been created to serve some specific purpose in an organization and there is little point in rearranging them when they are selected for permanent preservation. The original order should, as far as possible, be maintained.

Arranging records in this way seems to run counter to the ways researchers and others would use the information, that is by subject. However, it serves to protect the evidential value of the records, in the context within which they were created. Since records are usually produced to accomplish some purpose rather than to elucidate some subject, their rearrangement by subject or some other classification would obscure or lose the evidence of the activities of their source.

The order in which records are kept during their current life reveals much about the office of origin. Original order sometimes indicates a sequence of actions, shows administrative processes, reveals organizational relationships, and generally reflects how things are done in that particular office. Strict adherence to this principle means that the archivist should preserve the records in the condition they were maintained during active use, whether that condition was orderly or disorderly. In practice, the records must be accessible and the archivist should have no qualms about rearranging them so that they are intelligible and serviceable.

CLASSIFICATION

The classification of archives is based upon the principle of provenance. Subclassifications are by function, not by subject. It is essential that each group or series of records in an archive bears a unique reference so that it can be called up for reference or research. It is impossible to use the original references for the archival classification because there will be gaps in the sequence, since an appraisal and selection will have been carried out and because there is a good chance that individual departments or sections of organizations will have used similar or identical references (the reference 'GEN,' for example, is very common).

Each series should be given a short descriptive title, which should be based as far as possible on an existing series title given to the records by the creating organization. Titles may be amended at a later date to take account of changing circumstances.

LISTING

When records are transferred to the archives, a list of the contents of the series must be completed by the transferring organization. This list will enable the archives, the researcher and the transferring organization to know what the series contains and to identify readily any individual record required for reference. The list should reflect the arrangement that has been agreed upon by the archives and transferring staffs (see above). The choice of type of list for any particular series should be the outcome of evaluation of the specific nature of the records and of the uses to which they are likely to be put. There are a number of different types of lists:

- *Numerical*. This would be the normal arrangement for certain files, numbered reports, etc. Each transfer of files is listed in file reference number order and this original reference is also shown in the list itself.
- *Chronological*. This arrangement is applied especially to chronologically arranged volumes, periodical reports, etc.
- *Alphabetical*. Personnel files and other case papers are best filed alphabetically. Users will generally be looking for the names of particular persons, places, etc. and the original file reference order would therefore be unhelpful.
- *Hierarchical*. This arrangement is particularly suitable for series of records of an organization whose constituent parts have a definite hierarchical arrangement, such as committees and their subcommittees, military formations and units, etc.
- *Record type*. This arrangement will only be used rarely since in most cases different types of records require separate series. However, some collections, such as the records of a commission of inquiry, small research institution, etc., may be better arranged together in one series. Within this series the primary arrangement might be: minutes of meetings, papers considered at meetings, reports, correspondence, etc.

Descriptions

Files have a tendency to outgrow their original titles or contain abbreviations and technical phrases which may not be understood by the user. The list description, however, should not depart too far from the original title and should not be extended beyond a general statement of the subject of a file, volume, etc. The description should reflect as accurately as possible the contents of the piece without being too long or unwieldy.

The extent of the dates of each piece will depend upon the range of the records themselves, but generally it will be sufficient to give years only and not year/month or year/month/day. The dates must be the actual dates when the documents were compiled, the date of the earliest paper in the piece and the date of the latest paper. If a piece consists of, or includes copies of or extracts from, documents of earlier dates, such dates should (if cited) be included in the description of the piece rather than the date.

Introductory notes

Each series list should be prefaced by a brief introductory note, which will complement the list itself and furnish the user with essential information not given in the body of the list. The introductory note should contain the following information, where appropriate:

- *Name, origin and history of the creating body*. When a creating body is a government entity or a company it is usually sufficient just to name it, but for small departments, commissions, boards of inquiry, divisions or sections of organizations, etc., it will be necessary to give brief details of their origin, history and functions. For private collections an outline of the career of the person concerned should be given.
- *Legislative background to the records*. This will be necessary if the records were kept or created as a result of a particular statute or other piece of legislation.
- *Nature and form of the records*. This should be included where it is not obvious from the title of the series, for example correspondence with local authorities, minutes of meetings, etc.
- *Geographical scope*. It may sometimes be relevant to indicate whether the records relate to the whole of the country or to some part of it or to give some other indication of the geographical area covered by the records.
- *Preservation*. Any special circumstances affecting the preservation of the records, such as dispersal, accidental damage, or custody by a body which did not create them, are worth noting.
- *Selection*. If selection has been made in some special way, this should be stated. For example: specimens, sample, representative selection, collection of notable cases, etc.
- *Other means of reference*. Where there are indexes, or other finding aids produced by the creating organization, whether within the series or elsewhere, mention should be made of them.
- *Publications*. If the series has been used as a source for official publications, this should be mentioned. Attention might also be drawn to any other publications which would assist in understanding the records.
- *Related records*. Where related records exist in other series, they should be mentioned and the relationship explained.
- *Access*. A statement should be made of the period of access given to the records, especially if this differs from any general access rule.

Lists and introductory notes are best compiled by the organization that is transferring the records, since they will have a more detailed knowledge of their content, make-up, etc., but rules and guidelines for standard listing format should be formulated by the archives. The value of a standard form of list is great and conformity to the standard does not make the task of listing any more difficult.

ACCESSIONING

When the list has been compiled and agreed, and when the records have been numbered, packed in suitable archival boxes and labeled, formal arrangements for their physical transfer to the archives must be made. A simple transfer/accession form may be used. Through accessioning, the archives becomes the physical and legal owner of the records.

The archives should also keep a record of accessions; this may be easily achieved by using a register showing date of transfer, transferring organization, series and pieces references, description of series, agreed access arrangements, and location of the records in the archives repository. Other supplementary information may be kept, such as an alphabetical list of groups and numerical list of series within groups, showing the number of pieces within each series and the repository location.

FINDING AIDS

Finding aids are the keys to making the holdings in an archival collection accessible for use. A descriptive program to prepare appropriate finding aids should be designed with the following objectives.

- To provide information on all records in a repository. This can be in the form of summary finding aids such as guides and catalogs which concisely describe all groups and collections, or inventories describing records series within large or significant collections.
- To provide special information that may be needed about the records. Since different groups of records have different values, and, consequently, different uses, different types of finding aids are needed by different types of researchers. The descriptive program should be adapted to accommodate the special uses to which particular records series may be put.
- To provide specific information about particular records. While the second objective focuses on selecting the type of finding aid to be prepared, this emphasizes the degree of detail in the finding aid. The more intensive the description, the more likely it is that the quality of reference service is improved.
- To produce finding aids in a form that best facilitates use of the records and best reveals their significance and content. The card catalog is particularly flexible in that subject entries as well as record titles or series can be included. An on-line database of descriptive information can be searched and sorted in a variety of ways for the researcher.
- To make the finding aids readily accessible to the user. Depending on who may have access to the collection, these aids may be solely in-house reference service material, such as would be most appropriate in a business archives, or they may be published for external use, such as might be done by a university archives, or they may be a combination of both.
- 'Finding aid' is a term used generically to cover all types of archival descriptive documents. It may be comprehensive or limited in its coverage, general or detailed in its descriptive data, and may pertain to holdings of any size. A finding aid may be a catalog, guide, inventory, calendar, list, index, or similar document; it may be in paper, micro, or magnetic form.

The types of finding aids most suitable for the archives depend on how the archives will be put to use and the judgment of the archivist. For years a catalog, usually in card form, has been a basic finding aid in archives. Cataloging basically treats both single documents and extensive collections in such a way as a librarian would treat a single book or series of books. An adjunct to the catalog is the index which allows the material to be described in great depth. On-line indexing provides the most flexibility in meeting current and future needs.

Another useful tool is the accessions log. Because it records the type, amount and date of arrival of new materials to the archives, it constitutes the first record of new acquisitions and therefore is a fundamental means of control. Should the processing of a record collection and preparation of appropriate finding aids be delayed, the accessions log can be a preliminary descriptive tool.

An inventory of records series within an archival collection is the principal finding aid that reflects arrangement and, as such, is the most thorough single description of a collection since it combines the arrangement information with that of the content. Common elements in an inventory include:

- provenance, or the source of the records
- biographical sketches of the major persons mentioned in the records or historical overview of the office or unit whose records are being described
- the scope and general content of the records
- a description of the files within the series, including their order, inclusive dates, and volume

- a container listing, including physical location
- a guide to related materials on the topic or unit
- subject index to the content of the records if justified.

Some archives create a brief checklist or guide to their holdings in addition to the card catalog. A calendar may be produced which provides a chronological list of record items with a brief summary of the contents of each.

Although machine-readable records are not usually arranged in the traditional manner of paper or film-based collections, finding aids can be developed in the form of code books or indexes. These should provide a good general sense of the structure of a collection and as much specific information as possible. Essentially, this uses the same principles governing the preparation of finding aids for paper records.

ACCESS AND SECURITY

Archives have a dual responsibility: preservation and use. Preservation of records has little value in and of itself; the primary value is in their use. Access to the records by researchers and other users should be explicitly stated as policy.

The degree of access depends upon the type of repository. Public archives usually have generous access policies, which are usually mandated by statute, welcoming the general public as well as the serious researcher. College and university archives may also open their collections to those outside the institution. Private repositories vary in their access policies, often limiting access to a specific constituency.

The rationale for imposing restrictions on the use of a collection is based on privacy considerations. Such restrictions may be mandated by law or regulation as in certain public records or classes of information. Donors may impose restrictions to protect their own or others' privacy and interests. A repository may need to restrict access to protect itself from privacy suits should the information derived from confidential data be misused.

The two types of business archives present two possible access policies. A business archives housed within the company may feel under no obligation to open its archival information to those outside the company or office that deposited the material. However, if it is maintained as part of a research collection of an academic or historical archives, access is probably not as restricted.

Limited access is also important from a security standpoint. Archives staff should serve the users rather than allowing them to serve themselves. The stack areas should always be locked to prevent unauthorized access. More often than not, the theft of archival materials takes place during normal working hours. The level of access and value of the collection determines the extent to which users must be registered and properly identified before gaining access to the material. At the very least, users of any archives should sign a visitor's log.

Even though break-ins do not commonly occur at archival repositories, they can happen. The archivist is responsible for the security of the archives after closing as well as during normal working hours. Security devices, such as locking systems, security alarms, and surveillance equipment, should be installed. (See also Chapter 16.)

STORAGE REQUIREMENTS AND PRESERVATION TECHNIQUES

Archival materials are best stored in acid-free (also referred to as 'alkaline' or 'buffered') containers to retard deterioration of the records inside. They should be placed on steel shelving with baked enamel finishing or powder coating to minimize fire hazard. (Wood shelving should be avoided because of its acid content.) Boxes come in several sizes and shapes for different types of material. It is particularly important that they be acid-free because acidity causes destruction of the records. The acceptable range for archival storage containers and folders is a pH of 7.0 to 8.5 (neutral to basic). Acid-free containers are more expensive than standard records center boxes. Acid-free folders are also available.

Since an archives preserves records permanently, it is important to create a proper environment for long-term storage. The National Information Standards Organization (NISO) recommends a temperature range of 35–65°F (2–18°C), a relative humidity range of 30 to 50 percent, with the recognition that lowering the humidity whenever the temperature is at the high end is as effective in promoting stability as lowering the temperature if the relative humidity is high. High humidity promotes mold growth and accelerates acid deterioration of paper; low humidity will cause paper to desiccate. Microfilm, ideally, should first be processed by archival standards to ensure a longer life expectancy for the image. All records in an archives, whether paper, film, magnetic media, or other, require a constant temperature and humidity, protective casing, and a clean environment, and should be protected against fire, water, and other hazards.

All loose materials should be stored in protective containers where dust contamination is kept to a minimum. Whenever possible, paper records should be stored lying flat to reduce strain on the paper edge. If paper must be stored on edge, the containers should be packed firmly to prevent bending. The best storage for maps and posters are map cases in which they lie flat. Magnetic tape should be stored on end in boxes in tape cabinets or on hanging tape racks.

Photographs may be stored the same way as paper records, or mounted, if part of a collection that will be displayed. The mounting paper and process should be acceptable for long-term storage. Negatives should be kept separate from the photographs for backup reasons and should be stored in darkness in transparent jackets (sleeves) of cellulose acetate or polyethylene.

Only safety film should be allowed in the archives. Nitrate-based film is highly flammable, self-combustible, and deteriorates rapidly. While it has not been used for years, some older films may become part of the archives. These films should be examined to determine if they are on nitrate base. If so, they should be removed from the archives and recopied on to safety film as quickly as possible.

Paper

Many materials received into the archives require preparation and cleaning. Letters should be removed from envelopes and unfolded, since folding breaks down the paper and results in deterioration. Loose surface dirt should be gently removed. Paper clips, rubber bands, and staples should be removed. Although rust-proof paper clips may be substituted, it is preferable not to use them because they can tear or bend the paper. Pressure-sensitive tape should never be used to repair torn documents. Tape that is already on the records can be removed through a special process.

Paper deterioration caused by acidity is a serious problem for the archivist. Most paper now produced in the United States is alkaline, but in the past it has been acidic. Because acid can migrate from one piece of paper to another, even a small amount can contaminate adjacent papers. Thus the importance of acid-free folders and containers and of proper environmental conditions.

Ultraviolet radiation from natural sunlight and fluorescent light contributes to paper deterioration. It causes a bleaching action that can fade certain inks and colored paper, and it reacts with the wood fibers to turn paper yellow or brownish. This photo-oxidation process is further exacerbated by high temperatures and unfiltered air. It can be minimized by keeping paper records out of direct sunlight for any period of time, filtering fluorescent lighting with protective screens, maintaining light levels in record storage areas at 50 lux or lower and turning off lights when the areas are not being used, and using incandescent lighting, which emits less harmful light radiation, wherever possible.

Regardless of the storage conditions and containers, newspaper clippings deteriorate rapidly because of the especially high acid content of the wood from which newsprint is made. Clippings should be reproduced, preferably on acid-free paper, microfilm, or other enduring medium, and the copy substituted for the original.

If it is necessary to add identifying information to photographs or paper records, the archivist should use pencil to make the notations lightly and place a heavy glass under the document to avoid making impressions on the paper.

Records which are in very poor condition may be conserved either through encapsulation or lamination. Encapsulation involves sandwiching a document between sheets of polyester film without plasticizer and sealing the edges with 3M/415 double-faced, quarter-inch tape. This can be done in-house by the archivist. It increases the durability of the document without causing inherent changes to the paper itself, but it will not increase its permanence unless the acid content of the paper is first neutralized. Most importantly, it is completely reversible by carefully snipping the film edges to release the document. Lamination, once an acceptable technique, is no longer practiced by most conservators. It is generally an irreversible process requiring the services of a conservation specialist. Conservation laboratories are available to handle any difficult conservation measure such as tape removal, deacidification, fumigation, or lamination.

Microfilm

Microfilming documents is an acceptable preservation technique since silver halide film has a long life-expectancy when stored under proper conditions. It also substantially reduces space requirements. Microfilm should be produced in accordance with American National Standards Institute (ANSI) *Specifications for Photographic Film for Archival Records, Silver-Gelatin Type, on Cellulose Ester Base* (PH1.28), *Specifications for Photographic Film for Archival Records, Silver-Gelatin Type, on Polyester Base* (PH1.41), and stored according to *Practice for Storage of Processed Safety Photographic Film* (PH1.43). In non-US archives, the corresponding International Standards Organization (ISO) standards should be followed: *Photography-Processed Photographic Film for Archival Records Silver-Gelatin Type on Cellulose Ester Base – Specifications* (ISO 4331) and *Photography-Processed Photographic Film for Archival Records – Silver-Gelatin Type on Poly (ethylene terephtholate) Base – Specifications* (ISO 4332).

By adhering to these standards and to those governing the formats and reduction ratios of microfilm and microfiche, information that is now readable on standard micro-image equipment will be so many years hence.

To date there are no standards covering the archival usage of diazo, vesicular, dry process silver, or updatable microfilms. Diazo film, which is ammonia processed, will fade upon exposure to light. There can also be image loss after prolonged storage in the dark. Under correct storage conditions, however, diazo is likely to last for 100 years or more, making it suitable for long-term, although not archival, storage. Tests conducted on the stability of processed vesicular film indicate that it is suitable for medium to long-term storage. Thus diazo and vesicular film serve a useful function providing a cheap medium for duplicating original microfilm and will probably last for many years, but they should not be used for the archival storage of valuable original documents.

Dry process silver film is still a relatively unproven medium primarily used in computer-output-microfilm (COM) recorders. It is suited to medium to long-term storage. If archival data is transferred to COM using this process, it should be duplicated on to silver halide film. An alternative is to keep a wet process COM recorder on hand to output archival data directly to silver halide film.

Updatable microfilm, as with dry process film, is designed primarily to widen the appeal of microfilm rather than to serve as an archival medium, but is suitable at least for medium-term storage.

Color film, on the other hand, is specifically excluded from standards for archival microfilm and cannot be regarded as an archival medium. Color film dyes are subject to change over time, and color images will fade upon excessive exposure to light.

Magnetic media

Magnetic media is developed primarily as backup storage for computer data and not for archival preservation. Fixed and floppy magnetic disks provide adequate intermediate storage. Both are susceptible to physical damage from 'head crashes' or improper handling. They are hardware dependent, needing expensive disk drives to read and record data. They are also designed to be easily amended, erased, and updated, which can result in the alteration of valuable documents.

Magnetic tape is designed primarily for the short to medium-term storage of the kind of data that regularly needs to be processed on a computer; for example, financial data, statistics, etc. International standards have been written to cover the general dimensional requirements (ISO 1859) and the physical properties and test methods of unrecorded tapes (ISO 2690), but there are no standards regarding the production, recording, and storage of archival magnetic tape.

The two major drawbacks to retaining archival information on magnetic tapes are obsolescence and quality. The storage and transportation of unrecorded tapes prior to arrival at the computer center as well as of recorded tapes during usage can adversely affect the quality of the tape and therefore render the information unreadable. Every few years tapes should be unrolled and rerolled to prevent 'print through,' in which the data transfers from one layer to another on a tightly wound roll. Obsolescence affects the ability to access the data. Packing density, for instance, has changed over the years from very low to very high. This and other software and hardware dependencies, such as the major changes in tape drives over the years, can obsolete that part of the collection within a few years.

The only way to guarantee the preservation of machine-readable records is to output them on to a more stable medium such as silver halide (wet processed) computer output microfiche. This is undeniably expensive for large amounts of information and may be utterly impractical. Until such time as standards are in place to ensure that magnetic tapes meet archival requirements, the archivist should use duplicate tapes for reference rather than the original (as with microfilm), refresh (recopy) the tapes at regular intervals to ensure that they remain in good condition, and maintain them under proper environmental conditions (maximum 65°F to 70°F and 40 percent relative humidity).

Optical disk

Optical data disks offer the high storage capacity and rapid retrieval of magnetic media without the danger of erasing valuable information. The key to their archival life is the stability of the material from which the disks are made along with the availability of appropriate hardware and software. Since optical disks are a relatively new medium, their life expectancy is still unknown (outside of accelerated aging tests). Best estimates are that ablative (pit) and thermal (bubble) recorded disks have a read life of approximately ten years. Dye-based (color change) recordings may have a read life of up to 30 years, while element change recordings could last as long as 100 years.

If optical disks were ever to be proven archival, they would provide a very high storage capacity alternative to COM since computer data can be directly recorded on to them. As with magnetic tape, however, this would be a rather expensive alternative because of the hardware and software that is required to retrieve and read the information. To rival microfilm as an archival document storage medium, an optical disk system would probably need removable disks or disk packs so that the archivist would only need to purchase one recorder/player unit and could store hundreds of disks off-line, as with magnetic tape.

19

The opportunities and pitfalls of using technology in records management

Innovations in information handling technology have created new opportunities to improve the accuracy and availability of information. Word processing has spawned a revolution in document creation that has all but eliminated the typewriter, formerly the standard business tool for document preparation. In recent years, a large percentage of written information communication has been by facsimile (FAX), in addition to mail or courier, reflecting the new urgency of business. The rapid maturity of FAX also demonstrates the speed with which a truly useful technological tool can be assimilated into the mainstream of business practice.

These are but two examples of how new technology is revolutionizing the way organizations do business. New technologies, however, usually cannot just be substituted for previously manual tools with the resulting availability of information being magically improved. They need to be used in a broader context in system combinations that address

Table 19.1
How new tools replace the old

Information flow	Past	Future
INPUT	Manual	Digital scanning Direct computer input
CONTROL	Card indexes	Electronic databases Indexing and classification software
PROCESSING	Stacks of paper	Large screen, high resolution video monitors Workflow software
STORAGE	File folders, File cabinets	Optical disks
OUTPUT	Paper, mail	Local Area Networks (LANs) FAX/modems Electronic data interchange (EDI)

272

the entire information flow. For example, Table 19.1 illustrates how the new tools are being assembled into an imaging system to replace the standard hard copy system of document management.

THE SLOW AND STEADY COURSE TO TECHNOLOGY IMPLEMENTATION

Of course an organizational manager does not simply arrive in the office one morning and say, 'The past is over and now we are doing business as the future.' Since document management is critical to the health of every organization, this process has to be undertaken with care. We all need to explore along the way and try to find out what works and what doesn't without it costing the organization too much. Few organizations want to 'bet the business' on a wholesale move to the new technologies and unproven methods. Many will want to proceed 'slow and steady' and even the vanguards will still need years. The important thing for the records manager to understand is that this is the way the world is moving for the management of records. We have already discussed some of the values that a records manager can provide in the electronic office. But there is no question that this means a significant educational process in technology has to be undertaken by the records manager in order to maintain the role as the custodian of all recorded information.

In this chapter we will discuss two of the new technological tools that records managers can use to significantly improve the management of records and related information in their organizations. These two tools are automated records management systems and electronic document imaging systems.

THE EVOLUTION OF TECHNOLOGY IN THE OFFICE

Since the introduction of computers in the 1940s, there has been an evolution of manual business systems to electronic business systems. Each phase of this evolution can be traced to the sophistication of the hardware and software. Major improvements have been made in computer systems, but these developments have been almost exclusively to add, manipulate, distribute, store, and retrieve data. Recently, however, concepts of information and consequently the information professions are in a state of flux. Information technology is moving so rapidly that it is difficult to determine anything but the fact of constant change. This change goes deeper than the technology, the storage media, and the processes. Electronic technology has not only changed the office environment and jobs, the change is beginning to appear in the way we think about and use information.

As more people become first familiar, then creative, with computers, they cease to think of information as synonymous with the medium on which it is stored. Books are no longer knowledge; a long, single, documentary film is no longer the factual truth; 'the file on Jones' no longer has any clear meaning at all. Information is obviously contained in all of these, but less absolutely than it once seemed to be. Information is fluid. In offices, information can be divided, reassembled, transferred wholly or partly across files, databases, national borders.

Realizing this, we begin to see *all* information – in books, audio or video cassettes, archived files – as equally fluid, and we expect to have it all, consolidated and indexed, available to us. This becomes the true promise of computerization. With the foundations of a records management program in place and the initial streamlining and cost savings achieved, the real benefits can begin. Once the most awkward and amorphous area of information – records – is brought under control, it can be amalgamated with the other areas of the library, information technology, and communications, to provide a full information service to the organization. It is no longer practical to divide information according to its storage medium. It must all be brought together, for only then can the information which flows through computers, telephones, periodicals, files, and the mail room be managed as a single resource.

Many traditional records systems are controlled and managed through the use of automated records management systems. These systems can be configured to provide an organization-wide structure for the arrangement, location and retrieval of records on all media. The next step is the move to the much dreamed about world of on-line records storage and retrieval systems. Many organizations attempt to skip the first step of records organization and jump to the use of on-line storage and retrieval. Their projects often fail because they lack a proven indexing methodology and standards. Records managers can develop these standards and increase their own knowledge of what it takes to automate the management of records by first starting with an automated records management system.

AUTOMATED RECORDS MANAGEMENT SYSTEMS

What are automated records management systems?

From the sound of the name, you would think that 'automated' records management systems are systems that provide the complete automation of records. However, these systems are quite different in concept from hard copy systems, micrographic systems, magnetic media systems and optical memory systems. Those are recorded information handling systems. *Automated records management systems are electronic databases made up of data about the media* – whether it is hard copy, microform, magnetic, or optical memory. This data is accessed and updated to better manage and control the existence, location, retention, movement, and disposition of the media that the recorded information is on. The difference between this and the usual data processing systems is that data processing systems are made up of data extracted from the documents with the function of answering questions about the actual information in the documents.

Since over 90 percent of records in use today are in a hard copy format, most systems available have been focused on managing and controlling the special demands of paper systems. Computer assisted retrieval (CAR) of microforms and of optical memory systems, with their special indexing and control requirements, are actually types of automated records management systems. In the past they have so specifically addressed the needs of these systems that they were in fact part of them. The inflexibility of this arrangement has led to the development of separate software applications for the indexing and management of the images that are not so closely tied to the hardware.

A key breakthrough in the use of these systems has been the proliferation of local area networks (LANs). Low-cost software that runs effectively on these LANs is now available to manage records on any and all media. This software is relatively easy and fast to customize to the organization's needs and it is presented in a way so similar to other PC application interfaces that the learning curve for all users is quite manageable.

Elements of an automated records management system

Automated records management systems can be considered by discussing the application elements that can be automated in the management of records during their life cycle. We will discuss these general elements as they relate to all storage media with emphasis on paper systems. These elements do not reflect the actual way in which a system is configured. However, we need to understand the application first in order to put the technology in the context of the user's needs and not the other way around. Then we will equate them to a typical system configuration.

The elements discussed are:

1   Classification and indexing
2   Media label and program documentation creation

3 Location control
4 Security/confidentiality
5 Retention scheduling
6 Activity reports

Classification and indexing

The important job here is to provide a link between how a record is asked for and what is on the file caption. Some record series such as personnel files are usually filed and requested by the same caption; e.g., by employee name. Others such as insurance policy files have a policy number, but are sometimes asked for by the policyholder's name. In the latter case a cross-reference is required in the index between the name and the number. Still other record captions might be part of a subject arrangement.

Subject filing, which is thoroughly discussed in Chapter 15, is specific to an organization. Records managers and records management consultants tend to have their own custom approaches, but there are certain common elements:

1 All automated subject systems tend to have three levels of classification:
   * *primary headings* which are broad master categories of information like Financial, Personnel, Transportation, etc. These are not department headings but deal more with functions.
   * *secondary headings* which are also general headings but specific to a particular primary; for example, Personnel, Relocation. Personnel is the primary heading and Relocation the secondary.
   * *tertiary headings* are usually the file folder or other media captions; for example, Personnel – Relocation – Expense Limits. This folder would contain information on policy, procedures (and perhaps comparisons with other organizations), legislative and tax ramifications, etc.
2 A subject file index is used to code new documents and index new folders.
3 Pre-selected meaningful words in the file description (which includes the primary, secondary, and tertiary headings) or that are synonyms for words in the file description are sometimes indexed in a key word index. This makes the caption search more of a dictionary approach than the encyclopedic approach inherent in the file description. This more direct indexing is far faster for the computer to process.

Media label and program documentation creation

The system should automatically create a file caption label when a record is added to the database (used here to designate a computer file containing all file captions used by the organization). This ensures that the file caption on the computer exactly matches the caption on the medium. The media label should never be changed without editing the database.

Many forms are generated during the administration of the life cycle of a record that can be automatically produced by the computer system. These include a hard copy classification index to be used by people who require it but do not have access to a terminal; records transfer lists for records being sent from active files to an inactive record center; and a records disposal inventory for disposal authorization.

Location control

The first thing that a system must do is to designate where a folder, microform, or tape containing the desired record is stored when no one is using it. This may be in a file room, in a tape library, or in a person's office. It is not necessary to physically centralize all records whose captions are captured in the database. The important thing is that the central index accurately reflect where the record is at all times. This becomes much more complex when a record is removed from its storage place (sometimes called its home) when someone requests it.

Compounding the difficulty is the fact that records are frequently passed on from user to user for reference before they are returned home. The key to keeping track of files out of home is to make charge-out procedures simple and fast. If there is any delay in handling the records to update the database, users will find a way to go around the system and the file will be temporarily lost. By labeling folders with machine-readable codes, such as a bar code, at the time the file folder is prepared, the caption can be read into a computer quickly and accurately. Some organizations also bar code their employee security badges. *A bar code is a patch of thin and thick black lines that represents a number.* It is most commonly seen on grocery products and is used by supermarkets to identify products for item recognition by the computer at the checkout.

Later, when someone requests a file folder, the file clerk simply wands the bar code on the folder, and enters the person's user number (by wanding the security badge or by keyboard). If the person requesting the folder is authorized to have access to it, the name and location of the person is automatically recorded into the database along with the date and time of the release of the folder into the user's custody.

By using this charge-out system, the records manager knows the location of each file folder and can keep track of how active any particular folder is. This is a high priority for these systems; for location control, particularly with active case files, and for the continued retention of a file in an active filing area, particularly with subject files. File folders that have been kept by users for too long can be selected from the information stored on the disk and notices sent out for their return.

Security and confidentiality

Original records that are vital records or records that are on a fragile medium such as magnetic tape should not leave their homes. Such records should be specifically identified on the system and not allowed to be charged out. Further, some records contain sensitive material and should not be allowed to be viewed by all employees. Each record should have a security level. Each authorized user of a system should be assigned a security level If a user's security is lower than that of the record, access would be denied. Obviously unauthorized users would be denied access to the whole system. In extreme cases, even the file captions may be sensitive. In these cases they should be masked from all but users with a high enough security clearance.

Maintenance of the database for adding, editing, or deleting file captions is also a high security issue. These functions are denied to individuals with a low security clearance.

Retention scheduling

The system should be capable of maintaining an index of all retention requirements for the organization (see Chapter 9). Usually, this is accomplished by assigning retention periods for the office of record copy and the information copy, at the primary and secondary subject levels. These retention periods then automatically act on all files created under these master headings. All retention schedules are updated regularly. This allows automatic lists to be generated of records that are ready to be moved to inactive storage and lists of records ready for disposal. In this way, space requirements are kept to a minimum because records are transferred at minimum required active office retention. Time is saved because all records administration documents are generated automatically. Further, records governed by a computerized retention schedule are preferred by government officials charged with corporate regulation and by the courts themselves because such a schedule shows an organized picture of compliance in the 'normal course of business' rather than wholesale destruction of records when space becomes critical.

Records kept for legal, legislative or regulatory compliance should not be destroyed unless signed off by an authorized person in the department responsible for the records. The system should produce a disposal authority list for their signature.

Activity reports

The system keeps track of additions, deletions, transfers, charge-outs, etc. This allows a records manager to monitor activity levels to ensure appropriate staffing levels as things change. In addition, records that have not had any requests on them for a period of time (usually twelve months) can be transferred to inactive storage or destroyed if the schedule allows, thereby freeing up valuable office floor space.

General computer requirements

Automated records management systems can be configured on any of the three types of computers – mainframe, minicomputer, or microcomputer. For mainframes and mini-computers, 'off-the-shelf' software for records management is not very transferable from machine to machine. Although some off-the-shelf software is available, most organizations using this hardware for this application develop their own software. This leaves the records manager dependent upon the goodwill of the data processing department for development and future changes to the system.

Many successful systems have been set up on microcomputers. There is a growing availability of software from vendors. If microcomputers are installed in each major area of the organization (usually departmentally) to keep a database of their files, these microcomputers can be linked together using LANs. LAN technology enables many microcomputers to share the same database of information (assuming security clearance is high enough). By having all organizational microcomputers used for this application linked together in this way, an organization-wide automated records management system is in place.

Basic steps to selection and implementation of a system

In preparing to computerize any records management programs, certain steps, basic to all computerization projects, should be followed.

1 *Analyze* current procedures of the program. Computerization can solidify bad practices as easily as it can solve problems. It is imperative to analyze closely the whole program as it stands, keeping the purpose of it – the goals it is to achieve – in mind. Does it currently do what it is supposed to do? For example, are records stored and retrieved efficiently? Are they destroyed on time? Are the right ones destroyed, etc. It is the achievement of these goals that is to be automated, not the current procedures. If this is kept in mind, then unnecessary adherence to outdated or even pointless procedures will not be built into the software. Look also for specific problems in reaching those goals again, not in the procedures that automation can solve. Then, try to be creative and look for improvements and new uses of the information that automation might bring.

2 *List* exactly what the new system should accomplish. This list should include requirements both immediate and for the future. Also list all of the reports it should produce. (Include the facility to query the system for unique reports.)

3 *Learn* as much as possible about software uses and abuses.

4 *Build* a team of internal personnel to help evaluate the products. Include someone from the information systems (IS) department with knowledge of software and hardware, and the supervisors of the records management programs to be computerized.

5   *Consider* with the team, what the project should entail. This will include purchases and time – hardware, software, studies, trials, training, conversion, documenting new procedures, both within the records management department and with users.
6   *Budget* the money and time to be spent and the project.
7   *Evaluate* following the steps in the Appendix.

Once the software is selected, it will be necessary to plan carefully the implementation and conversion. (If, however, the records manager is in the position of purchasing and implementing the software before the records programs are begun, there will be, of course, no conversion from paper to electronic systems.) The plan should include:

- Where the new computer is to go. Does it need a room with a particular temperature and environment? Is there sufficient wiring for it?
- Who is to enter the data? If records management staff, do they have the time and training? If external or temporary staff, do they understand the data to be entered? Will their entries be checked?
- When will the conversion be done? During or outside of normal work hours? During holidays or slack times of year?
- How long should it take? Plan this very realistically! It takes time for people to learn the system to the point where they are entering data quickly; and it takes time to understand and work quickly with the reports produced. A rushed conversion will produce only mistakes and delays.
- How will users be educated? They will need explanations of new procedures and reports to follow and use. This should also be used as an opportunity to promote the use of the records management programs. Both to keep staff morale high and to educate users, demonstrations of the new system (when it is fully working) should be given.

Any computerization project will take a great deal of time and effort, especially at the planning stage, if the results are to be of any worth at all. There is no question that a well planned and implemented computerization project will bring major improvements in efficiency and services, and increased respect for the records management department. With these elements in mind let's now look at a typical automated records management system.

A typical automated records management system

For the sake of simplicity, we will consider how a single-user automated records management system would typically be configured.

The system would require the following hardware:

- a microcomputer with a hard disk
- a keyboard, bar code wand, and CRT
- a report printer (and, optionally, a label printer).

It would also require software that would be capable of providing:

- a master index
- a database of all file captions
- a directory of authorized users
- a records management administration program
- a retrieval and refiling system
- a reporting program.

Master index

The most important part of any automated records management system is the index. This is often referred to as the master index or the corporate classification system, or in government usually the subject file classification plan. We will refer to it here as the master index. In this index, we will maintain a master classification index of all subject headings or case file series types. This includes a table of subject descriptions, keywords, retention schedules, and disposal authority references.

Database of all file captions

It is imperative that all file captions be included in the database whether they are active, semi-active, or inactive. In most systems, there is more information about a record besides its file caption and number. These extra identifiers such as home, creation date, department, person responsible, security code, address, etc. are called fields.

Directory of authorized users

Every individual authorized to use the system or request folders is assigned a user number (usually about four digits) and added to the user directory. A simple ranking system defines which system functions (computer commands that allow search, charge-out, add, delete, etc. of files) and which folders are available to each user.

Records management administration program

Functions must be available to authorized users to administer appropriate action during the entire life cycle of a record – from creation to final disposition. In addition, manual filing tasks such as bring forwards, reserves, and flagging files that have correspondence to be filed on them, should be included.

Retrieval and refiling procedure

During the administration of the records management program employees of the organization will want to request records whether they are in active file rooms, inactive record centers, or out in use in an office. An adequate program and procedure must be in place to locate a record at any time. Applying bar coding to the file folders to make them machine readable will speed handling on charge-outs.

Reporting program

The system should be capable of printing file reports such as a listing of all files, of all files in use, of all files overdue, of all reservations, etc. In addition, statistical reports like the number of files created, number transferred, etc. should be available for program monitoring and staffing levels.

Summary

The advantages of automated records management systems could be summarized as follows:

- a complete, up-to-date index of all file subjects and captions
- faster and more flexible search and access for records regardless of media
- less personnel required to do mundane filing tasks and to fill out time-consuming forms for the records program administration
- savings in space as records are transferred on a timely basis and disposed of due to adherence to a minimum retention period schedule
- corporate standard filing and classification system

- reduced duplication of the creation and storage of files in an organization, through the use of office of record copy and information copy concepts
- better opportunity to have organizational records accepted into a court of law as admissible evidence with an organized approach to records retention in the normal course of business
- introduction of discipline in the handling of records (which becomes essential as an organization moves to automated storage systems such as optical disk)
- centralized control of the records management function.

While the advantages of using automated records management systems are many, perhaps the most significant advantage to the users of files and other recorded information is the knowledge that certain information even exists in the organization. And being able to easily locate and request this information (even if it exists in a hard copy format) is a significant step forward.

The technology described has been widely proven, is fairly inexpensive to purchase and implement and, if preferred, can be implemented on a phase-in basis. The costs and risks of failure are low and the benefits are high. A simple automated records management system provides an excellent foundation for the implementation of more sophisticated technologies. For records managers who are just learning their way around information technology, such a system can be an ideal place to begin.

ELECTRONIC DOCUMENT IMAGING SYSTEMS

The office of today is a complex society driven by a need to stay competitive in a world economy. Business and government are continually being pressed to become more productive in a world that is better informed and more demanding. Two important elements of productivity are economy and efficiency. Since information is the major resource in office work, technology is being continually sought to make the handling and management of information more available and more timely, but at the right price. We have seen how the implementation of an automated records management system can make most of the present time-consuming manual records management tasks more efficient. But to allow any organization to significantly reduce its processing times and increase customer service, the new technologies have to provide ways of doing things that cannot be done manually.

Technologies such as imaging enable a business to completely rethink the way it is doing business. The effect of this work re-engineering as it is called, is a higher level of customer service and product quality, all with reduced personnel. These business opportunities would not have otherwise been possible without the implementation of the technology tool.

What are imaging systems?

Understanding the application of imaging to business solutions today can be enhanced by reviewing how the evolution of computers in business has occurred. Initially, the introduction of computers changed the face of 'data' management. Computers were originally developed to handle large masses of numbers such as census statistics and accounting figures. In a business accounting application such as customer billing, the names and addresses of the customers, the dates of purchases, descriptions of goods, and their prices make up the information the computer requires as input before it can go about the business of billing. Calculations producing an invoice are performed as promptly as possible, so that the invoice can accompany the customer's order.

If all that was required was to output a bill to the customer, there would be very little need to store this information. However, customers often do not pay for goods the moment they receive them. In most cases information about what a customer owes must be stored for retrieval at a later date when the customer's statement of account is prepared. In the course of requesting and receiving payments on accounts, the organization begins to accumulate more information – information that is recognized as being valuable to assist managers in their decision making. Specialized management reports are produced and distributed internally to managers to aid in these decisions.

In this simple business example it is hard to imagine that there could be any further information needs beyond that which was instantly available on a computer screen of a sophisticated corporate database management system. In fact, there probably wouldn't be a need for anything more if in all business transactions all parties consistently agreed on the original terms of the transaction. However, customers forget small details like the fact that the sales representative told them that delivery charges would be extra; companies make mistakes entering data on their computers; and, unfortunately, dishonesty can play a part when money is involved.

Data on a company's computer derives from documents governing the details of the company's transactions. These documents serve to provide proof to watchful government eyes responsible for collecting taxes, enforcing environmental laws, or for ensuring free and fair trade practices. Ultimately, these documents are the instruments of evidence that are called upon in a court of law to settle disputes. As we have discussed in previous chapters, an instrument with clearly stated and legible terms, alterable only with difficulty, and dated and witnessed by the sign (signature) of both parties, holds the most weight as evidence in a court of law.

The physical form of these instruments is an essential attribute of what is good evidence. To further complicate matters, documents sometimes contain pictures, drawings, maps, and handwritten notations or signatures. These factors require a computer to somehow deal with a collection of data elements that form an *image*, rather than the one-dimensional strings of data dealt with in data processing systems. This requirement for an image caused fundamental difficulties in the transition to the use of computers to store and retrieve documents.

A picture or image of a document had to be captured by the computer instead of the traditional capture of alphabetic or numeric keystrokes. The image had to be stored on a medium that preferably could not be altered, or if it could be altered, would make it obvious that it had been altered. This was a new concept for interactive computer storage. The traditional magnetic media used in data processing certainly did not meet the criteria. There became such an emphasis on this issue – an appropriate storage medium – that when one was announced in the 1970s, imaging systems became popularly known by their medium – 'optical disk systems.' We now realize that the storage medium is only part of the overall imaging system.

The basic components of a simple imaging system are:

- Input scanner   These scanners digitize information on paper documents or microforms.
- Computer   Imaging systems have been developed for mainframe, mini and microcomputers. Many of the newer systems have been developed for PC LAN-based systems. The popularity of FAX boards in these machines has fueled a growth in this type of system.
- Monitor   Reading images on a screen is a different process than perusing documents in a file folder. A large, non-glare, high resolution monitor is required to clearly view a number of documents simultaneously. The ability to open up windows to also look at portions of other documents or run other applications is also needed.
- Optical memory   Most systems use optical disks for storage, but some systems use optical tape or individual optical cards. The disks are most popular

in 3.5, 5.25, 12 and 14-inch disk sizes. They are available in write once-read many (WORM) disks or rewritable disks.

- Printer
Most printers are high-speed laser printers. While part of the allure of an imaging system is to get rid of all of the paper, there are some innate advantages to using paper documents that require the ability to print out the imaged documents.

- Communications
As imaging systems are used in more and more mainstream business equipment applications an important component is the communications equipment that controls the sending and receiving of documents over local and wide area networks, as well as through long distance telephone services using FAX/modems. The interconnectability with other imaging systems and other business application software is critical to the expanding use of imaging systems.

- Software
The above hardware components are controlled by imaging application software. Many different approaches to imaging software are now on the market. They range from highly proprietary software/hardware arrangements to strictly application software that will run on a variety of operating systems. This application software provides many different functions for the end user. It is here that the indexing and classification is handled. Also if there is a flow of information between many users, the imaging application software usually controls the routing of documents from one user to another.

As you can see the unique parts of the imaging system are:

- the input scanners,
- the optical memory storage subsystems, and
- the software.

We will examine each of these in more detail to identify some of the opportunities and pitfalls in their use.

Input scanners

There are two basic types of scanners for the input of document information. Data can be input into a computer using a scanner that scans the document and 'captures' the text on the page. These scanners are called **optical character readers** (OCR) because they actually recognize the characters on the page and register them in computer storage the same way that they would be recognized if they were typed on a keyboard. A forerunner of the OCR scanner is the **bar code scanner** which is in public use in most food stores to read the pattern of lines or bar codes on the soup cans, detergents, tissue boxes, etc. that they sell. OCR scanners do not recognize the pictures, drawings, or maps referred to earlier.

To capture the pictures, drawings, and maps another type of scanner, usually referred to as an **imaging scanner**, is used. Imaging scanners recognize only white and black squares, laid out like a grid on the page. A simple example of this type of scanner is the one used in a FAX machine to capture a document image for digital transmission over phone lines. Imaging scanners are available to scan paper documents and various microforms.

Imaging scanners

Imaging scanners vary in their size and capabilities with the function they will be required to perform. For instance most imaging scanners are for paper documents. This stands to reason since over 90 percent of documents are still in a paper form and many will have to be converted to a digitized format to implement an imaging system. To illustrate how these scanners work, imagine a page with a grid with tiny square overlaid on it. Each square is read as either white or black and this is translated into computer digital language as 0 or 1. These squares (or dots) are referred to as picture elements or **pixels** when used in pictures with gray scales and **pels** when the image contains only black and white information, such as printing. The number of dots in the grid pattern controls how much like the original that the digital representation looks. The more dots on the page, the better the quality, or resolution, of the copy. This process is called bit-mapping or 'raster scanning.'

Scanners continue to improve with sophisticated new software to increase the resolution of their scanned images. The following summary outlines some pitfalls to watch for:

- Image quality

  Scanners vary in the number of dots per inch that they can scan. This measure, referred to as dots per inch (dpi), should be as high as possible (300 dpi plus) to ensure a good image. Low dpi scanners (under 200 dpi) can produce poor images that distort the information on the page or cause eye strain when images are viewed constantly.

- Speed

  High speed scanners can scan a letter-sized document in under 2 seconds. Typically, purchase of a high speed scanner can be justified if more than 500 pages are being scanned per day. This scanning speed can be significantly impacted by different sizes, quality, and color of documents. Include the smallest, thickest, most damaged and difficult to read documents in any testing of a scanner to get a true reading of the scanner's speed. Make sure that if the scanner has a transport that it will handle your particular range of documents.

- Reliability

  An imaging system will only function efficiently if images are being constantly input. Since the input of paper documents will probably be part of most systems for some time, any breakdown of the image scanner is critical. Knowing the service life and maintenance cycle and method are key elements to having a successful system.

- Indexing

  Although indexing is not a function of the scanner, it is imperative to realize that an imaging scanner will not recognize any of the text on the document and therefore the image will only be retrievable if it is accompanied by careful and time-consuming indexing. This can mean that while scanning can be done in under 2 seconds, the total time to capture an image including indexing might average more like 60–70 seconds. To minimize indexing, an OCR scanner can be used at the same time as the imaging scanner to recognize and register the text. This would allow full text searching of the scanned document. Unfortunately there are still some limitations to OCR scanning.

OCR scanners

The biggest pitfall in using OCR scanners is in their ability to consistently and accurately read, particularly at a high speed. Originally to increase the speed and accuracy with which they read, bar codes were carefully selected to represent alphabetic and numeric characters. Groups around the world got together to standardize on these represent-ations. While there are many standards, one of the most used is the Universal Product Code (UPC). UPC bar coding is used worldwide to code products with the same representations so that all retail store scanners will recognize the bar codes on all products from all suppliers. The bar codes represent a unique code for the particular product. The store's computers match this code with their database of prices and automatically assign the correct price to your bill as you check out. The codes can be keyed into the computer to achieve the same result, but the scanners speed up the checkout process.

It would be impractical to bar code all the information on all documents before they are scanned, so for business document scanning OCR scanners must actually read alphabetic or numeric characters. Original OCR scanners could only read stylized characters because they could not recognize the differences between some letters with accuracy. Recent technology has made this recognition far better, however, and some sophisticated OCR scanners can be trained to read handwriting. These advanced OCR scanners are being referred to as Intelligent Character Recognition (ICR) scanners because of the built-in software that lowers the error rates and makes the scanners able to recognize patterns in character formation and adapt to the peculiar style of the writer. But even though scanners are becoming more sophisticated they are still prone to making errors on input. Sometimes this error rate is so high that the time it takes in corrections is more than the time it would take to have the document rekeyed by a fast typist.

Potential issues with OCR scanners can be broken into four groups:

- Image quality

  This is a direct relationship between image quality and OCR accuracy. If the pixels that represent the data on the page do not have a high contrast to the background pixels, errors in reading tend to be high. A technology called **image enhancement** is used to 'clean-up' the image prior to scanning to improve readability by the scanner.

- Background noise

  Any marks or smudges on a document or image to be scanned can severely affect the ability and accuracy of a scanner. These marks complicate the print contrast ratio by interjecting noise thereby hindering the scanner's ability to distinguish between the data and the background. Even dirt or dust can interfere with the scanner's accuracy and efficiency. And small quantities of dirt and dust can add to the amount of storage space that an image will need for storage, adding up to a significant increase if this is typical of the range of documents that are being scanned. Some 'prepping' software is available to digitally filter out some of this noise and ensure a more accurate read result.

- Touching characters

  OCR scanners read best when the black text is clearly separated by white space. Touching characters confuse the scanner leading to either an inability to read or errors in reading. This is particularly a problem in trying to read handwriting. Hand printed documents can be read successfully after 'training' the scanner on the author's letters, but cursive writing is another issue.

- Substitutions

  One of the most serious problems with OCR scanners is when they misread a letter and substitute a wrong letter. These substitutions are very difficult to detect. Newer scanners work with recognition software that has rules and parameters to make decisions about what a letter will probably be given in its context if it is not clearly recognizable.

Input of documents into an imaging system

The whole document input process to an imaging system must be studied carefully. We have already discussed some of the pitfalls of image scanners. But the input procedure should be looked at as a whole since it is by far the most expensive part of the process. The steps in the input procedure are:

- Image preparation — Paper documents must have staples and clips removed, have rips repaired and be put in the proper order before the scanning begins. This procedure is the same as the preparation for microfilming.

- Scanning — We have discussed some of the pitfalls to consider when using scanners. However the scanning procedure also includes preliminary indexing (usually in batches for future comprehensive indexing), and the inserting of appropriate certificates of authenticity as prescribed by applicable laws and regulations controlling the admissibility of the image storage. Images should be checked after scanning against the originals in order to verify that all images have been properly captured. Documents can be missed in the process. The paper can twist or skew as it is being fed through a scanner if it is not properly fed. This skew can blur the resulting image or cause unnecessary extra storage space to be taken up by the compressed image. The integrity of the images must be carefully verified at the time of scanning to ensure that they can be properly retrieved, viewed or printed when required.

- Indexing — Many organizations have a hard time keeping track of the file folders that they create. Indexing documents for later retrieval is 50 times as complex (assuming 25 documents per folder, two sides). An index of file folder titles is not sufficient if there are more than ten pages in the folder. Then a page index is required which has a listing of the folder contents in enough detail to identify the required document(s). Keywords can be added to assist in future retrieval, since it must be remembered that raster scanning does not recognize the content of the document as does OCR scanning. However, while documents that have been scanned with an OCR scanner can be found through a full-text search, it has been found that a classification structure for the indexing of the documents is also critical to future fast retrieval.

  One of the most difficult jobs for most organizations is developing an appropriate indexing and classification structure that can be easily understood and used by all of the users. Some software is very limiting in how this classification can be done. Since images on an optical disk cannot be perused like documents in a file folder or stacks of paper on a desk, the indexing is the only link to finding the image in the future.

  Where file numbers are used in case file systems, indexing can be relatively straightforward, particularly if the type of documents are relatively standard from case to case. Volume of documents is usually the indexing battle with these case files. Usually high-volume scanning and indexing at the point of creation or receipt by input specialists is the best way to minimize costs and maximize throughput. On the other hand reference files, subject files and project files usually do not present the same crushing volume of documents but can require very complex indexing. In fact, this type of documentation normally has to be classified and indexed by the end user responsible for its creation or the addressee if it is created outside the organization. Few organizations have scanners at every workstation, so work has to be scanned at central scanning stations, batched electronically, and then routed electronically to these 'subject experts' for their classification and indexing.

● Storage

Once the image is captured, it needs to be stored in a format that is accessible by the applicable users' computer displays. Magnetic storage is fast and readily accessible. However, magnetic storage is used only initially when the image is created until it is moved to optical storage and then again when an image is requested for viewing. The image while viewed is stored in magnetic memory as a temporary image only, with the permanent image remaining etched in the optical memory. The hand-off to optical storage after scanning is done because magnetic storage is not appropriate for long-term document storage and it does not meet the unalterable media requirement for official organizational documents.

Since image files consume large chunks of storage, the image files are compressed before they are stored. There are standard compression ratios developed to meet the needs of open computer systems. Obviously as the images are retrieved, the image files also have to be decompressed in order to be viewed on a monitor. Specially written computer algorithms to speed the compression and decompression processes are used so that this procedure does not slow either the input or retrieval process significantly. These algorithms minimize space most when there is a large amount of uninterrupted white space on the document to be scanned. Forms should be designed to keep the use of boxes to a minimum and the layout should create as many uninterrupted white spaces as possible.

Optical memory storage subsystems

As we have discussed, there are many types of optical storage media. While optical disks are the main storage media for business documents, credit card sized **optical cards** are used where large amounts of information needs to be portable and easy to distribute. For example, applications such as patient records leave an individual free to travel and still have their detailed medical history with them. Other optical media include optical strips and optical tape. These media are mostly used for data backup rather than for document storage.

Even though optical memory storage systems provide incredible amounts of storage as compared with magnetic memory, many organizations are still startled by the amount of storage required to store document images. The reason is that image documents take much more storage space than text documents such as word processing files. For example, one million text documents can be stored in one gigabyte of storage space. However, fewer than 20 000 image documents can be stored on one gigabyte disk. Also disks are rarely filled to capacity when they contain active documents. This allows documents that are related to those on the disk to be added to that same disk at a later date so that when retrieving related information, time-consuming mechanical switching back and forth of disks is minimized.

Optical memory systems use a high-powered laser to record information on the optical surface, or substrate. They then use a low-powered laser to read the information. The information is stored using binary digital techniques. As we have discussed, optical disks are the most popular optical media for the storage of business documents. They are available in a number of sizes and formats. Most are produced using one of four technologies.

Write once read many

Write once read many (WORM) disk recording is the main technology for records management applications. Records managers prefer the unalterability of these disks and their relatively long read life for the rigorous demands of document storage. These are the disks preferred by regulators and the courts for the admissibility of documents because of their unalterability.

Erasable/rewritable

Erasable or rewritable disk recording allows end users to produce disks in sizes similar to floppy disks – 3.5 and 5.25 inches. In fact, the magneto-optical technology which is most common for this type of disk is a hybrid of magnetic and optical storage. These disks are used where the end user needs to modify documents frequently. This saves significantly on disk space by allowing the reuse of the existing space. The fact that the disks can be altered leaves them poor choices for the storage of organizational official documents. They can have their place, however, in a storage management strategy that has all official documents on WORM disks and daily user copies stored closer to the user systems on a combination of magnetic disks and erasable optical disks. This storage management strategy speeds the images into the hands of the most frequent users, allows them reference yet effects just one update to the WORM disk at the end of the day if any modifications are made to an existing document.

CD-ROM

Compact disk–read only memory (CD-ROM) disk recording is usually done by publishing houses that master an original disk and then produce 4.72 inch disk copies in the hundreds or thousands for distribution. Encyclopedias, dictionaries, books, and other library type material are being published in this format. Many software vendors also distribute their software in this format. Since these disks as yet cannot be recorded economically by end users, their use in records management is limited to reference information.

CD-R

Compact disk–recordable (CD–R) disk recording is now available for end users to master and duplicate their own 4.72 inch CDs. The storage capacity and disk recording speed of these systems is not as efficient as the larger disk WORM systems, but the relatively low price and flexibility of these systems make them attractive especially for small LAN-based systems.

Optical disk systems are used in the management of records and related information in organizations for two primary purposes. We have discussed the recording of source documents such as paper or microfilm documents. The other purpose is to record computer generated information. This technology, often referred to as computer output to laser disk (COLD), is growing in its use for the downloading of computer reports for distribution within the organization. Many records managers are using this technology as a replacement for computer output microfilm (COM), because the resulting disk has nearly the permanence of a microform, can also be duplicated at a low cost, yet is in a digitized format allowing interaction with other computers.

Imaging application software

As scanners and optical disk storage subsystems become more refined, the technological emphasis on the hardware will be eclipsed by the software advances. In other words, scanners and optical disk storage subsystems are becoming standard hardware selections in the same realm as computers, monitors and printers. The selection of any of these hardware components no longer has to be predicated on their compatibility with the software. Yet advances in imaging software are far from over. We are just beginning to understand our needs and have them incorporated into software in the various applications that have been attempted, let alone the hundreds that haven't.

Despite how far we have to go, imaging application software has evolved significantly from the mid eighties. At this time the software was tightly tied to the hardware sold with it. Since optical disk systems were used primarily as storage and retrieval systems, most of the functions built into the systems were rudimentary at best. The combination hardware/software systems were inflexible and also very expensive, often in the millions of dollars. The shift in demand from large stand-alone systems to the integration of imaging with the other office information access and retrieval systems in the early nineties changed all of this. Organizations demanded to use their existing hardware and networks to run their imaging applications. They were interested in imaging software that could run on these open systems and they wanted to view images simultaneously with data, text and video files.

The software that has resulted can be broken down into two categories: transaction processing, and ad hoc.

Transaction processing software

This software is the key part of a transaction processing imaging system. These systems are characterized by large volume form processing in the large case file applications such as those found in banks and insurance companies. The claims process at an insurance company or the process used in banks for routing and viewing check images are examples. As we discussed earlier, the indexing requirements of this type of system are less complex and usually amount to a number and name and perhaps a few keywords. These simple indexing requirements lend themselves to selective windows from which a user can choose an index term. Often documents in this type of system are bar coded or magnetically encrypted with information to describe their document number, form number or other simple information which can be automatically read and indexed by the computer.

A primary function of this type of software is to control getting a document routed from one department or process to another. This work flow must be defined for each document. Given the sheer volume of the documents involved in this type of system, the emphasis is on speed. The software then controls the transmission of documents around the office. It allows the images to be stored on various media including magnetic disk or tape, WORM disks or erasable optical disks while workers process them and then pass them on to the next person. Documents can be sent in a sequence like that of a loan application approval process or a workers compensation claim adjudication or they can be sent to several workers simultaneously for processing and later amalgamation.

The software sets work priorities so that arriving documents can be put on hold while more pressing work is processed or they can be moved up to first in the queue if they hold priority. They can also be put on hold at the workstation awaiting other related documents to arrive. A calendaring system puts the holding documents back in the queue when all the work has been accumulated or when the priority of the work is next. Throughout the process appropriate security clearance to all or part of the document can be controlled by the software. Recent innovations have allowed the annotation on images with hand-written notes, typed memos and even voice instructions or comments.

Work flow software has become so popular that it is sometimes not even bundled with an imaging software but stands alone as a discreet software application. This type is usually designed to aid in the re-engineering of the office. It simplifies the preparation of 'as is' flow charts and allows their manipulation until the work flow process under review is in its most efficient configuration.

Ad hoc software

The second kind of imaging software supports an ad hoc imaging system. In these systems routing is usually the secondary function with the primary focus on the management of a variety of reference documents. These documents are rarely form documents and could include virtually anything produced in or received by the office such as text, spreadsheets, drawings, photos, newspaper clippings, video clips or voice messages. It is the content of the documents that is important and not the work flow process. These documents are used simultaneously by a work group to do such things as prepare a research report, financial report, evaluation or proposal. Usually each person in the work group works on a different aspect of the project and will want to file the data in a different way. This necessitates having different field names for categorizing the same document. In fact the indexing of these documents is quite a bit more complex than is usually found in the transaction processing systems. The software needs to accommodate a classification structure as well as the ability to develop keyword indices. Full text searching is often a requirement for image documents that have gone through an OCR scanning.

Unlike transaction processing imaging software that is often developed to run on mini and mainframe computers because it is serving users organization-wide, ad hoc imaging software is usually resident on a PC LAN-based system where it services a small work group. In this configuration the software is the key element of the system. And as the trend to more open systems expands to include interoperability between PCs, mini and mainframe computers the trend will be to software that will run on any of these machines and allow free exchange of images, text, sound and video files organization-wide. This eventuality will mean that an organization-wide classification hierarchy for documents will need to be developed to facilitate the interchange of documents. In addition, the imaging software will need to be compatible. This will likely lead to organizations establishing application software standards like they have for word processing, spread-sheets and presentation software.

Technological pitfalls to imaging systems

There are several technological pitfalls that lead to disappointing performance in an imaging system.

Interchangeability/interconnectability

Being able to select standard peripheral devices and plug them into other standard computers to put together an imaging system is a critical requirement. Imaging systems should not depend on proprietary hardware or hardware/software combinations. Off-the-shelf components and shrink-wrapped imaging software are good choices for the future.

Processing speed

As imaging software becomes more complex and as the number of applications and number of people using them multiply, the speed of the processor continues to be critical especially in network servers. The move to full motion video and sound has also pushed requirements for faster processing speed in desktop computers.

Throughput

Many users have complained about the speed with which an image is brought up on the screen. Sometimes this slowness is a result of changing platters in a mechanical optical disk juke box configuration. However, often it is a reflection of a too narrow bandwidth on the network. Data strings typical of data processing applications might speed through present communications channels. But the large chunks of information that form document images require a much wider bandwidth to achieve the same transfer rates.

Visual displays

Imaging systems need larger, high resolution monitors to view multiple document images clearly. These displays can significantly slow down the whole delivery of an image to a workstation because it takes longer for them to redraw or 'refresh' the screen display. Video accelerator boards have helped somewhat in this battle, but larger color screens can still be slow to display an image for this reason. Many organizations have chosen large, high-resolution, gray scale monitors instead of color monitors to speed image delivery. Of course it also helps that they are less expensive.

Scanning and OCR

We have already discussed the various difficulties brought on by limitations in scanning and OCR technologies. Because it can so seriously affect the success of an imaging initiative much work is being done in this area to overcome some of the obstacles.

Summary

Often the records manager is not in control of the development of the corporate strategy for imaging. In fact, often no one is in control of the strategy and systems proliferate as department managers acquire these tools on an as needed basis. The responsibility to 'headman' this strategy should reside with the group in the organization that is responsible for information systems. They must be in a position to build the imaging strategy to fit on the computer platform(s) that will be in place when the imaging system comes on stream. This does not mean that the organization should be trapped with the limitations of its current technology. It does mean, however, that the hardware requirements of the imaging system should be carefully selected to mesh with the hardware requirements of the rest of the information systems within the organization.

A records manager can be a key player in the development and implementation of an imaging strategy. Successful electronic imaging systems are often predicated on the existence of a formal records retention schedule covering records on all media and used in the normal course of business. This not only keeps the organization's eye on the regulatory ball, but it minimizes the documents that need to be converted to electronic images. It also is a key element in the legal admissibility of optical disk records into a court of law. The best position for an organization is to establish and follow standards for records retention on paper, microfilm, magnetic and optical records – basically all media. They should consider a document to be the same no matter what media it is stored on.

The records manager and the organization's legal counsel are critical players in making sure that the operating policies and practices of the electronic imaging system will be judged by a court to be accurate, reliable and trustworthy. Organizations should not be lulled into a sense of comfort that optical disk records have been admitted into courts of law. In order to ensure that *their* optical disk records will be admitted, they must ensure that recording methods and the resulting records comply with stipulated foundational requirements for this type of media. The core regulations that set out the conditions which affect the admissibility in evidence of records stored on alternative media to paper in the United States are the Uniform Photographic Copies of Business and Public Records as Evidence Act (UPA) and its federal counterpart, the Federal Business Records Act.

In addition to the retention and admissibility issues records managers can add value to the process through obtaining expertise in indexing and classification. An electronic imaging system alone will not solve all the indexing and classification problems. In fact, in an electronic environment the organization and control of information are even more critical than in a paper environment. In an electronic environment classification is often the only means of access to documents. If careful consideration is not given to the manner in which documents are to be classified, access to documents will prove to be more difficult than in a manual system. Business document images should be viewed as another data type available on the computer network. Their indexing and classification should be part of the overall scheme that includes text documents, spreadsheets, relational databases, etc. Maximum benefits from an imaging system are realized through the integration with other systems and data types. This integrated environment allows the end user to search across a network for information that is available on any given subject, in any data format.

The implementation of imaging systems was not always as focused on user needs. In the 1980s, a prevalent ingredient for the implementation of an imaging strategy was an autocratic leader pushing the administrative practices of the organization from the top down. This, however, is not the typical model of an organization as we near the turn of the century. As we have discussed, senior managers are pressing their departments to be profit centers and want their managers to be entrepreneurs. This means making them not only responsible for getting results but how they get results. This organizational model does not foster organization-wide thinking, nor independent risk-taking, in the management of information. The IS department should ensure some consistency, but the day-to-day management of the information must be done by the department managers. That makes them and their workers key players in imaging strategy planning as well.

It follows then that the speed with which organizations move to less dependency on paper for business records is controlled by the masses, not senior management. With the realization that the people doing the office work have to feel comfortable with the new technologies, the whole game has changed and so has the agenda. Electronic imaging should not be viewed as solely a storage and retrieval system, or as a replacement for an existing manual system. Imaging should be viewed as a tool which when properly applied can improve the management of documents within a business process. Potential imaging applications should be evaluated in light of the overall business process.

To motivate the workers to learn and use these technologies, they must see how it will be profitable to them. Since factors such as workload, computer literacy and personal motivation vary from person to person so will the motivation to move to less dependency on paper. While there must be organization-wide advocacy of change, the opportunity and the tools must be presented independently to each individual for them to integrate at their own comfortable pace.

Most imaging systems installed to date have not started with this premise. Many organizations have started with exactly the opposite premise. They have mandated the use of the new technologies and policed the 'offenders' at the photocopy machine trying to make and store illicit paper copies. Herein lies the single most important reason for the stunted growth of imaging systems to date. The majority of people in the office haven't wanted them. Document management pervades the office worker's routine of receiving, creating, processing, communicating and recording information. It is common sense that users will only want document imaging if it integrates with other existing applications. Document management systems based on a platform of networked PCs are essential for this independent pursuit of records automation. It integrates a worker's needs in one place with one common way of doing things, which means it is easier to learn and use.

Appendix

Steps to the selection and contracting of services/products/consultants

The following steps are applicable to any contracted service, for example commercial storage; a microfilm bureau; the purchase, installation, and maintenance of any equipment, consulting services, data processing bureau, etc.

Education

Become thoroughly familiar with the product or type of service, with what it can and cannot be expected to accomplish.

- Read books and articles on the subject.
- Purchase copies of the appropriate standards and codes.
- Attend seminars and lectures on the subject.
- Talk to any local experts on the subject, and to experienced users of such products or services.
- Find the organization of professionals in that subject and ask if they have published advice for potential clients.

Preparation of a request for proposal (RFP)

The RFP should clearly outline what product or service is desired. It is as much for the client as for the vendor, for it will force the clarification of the whole purchasing situation long before any trouble can begin. In requesting the pricing of services, it is helpful to specify that common terms be used so that comparison of comparable services is assured. Write a short but complete description of the service/product needed, including details of:

- the problem it is to solve (for example, boxes to be stored per year, tapes per day to be exchanged, office to be computerized, people to be trained, etc.)
- any other solutions already tried
- any limitations to new solutions
- an approximation of the amount of money to be spent on the product/service.

Include with the RFP:

- a copy of your organization's most recent annual report
- any of the legal or purchasing department's procedural rules or requirements for contracts or purchases.

Submission of the RFP

The RFP should be sent to a number of vendors as a request for a quotation or proposal to supply the service/product. In the covering letter also ask:

- that they respond within a given period of time
- that they send a copy of their most recent annual report
- that they submit the names, addresses, telephone numbers, and contact people of at least three client references, each of whom has purchased a product/service similar or identical to the one under consideration.

Shortlisting the vendors

Take sufficient time and ask for any needed advice on the evaluation of the proposals. Keep the list to two to five vendors:

- Ask for any further documentation, samples, brochures, explanations, demonstrations, etc. necessary to understand and evaluate fully.
- Visit the vendors' sites, if they will be providing a service, for example, storage facilities, microfilming bureau, etc.
- Visit each of the client references, view the products/services they received from the vendor, ask for their honest opinion of the vendor's service, maintenance, support, reliability.
- Ask for the vendor's bank and credit references and check financial viability.

Negotiation of the contract

After selecting the vendor, let the legal department or advisor to the organization negotiate the contract (or ask them to review the one negotiated by the records manager). Insist that the contract include:

- a certificate or letter of compliance with the relevant standards, which must be cited by number and title
- a full maintenance agreement
- a guarantee, on large orders, that parts and supplies will be available, at a fixed price, for a certain number of years
- an insurance agreement that covers the value of the information, not just the tape or papers on which it is stored.

Periodic review

All contracts and services should be reviewed at least annually. If the service or products are not satisfactory, either:

(a) cancel or decline to renew the contract;

or

(b) meet with the vendor, tell them the product/services are unsatisfactory, and give them a limited period of time to try to make improvements. If they fail, cancel the contract and look for someone better.

Index